AutoCAD® Release 12 for Beginners

Vic Wright

Kurt Hampe

Ashim Guha

NRP

NEW RIDERS
PUBLISHING

AutoCAD Release 12 for Beginners

By Vic Wright, Kurt Hampe, and Ashim Guha

Published by:
New Riders Publishing
11711 N. College Ave., Suite 140
Carmel, IN 46032 USA

Printed in the United States of America 1 2 3 4 5 6 7 8 9 0

Library of Congress Cataloging-in-Publication Data:

```
Hampe, Kurt, 1968-
        AutoCAD release  12 for beginners / by Kurt Hampe, Vic
Wright, Ashim Guha.
                p.      cm.
        Includes Index.
        ISBN 1-56205-056-7 : $19.95
        1. Computer Graphics.  2. AutoCAD (Computer program)    I.
Wright, Victor E.   II. Title
T385.H3297   1992
620'.0042'02855369--dc20
```

Publisher
David P. Ewing

Associate Publisher
Tim Huddleston

Acquisitions Editor
Brad Koch

Product Director
Kevin Coleman

Managing Editor
Cheri Robinson

Production Editors
Peter Kuhns
Rob Tidrow

Editors
Margaret Berson
Cheri Robinson
Nancy Sixsmith
Lisa D. Wagner

Technical Editors
Kurt Hampe
Richard Howard
Don Strimbu
Peter Tobey

Book Design
Scott Cook

Production
Claudia Bell
Jeanne Clark
Michelle Cleary
Christine Cook
Mark Enochs
Tim Groeling
Denny Hager
Carrie Keesling
Phil Kitchel
Bob LaRoche
Laurie Lee
Cindy L. Phipps
Caroline Roop
Linda Seifert
Julie Walker
Christine Young

Editorial Assistant
Karen Opal

Acquisitions Assistant
Geneil Breeze

About the Authors

Vic Wright is Vice President, Engineering for Challenger Lifts Division of VBM Corporation, a manufacturer of automotive lifts in Louisville, KY. Mr. Wright is a mechanical engineer registered in Kentucky, Tennessee, and Indiana. Before joining VBM Corporation, he spent 18 years in the A/E/C field as a project manager with a mechanical contractor and an architectural, engineering, and construction management firm. He has written two books: *TK Solver for Engineers* and *The Best Book of AutoCAD*. He also writes monthly columns for *CADENCE*, *MCN*, and *Design Management* magazines. Mr. Wright has been an AutoCAD user since 1983.

Kurt Hampe is a graduate of Kentucky Polytechnic Institute. Mr. Hampe worked as a programmer before becoming a teacher. He has held teaching positions at Kentucky Polytechnic, the Marion County Adjustment Center where he taught inmates to use computers, and Corporate Computer Training Center. While at the training center, Mr. Hampe began writing and editing technical manuals and books.

Ashim Guha received his bachelor's degree in Mechanical Engineering from M.S. University, Bawate, India and his master's degree in Mechanical Engineering from Boston University, Boston, Massachusetts.

Acknowledgments

The author would like to thank the staff members of Autodesk, Inc. for their help and support in the writing of this book.

Special thanks also to the members of the Autodesk forum of CompuServe, for their help in locating topics that needed to be covered in this book, and for providing answers to many questions.

New Riders Publishing would like to thank the following people and companies for their contributions to this book:

Kevin Coleman, for developing the revision and update for this edition of the book and for directing the authors and technical editors who contributed text and ideas.

Brad Koch, for putting together the authoring team and riding herd over everyone involved in the project.

Cheri Robinson, for managing us all.

Peter Kuhns and Rob Tidrow, for coordinating the editing team and for tracking the book throughout the production process.

The editorial staff at New Riders Publishing, including Margaret Berson, Nancy Sixsmith, and Lisa Wagner.

Karen Opal, for editorial assistance wherever needed.

Geneil Breeze, for managing the flow of materials from original submission to author review.

NRP extends special thanks to the members of Prentice Hall Computer Publishing's production and manufacturing staff. Their graciousness and extraordinary efforts are deeply appreciated.

Thanks also to the following vendors for providing hardware, software, and video support: Contrade; Videomania, Inc.; Truevision; Video Support Associates; Graphical Softwares, Inc.; Hercules; and Technical Designs, Inc.

Trademark Acknowledgments

New Riders Publishing has made every attempt to supply trademark information about company names, products, and services mentioned in this book. Trademarks indicated below were derived from various sources. New Riders Publishing cannot attest to the accuracy of this information.

Autodesk 3D Studio, Autodesk Animator, Animator Pro, AutoFlix, and CHAOS are trademarks of Autodesk, Inc.

AutoCAD and AutoShade are registered trademarks of Autodesk, Inc.

Microsoft Project is a registered trademark of Microsoft Corporation.

RenderMan is a registered trademark of Pixar, used by Autodesk under license from Pixar.

Targa is a registered trademark of Truevision.

Trademarks of other products mentioned in this book are held by the companies producing them.

Warning and Disclaimer

This book is designed to provide information about the AutoCAD computer program. Every effort has been made to make this book as complete and as accurate as possible, but no warranty or fitness is implied.

The information is provided on an "as is" basis. The author and New Riders Publishing shall have neither liability nor responsibility to any person or entity with respect to any loss or damages arising from the information contained in this book or from the use of the disks or programs that may accompany it.

Table of Contents

Introduction

If you have this book in your hand, you need to learn AutoCAD. Maybe you are a student studying for a career in drafting or engineering. Maybe you are a 20-year drafting veteran and have just had your drafting board replaced by a computer workstation. Whatever your situation, if you are faced with the task of learning the large, complex computer-aided drafting and design program called AutoCAD, this book is for you.

What You Will Learn From This Book

AutoCAD Release 12 for Beginners acquaints you with the AutoCAD program, but it does not try to dump everything about AutoCAD on you all at once. First, it teaches you the basic AutoCAD commands and skills you need to get started and to feel comfortable using the program. As you become more comfortable with AutoCAD, the book builds upon the basics with methods of drawing more efficiently and accurately than with your pen and paper. As you proceed, you learn to use some of the uniquely powerful techniques that give AutoCAD such an advantage over manual drafting. Most of AutoCAD's commands and features are covered in *AutoCAD Release 12 for Beginners*, but some of the more advanced commands and features are left for other New Riders Publishing books to cover.

What This Book Covers

The first two chapters of the book cover the basics that you need to get started. Chapter 1, "Setting Up," guides you through the setup process for this book. Then, Chapter 2, "Using AutoCAD Menus and Commands," introduces you to how the AutoCAD program works and how to use menus, dialog boxes, and the command line to tell the program what you want it to do. You learn the basic commands for drawing points, lines, arcs, circles, and text, and how to erase or undo errors. With these basic commands, you can draw almost anything. What you learn in the rest of the book is how to draw more accurately and more efficiently.

The next four chapters of the book concentrate on accuracy and efficiency. In Chapter 3, "Drawing Accurately," you will become skilled with AutoCAD's commands and controls for drawing accuracy, enabling you to place points exactly where you want them. Chapter 4, "Basic Drawing and Editing," introduces you to commands for producing drawings quickly, with a minimum of effort, and how to make changes to your drawings. In Chapter 5, "Drawing Setup and Screen Control," you apply this accuracy and efficiency to larger objects and drawings, learning how to draw big things on the small computer screen. You learn to display and work on any part of any size drawing at any scale. You also learn to subdivide the screen so you can see several portions of the drawing at once. In addition, you learn how to make the drawing setup process quicker. Finally, Chapter 6, "More Drawing Commands," carries efficiency in drawing to new levels. You learn more advanced methods of using the basic drawing commands, as well as many commands that make drawing objects much quicker and easier than in manual drafting.

Chapters 7 and 8 teach you the real power of AutoCAD—making changes quickly and easily, and eliminating drawing repetition. Chapter 7, "Enhancing and Correcting Your Work," features commands that can be used to make changes and correct mistakes much more efficiently than simply erasing or undoing and then redrawing. Chapter 7 also shows how to set up and organize your drawing to add color and linetypes to objects and to organize objects in layers that can be used like manual overlay drafting.

Chapter 7's editing commands also can be used for constructive purposes, changing construction lines to become part of the finished drawing. Chapter 8, "Editing Constructively," features more advanced constructive editing commands, nearly all of which duplicate existing objects or create new objects.

By the time you finish Chapter 9, "Drawing Power: Blocks and Xrefs," you learn one of AutoCAD's most powerful and efficient features: creating symbols and complex parts and repeatedly inserting them easily as *blocks*. You can even use an entire existing drawing as an inserted block.

The next two chapters of the book cover those tasks involved in finishing up and plotting a drawing. In Chapter 10, "Dimensioning Drawings," you will learn to use AutoCAD's dimensioning to generate accurate dimensions from an accurate drawing. You also learn to control the style of dimensions that *your* drafting standards dictate.

In Chapter 11, "Composing, Annotating, and Plotting," you will put it all together to compose a drawing for plotting. You will learn how to scale, annotate, crosshatch, and plot a finished, professional drawing.

The last chapter in the book is an introduction to AutoCAD's three-dimensional drawing features and commands. In Chapter 12, "Drawing into 3D," you will not really be a beginner any more, so you will be quite comfortable experimenting with some of AutoCAD's 3D capabilities. You will be introduced to AutoCAD's 3D concepts, use 3D extrusions and surfaces to draw a table, and learn to view the 3D model from any angle or perspective.

In Appendix A, "AutoCAD System Variables," contains a table of system variables. Appendix B, "Installation, Configuration, and Troubleshooting," contains information on installing, and configuring AutoCAD, and on troubleshooting AutoCAD problems. Appendix C, "DOS Basics and Performance," is a review and explanation of basic computer skills, file handling, and terminology needed for using AutoCAD.

Getting the Most from This Book

If you simply read the book, you will learn a great deal about AutoCAD. The introduction of each chapter lists the AutoCAD commands that the chapter covers, followed by explanations of the concepts of the chapter's topic. As each command is introduced, its use is discussed and a reference to the command is shown, like the following reference to the LINE command.

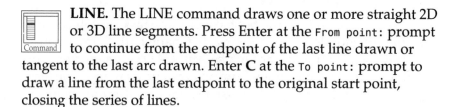 **LINE.** The LINE command draws one or more straight 2D or 3D line segments. Press Enter at the From point: prompt to continue from the endpoint of the last line drawn or tangent to the last arc drawn. Enter **C** at the To point: prompt to draw a line from the last endpoint to the original start point, closing the series of lines.

The From point: and To point: lines show you how the command prompts you for input.

The Options Lists

Many commands have a number of options you can choose when prompted for input. These options also are shown for easy reference, like the following LINE Options list.

LINE Options

- **From point:**. At this prompt, you need to specify the first point of the first line.

- **To point:**. At this prompt, you need to specify a new point to draw a line from the previous point to the new point.

- **Continue.** Select Continue from the screen menu or press Enter at the From point: prompt to continue a line from the endpoint of the most recently drawn line or arc.

- **Close.** Enter **C** (Close) at the To point: prompt to close a series of line segments, connecting the last endpoint to the original start point.

- **Undo.** Enter **U** at the To point: prompt to undo the last line segment and return to the previous point.

Following the introduction of most commands is a practice exercise. The exercises are designed so that you can use your copy of AutoCAD to go through them step by step. You can just read the exercises, but to get the most from this book, you need to sit down at a computer and try the practice sessions.

If you have never worked with AutoCAD before, you should work through the exercises in chapter sequence, from the front of the book to the back. If you already have some experience with the program, you may prefer picking and choosing your topics. Most chapters are designed so that you can work through them without having to finish previous chapters. If prior material is needed, the exercises tell you.

How Exercises Are Shown

The following is a sample exercise. The exercise tells you exactly what keys to press or picks to make, and comments tell you about what you see on the screen as you work. AutoCAD's screen display text and your input are in computer-style type on the left of the exercise. Prompts are shown like the Command: prompt in the following exercise. Prompts, including operation system prompts, are shown as they appear on your screen, although the exercises abbreviate or omit portions of the command dialogue for simple commands, for command dialogue that is unimportant or that scrolls by, and for familiar or repetitive sequences. Necessary commands, prompts, and input always are shown.

Blue type indicates what you need to enter. *Press Enter* or ↵ means to press the Return or Enter key on your keyboard. AutoCAD prompts refer to Enter as the RETURN key, but most keyboards label it as Enter, which is how it is shown in this book.

Example Exercise

```
Command: ZOOM ⏎
```
```
All/Center/Dynamic/Extents/Left/                 Selects the Last option
Previous/Window/<Scale(X)>: L ⏎
```
```
Lower left corner point: Press Enter          Defaults to current corner
```
```
Magnification or Height <9.0000>:
8.5 ⏎
```
```
Command: Press F6                             Turns on coordinate display
```
Select Draw, *then* Line

Draw a line from 1,1 to @0,3.

```
From Point: 1,1 ⏎
```
```
To Point: @0,3 ⏎
```
```
To Point: Press Enter                         Ends the LINE command
```

Comments are shown in the book's normal text font, and instructions are shown in italic. Menu items, labels, or dialog boxes are shown in normal text, such as "*Select* Draw *then* Line." Select means to pick the menu item(s) shown. If more than one menu item is shown, select them in the order shown.

Input that you should enter is shown in blue type. Type input exactly as shown and press Enter as indicated with ⏎, watching carefully for the difference between the numbers 0 or 1 and the letters o or l. The @ is the @ character, which is above the 2 on your keyboard. Keyboard keys are shown like Ctrl-D for the Control-D combination, F6 for function key six, or *Press Enter* and ⏎ for the Enter key.

Exercises and Your Graphics Display

The illustrations in this book were developed on a VGA (Video Graphics Array) display with 640×480 resolution. If you are using a different display, you may need to zoom to get an appropriate view for an exercise. You also may need to adjust your aperture size when using object snap modes if your screen resolution is extremely high or extremely low. If your display is configured for a white background, the color that AutoCAD calls white appears black on your screen.

 For clarity, the AutoCAD grid is not shown in most of the illustrations.

Notes and Tips

AutoCAD Release 12 for Beginners features two special "sidebars," which are set apart from the normal text by icons. The book includes "Notes" and "Tips."

 A *note* includes "extra" information that you should find useful, but which complements the discussion at hand instead of being a direct part of it. A note may describe special situations that can arise when you use AutoCAD under certain circumstances, and may tell you what steps to take when such situations arise. Notes also may tell you how to avoid problems with your software and hardware.

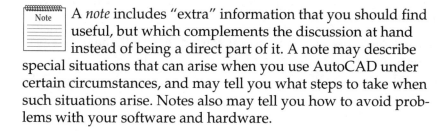 A *tip* provides you with quick instructions for getting the most from your AutoCAD system as you follow the exercises and discussions.

Prerequisites for This Book

To use this book, you need to have a copy of AutoCAD Release 12 installed and configured and have a graphic display and a mouse or digitizer tablet, all configured for AutoCAD. If you need information on configuration, see Appendix B.

AutoCAD Release 12 for Beginners was written for AutoCAD Release 12.

For DOS systems, PC- or MS-DOS 3.0 or a later version is recommended, but you can use any system that runs AutoCAD. If you are using a non-DOS version of AutoCAD, you may see minor differences between the illustrations and AutoCAD's screen display. If you are using UNIX, use lowercase letters to enter all file names shown in the book's exercises.

Bon Voyage

AutoCAD is a big program, and it can do an amazing number of things. It will eventually make your engineering or drafting job much easier to do, although you may not think so at first. The time it takes to lay out and draw original objects still may be the same, but when you need to do repetitive drawing, dimensioning, 3D, or everyday revisions, AutoCAD leaves manual drafting far behind.

You are probably impatient to get started. After all, the best way to learn AutoCAD is to *use* AutoCAD. So turn the page and get started!

Setting Up

This chapter introduces the AutoCAD program, some of its basic features, and a brief description of the equipment you need to run the program. In addition, you read about the following:

- The basic components of a CAD system
- Starting the AutoCAD program
- The elements of the AutoCAD user interface
- Beginning a new drawing
- Saving the current drawing
- Ending the program

Introducing AutoCAD Release 12

AutoCAD Release 12 is the latest version of the most widely used CAD (Computer Aided Drafting) system of all time. AutoCAD workstations outnumber all other CAD workstations combined, and AutoCAD users outnumber all other CAD users. AutoCAD is the CAD system of choice in educational institutions, industrial firms, architectural and engineering design firms, government agencies, and other organizations that have chosen to automate drafting and design tasks. Whether you are a veteran user of some other CAD system, or just beginning to learn about CAD in general, your decision to learn AutoCAD opens many doors.

AutoCAD started as a simple program and has evolved into a complex one. Each release, or version, including Release 12 added new capabilities. If you have used an earlier version of AutoCAD, you will notice that Release 12 differs somewhat in its "look and feel" from earlier versions. Release 12 incorporates Autodesk's own GUI (Graphical User Interface), which makes AutoCAD easier to use. Release 12 also has new facilities for editing drawings.

Although Release 12 is more powerful than any previous version, you will find it easier to use.

The Components of a CAD System

A CAD system consists of hardware and software components. The hardware consists of a computer, a graphics display, a pointing device, and perhaps a plotter or printer. The software consists of the computer's operating system, the AutoCAD program, and perhaps additional programs developed by third party developers. The *AutoCAD Installation, Interface, and Performance manual* describes these components in detail, as does Appendix B of this book. Review the *AutoCAD Installation, Interface, and Performance manual*, Appendix B, or both to ensure that your CAD system is complete. You also need to be familiar with your computer's operating system.

Understanding the Computer and Operating System

The central hardware component of your AutoCAD workstation is a computer. AutoCAD is available for several different computers and operating systems, including IBM PC-compatibles, Apple Macintosh, Sun engineering workstations, and VAX minicomputers. Although this book discusses the DOS 386 version of AutoCAD, which is used on IBM PC-compatibles, AutoCAD is essentially the same regardless of the computer platform.

Any computer that you might use to run AutoCAD has an operating system. An operating system is a group of programs that manages the hardware components of the computer. When you want the computer to do something, you type or use the mouse to submit a command to the operating system. When the operating system receives the command, it issues the appropriate instructions to one or more hardware components. The operating system stores data on disks in the form of files. By using files, the operating system can manage and retrieve the data when you enter the appropriate command. The operating system also coordinates hardware and data for programs. When a program runs, it communicates with the operating system. You talk to AutoCAD, AutoCAD talks to the operating system, and the operating system talks to the computer.

Understanding the Graphics Display

The graphics display system consists of a graphics controller and a compatible monitor. The graphics controller may be a plug-in board, or it may be integral to your computer. A standard VGA graphics display is suitable, even for production use, but many users upgrade their computers with high-resolution, high-performance graphics displays. The illustrations in this book were produced at the standard VGA resolution of 640×480 pixels.

Some graphics display manufacturers supply a custom software driver that enables AutoCAD to take advantage of special features of their hardware. If you are using such software, your screen displays may differ slightly from those in this book.

Understanding the Pointing Device

The pointing device is the device you use to provide graphic data points to AutoCAD. The pointing device may be a mouse, trackball, joystick, or digitizer tablet with a cursor or stylus. AutoCAD displays a pointer on the screen that follows the motion of the pointing device. You can, in fact, operate AutoCAD with the arrow keys on your keyboard, but a mouse or digitizer is much easier to use.

Working with Printers and Plotters

The computer, graphics display, and pointing device are essential components of an AutoCAD workstation—you need all three to create and edit drawings. If you want to produce plots of your drawings at your own workstation, you also need a printer or plotter. If you do not have a plotter or printer, you can transfer a drawing file to another workstation that is equipped for printing.

Installing AutoCAD Release 12

The DOS 386 version of AutoCAD consists of a large, main program and a number of supporting files. The main program file is too large to fit on a single floppy disk for distribution. As a result, it is split into several files and compressed. To execute, the main program must be assembled from its component files. The first disk in the series of distribution disks includes an installation program that copies files from the distribution disks to your hard disk, decompresses the files, and assembles the main program. This process is explained in detail in the *AutoCAD Installation, Interface, and Performance manual*, and in Appendix B of this book. If you have not installed AutoCAD, you should do so at this point.

Setting Up AutoCAD for Exercises in This Book

After installing AutoCAD, follow the steps in the next exercise to make a directory named AB for this book's drawing and configuration files. If you create this directory, you ensure that any AutoCAD settings used for this book's exercises do not interfere with other projects. When you create drawings by following the exercises, you will store them in this directory. You do not have to use the same file names that appear in this book, but doing so ensures that your drawings on-screen match the book's illustrations (screen shots). The illustrations for this book were created by actually following the exercises and capturing the screen display at various stages.

Even if you are an experienced DOS user and have some experience with AutoCAD, you need to make some preparations before moving on to any of the following chapters. You should start by performing several exercises in this chapter, beginning with the "Making the AB Directory" exercise, which appears in a later section.

The setup for *AutoCAD Release 12 for Beginners* requires you to create a directory—named AB—on your hard disk. The book is designed to ensure that the AutoCAD settings you use for the book's exercises do not interfere with any other AutoCAD settings or projects that you may have under way.

Creating Directories

This book assumes that you are using the DOS operating system version 3.3 or later, that you are running AutoCAD on a hard disk drive named drive C.

> **Note** Your drive letter or subdirectory names may differ from those shown in this book. If they do, substitute your drive letter and directory names wherever you encounter drive letters (such as C) or the directory names (such as \ACAD) in the book. If you are using an operating system other than DOS, your directory creation and setup will differ from those shown in the following pages. Even so, you should set up a directory structure that is similar to the one shown in this chapter.

Making the AB Directory

The book's setup also assumes that you work in the AB directory. You need to make an AB directory on your hard disk and then place a copy of your AutoCAD configuration file into this directory. By copying the configuration file into the working directory, you create a self-contained AutoCAD environment. To begin this task, make the hard disk's root directory the current directory. In the following exercise, you make the AB directory.

Before you begin the following exercise, note that the input you type at the `c:\>` command prompt is shown in `blue text`. After you type the blue input, press Enter to execute the command.

Making the AB Directory

Change to the root directory of drive C and perform the following steps:

`C:\> MD \AB ↵`	Creates the directory
`C:\> DIR *. ↵`	Displays a list of directory names, as shown in the following listing

```
Volume in drive C is DRIVE-C
Directory of  C:\
ACAD      <DIR>  12-01-88   11:27a
DOS       <DIR>  12-01-88   11:27a
AB        <DIR>  12-01-88   11:27a
```

Your disk may show other directories, as follows:

```
123       <DIR>  12-01-88   11:27a
DBASE     <DIR>  12-01-88   11:27a
5 File(s) 48753472 bytes free
```

The ACAD subdirectory contains the AutoCAD program files, configuration files, and standard support files. The DOS subdirectory contains the DOS operating system files. The AB subdirectory contains the configuration files, prototype drawings, and other support files that are required for the *AutoCAD Release 12 for Beginners* exercises. Your directory listing almost certainly will be different from the one shown here.

Setting Up the AutoCAD Configuration Files

AutoCAD requires a *configuration file*—a file named ACAD.CFG, which specifies the hardware devices (such as video display cards and plotters) that you use with AutoCAD. This file is created the first time you run AutoCAD. The following exercise assumes that AutoCAD's configuration file resides in the ACAD directory. If your configuration file is not in the ACAD directory, substitute the correct directory name for \ACAD in the following exercise. By copying the ACAD.CFG file to the AB directory, you establish a separate AutoCAD configuration for this book. If AutoCAD has not yet been configured, see Appendix B of this book or your *AutoCAD Installation, Interface, and Performance Guide* for more information on configuring the program.

Configuring AutoCAD is a simple process of answering a series of prompts to tell AutoCAD what devices you are using, how they are connected, and your preferences for several optional settings that control AutoCAD's behavior.

Copying the AutoCAD Configuration File to the AB Directory

`C:\> CD \ACAD ⏎`	Make the ACAD directory current
`C:\ACAD> COPY ACAD.CFG \AB ⏎` `1 File(s) copied`	Copies the AutoCAD configuration file from the ACAD directory to the AB directory

Using a Batch File To Start AutoCAD

Now you can create a simple batch file that starts AutoCAD so that it does not conflict with your current AutoCAD setup, and which keeps your drawing exercise files in one place. The batch file loads AutoCAD directly from your ACAD directory to avoid conflict with any ACAD.BAT batch file that you might already have. The batch file avoids conflicts by ensuring that the settings of two of AutoCAD's environment variables—named ACAD and ACADCFG—are correctly set when you run AutoCAD and then are cleared when you exit from AutoCAD. This section shows you how to make a batch file named AB.BAT to use with the directory you have created. For more explanation of start-up batch files and of the settings shown in this section, see Appendix B.

 If you are using an operating system other than DOS, you can create a similar shell file rather than the batch file. See the *AutoCAD Installation, Interface, and Performance Guide* for details.

After you create the AB.BAT batch file, you can start AutoCAD from any directory by entering \AB at the DOS prompt. The backslash enables you to enter the AB batch command from any directory; if the AB.BAT file is placed in a directory on your path, you can omit the backslash.

The AB batch file sets the ACAD and ACADCFG settings, makes the AB directory current, and starts AutoCAD. When you exit from AutoCAD, the batch file clears ACAD and ACADCFG and returns you to the root directory. Your configuration may require additional settings. The AB.BAT file requires at least the following eight lines:

```
SET ACADCFG=\AB
SET ACAD=\ACAD\SUPPORT;\ACAD\SAMPLE;\ACAD\FONTS;\ACAD\ADS
CD \AB
\acad\ACAD %1 %2
SET ACAD=
SET ACADCFG=
CD \
```

In the third line of the file, the %1 and %2 are *replaceable parameters*. These parameters are used in batch files as place holders for any command-line options that a program might take. Because AutoCAD can take two optional parameters (which can set a default drawing or script or enter AutoCAD's configuration when you start AutoCAD), this batch file includes two place holders.

See the *AutoCAD Installation, Interface, and Performance Guide* for more information.

> **Note** The sample AB.BAT file supports the default directories suggested by the AutoCAD installation program. If your AutoCAD support files are not installed in the AutoCAD program directory, or your font, support, sample, and ADS files (if installed) are not in the ACAD\FONTS, ACAD\SAMPLE, ACAD\SAMPLE, and ACAD\ADS directories, then change the SET ACAD= line. If your font, sample, and support files are combined in the ACAD\SUPPORT directory, for example, delete ;\ACAD\SAMPLE and ;\ACAD\FONTS and use SET ACAD=\ACAD\SUPPORT;\ACAD\ADS.

> **Note** If your AutoCAD program files are not in a directory named \ACAD, then substitute your directory name for acad where shown in lowercase letters in the preceding listings and the following exercise.

Creating the AB.BAT File

The best way to create your batch file is to use a word processor or text editor in ASCII-text mode. If you prefer, however, you can use the following technique, which utilizes the DOS COPY command. This technique copies the characters you type at the keyboard to create the specified AB.BAT file. The keyboard is referenced as CON in the exercise because it (along with the video device) is the CONsole—the default DOS input/output device.

As you create your version of the AB.BAT file, be sure to make any changes and add any extra lines you need. To enter the ^Z character shown in the exercise, hold down the Ctrl (Control) key while you press Z, and then press Enter.

Creating the AB.BAT Batch File

`C:\ACAD> CD\ ↵`	Returns to the root directory
`C:\> COPY CON AB.BAT ↵`	Creates a file named AB.BAT containing the following lines of keyboard input
`SET ACADCFG=\AB ↵`	Sets the ACADCFG environment variable

The following line sets the ACAD environment variable:

`SET ACAD=\ACAD\SUPPORT;\ACAD\SAMPLE;\ACAD\FONTS;\ACAD\ADS ↵`	
`CD \AB ↵`	Makes AB the current directory
`\acad\ACAD %1 %2 ↵`	Starts the AutoCAD program
`SET ACAD= ↵`	Clears the ACAD setting
`SET ACADCFG= ↵`	Clears the ACADCFG setting
`CD \ ↵`	Returns to the root directory after you exit from AutoCAD
`^Z ↵`	Ends the COPY command and creates the AB.BAT file
`1 File(s) copied`	Confirms that the AB.BAT file was written to disk

Now you can start an *AutoCAD Release 12 for Beginners* session from any directory on your hard drive simply by entering \AB. For more information on the startup batch file's settings, see Appendix B.

> **Note** If the root directory is on the path specified by your AUTOEXEC.BAT file, you can omit the backslash and just enter **AB**. If you want to keep your root directory uncluttered, you can move the AB.BAT file to any other directory on your path.

Using the AB.BAT File

With these file-handling chores out of the way, you can now use the AB.BAT file to start up AutoCAD.

Starting AutoCAD

```
C:\> \ABA ↵                                    Begins AutoCAD
```

Your screen displays a new drawing (see fig. 1.1).

> **Note** If your system displays a `Bad command or filename` error message when you try to start AutoCAD with the AB batch file, make sure that you have specified the correct path to the AutoCAD executable file. If AutoCAD is installed on a different drive than the AB subdirectory, you must also put the correct drive letter before the first backslash on the `\acad\ACAD %1 %2` line of the AB batch file. If the ACAD.EXE file is located in the ACAD12 directory on drive E, for example, use the following command:

```
E:\ACAD12\ACAD %1 %2
```

As soon as you enter \AB from the operating system, the batch file takes control of your computer. The batch file makes AB the current directory, and the AutoCAD program displays the opening screen.

Creating CAD Drawings and Files

If you work on a drawing board, you define "drawing" as using pencil lead or ink to place geometric symbols and text on a sheet of paper or Mylar. The sheet of Mylar is the input surface, storage device, and display mechanism. A CAD system can produce a similar drawing, but the sheet of paper or Mylar covered with marks is not the CAD drawing—it is a plot of the drawing. The drawing resides electronically on the computer's hard disk in the form of a list of points and parameters. In computerese, this list is called a *file*. Because AutoCAD "knows" how to create this file, and how to display it in the form of a drawing, it is commonly called a *drawing file*. If you tried to view an AutoCAD drawing with most other programs, the drawing file would appear as gibberish.

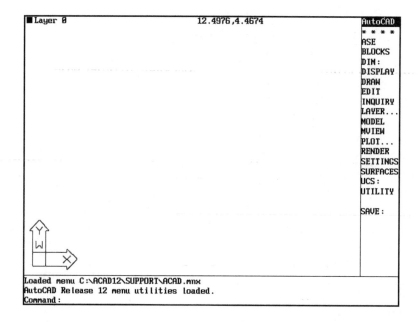

Figure 1.1:

The AutoCAD opening screen.

If you have seen or used an earlier version of AutoCAD, you might notice Release 12 does not display the familiar "main menu" when it starts. AutoCAD no longer includes the "main menu" because all of its tasks now can be accessed using the pull-down menus of AutoCAD's GUI. Instead of displaying the main menu at startup, AutoCAD immediately invokes the drawing editor, enabling you to begin drawing immediately.

Notice that AutoCAD displays a banner in text form while the program loads. It then displays the drawing editor screen, with the Autodesk logo and the program banner superimposed. After a short delay, the logo and banner disappear and the word Command: appears at the bottom of the screen, ready to accept commands.

Although you can begin drawing immediately, AutoCAD uses temporary files to store your drawing until you have named it. You do not have to name your drawing immediately, but when you want to save the drawing or end the drawing session, AutoCAD prompts you for a name so that it can permanently save the file.

Interacting with AutoCAD

AutoCAD is an interactive graphics package. In other words, you submit commands to AutoCAD and it displays the results. You can issue AutoCAD commands in several ways; AutoCAD uses several methods for displaying results and sending messages to you. Although the next chapter describes AutoCAD's user interface in detail, the following sections describe some basic concepts.

Examining the AutoCAD Screen

AutoCAD displays the results of your commands in both text and graphics form on-screen. The largest part of the screen is occupied by the drawing area, which is where your drawing appears. Below the drawing area is a command line. The AutoCAD command line enables you to enter a command and additional information needed for the command. The command line also displays short messages in text form. At the top of the screen is a status line used to display various settings, and along the right side of the screen is a menu, from which you can pick commands.

Using Pointers

As you can see in figure 1.2, AutoCAD displays a set of crosshairs on the screen that extends from the top to the bottom of the drawing area, and from the left side to the right side. This pair of crosshairs is the *crosshair pointer*. When you move the pointing device—mouse or digitizer cursor—AutoCAD moves the crosshair pointer.

If you move the pointing device so that the crosshair pointer moves out of the drawing area into the status line, the pointer changes to an *arrow pointer*, and the status line changes to a menu bar. If you place the arrow pointer on one of the words in the menu bar, AutoCAD highlights it in reverse video. If you then click (press and release once) the left mouse button, AutoCAD displays a pull-down menu from which you can pick a command in the same manner. Some commands execute immediately; others display additional menus. Figure 1.3 shows the arrow pointer and the menu bar.

Figure 1.2:

The drawing area with the crosshair pointer.

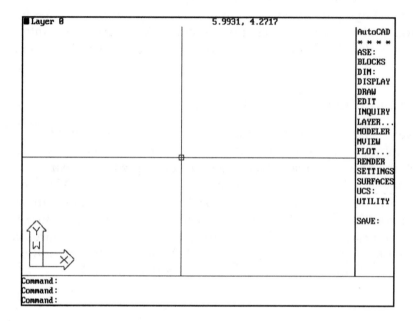

If you move the pointing device so that the crosshair pointer moves onto the right side of the screen menu area, the crosshair pointer changes to a *menu pointer*, which is a reverse video block (see fig. 1.4). You can move the menu pointer by moving the pointing device and pick commands by clicking the left mouse button (or the data button on a digitizer).

Working with Dialog Boxes

Before it can execute some commands, AutoCAD requires additional information. When you enter one of these commands, AutoCAD requests the information in one of two ways. The first method is to display a series of prompts in the command prompt area. Prompts are always displayed in a specific order, and the only way to correct an error is to repeat the command. Another way AutoCAD requests additional information is by displaying a dialog box, such as the one shown in figure 1.5.

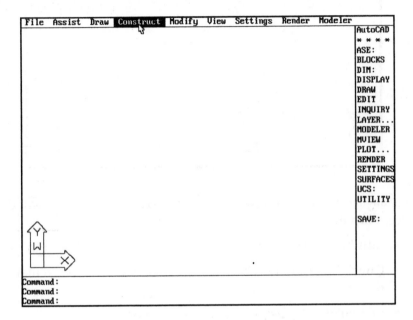

Figure 1.3:

The arrow pointer in the menu bar.

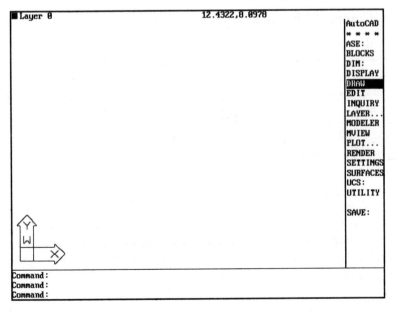

Figure 1.4:

The menu pointer in the screen menu.

Figure 1.5:

A typical dialog box.

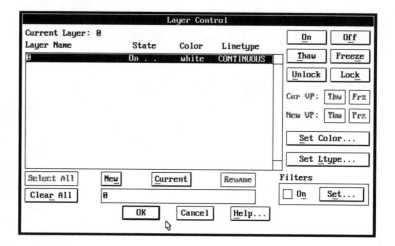

A *dialog box* uses the following elements to display messages and accept input:

- **Edit boxes.** This element accepts numbers or text or both

- **Check boxes.** Use a check box to turn on or off a particular feature

- **List boxes.** Use list boxes to choose an option

- **Command buttons.** This element causes immediate action

A dialog box enables you to enter necessary information in any order you want, rather than in the order given by prompts. In addition, you can change the entries in a dialog box as many times as necessary; the information is not transmitted to AutoCAD until you choose the OK box or press the Enter key.

Some commands always display dialog boxes; others display dialog boxes or prompts depending on AutoCAD's configuration.

Note

Some commands switch the display to a text screen to display prompts when text is displayed, rather than display a dialog box. After the command executes, the text screen may remain active. To return to the graphics screen, press the F1 key.

Using the File Menu

The first pull-down menu in the AutoCAD menu bar is the File menu (see fig. 1.6). This menu contains commands that create new drawings, open existing drawings for editing, save drawings, exit AutoCAD, and perform other file operations. Display the File menu and skim over the contents. The File menu's most important commands are described in the sections that follow.

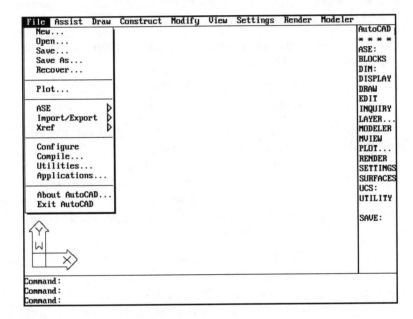

Figure 1.6:

The File menu invoked from the menu bar.

Displaying the File Menu

Move the cursor to the top of the screen	Displays the pull-down menu bar
Choose File	Displays the File pull-down menu

Beginning a New Drawing

Although you can begin drawing as soon as you start AutoCAD, you must name your drawing before you can save it. You can assign a name to a drawing in one of several ways:

- You can enter a drawing name after the ACAD command when you start AutoCAD

- You can start AutoCAD without entering a drawing name, and then pick the New command from the File menu

- You can begin drawing, and then pick the Save or Save as command from the File menu

- You can enter the New, SAVE, SAVE AS, or QSAVE commands from the keyboard

The exercise that follows uses the New command from the File menu. (Most of the exercises in this chapter use the New command.) Exercises are based on the AutoCAD GUI—you pick commands from menu bar pull-down menus. In later exercises you read about other ways to enter commands. In all cases, you can key in commands if you want, but the GUI generally requires fewer keystrokes.

When you pick commands from the menus, AutoCAD echoes the command in the command line. As you pick commands, observe the command echo—you soon will learn the names of the commands that you use. In any case, AutoCAD uses the command prompt area to display prompts and option lists for commands that do not use dialog boxes. To experiment with these menu commands, name your drawing in the next exercise.

Creating a New Drawing

Move the cursor to the top of the screen	Displays the menu bar
Choose File	Displays the File pull-down menu bar
Choose New	Displays the Create New
In the New **D**rawing Name *edit box,* *type* SAMPLE *and press Enter*	Drawing dialog box (see fig. 1.7)

Figure 1.7:

The Create New Drawing dialog box.

If you make any changes to the current drawing and then choose File, New, AutoCAD displays the Drawing Modification dialog box shown in figure 1.8. This dialog box enables you to save changes, confirm the deletion of changes, or cancel the New command.

Figure 1.8:

The Drawing Modification dialog box.

If you choose **S**ave Changes, but you have not assigned a drawing file name for the current drawing, AutoCAD displays the Save Drawing As dialog box. Assign a drawing name to the current drawing in this dialog box. The Create New Drawing dialog box displays again so that you can assign a name to the new drawing.

Editing an Existing Drawing

You rarely can complete a drawing in a single session. Usually, you must begin and end drawing sessions several times before a drawing is complete. Even when the drawing can be called complete, you probably will need to change it because of revisions or changes in the design.

To edit an existing drawing, you must open its drawing file. In other words, you must instruct AutoCAD to read the specified drawing file, and display it on-screen. To open a drawing file, choose the Open command from the File pull-down menu. When you do, AutoCAD displays the Open Drawing dialog box, which lists the available drawing files (see fig. 1.9). You can pick a drawing file from the list in the dialog box, or type a file name.

Figure 1.9:

The Open Drawing dialog box.

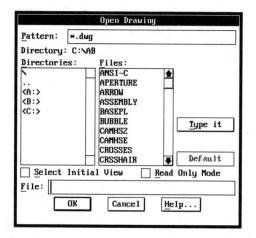

In the next exercise, study the elements of the dialog box. The **P**attern box accepts a parameter that filters out all file names except those matching the pattern. The default pattern for the Open Drawing dialog box causes only drawing files to be displayed in the files list box. The Directory line lists the current directory. The **D**irectories list box contains a list of the disk drives and directories. The **F**iles box contains a list of files in the current directory that matches the extension specified in **P**attern. The **T**ype it button tells AutoCAD to remove the dialog box and prompts you for the file name in the command prompt area. The Default button tells AutoCAD to enter the default pattern or file name, depending on the cursor's position.

If you check the **S**elect Initial View option box, AutoCAD lets you select an initial view of those saved in the drawing. If you check the **R**ead Only Mode box, AutoCAD displays the drawing, but does not allow you to save changes. If you want, you can type the file name in the **F**ile box, rather than pick the file name from the **F**iles list. If you choose a file name, AutoCAD types the name in the **F**ile edit box. When you click on the OK button, AutoCAD

executes the Open command using the parameters you specified.
If you click on Cancel, AutoCAD aborts the command and returns
to the previous screen display.

Opening a Drawing

Choose File, *then* Open	Displays the Open Drawing dialog box
In the File edit box, enter `C:\ACAD\SAMPLES\ADESK_B`	Opens the sample drawing ADESK_B.DWG in the samples directory of AutoCAD

If you double-click on a file name in the Files box (by
pressing and releasing the left mouse button twice in rapid
succession), AutoCAD selects the file and opens the file.
You do not have to press Enter or click on the OK button when
you double-click on a file name.

Saving a Drawing

When you edit a drawing, whether you are entering new elements
or changing existing ones, AutoCAD does not change the current
drawing file. It stores the changes in a series of temporary files on
disk and in memory. When you end a drawing session, or instruct
AutoCAD to save the drawing, AutoCAD posts the net effect of
all your changes to the drawing file. If you turn off the computer
or suffer some sort of disaster, such as loss of power, you lose any
changes that have not been posted to the drawing file. Thus, it is
essential that you save your changes at regular intervals.

The File menu contains two commands that save changes and
enable you to continue with your work. The first command, Save,
issues the QSAVE command. QSAVE does not display a dialog
box or issue any prompts unless you have not named your drawing. AutoCAD assumes that you want to save the current drawing
file without changing its name. To use this command, your

drawing must have a name. If you choose this command before a drawing file name is assigned, AutoCAD behaves as if you had chosen the second save command, Save as.

The SAVEAS command displays the Save Drawing As dialog box (see fig. 1.10). This dialog box is virtually identical to the Open Drawing dialog box—it has no Select Initial View or Read Only Mode check boxes, and the dialog box title differs from Open Drawing.

Figure 1.10:

The Save Drawing As dialog box.

To save a drawing, simply follow this step:

Saving a Drawing

Choose File, *then* Save

Saves the drawing to its current name

Exiting AutoCAD

You cannot just turn off the computer when you are finished drawing. Instead, you must tell AutoCAD that you want to end your drawing session, and then let AutoCAD perform its housekeeping chores. To end a drawing session, choose Exit AutoCAD from the File menu. AutoCAD issues the Quit command and then displays the Drawing Modification box if you have changed the drawing since it was last saved. If you have not changed the drawing since it was last saved, AutoCAD ends immediately, and returns you to the operating system prompt.

Setting AutoCAD Release 12 for Beginners Defaults

To make absolutely sure you are using the same default settings in AutoCAD as this book uses, follow the steps in the next exercise to set up AutoCAD so that it does *not* use a prototype drawing (see fig. 1.7). A prototype drawing is a drawing that AutoCAD uses as a template for creating a new drawing. All the AutoCAD settings that are stored in a drawing file, other drawing information, and any entities are transfered to the new drawing from the prototype. Without a prototype drawing, AutoCAD begins all new drawings with the same settings as the initial default ACAD.DWG.

Starting a New Drawing

Start AutoCAD with the AB.BAT file	
Move the cursor to the top of the screen	Displays the pull-down menu bar
Choose File	Displays the File pull-down menu
Choose New	Displays the Create New Drawing dialog box
Click on the box to the left of No Prototype, *then on* Retain as Default	Places X's in the boxes, turning on their settings
Choose OK	Closes the dialog box and saves your settings
Choose File, *and then* Exit AutoCAD	Leaves AutoCAD

You can enter the NEW command at the AutoCAD command prompt if you prefer. Many of AutoCAD's commands can be accessed from the pull-down and screen menus or from the command line. However, the commands sometimes act differently depending on how you access them. The differences between command access methods will be discussed as you learn about AutoCAD's commands and menus in the next chapter.

You can use the REINIT command to bring up the Re-initialization dialog box. Here, you can re-initialize your digitizer if it becomes inactive for some reason. You can also re-initialize your plotter if you forget to turn it on before starting AutoCAD. Any time your screen becomes "scrambled," you can re-initialize it by entering RE-INIT followed by the number eight.

Summary

In this chapter, you learned how to start the AutoCAD program, and how to assign file names to drawing files. You learned some basic concepts of AutoCAD's GUI—Graphical User Interface. With this information, you can view the sample drawings included with AutoCAD for a preview of what you can accomplish with AutoCAD.

Using AutoCAD Menus and Commands

In this chapter, you learn to communicate with AutoCAD, and how to use five basic drawing commands. You learn the following concepts:

- How the AutoCAD program works

- How to use menus, dialog boxes, and the keyboard to tell AutoCAD what you want it to do

- How to specify points, angles, and distances

- How to draw points, lines, arcs, circles, and text

- How to erase or undo errors

- How to get help and list drawing information

- How to save, end, or quit a drawing

In Chapter 1, you learned how to start the AutoCAD program, how to assign drawing-file names, and how to leave the AutoCAD program. This chapter has two primary topics: to provide an overview of ways to interact with AutoCAD and to introduce you to enough basic commands to create simple drawings. With the five drawing commands introduced in this chapter—Point, Line, Arc, Circle, and Text—you can draw almost anything with AutoCAD. The rest of the book builds on this foundation to show you how to draw more efficiently and more accurately. Along with the five basic entity drawing commands, this chapter covers the REDRAW, U (undo), ERASE, OOPS (unerase), LIST, HELP, SAVE, END, and QUIT commands.

AutoCAD's User Interface

Like most computer programs, AutoCAD has a *user interface*, which makes it possible for you to interact with the program. The user interface consists primarily of the following:

- A command entry and prompt line

- A status display line

- Dialog boxes

- Menus (screen, pull-down, icon, buttons, and, if you have a digitizer tablet, a tablet menu)

AutoCAD was developed around a command-prompt inter-face, with a provision for menus to make command entry easier. An AutoCAD menu displays a set of commands or choices, usually related, when you select it. You select a command from a menu by moving the pointer to the menu, and picking a menu item. AutoCAD generally echoes the command on the command line.

If you have a digitizer for a pointing device, you can use AutoCAD's tablet menu to enter the command (see fig. 2.1).

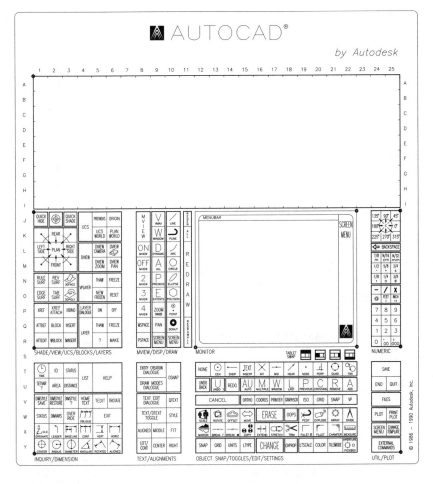

Figure 2.1:

AutoCAD's digitizer tablet menu.

The User-Interface Components

Figures 2.2 and 2.3 illustrate the AutoCAD components described in the following pages.

- **Drawing Area.** The *drawing area* is in the middle of your monitor's display (where the drawing appears). It is similar to a window that looks onto an infinite drawing surface. Using AutoCAD's display commands, you can pan this "window" around on your drawing, *zoom in* closer to see more detail, and *zoom out*, away from your drawing, to see more of the drawing area.

Figure 2.2:

AutoCAD's status line, command line, and drawing area.

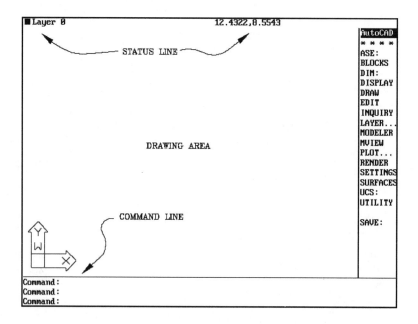

Figure 2.3:

AutoCAD's screen menu and pull-down menus.

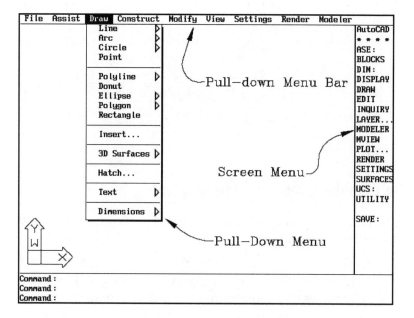

- **Command Line.** The *command line* is a command prompt (usually containing one to three lines) and command entry area, located below the drawing area. The number of lines you see on your screen depends on your system configuration. Command prompts appear in this area as you work. When you use the keyboard to type commands and responses to prompts, your input also appears on the command line.

- **Status Line.** The *status line*, located at the top of the display, shows the status of several drawing settings, as well as a coordinate display. You learn to watch the status line as your work in AutoCAD becomes more complicated and more precise.

- **Context-Sensitive Screen Menu.** The *screen menu* is the vertical menu along the right edge of the drawing area. Selecting an item from the screen menu executes a pre-defined command or choice; selecting some menus displays other menus with more sets of choices. The screen menu page that first displays when you enter the AutoCAD drawing editor is the *root menu*. At the top of every screen menu is the option shown as [AutoCAD]. When you select this option, you always return to the root menu. The screen menu is context-sensitive. It changes to reflect the command currently in progress, regardless of how the command was entered.

- **Pull-Down Menus.** As you move the pointing device (mouse, digitizer puck, or stylus), a crosshair cursor moves across the drawing area. When you move the cursor to the status line, the *pull-down menu* bar appears. When you select one of the labels on the pull-down menu bar (by pressing a button on your pointing device), it "pulls down" a menu with several command selections. (Pull-down menus are sometimes called *pop-down menus*.)

- **Cascading Menus.** Some commands listed in pull-down menus do not cause immediate execution of the command, but instead cause the display of another menu. You can identify these commands by the presence of a triangle at the end of the menu item. When you move the arrow pointer to the triangle, a submenu appears, overlapping the menu from which it was called. If you move the pointer vertically within the submenu, a reverse video highlight follows the pointer. If you move the arrow pointer to the right and out of the submenu, the highlight disappears, but the submenu remains in place. If you move the arrow pointer back into the previous menu, the submenu disappears. While a submenu is displayed, the command from which it was called remains highlighted, enabling you to see the chain of menu selections leading to the current command. Notice that you do not have to pick a menu command to display a cascading menu—you only have to move the arrow pointer to the triangle.

- **Dialog Boxes.** Many AutoCAD operations that involve making or checking several settings can be done at once by using a *dialog box*, which is an interface that simultaneously shows the status of a number of settings and enables you to provide input by clicking, selecting settings, and typing text (see fig. 2.4). Commands that prompt for file names also make use of dialog boxes to show lists of file names from which to select.

Figure 2.4:

Running Object Snap dialog box.

- **Icon Menu.** An *icon menu* shows an array of graphic images on-screen (see fig. 2.5). *Icons* are simple pictures or diagrams that graphically depict commands or functions. When you select the small box to the left of an icon, the computer executes the associated command or commands.

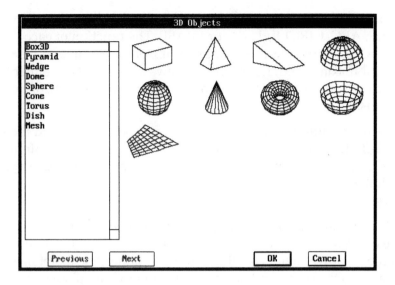

Figure 2.5:
An icon menu.

- **Tablet Menu.** If your system includes a digitizing tablet, you
  can use the AutoCAD *tablet menu* to enter commands with
  the digitizer. Many of AutoCAD's most common commands
  are identified by a command name and an icon on the tablet
  menu. The tablet menu puts most commands within view
  simultaneously.

These menus are defined in a menu file, which can be customized
to suit your preferences. The standard AutoCAD menu, which is
the default normally loaded in new drawings, is defined as the
ACAD.MNU file. This menu is commonly called the ACAD
menu.

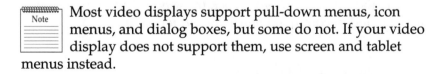 Most video displays support pull-down menus, icon
menus, and dialog boxes, but some do not. If your video
display does not support them, use screen and tablet
menus instead.

AutoCAD Command Entry Methods

Regardless of the menu or command-entry method you use, you
invoke AutoCAD's commands by using easy-to-remember words

and symbols. Each command consists of a single word, such as LINE, ARC, CIRCLE, TEXT, or ERASE. The function of each AutoCAD command is often apparent from its command name—the LINE command, for example, draws a line. You can either type commands at the keyboard or select them from one of the menus.

To enter a command with the keyboard, type its name and then press Enter, Tab, space bar, or the Enter button on your pointing device. For your convenience, AutoCAD treats all of these keys as Enter keys (except when you enter a string of text—you must press Enter).

If you use the screen, pull-down, or tablet menus, you can select the command you want with your pointing device. The screen and pull-down menus list the command names; the tablet menu often lists the command name, in addition to a small icon that symbolizes the commands. On the tablet menu, you pick a command's box with your pointing device to issue the command. On the screen and pull-down menus, you must display the menu page where the actual command is located, but menu pages are grouped by function. For example, the LINE command appears on the DRAW page of the screen menu and on the Draw pull-down menu, so you can select DRAW and then LINE: with your pointing device to issue the LINE command.

The exercises in the first part of this book instruct you to use the pull-down menus listed in the menu bar because their options are usually more descriptive than screen menus, and they are faster to use than typed commands. Later in the book, exercises will contain more general instructions that do not specify how to enter the command. By the time you reach those exercises, you decide which method of command entry you prefer.

Using a Mouse or Digitizer

You use the pointing device to select an item from a menu and to enter data points. As you move the mouse, puck, or stylus, a pointer moves across the drawing area. To select a menu option from the screen menu, move the pointer to the far right of the drawing area and onto the screen menu area. A menu option is then highlighted. To highlight other menu options on the screen menu, move the pointer up or down on the screen menu.

To activate a highlighted command menu item, press your pointing device's *pick button*. On a mouse, the pick button is usually the left button. On digitizer pucks, the pick button is usually located at the top of the puck (farthest away from you). If you use a stylus with the digitizer, pressing down on the stylus tip or pressing a button on the side of the stylus acts as the pick button. Whenever you are prompted to select a menu item or to pick a point, use the pick button to do so.

> **Note** Digitizer vendors and some users may refer to the pick button of a digitizer cursor as the *data button*. The data button may be the one with a 0 or it may have a specific color. Check the instructions that came with your digitizer.

To pick points in the drawing area with your pointing device, you move the pointer to where you want to pick a point, and then press the pick button. If a command is active and expecting a point, it uses the point picked at the pointer location.

To select pull-down menu items with your pointing device, move the pointer to the status line (located at the top of your screen). The status line changes to display the pull-down menu page labels. Move the pointer to the desired menu page label, pick the label to display the page, and then pick again to select the desired item from that page.

To select a tablet menu item with your pointing device, move the cursor to that item's box and pick to select it.

> **Command** **TABLET.** The TABLET command configures the digitizing tablet. Configuring defines the tablet areas for tablet menus and defines the screen pointing area. The tablet menu template supplied with AutoCAD works with the ACAD menu file. The screen menu contains a selection that automates tablet configuration. To use it, attach your template to your tablet, select SETTINGS, select TABLET: Config (or Re-Cfg), and follow the prompts you see.

| Note | If your pointing device has other buttons in addition to the pick button, menu items can be assigned to them. In the ACAD menu, the first additional button (the right button on a mouse) acts as an Enter key. The second button (the middle button on a three-button mouse) accesses the Assist cursor menu, which contains object snap modes, point filters, and the calculator function. |

Canceling Commands and Menus

Some AutoCAD commands can be aborted by pressing Enter. Other commands require that you use a special cancel character, the Control and C keys on your keyboard (shown as Ctrl-C) to abort or cancel the command. To issue Ctrl-C to cancel a command, hold down the Control key and press the letter C (either uppercase or lowercase), then release both keys. This cancels most commands, although some require you to press Ctrl-C twice.

If you display a pull-down menu, and you want to remove it from the screen, you can move the arrow pointer off the menu and press the pick button, or you can press Esc on the keyboard. Pressing Enter removes the menu, but also repeats the last command entered.

If a dialog box is displayed, you can cancel it by picking the Cancel button or pressing Esc. Do not press Enter—it either causes AutoCAD to complete the command with the settings currently entered in the dialog box, or it has no effect.

Trying AutoCAD's User Interface

The following exercise introduces you to AutoCAD's menu structure. After your operating system is booted, start AutoCAD. Then follow the steps in the following exercise to move through AutoCAD's interface. Experiment with the different types of menus and notice the prompts that appear at the bottom of your display. Press Ctrl-C to cancel commands after you select them from the menu. Whenever you need to press Enter, the exercise text shows the bent arrow character ⌐.

Using AutoCAD's Interface

`C:\> CD \AB` ↵	Puts you in your working directory
`C:\AB> \AB` ↵	Starts AutoCAD
`Command: LINE` ↵	Issues the LINE command from the keyboard
`From point:` *Press Ctrl-C* `*Cancel*`	Cancels the LINE command
From the screen menu, choose AutoCAD	Refreshes the screen menu
From the screen menu, choose DRAW	Displays the DRAW screen menu
From the screen menu, choose LINE:	Displays the LINE: screen menu
`Command: _LINE From point:` *Press Ctrl-C* `*Cancel*`	Cancels the LINE command
Choose Draw	Displays the pull-down Draw menu
Choose Line, *then* Segments	Selects multiple, connected Line segments
`Command: _LINE From point:` *Press Ctrl-C* `*Cancel*`	Cancels the LINE command

If you have a digitizer, select Line from the tablet menu. Then press Ctrl-C to cancel the LINE command. Select AUTOCAD from the screen menu.

Choose Modify, *then* Erase	Displays the Erase cascading menu
Click on Select	Starts the ERASE command
`Command: _erase`	Types the ERASE command
`Select objects:` *Press Ctrl-C* `*Cancel*`	Cancels the ERASE command
Choose File, *then* Exit AutoCAD	Displays the Drawing Modification box
Click on Discard Changes	Exits AutoCAD without saving the current drawing

The operating system prompt returns.

You can see that AutoCAD offers several ways to enter a command. It does not really matter which menu or method you use to invoke a command. You can type the commands at the command prompt or choose your favorite menu to execute them.

Before you learn AutoCAD's drawing commands and explore more of the user interface, you should have a basic understanding of the way points and coordinates are used in AutoCAD. Chapter 3 examines those subjects in detail, but the following is a brief overview.

Coordinates and Points

When you draw at the board, you use a variety of techniques to locate lines, circles, arcs, and text. In some cases, you measure from another feature with a scale—so many units to the right, so many units up. In other cases, you locate key points. For example, you might begin a line at the intersection of two other lines or you might draw a group of construction lines, and then trace over sections of those construction lines. In many cases, you can "eyeball" the points that define entities.

AutoCAD, or any other CAD program, requires numeric data in one of several specific formats. Because AutoCAD is interactive, you can draw in much the same manner as you do at the board. There are times, however, when you must furnish graphic data in a certain format to perform a given task.

Using Coordinates

The AutoCAD drawing world is based on a three-dimensional Cartesian coordinate system. That is, a point is located in space by specifying its distance from an origin, along three perpendicular axes: the X, Y, and Z axes.

The World Coordinate System

The two axes used for 2D drafting are the X axis and the Y axis. Unless you change the coordinate system, the *X axis* is horizontal and the *Y axis* is vertical on the display. (The *Z axis*, for 3D design, is perpendicular to the plane formed by the X,Y axes, extending into and out of the display.) AutoCAD's default coordinate system is called the *World Coordinate System (WCS)*. Figure 2.6 shows the orientation of the axes relative to the screen display. The icon at the lower left corner of the drawing area shows the orientation of the axes.

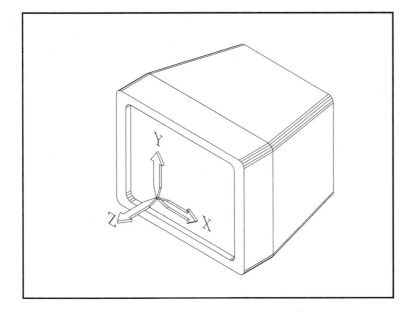

Figure 2.6:

The orientation of X, Y, and Z axes relative to the screen.

The intersection point of the X and Y axes in a Cartesian coordinate system is called the *origin*. The origin of the default WCS is often referred to as the *world origin* (or *global origin*). Throughout this book, the world origin is referred to as simply *the origin* or as the *0,0 coordinate*.

When you enter a point, whether by picking it visually or by typing it at the command line, AutoCAD reads the point as a set of numbers in the form X,Y,Z. In 2D drawings, you can omit the Z value because AutoCAD automatically assigns it a value of 0.

The coordinates of the origin are 0,0. As you look at the screen, X coordinate values to the right of the origin are positive; X coordinates to the left of the origin are negative. Y coordinate values above the origin are positive; Y coordinate values below the origin are negative. The origin is initially placed at the lower left corner of the drawing area, but you can move it up and/or right to make room to draw in negative coordinate space. For example, a coordinate of 6,-2 represents a point six units to the right of the origin and two units below it, as shown in figure 2.7. (One default unit is assumed to represent one inch, but it can represent any unit you need. The assumption for units in this book is inches.)

Figure 2.7:

Sample coordinates 6,-2.

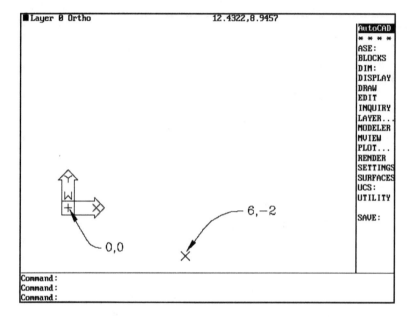

Absolute Coordinates

The coordinate discussed previously is called an *absolute* coordinate because it is expressed as a distance from the origin. When prompted for a point, you can enter absolute coordinates by typing them on the command line. Type the X value of the coordinate, insert a comma, type the Y value of the coordinate, and then press Enter. For example, the following example enters an absolute coordinate 3.5 inches to the right of the origin (in the X direction) and 4.25 inches above it (in the Y direction).

```
From point: 3.5,4.25
```

Relative Coordinates

Each time you type or pick a point, the new point becomes the *last point* input. AutoCAD remembers the last point, so you can easily enter new points relative to its location. *Relative coordinates* are based not on the origin, but on the last point. To enter a relative point, precede the X,Y pair with the @ (at sign). The following coordinate specifies a point six inches directly to the right of the current last point:

```
From point: @6,0
```

Use relative coordinates when you know the X and Y distances from your last point to the next one—for example, when you want to draw a horizontal or vertical line exactly six inches long. Relative coordinates are often easier to enter than absolute coordinates. If your last point is 3.55261,2.98741 and you want to draw exactly 3.5 inches straight up along the Y axis, it is much simpler to enter @0,3.5 than it is to enter the absolute coordinates 3.55261,6.48741.

Polar Coordinates

The third form of coordinate entry you can use in AutoCAD is polar specification. A *polar coordinate* is expressed as a distance and a direction angle from the origin. To specify a polar coordinate, type the distance, followed by a left angle bracket (<) and the angle. To locate a point based from the last point (relative polar), precede the distance < angle with the @ symbol. For example, to specify a relative polar point 3.75 inches from the last point at an angle of 45 degrees, enter the following:

```
@3.75<45
```

You can abbreviate entries of distances, points, and other numbers by omitting insignificant leading and trailing zeros and decimal points. For example, enter 0.25,75.0000 as .25,75 to save typing.

Pointing with Pointing Devices

The final method you can use to enter points is the simplest and the one you will use most often. You can use your mouse or pointing device to pick a point on the display at the current cursor location. If AutoCAD is expecting a point, it receives the coordinates of the selected point and acts upon them accordingly. If it is not expecting a point, AutoCAD generally ignores the point pick. You can tell when AutoCAD expects a point by the prompt it displays in the command prompt area: From point:, for example.

Because it is the simplest to understand, this last method of point entry is the one you use in this chapter. In later chapters, you work with absolute, relative, and polar point specifications when creating exact drawing geometry.

The Coordinate Display

At the outset, you should learn to use one of AutoCAD's most important drawing aids: the *coordinate display*. Slightly to the right of the center of the status line is a pair of numbers separated by a comma. The first number is an X coordinate, the second is a Y coordinate. As you move the pointing device and the crosshair pointer, the numbers change, indicating the current position of the crosshair pointer in the current coordinate system. At this point, they indicate coordinates in the WCS.

By pressing the F6 key, you can change the operation of the coordinate display. By default, AutoCAD continuously updates the coordinate display as you move the pointing device. If you press F6 once, the coordinate display will only update when a point is picked. When the coordinates are on and you are using a command that sets a point and accepts points thereafter, the coordinate display changes to display the relative polar distance from the previous point. If you press F6 again, the coordinate readout changes back to display the absolute X,Y position of the cursor.

The coordinate display is the counterpart to the scale you use at the board. You can use it in conjunction with other drawing aids (covered in the next chapter) to draw what you want, where you want it.

A Basic Drawing Command

The simplest command that accepts a single point is the POINT command.

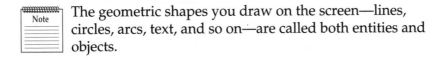

POINT. The POINT command draws a point entity with X,Y,Z coordinates anywhere in space. Points are commonly used for reference marks and as nodes to snap to with the NODe object snap mode. (See Chapter 3 for an explanation of object snap modes.)

When you use the POINT command, AutoCAD asks you to locate the point you want. You can pick the point with the cursor or enter the coordinates from the keyboard. AutoCAD uses the coordinates you specify to create a *point entity* (an object called a point) in the drawing at the coordinate location.

> **Note**
> The geometric shapes you draw on the screen—lines, circles, arcs, text, and so on—are called both entities and objects.

Although the default point entity is displayed as a dot, you initially see a small cross mark, called a *blip*. Each time you enter a point in AutoCAD, its location is temporarily marked by a blip. When you redraw the screen (the REDRAW command cleans up the display), the blips disappear. Actually, a true point would be invisible on the screen. By default, AutoCAD displays a single pixel (dot) as the symbol for a point, and offers a choice of other, more visible symbols.

REDRAW / REDRAWALL. The REDRAW command redraws the current viewport, cleaning up blips, redrawing the grid (if shown), and redrawing images that may have missing pieces because of previous edits. Use REDRAWALL to redraw all viewports. 'REDRAW and 'REDRAWALL execute these commands transparently.

When you execute a REDRAW command, the point entity remains on the screen. Unlike blips, points remain part of the drawing (and are visible on the display) until they are erased.

Try the following simple exercise, creating a few points and comparing them with blips:

POINTS versus Blips

Start AutoCAD with the AB batch file.

Choose File, *then* New	Starts a new drawing
New Drawing Name: **SAMPLE** ↵	Calls the new drawing SAMPLE
Choose Draw, *then* Point *or just type* **POINT**	Prompts for a point
Command: _point Point: *Pick a point* *with the cursor*	Shows picked point with a blip
Command: - Point	Repeats automatically if you used the pull-down menu; otherwise, press Enter to repeat the command.
Command: Point: 1,1 ↵	Enters an absolute coordinate using the keyboard
Command: Point: @4,0 ↵	Enters a relative coordinate by using the keyboard
Command: point Point: *Press* *Ctrl-C* *Cancel*	Cancels the repeating command
Choose View, *then* Redraw	Redraws the screen
Command: - redraw	

The blips disappear and the points remain as dots. You can type R and press Enter instead of typing **REDRAW**.

You can control the style and the size of your points by setting system variables. (Appendix A contains a table of system variables.)

Now that you are familiar with entering points, it is time to move on to the commands that you use most often: LINE, ARC, CIRCLE, and U (undo).

Understanding Lines, Arcs, Circles, and Undo

The three most common entities in drawings are lines, arcs, and circles. A line is the the most common entity found in a drawing; AutoCAD's LINE command is the one you probably use most often.

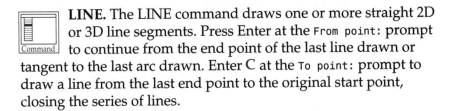

LINE. The LINE command draws one or more straight 2D or 3D line segments. Press Enter at the From point: prompt to continue from the end point of the last line drawn or tangent to the last arc drawn. Enter C at the To point: prompt to draw a line from the last end point to the original start point, closing the series of lines.

Using the LINE Command

The LINE command is simple to use. AutoCAD prompts you for the line's starting point; it then continues to prompt you for succeeding points until you end the command by pressing Enter or Ctrl-C. As you enter points, AutoCAD draws line segments between the end point and the newly entered point. LINE is a simple yet versatile command with three options.

LINE Options

- **From point:.** Specify the first point of the first line.

- **To point:.** Specify a new point to draw a line from the previous point to the new point.

- **Continue.** Select Continue from the screen menu or press Enter at the From point: prompt to continue a line from the end point of the most recently drawn line or arc.

- **Close.** Enter C (Close) at the To point: prompt to close a series of line segments, creating a line from the last end point to the first point of the series.

- **Undo.** Enter U at the To point: prompt to undo the last line segment back to the previous point.

Try out the LINE command to see how it works.

Drawing with the LINE Command

Continue from the previous exercise.

Choose Draw, *then* Line, *then* Segments	Starts the LINE command
From point: *Pick a point*	Specifies the beginning point of the line; a blip also appears
To point: *Pick another point*	Picks the end point of the segment

Notice that the line rubber-bands from the last point to the cursor.

To point: @2<45 ⏎	Enters a relative polar point
To point: U ⏎	Undoes the previous line segment
To point: *Pick a point*	
To point: *Press Enter*	Ends the LINE command
Command: *Press Enter*	
LINE From point: *Press Enter*	Starts the new line at the last pick point
To point: 2,2 ⏎	Enters an absolute coordinate by using the keyboard

`To point: @2,1 ↵`	Enters a relative coordinate by using the keyboard
`To point: C ↵`	Closes the line segments from the last pick point to the first in the series and terminates the line command

In this exercise, you added two line entities to your drawing. Notice that AutoCAD indicated what it is drawing by showing you a rubber-band line from the previous point to the cursor position. This rubber-band cursor enables you to visualize how the line will appear if you pick a point at the current location of the crosshair pointer.

You also saw that the LINE command's U option undoes the previous line segment and enables you to continue drawing line segments. You can enter U repeatedly to undo several line segments. Undo makes it easy to remove incorrect segments without having to exit and restart the LINE command.

Before you learn about the ARC and CIRCLE commands, take a moment to learn about another form of undo: the U (undo) command.

U (undo). The U (undo) command reverses the effects of the previous command.

The U command reverses one entire command. For example, if you use the LINE command to draw ten line segments, the U command from the Command: prompt undoes the entire LINE command—all ten segments—in one step. By using the LINE command's U option, you can undo only one line segment at a time. Although the U option of the LINE command works only within the LINE command, the U command works for any AutoCAD command.

Using Undo

Try using the U command to undo your last LINE command. Then undo the points you created with the earlier POINT command.

Using the U (Undo) Command

Continue from the previous exercise.

Choose Assist, *the* Undo	Removes the last series of lines
U GROUP	Prompts with the name of the undone command
Command: *Press Enter*	Repeats the U command
U GROUP	Removes the previous series of lines
Command: *Press Enter*	
U GROUP	Removes the last point you created

Continue to press Enter, reversing the POINT commands until your drawing is clear of all entities. With the last point undone, AutoCAD prompts:

Everything has been undone

Command: *Press Enter*

Further attempts to repeat the command cause AutoCAD to prompt:

U Nothing to undo

 Note Entities that were drawn with menu commands rather than keyboard commands cause AutoCAD to respond with GROUP rather than entity.

Now that you have a clear display again, take a look at two more drawing commands: ARC and CIRCLE.

ARC. The ARC command creates a circular arc. You can choose the arc's dimensions and location by specifying virtually any combination of the Start point, Second point, End point, Center, Angle, Length of chord, Radius, and Direction options. The default is a three-point arc that uses a starting end point, a second point on the arc, and the other end point.

The default three-point arc option prompts are shown in the previous command definition. Press Enter at the start point prompt to continue a new arc tangent to the last arc or line drawn. At each step, the prompt displays the options available.

Other options are discussed in later chapters. For now, experiment with the three-point ARC command to see how it works. Then use the U command again to undo all of the arcs and return to a clear display.

Using the ARC Command

Continue from the previous exercise or begin a NEW drawing named SAMPLE from the File menu.

Choose Draw, *then* Arc, *then* 3-point Or type **ARC** ⏎	Issues the prompt
`Command: _arc: Center/<Start point>` *Pick a point*	Selects the arc's start point
`Center/End/<Second point>:` *Pick a point*	Selects the arc's second point and draws a rubber-band arc
`End point:` *Pick another point*	Draws the arc
`Command:` **ARC** ⏎	
`Center.<start point>:` *Pick another start point*	
`Center/End/<Second point>:` *Pick a second point*	
`End point:` *Pick another end point*	
`Command:` *Press Enter*	
`ARC Center/<Start point>:` *Press Enter*	

Instead of picking a start point, press Enter to use the end point of the last arc.

`End point:` *Pick a point*	Prompts only for an end point, drawing the new arc tangent to the last
`Command:` *Press Enter*	
`ARC Center/<Start point>:` *Press Enter*	Starts another tangent arc
`End point:` *Pick an end point*	
`Command: U ⏎`	

Continue entering U until all the arcs are gone.

Although the ARC command has a number of options, the command itself is simple to use. When prompted to do so, provide the point or distance requested. When you give AutoCAD the information it needs, it draws the arc.

Like the LINE command, AutoCAD indicates where it will draw the arc (if you pick a point) by dragging a temporary arc with the cursor. AutoCAD drags or rubber-bands to give you feedback whenever it can.

CIRCLE. The CIRCLE command can draw circles by using nearly any geometric method. The most common method (the default) is to specify the center point and radius. You can drag and pick the size of the circle on the screen if the DRAGMODE system variable is set to On or AUTO (the default).

Like the ARC command, the CIRCLE command provides several ways to specify how to draw it. In addition to the default center point and radius shown in the command definition, you can create a circle by specifying the center point and diameter, by specifying three points on the circumference, by specifying two points to indicate the diameter, or by specifying two points (on a line, circle, or arc) that are tangent to the circle and a radius. These options are discussed further in a later chapter.

To enter the radius, type in a distance value when prompted or specify a point that is on the circle's circumference. You can specify a circumference point by picking it or typing its coordinates. The distance from the center point to the circumference point defines the radius.

Try out the CIRCLE command. Place a few circles, and then remove them by using the U command.

Drawing Circles by Using the Center Point and Radius

Continue from the previous exercise or begin a new drawing named SAMPLE from the main menu.

Command: **CIRCLE** ↵

CIRCLE 3P/2P/TTR/<Center point>:
Pick a center point

Diameter/<Radius>: **1.5** ↵   Draws a circle with a 1.5" radius

Command: *Press Enter*

CIRCLE 3P/2P/TTR/<Center point>:
Pick a center point

Diameter/<Radius><1.5000>:
*Pick a point that falls on the circumference
of the circle*

Notice the default radius length of 1.5". This will be replaced by your new radius length.

Command: *Press Enter*

CIRCLE 3P/2P/TTR/<Center point>:   Specifies a center point
2.5,3 ↵

Diameter/<Radius> <1.8381>:@1,0 ↵   Specifies a point that is one inch
                                             to the right of the center point,
                                             uses relative coordinates

Command: **U** ↵

Continue to UNDO until all of the circles are gone.

You now have the basic tools for creating a drawing.

Creating Real Drawings

Now, you get an opportunity to use what you have learned to draw a simple shear plate. Pick eight points with the cursor to draw the plate shown in figure 2.8. Do not concern yourself with exact dimensions yet—instead, estimate the points as if you are drawing freehand. Do not worry if your figure is not precise or perfect—the next chapter shows you how to control drawing accuracy. Unless specific menu instructions are given, type the command names or select them from the screen, pull-down, or tablet menus. If you make a mistake, press U and try again.

Figure 2.8:

The shear plate outline.

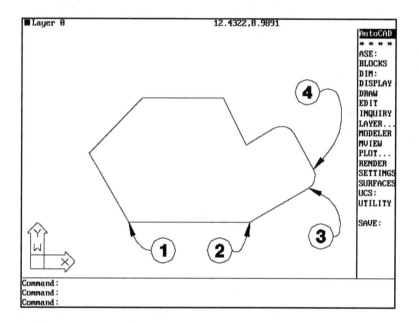

The Shear Plate

Choose File, *then* New, *then* Discard Changes

In the New Drawing Name: edit box, enter SHEARPL.

Command: LINE ↵

From point: *Pick point* ①
(see fig. 2.8)

To point: *Pick point* ②

To point: *Pick point* ③

To point: *Press Enter*

Choose Draw, *then* Arc, *then* 3-point

Command: _arc Center/
<Start point>: ↵

Uses the last line end point as
the arc start point

End point: *Pick point* ④

Command: **LINE** ↵

From point: *Press Enter*

Starts the line at the last arc end
point; draws the new line
tangent to the arc end point

Length of line: *Pick point for the
length of the line*

It does not matter where you pick, as long as you are the correct distance
from the arc end point. The line will be tangent to the arc.

To point: *Press Enter*

From the screen menu, choose AUTOCAD,
then DRAW, *then* ARC, *then* CONTIN:

Starts the arc at the end point
of the line

End point: **DRAG** *Pick the end point
of the arc*

Command: **LINE** ↵

From point: *Press Enter*

Length of line: *Pick point for the length*

Draws tangent to the arc

To point:

Continue drawing around the perimeter of the part, finally closing it
back at point one with the LINE command.

You continued the last line tangent to the previous arc by pressing
Enter in response to the From point: prompt. When you draw
tangent lines, a rubber-band line extends, tangent to the arc, in
addition to the normal rubber-band line from the last point to the
cursor. The value you enter or the point you pick at the prompt
indicates the length of the line that AutoCAD draws along that
tangent.

The perimeter of the shear plate is now complete, including the rounded corners. Finish the drawing with two circles and a slot. Begin with the two circles at the bottom of the shear plate and then approximate the slot by using the ARC and LINE commands. Your drawing should look like the one in figure 2.9.

Figure 2.9:

The shear plate with holes.

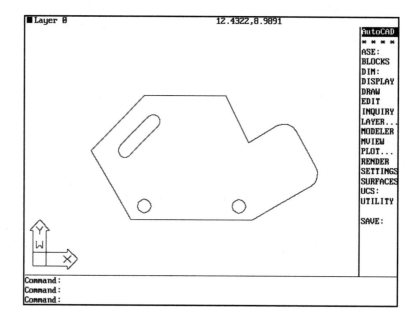

Adding a Slot and Circles to the Shear Plate

Continue from the previous exercise.

Choose Draw, *then* Circle, *then* Center, Radius

Command: _circle 3P/2P/TTR/
>Center point>: *Pick the center point of the left circle*

Diameter/<Radius>: .375 ⏎   Specifies a radius

Command: *Press Enter*

CIRCLE 3P/2P/TTR/<Center point>:   Specifies the second center point
@3.5,0 ⏎   using relative coordinates

Diameter/<Radius> <0.3750>: *Press Enter*   Uses the default radius size to
                                            get an identical circle

```
Command: ARC ↵
```

Draw one of the arcs that makes up the slot.

`Center/<Start point>:` *Pick the start point*

`Center/End/<Second point>:` *Pick the second point*

`End point:` *Pick the end point*

`Command:` **LINE** ↵

`From point:` *Press Enter*   Starts tangent to the last arc

`Length of line:` *Pick point for length of the first slot line*

`To point:` ↵   Ends the LINE command

`Command:` **ARC** ↵

`Center/<Start point>:` *Press Enter*   Starts the arc at the line's end point

`End point:` *Pick the end point*

`Command:` LINE ↵

`From point:` *Press Enter*   Starts at the end point of the last arc

`Length of line:` *Pick point for length for the second slot line*

`To point:` *Press Enter*   Ends the LINE command

Notice that the end points of the slot do not line up exactly, so you need better control over the accuracy of pick points (this subject is covered in the next chapter). If you want, you can undo the last line and try to replace it with a line that fits better.

You have now completed the main portion of the shear plate drawing. Before you experiment with a few more AutoCAD commands, however, save your shear plate drawing so you can work with it again. To save it, use AutoCAD's SAVE command.

Saving Your Work

When you edit a drawing in AutoCAD, changes or additions to the drawing are stored temporarily. Sometimes your drawing data (and everything in memory) can be lost because of accidents, such as power failures. Therefore, you need a way to store a permanent copy of the drawings you create. The SAVE command in the File menu enables you to safely store these drawings.

SAVE. The SAVE command saves your drawing to a file on disk. The current drawing's path and file name is the default, but you can specify another file name or path and file name. When saving to the default drawing name, the SAVE command renames the previous drawing file with a BAK extension.

The SAVE command copies the drawing data from memory into a disk file. All you have to do is supply the name of the drawing; AutoCAD automatically adds the DWG file extension. If you press Enter instead of supplying a file name, AutoCAD saves the drawing under the current drawing name.

Using Dialog Boxes

When you use the SAVE command, AutoCAD displays the Save Drawing As dialog box, shown in figure 2.10. It enables you to select disk drives, directories, and files by using the cursor. When you use a file dialog box to save a file, the current drawing file name automatically appears at the bottom of the dialog box. If you want to use the same name, press Enter. If there is no current drawing file name set, AutoCAD displays a bar cursor in the File: edit box, inviting you to type in a name. If you want to save the file under a name other than the current name, double-click on the current file name and enter a new one.

Use the SAVE command to save your shear plate drawing.

Using SAVE To Save Your File

Type **SAVE** *or select it from*   The dialog box appears
the pull-down menu

Press Enter to save the drawing
with its original name.

```
┌─────────────────────────────────────┐
│          Save Drawing As             │
│  Pattern:  *.dwg                     │
│  Directory: C:\AB                    │
│  Directories:      Files:            │
│  \                                   │
│  ..                                  │
│  <A:>                                │
│  <B:>                                │
│  <C:>                                │
│                          ┌─────────┐ │
│                          │ Type it │ │
│                          └─────────┘ │
│                          ┌─────────┐ │
│                          │ Default │ │
│                          └─────────┘ │
│  File: SHEARPL2                      │
│      ┌────┐  ┌────────┐  ┌───────┐   │
│      │ OK │  │ Cancel │  │ Help..│   │
│      └────┘  └────────┘  └───────┘   │
└─────────────────────────────────────┘
```

Figure 2.10:

The Save Drawing As dialog box.

Now that your drawing is safely stored on disk as SHEARPL.DWG, it is time to learn about the ERASE command, which is one of AutoCAD's most-used editing commands.

The Editing Process

Just as you need an eraser to make changes or corrections to a drawing you create manually, you also need a set of tools to edit a CAD drawing. AutoCAD provides a wide range of commands for making changes to existing drawing entities. AutoCAD has more commands for editing objects than it does for creating new ones. All of AutoCAD's editing commands are located on its EDIT screen menu, and most of them appear on the Modify pull-down menu and on the tablet menu.

One of the most useful (and necessary) commands for a beginning AutoCAD user is the ERASE command. Just as its name implies, the ERASE command erases lines, arcs, circles, text, or any other type of entity you create. The ERASE command prompts you to select the items to be erased, and after you press Enter to confirm the selection, AutoCAD removes the entities.

ERASE. The ERASE command deletes selected entities from the drawing.

Creating Selection Sets

Like many of AutoCAD's editing commands, the ERASE command works on a selection set. A *selection set* is nothing more than a collection of drawing entities that you build by specifying which entities are to be part of the set. You usually specify them by selecting the entities with the pointer. For example, when you invoke the ERASE command and then pick a line to be erased, the line is placed into the selection set. AutoCAD highlights selected entities (it displays them as dotted or dashed) to indicate that they are in the set.

When you have selected all the entities you want to erase, press Enter to indicate to AutoCAD that your selection is complete. In the case of the ERASE command, the entities in the selection set are then erased.

AutoCAD offers a number of ways to select entities (Chapter 7 explores them in more detail). When you enter **ERASE**, the full-screen crosshair cursor is replaced by a small box cursor. This selection cursor is called the *pick box*. To select an entity and make it a part of the selection set, place the pick box anywhere on the entity and click the pick button. The pick box must touch the entity for AutoCAD to select it.

Use the ERASE command to remove the slot you just created on your shear plate. Then, to confirm that the U command really reverses the effect of the previous command, use it to bring back your slot.

Picking Entities with ERASE

Continue from the previous exercise, or use the File menu's Open command to open the SHEARPL drawing

Choose Modify, *place the pointer on the triangle next to Erase*	Displays the Erase submenu
Choose Select	
Command: _erase	
Select objects: *Pick the first slot arc*	
Select objects: 1 found	
Select objects: *Pick the second slot arc*	
Select objects: 1 found	
Select objects: *Pick the first slot line*	
Select objects: 1 found	
Select objects: *Pick the second slot line*	
Select objects: 1 found	
Select objects: *Press Enter*	Confirms the selection set, erases the entities
Command: R ↵	Cleans up the drawing display

A fast way to redraw is to type R and press Enter

Command: U ↵	
REDRAW	Displays the name of the command undone
Command: U ↵	
ERASE	Reverses the ERASE command

If you wonder how to remember everything about AutoCAD, take heart. You do not have to remember it all—you just need to know where to find information; AutoCAD offers you help to find the information you need. Before completing the shear plate drawing, take a moment to explore AutoCAD's built-in help feature.

Using Help in AutoCAD

AutoCAD is a relatively easy program to use after you understand a few basics. It can be overwhelming at first in its complexity: AutoCAD has 118 standard commands, and 172 standard system variables. Even the most experienced user can have a hard time remembering all the possibilities. Fortunately, AutoCAD includes an on-line help system that provides information on each of those commands and variables.

HELP / ?. The HELP command (you can type **HELP** or **?**) displays information on commands, point and coordinate input, and entity selection. If you type **HELP** or pick Help! from the Assist pull-down menu, AutoCAD displays the Help dialog box (see fig. 2.11), which contains a list of commands. If you enter '**HELP** or '**?** during another command, AutoCAD displays the Help dialog box with information about the current command and resumes the command when you pick OK.

Figure 2.11:

Help dialog box.

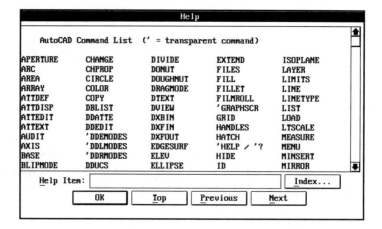

Help
AutoCAD Command List (' = transparent command)

APERTURE	CHANGE	DIVIDE	EXTEND	ISOPLANE
ARC	CHPROP	DONUT	FILES	LAYER
AREA	CIRCLE	DOUGHNUT	FILL	LIMITS
ARRAY	COLOR	DRAGMODE	FILLET	LINE
ATTDEF	COPY	DTEXT	FILMROLL	LINETYPE
ATTDISP	DBLIST	DVIEW	'GRAPHSCR	LIST
ATTEDIT	DDATTE	DXBIN	GRID	LOAD
ATTEXT	DDEDIT	DXFIN	HANDLES	LTSCALE
AUDIT	'DDEMODES	DXFOUT	HATCH	MEASURE
AXIS	'DDLMODES	EDGESURF	'HELP / '?	MENU
BASE	'DDRMODES	ELEV	HIDE	MINSERT
BLIPMODE	DDUCS	ELLIPSE	ID	MIRROR

Help Item: [   ] [Index...]

[OK] [Top] [Previous] [Next]

Using the HELP Command

Continue from the previous exercise.

Choose Assist, *then* Help!	Displays the Help dialog box
In the Help Item: *edit box, enter* ERASE	Replaces the list of commands with information on the ERASE command
Click on Index	Displays the Help Index dialog box, with ERASE highlighted
Click on the down arrow	Moves the command list down one command
Click on the up arrow	Moves the command list up one command
Click and hold on the square inside the slider bar between the up and down arrows, then move the point up and down	Scrolls through the command list
Click on a command in the list	Selects the command you want help with
Click on OK	Displays the Help dialog box with information on the selected command
Click on Index	
Pattern: LINE* ↵	Displays all help screen names that begin with LINE
Click on Cancel	Cancels Help Index dialog box
Click on OK	Exits the Help dialog box

The help screen for ERASE tells you about the command, gives you the format for use, and provides tips on how to use it. Finally, the help screen tells you where to look in the *AutoCAD Reference Manual* to find more information on the command.

Some commands can be prefaced with an apostrophe (') to execute them *transparently*. A transparent command can interrupt another command. If you are in the middle of a command (such as ERASE) and enter 'HELP or '?, HELP interrupts the command and displays the Help dialog box. When you exit HELP, it returns to the interrupted command.

Using Transparent Help

```
Command: LINE ↵
From point: '? or 'HELP ↵                    Opens Help dialog box with
                                             information on LINE

Click on OK                                  Exits Help dialog box
From point: Press Ctrl-C                     Cancels LINE command
```

Notice that help did not interrupt the LINE command.

Feel free to use HELP as you work through this book.

Adding Notes to Drawings

Drawings are usually made up of more than just lines, arcs, and circles. The vast majority of drawings also include notes, dimensions, symbols, and other data that help explain the body of the drawing.

Using the TEXT Command

The most common type of annotation on a drawing is *text*, which includes notes, item numbers, information in the bill of material, and other text. AutoCAD provides the TEXT command for entering text in the drawing.

TEXT. The TEXT command draws a single text string on screen after you enter a line of text input. (Another text command, DTEXT, dynamically shows text characters on the screen as you type them.)

TEXT Options

- **Start point.** Specify the bottom left corner of the first character of the text string. This option is the default left text justification.

- **Justify.** The Justify option prompts for 14 other text justifications (discussed in a later chapter).

- **Style.** The Style option changes the current text style. (Styles are discussed in Chapter 6.)

- **Press Enter.** When you press Enter instead of entering an option number, AutoCAD highlights the last text string drawn and defaults to that string's style, height, and rotation. AutoCAD then prompts for a new text string, which is placed directly below the highlighted text.

- **Height.** Enter the text height (the default is 0.2).

- **Rotation angle.** Specify the angle for the text (the default is 0).

- **Text.** Type a text string and press Enter to complete the command and draw the text.

To use the TEXT command, select it from AutoCAD's DRAW screen menu, from the Draw pull-down menu, from the tablet menu, or type TEXT at the command prompt. You provide AutoCAD with five items of information about your line of text: the alignment of the text, its reference point, text height, text rotation, and the text string itself. After you supply this information, AutoCAD makes the text a part of your drawing. The results are shown in figure 2.12.

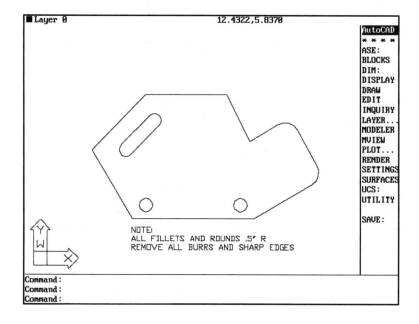

Figure 2.12:

The annotated shear plate.

You can add a few notes to your drawing by using the TEXT command's default alignment, text height, and rotation.

Using the Text Command

Command: **TEXT** ⏎

Justify/Style/<Start point>: *Pick a startpoint for the text (see fig. 2.12)*

Height <0.200>: .1875 ⏎ — Specifies the text's height

Rotation angle <0>: ⏎ — Accepts the default rotation of 0

Text: **NOTE:** ⏎ — Specifies the first line of text

Command: *Press Enter* — Repeats TEXT command

TEXT Justify/Style/<Start point>: *Press Enter* — Starts a new line of text below the first

Text: **ALL FILLETS AND ROUNDS .5" R** ⏎

Command: ⏎

TEXT Justify/Style/<Start point>: ⏎

Text: **REMOVE ALL BURRS AND SHARP EDGES** ⏎

Command: **QSAVE** ⏎ — Saves the drawing to the same name

You have created a drawing using lines, circles, arcs, and text. Now exit AutoCAD and save your drawing.

Using Exit AutoCAD to End a Drawing Session

Command: **END** ⏎

The END command saves all drawing changes and returns you to the operating system. If the current drawing doesn't have an assigned name, the Create Drawing File dialog box displays, enabling you to save your drawing to a file.

Summary

By now, you should be fairly familiar with AutoCAD's user interface: prompts on the command entry line, status displays, dialog boxes, and various menus.

You can draw points, straight lines, arcs, and circles, and annotate your drawings with text. You can erase unwanted entities and correct mistakes with OOPS and U (undo). You can clean up your screen with REDRAW and list entities. If you get lost, you can seek help.

If you put down this book right now, you can draw just about anything you want in AutoCAD, but you have just scratched the surface. In the next chapter, you will learn some techniques to make your drawing accurate and explore more efficient commands and methods.

Drawing Accurately

In this chapter you learn how to use AutoCAD's drawing aids so that you can draw faster, easier, and more accurately. Instead of typing points, distances, and angles, you learn how to perform the following:

- Check coordinate points and distances
- Lay out points that fall on a regular grid
- Draw at 90-degree angles
- Snap to geometric points on existing objects in your drawing
- Use dialog boxes to control various drawing aid settings
- Align points with XYZ point filters
- Relocate and control the AutoCAD drawing coordinate system

Overview

In Chapter 2, you created a simple drawing using AutoCAD's user interface, including its pull-down menus, screen menus, the keyboard, and pick points. Although you used a CAD program that stores points with an accuracy of 16 significant digits, you drew in "freehand"—you did not give AutoCAD precise measurements and coordinates when you drew the shear plate. Figure 3.1 shows the shear plate drawn with accurate dimensions.

Figure 3.1:

An accurate shear plate, with dimensions.

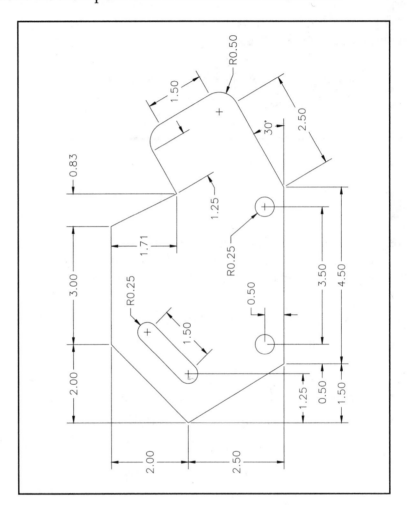

In this chapter you learn to use the following commands:

- **GRID.** This command configures and displays a grid on the screen.

- **SNAP.** This command is used to force the crosshairs to move at specific intervals.

- **ORTHO.** This command enables you to draw quickly and easily at 90-degree angles

- **DDRMODES.** This command's dialog box controls the drawing aids settings

- **OSNAP.** This command and object snap modes enable you to "lock on" to existing points of objects in your drawing

- **UCS.** This command and the DDUCS dialog box enable you to relocate the coordinate system

- **UCSICON.** This command enables you to control the display of the UCS icon

- **ID.** This command is used to select a point of reference for commands that need a start point

- **DIST.** This command is used to measure the distance between two points

Before reading about AutoCAD drawing aids that can improve your accuracy, take a moment to consider why accuracy is more important in a CAD drawing than in manual drafting.

Accuracy and AutoCAD

When you create a drawing manually, the drawing contains some inaccuracy because of paper instability, the width of the pencil lead or pen tip, the way in which the pencil is held, and other factors. To the naked eye, however, the drawing looks accurate. When dimensioning a manual drawing, you use values that you have calculated, and everyone understands that dimensions take precedence over the scale of the geometry. As veteran designers say, "Do NOT scale the drawing."

If you key in exact values when you use AutoCAD to lay out a drawing, AutoCAD records those values so that the completed drawing geometry is accurate to 16 decimal places. The plot paper still stretches with environmental changes, however, and the pen width affects accuracy. Why then, is it more important to be as accurate as possible when you work in a CAD drawing?

One of the most useful features of CAD is *automatic dimensioning*. When you are ready to add dimensions to your drawing, you do not need to calculate them, measure distances, or remember the values you used when you created the drawing. AutoCAD calculates dimensions from the definitions of drawing entities and displays those dimensions to the number of decimal places you specify. Dimensioning a drawing is a simple process of pointing and clicking.

Because the drawing geometry determines the dimensions, however, your dimensions are only as accurate as your input. If you use precise values when you create the geometry, the dimensions are accurate. If you round off numbers, your dimensions reflect that inaccuracy. Consequently, you should always use precise values or the accuracy aids that this chapter presents to ensure that your drawings are as precise as possible.

Using Coordinates, Grid, and Ortho To Obtain Accuracy

AutoCAD offers a number of drawing aids that correspond to conventional drawing tools. These aids can measure, serve as automatic scales, electronic drafting machines, straightedges, and triangles.

Coordinate entry, the first of AutoCAD's tools for accurate drawing, was discussed in Chapter 2. You learned the different ways in which you can specify coordinates when prompted to do so by AutoCAD. Coordinate entry is a major part of drawing in AutoCAD. Table 3.1 lists examples of the various forms of point entry.

Table 3.1

Coordinate Entry Examples

Example	Type	Description
4.5,3.25	Absolute X,Y	4.5 units to right, 3.25 up from 0,0 origin

Coordinate Entry Examples

Example	Type	Description
-2,0	Absolute X,Y	2 units to left from 0,0 origin
@4.5,3.25	Relative X,Y	4.5 units to right, 3.25 up from last point
@-2,0	Relative X,Y	2 units to left from last point
6.5<45	Absolute polar	6.5 units from 0,0 origin at 45 degrees (Release 11 only)
2<0	Absolute polar	2 units to right of 0,0 origin (Release 11 only)
@6.5<45	Relative polar	6.5 units from last point at 45 degrees
@2<0	Relative polar	2 units to right from last point
@		Accepts the last point picked as the start point of the command

Note
The default base 0-degree angle is horizontal, extending from 0,0 to the right. Angles are measured counterclockwise from the base angle.

The type of coordinate entry you use most depends on the type of drawings you create. When you begin to use AutoCAD on a regular basis, you will probably use relative coordinates most often because most drawings employ width and length (X and Y offsets), and distances and angles. CNC programmers, however, may prefer absolute coordinates.

Although coordinate entry using the keyboard guarantees accuracy, typing points is slow and tedious. Drafting would be much easier if you could indicate the general vicinity of the desired point and AutoCAD calculated the exact coordinates.

Entering Coordinates at Regular Intervals

The SNAP command enables you to set an increment to which your cursor jumps, or *snaps*. In some cases, SNAP eliminates the need to type coordinates, which speeds drawing time considerably. If you design a printed circuit board, for example, you can set the snap grid to 0.01 inches; if you design a brick or concrete block building, you can set the snap grid to four inches. The snap grid ensures that your drawing contains only those points that correspond to job requirements.

SNAP. The SNAP command restricts cursor crosshair movement to the snap increments. Use SNAP to specify the increment value (default is 1.0 drawing unit). The Aspect option enables you to specify different X and Y increments. The Rotate option enables you to offset the snap base point or rotate the snap grid. The Style option enables you to select a normal or an isometric snap grid. You can use SNAP or Ctrl-B (and F9 on DOS systems) to turn on and off snap. The DDRMODES dialog box also controls snap.

The snap increment is set using the SNAP command. The simplest way to turn snap on and off is by using the F9 function key. When snap is turned on, the status bar at the top of the screen displays the word SNAP to indicate that it is on (see fig. 3.2). The SNAP indicator in the status bar is near the left edge of the display, just to the right of the current layer indicator.

As you type the commands in the steps below, notice that the associated screen menu appears for each command you type. If you want to issue a command twice in succession, you can type the command once and pick the command off the newly displayed screen menu the second time. This saves you time. You can also press Enter to reissue the last command, which may be faster still.

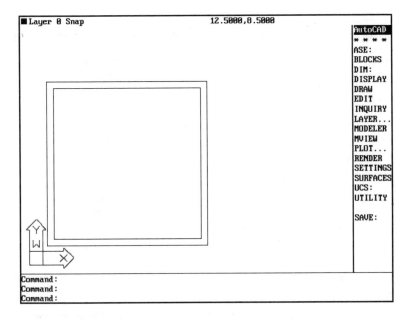

The SNAP command has the following options:

- **Snap spacing.** This option enables you to enter a value to set the snap increment and to turn on snap.

- **ON.** This option turns on snap.

- **OFF.** This option turns off snap (the default).

- **Aspect.** The Aspect option sets different horizontal (X) and vertical (Y) snap increments. (This option is not available in isometric mode; see the Style option.)

- **Rotate.** The Rotate option rotates the snap grid (and crosshairs) by any specified angle about a specified base point. See the Ortho section of this chapter for an exercise example.

- **Style.** Isometric sets an isometric snap grid style (aligns snap points to a 30-, 90-, or 150-degree grid). Standard sets the normal (default) snap style.

In the steps that follow, practice using the SNAP command and coordinate entry.

Using SNAP and Typed Coordinates To Draw Accurately

Start AutoCAD from the AB directory (your AutoCAD for Beginners directory) and create a new drawing named SAMPLE

```
Command: LINE ↵
From point: 1,1 ↵
To point: 7,1 ↵
To point: @0,6 ↵
To point: 1,7 ↵
To point: C ↵                          Closes the series of lines and
                                       ends the command

Commmand: SNAP ↵
Snap spacing or ON/OFF/Aspect/Rotate   Sets X, Y spacing to
/Style <1.0000>: .25 ↵                 .25 units
```

Move around the cursor and notice how it jumps in 1/4-inch increments.

Now draw a square one snap increment inside the existing square.

```
Commmand: LINE ↵
```

`From point:` *Pick a point .25" to the right and above the lower left corner of the square*

Continue to pick points drawing a 5.5" square .25" (1 snap increment) inside the 6" square:

`To point:` *Pick above and left of lower right corner*

`To point:` *Pick below and left of upper right corner*

`To point:` *Pick below and right of upper left corner*

`To point:` *Pick start point*

`To point:` *Press enter*   Ends the LINE command

SNAP is much easier to use than entering coordinates from the keyboard. The more you can avoid entering coordinates, the faster you can draw.

Note

Coordinates and distances entered from the keyboard, as well as object snap modes, override the snap setting.

What SNAP lacks is a frame of reference. If you have to count snap increments to verify a distance, SNAP is not doing you much good. AutoCAD has two tools that you can use as a frame of reference: the dynamic coordinates display and the drawing grid.

Controlling Accuracy with the Coordinate Display

You already learned that the coordinate display on the status line updates to display the last coordinate when you pick a point. The *coordinate display*, located just to the right of center on the status bar, displays an X,Y value using the current unit settings. (If you work in feet and inches, the coordinate display is also in feet and inches.)

Instead of displaying X,Y coordinate values, the coordinate display often shows relative polar coordinates when used in commands. If you invoke the LINE command, for example, and the coordinate display is turned on, an X,Y coordinate value appears at the From point: prompt. After you pick the first point, however, the display changes to relative polar coordinates. The polar display shows the distance and angle from the last point. This is the default, with the coordinate display on whenever polar coordinates make sense for the current prompt. When polar coordinates are displayed, the crosshairs are followed by a rubber-band cursor anchored to the last point.

When you start a new drawing, the coordinate display is in *dynamic* mode. The coordinate display shows the current X and Y coordinates of the crosshair. As you move the crosshair, the coordinate display is continuously updated. You can use the coordinate display to help you pick exact points without having to type the coordinates.

If you do not want the coordinate display to be continuously updated, you can press F6 to change to *static mode*. In static mode, the coordinate display is updated only when you pick a point.

You can activate a final mode, called *relative polar*, by pressing F6 while in static mode. In relative polar mode, the coordinate display is continuously updated as you move the crosshair, just like dynamic mode. When a rubber-band cursor is displayed, however, relative coordinates show the distance and angle from a first pick point to the current crosshair location. If you press F6 while relative polar coodinates are displayed, you will cycle back to the first mode (dynamic).

When you combine the SNAP command with the coordinate display, you can save quite a bit of time, as the following exercise shows.

Snapping to the Coordinate Display

Continue in the previous drawing or begin a new drawing named SAMPLE.

```
Command: SNAP ↵
```

`Snap spacing or ON/OFF/Aspect/Rotate/` `Style <0.2500>: .5`	Sets SNAP spacing to .5 units

```
Command: LINE ↵
From point: Move the cursor
```

Notice that the coordinates display changes.

Move the cursor until the coordinate display shows 8.0000,1.0000, and then pick a point

```
To point: Move the cursor to the right
```

Notice the rubber-band line and the coordinate display.

`To point: ` *Press F6*	Turns off the coordinate display
`To point: <Coords off>` *Press F6*	Turns on the coordinate display again to polar coordinates

Move the cursor until the display reads 3.000<0 and then pick the point

`To point: ` *Move to 6.000<90 and pick a point*

`To point: ` *Move to 3.000<180 and pick a point*

To point: *Move to 6.000<270 and pick a point*

To point: *Press Enter*   Ends LINE command

Command: **CIRCLE** ⏎

3P/2P/TTR/<Center point>: *Pick 8.5000, 1.0000 using the coordinate display as a guide*

Diameter/<Radius>: *Pick at 0.5000<180*

Command: **CIRCLE** ⏎

3P/2P/TTR/<Center point>: *Pick 10.5000,1.0000*

Diameter/<Radius>: *Press F6*   Turns the coordinate display to
                                          absolute coordinates

*Move the cursor to 11.000,1.000
and pick the point*

Command: *Press F6 twice*   Turns the coordinate display off
                                          and then to polar

Using GRID To Find Points

A grid often is more useful than the coordinate display because it provides a visual frame of reference on the drawing. A *grid* is a square or rectangular array of temporary dots on the drawing screen. By coordinating the grid spacing with the snap increment, you can easily estimate distances and identify points that fall on the grid or snap spacing. The GRID command sets the spacing between grid dots in both the X and Y axes. The grid spacing can be set to any value, or it can be set to different spacing values for the horizontal and vertical increments.

GRID. The GRID command defines and displays a reference grid of dots that can be spaced to any X,Y increment. You can use the GRID command to set the increment, and then turn the grid on or off. You also can turn the grid on and off by using Ctrl-G, the F7 function key on DOS-based systems, or the DDRMODES dialog box.

As with many AutoCAD drawing aids, GRID is turned on and off by using either a control character (Ctrl-G) or a function key (F7). The screen is redrawn each time the grid is turned on or off.

GRID Options

- **Grid spacing (X).** This option enables you to set and turn on the X,Y grid increment. Enter 0 to make the grid spacing equal to the snap spacing (changing automatically when snap changes). If you enter a number followed by an X, AutoCAD sets the grid to the current snap increment times the number.

- **ON.** This option makes the grid visible.

- **OFF.** This option makes the grid invisible.

- **Snap.** The Snap option sets the grid increment equal to the current snap increment, the equivalent of entering 1X for the grid spacing. The Snap option does not automatically change the grid as snap changes.

- **Aspect.** The Aspect option sets different increments for horizontal and vertical grid.

The angle and base point of the grid are controlled by the SNAP command's Rotate option. If you set snap to an isometric style, the grid follows. This option is useful for aligning snap and grid to your drawing geometry, but the UCS command, which is discussed later in this chapter, offers a better method of controlling the grid rotation and snap.

Although the GRID command's Snap option sets the grid spacing equal to the snap increment, set the grid and snap to different values, such as a grid spacing of one and a snap increment of .25, .125, or .2. This setting enables you to count snap increments easily between grid dots without having an overly dense grid.

The following exercise illustrates how using the GRID and SNAP commands decreases drawing time and increases accuracy.

Using AutoCAD's GRID

Continue using the previous exercise, or choose File, New to begin a new drawing named SAMPLE.

```
Command: SNAP ↵
```
```
Snap spacing or ON/OFF/Aspect/          Sets a new snap spacing
Rotate/Style <0.2500>: .5
```
```
Command: GRID ↵
```
```
Grid spacing(X) or ON/OFF/Snap/         Sets the X,Y grid spacing to 1
Aspect <0.0000>: 1 ↵                    and turns the grid on
```
*Move the crosshair pointer to
verify that snap is set to one-half
of the grid setting.*

If you are beginning a new drawing, use LINE to draw a 6" square with the lower left corner at 1,1. Pick the dot at 1,1, and then six dots to the right, six up, six to the left, and six down at 1,1 again.

```
Command: SNAP ↵
```
```
Snap spacing or ON/OFF/Aspect/Rotate    Sets a new spacing
snap/Style <0.5000>: .25
```
Notice that the grid does not change, although snap changed.

```
Command: GRID ↵
```
```
Grid spacing(x) or ON/OFF/Snap/Aspect   Changes the spacing to match
grid<1.0000>: S                         the snap increment
                                        automatically
```
```
Command: GRID ↵
```
```
Grid spacing(x) or ON/OFF/Snap/Aspect   Leaves the snap at
<0.0000>: 1 ↵                           .25 and sets the grid to 1
```
Now use the grid to locate a circle at the center of the 6" square.

```
Command: CIRCLE ↵
```
3P/2P/TTR/<Center point>: *Pick the grid
dot at the center of the 6" square*

*Diameter / <Radius>: Pick ①, on the snap
increment halfway between grid dots (see fig 3.3)*

By setting grid and snap to appropriate values, you often can reduce or eliminate the need to use coordinate entry when you draw. Whenever the majority of points in your drawing fall on consistent increments, use snap and grid to reduce your drawing time. Do not be afraid to reset snap and grid if you need different values.

Figure 3.3:

Drawing with snap and grid.

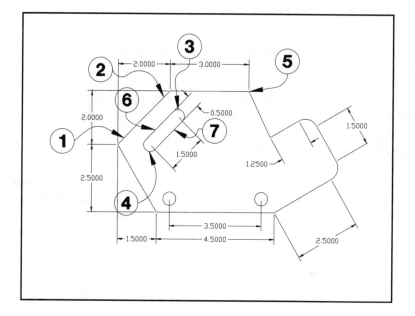

A quick way to trigger a redraw is to turn on or off the grid by using Ctrl-G or F7.

 If the grid is set too dense, it takes a long time to redraw. Press Ctrl-C to cancel a slow grid redraw.

 Occasionally, your drawings might consist mainly of horizontal and vertical lines. Aside from the convenience of Snap and Grid, another drawing aid is designed specifi-cally for this purpose.

Using Ortho To Draw Horizontal and Vertical Lines

Ortho, which stands for *orthogonal*, enables you to constrain lines to be drawn (or relative points located) horizontally or vertically with respect to the current snap grid. When ortho is turned on, you still can move the crosshair pointer to any location on the display and pick a point, but the rubber-band cursor extends either horizontally or vertically from the last point to one of the crosshairs (the one farthest away). When you pick the second point of a line or distance, AutoCAD calculates the coordinates of a point that will yield a vertical or horizontal line.

ORTHO. It constrains lines and distances so that they are parallel to the crosshairs. You can turn ortho mode on or off using the ORTHO command or by pressing Ctrl-O or F8. You can also use the DDRMODES dialog box to set ortho. By default, ortho mode is off.

ORTHO Options

- **ON.** This option turn ortho mode on.

- **OFF.** This option turns ortho mode off.

Ortho makes it easy to draw right angle lines, polyline segments, and other entities. With the CIRCLE command, ortho on causes the radius point to be horizontally or vertically aligned with the center point. Ortho on also constrains point picking any time AutoCAD displays a rubber-band cursor. When ortho is turned on, the word ORTHO appears at the left side of the status bar.

If you want to constrain lines to 90-degree increments, but with a rotated snap grid, use the SNAP Rotate option and ortho rotates to follow the grid.

To see how ortho works with snap, draw two rectangles—one horizontal and the other rotated at 30 degrees. As you draw, notice that you only have to position the crosshairs precisely in one axis with ortho on, because the other axis is constrained. This makes drawing much easier and quicker.

Drawing with Ortho On and a Rotated Grid

Start a new drawing called SAMPLE.

```
Command: SNAP ↵
```

```
Snap spacing or ON/OFF/Aspect/
Rotate/Style <1.0000>: .25
```

```
Command: GRID ↵
```

```
Grid spacing(X) or ON/OFF/Snap/
Aspect <0.0000>: 1
```

```
Command: LINE ↵
```

`From point:` *Pick any point on*
the drawing

`To point:` *Move the cursor*

`To point:` *Press F8*   Turns ortho mode on

Move the cursor

Notice that the rubber-band line is now constrained to follow the snap axes as you move the cursor.

Pick points to draw a 4"x 2"
rectangle, using the grid and snap
as a guide

`To point:` *Press Enter when you*
complete the rectangle

`Command: SNAP` ↵   Rotate the snap axes by 30
                                                           degrees

```
Snap spacing or ON/OFF/Aspect/
Rotate/Style <0.2500>: R ↵
```

`Base point <0.0000,0.0000>:` *Press Enter*   Accepts the default base
                                                           point

Do not change the base point

`Rotate angle <0>: 30` ↵

`Command: LINE` ↵

`From point:` *Pick a point anywhere*
in the drawing

`To point:` *Draw another 4"x 2"*
rectangle, rotated 30 degrees off
horizontal

`To point:` *Press Enter*   Ends the LINE command

When you finish, the rectangles appear as shown in figure 3.4.

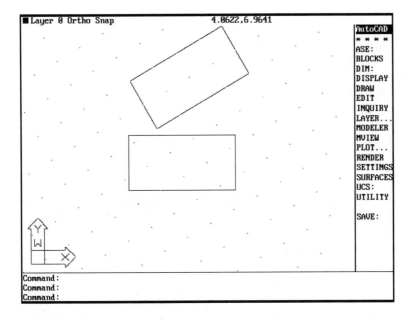

Figure 3.4:

Orthogonal and rotated rectangles.

The coordinate display is somewhat crippled when you use a rotated grid because the coordinate axes do not rotate with the snap, grid, and crosshairs. Nevertheless, relative polar coordinates are useful, and you can draw accurately with appropriate snap and grid settings.

Ortho is a drawing aid you turn on and off frequently. Turn ortho on when you draw horizontal and vertical lines, and off when you draw at other angles.

Tip: If ortho mode is on, you can override it by entering coordinates from the keyboard or by using object snap modes. Keep ortho on when working in isometric mode to align lines with the isometric grid.

Using the Drawing Aids Dialog Box

Although the function keys, commands, and control keys used to control the snap, ortho, and grid drawing aids become second nature with time, the Drawing Aids dialog box consolidates all of them into one handy tool. You can choose Drawing Aids from the Settings menu, or type 'DDRMODES to display the dialog box, as shown in figure 3.5.

Figure 3.5:

The Drawing Aids dialog box.

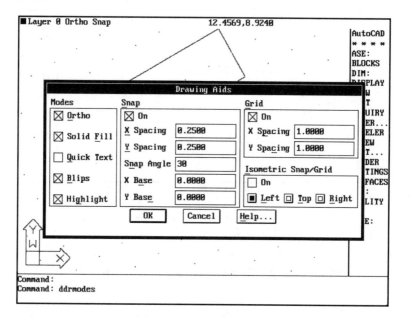

To turn a mode on or off, move the arrow pointer to its check box and click the left button. To change the value of the snap or grid spacing, click on the appropriate number and edit the value, or double-click on the number (it will be highlighted in reverse video), and type a new value.

DDRMODES. The DDRMODES (Dynamic Dialog dRawing MODES) dialog box controls drawing aids settings such as snap (default off, 1.0), snap angle (default 0), grid (default off, 0), axis (default off, 0), ortho (default off), blips (default off), isoplane (default left), and isometric mode (default off).

The DDRMODES command displays the Drawing Aids dialog box. The Drawing Aids dialog box enables you to set all of your drawing modes visually, so that you can see and compare all the drawing modes at once.

Use control keys and function keys if you need to turn on or off individual settings or change isoplanes. Control and function keys are faster than using the dialog box.

DDRMODES can be executed transparently by entering 'DDRMODES within another command or by selecting Drawing Aids from the Settings pull down menu. If DDRMODES is activated transparently, however, some DDRMODES changes do not take effect until the command or current step is completed. If you use 'DDRMODES transparently, for example, you do not need to end a LINE command to rotate the snap grid.

Now that you know how to use some of AutoCAD's drawing aids to make drawing easier and more accurate, redraw the shear plate using these new tools. Use the DDRMODES dialog box for your settings.

Redrawing the Shear Plate Accurately

Start AutoCAD from the AB directory, then begin a new drawing named SHEARPl2.

Set GRID to 1

Set SNAP to .25

As you work through the exercise, check periodically the SNAP indicator on the status line to make sure snap stays on through the rest of the exercise.

```
Command: LINE ⏎
From point: 4,2 ⏎
To point: <Ortho on> Press F8          Turns on ortho

Press F6 twice                         Turns off the coordinate display
                                       and activates polar coordinates
```

Pick at 4.5<0

`To point:` *Press Enter*

Now rotate the snap grid 30 degrees so that you can draw the shear plate's right end.

`Command: SNAP` ↵

`Snap spacing or ON/OFF/Aspect/`
`Rotate/Style <0.2500>: R` ↵

`Base point <0.000,0.000>: @` ↵   Sets the base to the last point

`Rotate angle <0>: 30` ↵   Sets a new rotation angle

`Command: LINE` ↵

`From point:` *Press Enter*   Begins at the end of the last line

`To point:` *Pick point 2.5 along the X snap axis, at coordinates 2.5<30*

`To point:` *Press Enter*

`Command: ARC` ↵

`Center/<Start point>:` *Press Enter*   Continues tangent to the line

`End point: <Ortho off>` *Press F8*   Turns off ortho

Use snap to pick at the end of the arc at ① (see fig. 3.6), at coordinates 0.7071<75

`Command: LINE` ↵

`From point:` *Press Enter*

`Length of line:` *Move cursor and use snap to draw 1.5" along the Y snap axis, at coordinates 1.5<120*

`To point:` *Press Enter*

`Command: ARC` ↵

`Center/<Start point>:` *Press Enter*   Continues tangent to the line

`End point:` *Pick the end of the arc at ②, at the coordinates 0.7071<165 (see fig. 3.6)*

`Command: LINE` ↵

`From point:` *Press Enter*

`Length of line:` *Use snap to draw -1.25" along the X snap axis, at coordinates 1.25<210*

`To point:` *Press Enter*

After you finish drawing the shear plate with accurate pick points, it should look like figure 3.6.

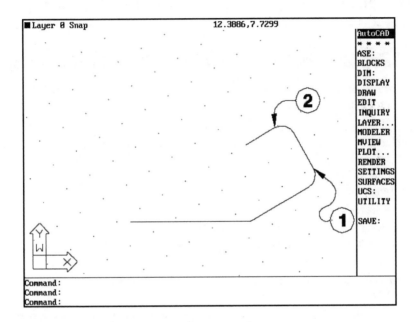

Figure 3.6:

Partial shear plate with rotated snap grid.

The next object you draw is the slot. You can use another rotated snap grid, but changing AutoCAD's coordinate system is a better method of drawing, relative to an offset base and angle.

Working with Drawing Aids

As you continue to redraw the shear plate in the following exercise, you use a combination of grid, snap, ortho, and the coordinate display. In addition, use the DDRMODES dialog box command to set these drawing aids.

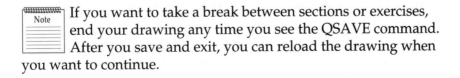 If you want to take a break between sections or exercises, end your drawing any time you see the QSAVE command. After you save and exit, you can reload the drawing when you want to continue.

Applying Grid, Snap, and Ortho

First, practice using grid, snap, ortho, and the coordinate display.

Using DDRMODES To Continue the Shear Plate Drawing

Continue from the previous exercise or start ACAD from the AB-ACAD directory, then begin a new drawing named SHEARPL2.

Command: *Type* **DDRMODES** *and press Enter or choose* Settings, *then* Drawing Aids	The Drawing Aids dialog box appears
Open S**n**ap Angle *by clicking on the 30 in the box to the right of the snap angle prompt*	
Backspace to delete the 30, then type **0**	
Open X B**a**se *by double-clicking on the 8.5000 in the box to the right and then type* **0**	Sets the X base to 0
Open Y Bas**e** *and enter* **0**	
Turn on ortho by clicking on the **O**rtho *box*	Selects ortho
Click on OK	Accepts the settings and closes the dialog box
Command: **LINE** ⏎	
From point: *Use coordinates and snap to pick 4,2*	
To point: **@-1.5,2.5** ⏎	

The typed relative coordinates override ortho

To point: **@2,2** ⏎	
To point: *Pick with the coordinates at 3<0 (absolute coordinates 7.5,6.5)*	
To point: **ENDP** ⏎	Activates the ENDP object snap mode
of *Close the boundary by picking the line at point* ① *(see fig. 3.7)*	

As you can see, object snap mode overrides ortho when ortho is on.

To point: *Press Enter*	
Command: **QSAVE**	Saves the file to the same name

Figure 3.7 shows the completed shear plate boundary.

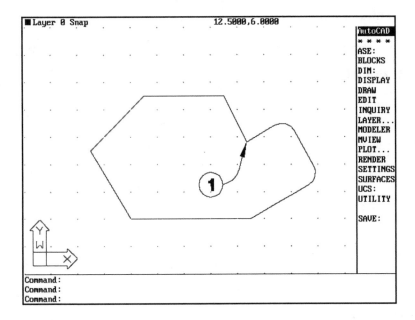

Figure 3.7:
Finishing the shear plate boundary.

Specifying Existing Points and Coordinates

The drawing aids described in previous sections help you enter coordinates precisely. In many cases, however, you are not concerned with the coordinates of the points that define a drawing entity. Rather, you are concerned with the relationship between a new entity and one or more existing entities. For example, you may want to begin a line at the end of an existing line, the center of a circle, or the intersection of a line and an arc.

AutoCAD enables you to enter points for new objects without knowing their coordinates. You can pick points that define existing objects and points that define features of existing objects. The drawing aid that AutoCAD provides for this purpose is object snap. *Object snap* enables you to specify a point by specifying a type of feature and selecting one or more entities in the drawing.

For example, you can snap a new point to the exact endpoint of an existing line by picking any point on half the line nearest the desired end (see fig. 3.8).

Figure 3.8:

Object snap examples.

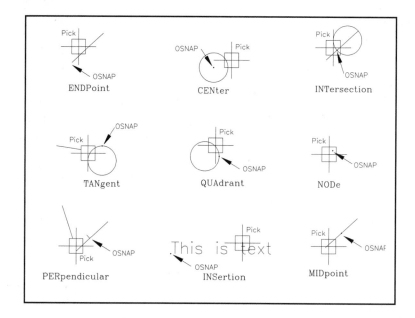

Using Object Snap

You use object snap to tell AutoCAD to search for one or more features or types of points. When prompted for a point, you pick a point in the general vicinity of the point you want, and AutoCAD searches for a point that resembles the settings you specify. You can use object snap in two ways—running object snap modes and object snap overrides. Running snap modes are set with the OSNAP command, and remain in force until changed with another OSNAP command. Object snap overrides are set in response to the prompt that requests a point, and remain in effect only for the response to that prompt.

Using the OSNAP Command

You use the OSNAP command to set running object snap modes. Initially, the default object snap mode is NONe. That is, AutoCAD does not search for any particular kind of point. Instead, it uses the point you actually pick. If you set a running snap mode, AutoCAD searches for the specified kinds of points in the vicinity of the point you pick. You can tell when a running object snap mode is in effect if an aperture box replaces the select box at the intersection of the crosshair pointer when AutoCAD prompts you for a point. The aperture box defines the area in which AutoCAD will search for object snap features. That is, the aperture must touch or enclose an entity to snap to it.

OSNAP. The OSNAP command sets one or more "running" object snap mode(s), which affect all subsequent points entered until OSNAP is reset. The available modes are as follows:

CENter

ENDPoint

INSertion

INTersection

MIDpoint

NEArest

NODe

NONe

PERpendicular

QUAdrant

QUIck

TANgent.

You can enter another object snap mode to override a running mode for a single point.

AutoCAD provides twelve object snap modes:

- **CENter.** The CENter mode snaps to the center of an arc or circle.

- **ENDPoint.** The ENDPoint mode snaps to the end of a line or arc.

Note Whenever you abbreviate ENDPoint, make sure you abbreviate it as **ENDP**, not END, so that you do not accidentally end your drawing.

- **INSertion.** The INSertion mode snaps to the insertion point of a shape, text string (the start point), attribute, attdef, or block insert.

- **INTersection.** The INTersection mode snaps to the intersection of any combination of two lines, arcs, or circles.

- **MIDpoint.** The MIDpoint mode snaps to the midpoint of a line or arc.

- **NEArest.** The NEArest mode snaps to nearest point on a line, arc, circle, or point.

- **NODe.** The NODe mode snaps to a point entity.

- **NONe.** The NONe mode prevents object snapping. NONe is the default.

- **PERpendicular.** The perpendicular mode snaps to a point on a line, arc, or circle perpendicular to the entity being drawn. In the case of a circle or arc, the entity drawn is actually perpendicular to an imaginary tangent line.

- **QUAdrant.** The QUAdrant mode snaps to the nearest quadrant (0-, 90-, 180-, and 270-degree points) of a circle or arc. In a rotated block insert, the quadrants rotate with the block.

- **QUIck.** When combined with other modes, QUIck snaps to the most recently created entity that matches one of the modes used within the selection range. Otherwise, object snap snaps to the closest matching entity, regardless of when it was created.

- **TANgent.** The TANgent mode snaps to a point on an arc or circle that forms a tangent to the lastpoint.

Remember that you can set several modes at one time. For example, you can set the multipurpose mode INT,END,CEN. Such a multipurpose mode probably works for nearly all object snap picks you do, and you can override it for a single pick by entering another temporary mode when you need to. The next exercise illustrates multiple running object snap modes.

Using the Running Object Snap Dialog Box

You can set running object snap modes with the Running Object Snap dialog box, which is displayed by the Object Snap selection on the Settings pull-down menu. The dialog box contains two blocks. The Select Settings block contains a check box for each object snap mode. The Aperture Size box contains a slider bar to set the size of the aperture. Figure 3.9 shows the Running Object Snap dialog box.

```
┌───────────────────────────────────┐
│        Running Object Snap         │
│ Select Settings                    │
│  ☐ Endpoint      ☐ Insertion       │
│  ☐ Midpoint      ☐ Perpendicular   │
│  ☐ Center        ☐ Tangent         │
│  ☐ Node          ☐ Nearest         │
│  ☐ Quadrant      ☐ Quick           │
│  ☐ Intersection                    │
│ Aperture Size                      │
│                                    │
│    Min        Max                  │
│                         ┌──┐       │
│  ◄├──────┤──►│          └──┘       │
│                                    │
│  ┌─────┐  ┌────────┐  ┌────────┐   │
│  │ OK  │  │ Cancel │  │ Help...│   │
│  └─────┘  └────────┘  └────────┘   │
└───────────────────────────────────┘
```

Figure 3.9:

The Running Object Snap dialog box.

Object Snap Overrides

An object snap override temporarily revokes the current running object snap mode. When you set a running mode—including the default of NONe—it stays in effect until you change it by using the OSNAP command again. Suppose, for example, that you have used OSNAP to set a running object snap mode of ENDPoint.

Each time you pick a point, AutoCAD searches for an endpoint. Later, you want to pick the intersection of a line and arc. You either enter INT at the Command: prompt or select the row of stars on the screen menu, select INTersection, and then pick the desired intersection point. For that one point pick, AutoCAD looks for an intersection. It then reverts to the previous mode, which is ENDPoint.

AutoCAD searches for the closest point to the crosshairs that meets one of the running snap modes or snap overrides. If it finds none of these points, the following prompt appears:

No mode(s) found for specified point.

It then reprompts for the point and discards the modes you specified.

When you use multiple modes, make sure you can use the aperture to select the desired entities, without interference from other entities. You can adjust the aperture size for better control.

 You do not need to type the complete object snap mode name; you can enter just the first three characters. You can respond, for example, to AutoCAD's request for a point by typing the following:

END,QUA,MID,CEN,INT *Press Enter*

Generally, you specify more than one object snap mode only when you use running object snap modes. Object snap overrides are temporary and affect only the next point selection. *Running object snap modes* affect all point picks until they are reset. When you are using object snap with a single pick, you know what mode to use. When you use a running object snap mode, however, you can use a multipurpose mode such as INT,END,CEN. A multipurpose mode probably will work for nearly every object snap you need. If not, you can override multipurpose modes for a single pick by entering another temporary mode.

If you have a mouse or puck, click on button one to display a menu of object snaps at the current cursor position.

 Object snap modes provide the exact snap point to AutoCAD, but the coordinates display on the status line updates to the pick point you use, not the calculated point.

Using the Coordinate System

In Chapter 2, you learned that the default Cartesian coordinate system in AutoCAD is called the World Coordinate System, or WCS. The origin of the WCS at 0,0 is called the World Origin, or Global Origin. Recall that you can use SNAP to rotate or offset the snap grid, but the coordinate readout shows the position of the crosshair pointer relative to the WCS origin (0,0) without rotation. If the snap grid is both rotated and offset, the coordinate readout can be confusing, even though you can use the snap grid to place points precisely.

You can use the UCS (User Coordinate System) command to define a new coordinate system, locate the origin, and orient the axes the way you want. A UCS looks and works the same as the WCS—snap, ortho, grid, crosshair pointer, and coordinate readout all perform their expected functions. A rotated or offset UCS accomplishes everything that a rotated snap grid does, and retains the full functionality of the coordinate display.

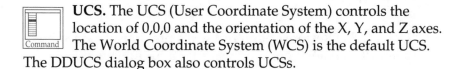

UCS. The UCS (User Coordinate System) controls the location of 0,0,0 and the orientation of the X, Y, and Z axes. The World Coordinate System (WCS) is the default UCS. The DDUCS dialog box also controls UCSs.

Using the UCS Command

Use the UCS command to create a coordinate system with an origin and axis orientation that is different from the WCS. Each UCS you create with the UCS command can be saved by name so that you can move easily between different coordinate systems.

The UCS command is useful in two-dimensional drawing for two main reasons. The first reason is to relocate the origin for easier coordinate entry. If you create a civil engineering drawing based on offsets from a number of different base points, for example, each base point can be set up as the origin (0,0) for a separate UCS. When you need to reference a point from one of the base points, you simply restore its UCS and enter absolute coordinates.

A second reason to use a UCS is to rotate the X,Y axes. This process is similar to rotating snap, but your coordinate system also rotates. If you draw an object whose normal lines are rotated 30 degrees off horizontal, for example, it makes sense to create a UCS that is rotated 30 degrees. This simplifies coordinate entry when you draw the object.

UCS includes fourteen options, several of which you use only for 3D work. The options used for 2D include the following:

UCS Options

- **Origin.** Specify a new UCS origin point at Origin, without changing orientation.

- **Z.** Use Z to specify a new UCS by rotating the X and Y axes about the Z axis.

- **Previous.** The Previous option restores the previous UCS. Repeat this option to back up 10 previous coordinate systems in paper space or 10 systems in model space.

- **Restore.** The Restore option restores a previously named and saved UCS. Enter a question mark for a list of named UCSs.

- **Save.** This option saves the current UCS. You specify a name (up to 31 characters). Enter a question mark for a list of named UCSs.

- **Delete.** The Delete option deletes a saved UCS by name. Enter a question mark for a list of named UCSs.

- **?.** This option lists named UCSs. You can use wild cards to create a specific list. A current unnamed UCS is listed as *NO NAME* unless it is the WCS, which is listed as *WORLD*.

- **World.** The World option restores the WCS.

For the options of the UCS command that relate to 3D coordinates, refer to the *AutoCAD Reference Manual*, or to *Inside AutoCAD* (New Riders Publishing).

 In the WCS, or a named UCS identical to the WCS, the grid extends to the drawing limits. In a UCS other than the WCS, the grid extends to the current view edges.

Using The UCS Icon

You have probably noticed the X,Y icon that appears at the bottom left corner of the drawing display. This UCS icon displays the current orientation and location of the coordinate system. The UCS icon can be turned on and off using the UCSICON command.

UCSICON. The UCSICON (User Coordinate System ICON) command graphically indicates the origin and orientation of the current UCS. The default shape of the icon is an L-shaped pair of X,Y arrows. If the UCS is the same as the WCS, a w displays in the icon. If the icon is displayed at the UCS origin, a cross (+) displays in the icon. The icon changes shape in paper space and 3D perspectives. Paper space and 3D perspectives are discussed in later chapters

The UCSICON options control its visibility and location.

UCSICON Options

- **ON.** This option turns on the UCS icon display.

- **OFF.** This option turns off the UCS icon.

- **All.** The All option displays the UCS icon in all multiple viewports.

- **Noorigin.** The Noorigin option always displays the UCSICON at the lower left corner of the viewports.

- **ORigin.** The ORigin option displays the UCS icon at the 0,0 origin of the current UCS, unless the origin is off-screen or too close to the edge for the icon to fit. The icon then displays at the lower left corner of the viewport.

The shear plate slot is easier to draw with an offset and rotated UCS. Draw the slot to see how the UCS and UCSICON commands work.

Creating and Rotating a User Coordinate System

Continue from the previous exercise. Offset the UCS to center it at ① (see fig. 3.10).

Command: **UCS** ↵

Origin/ZAxis/3point/Entity/View/X/Y/Z   Selects the Origin
/Prev/Restore/Save/Del/?/<World>: **O** ↵ option

Origin point <0,0,0>: *Pick 3.75,4.5*

The following steps rotate the UCS about the Z axis about the origin.

Command: **UCS** ↵

Origin/ZAxis/3point/Entity/View/X/Y/Z   Selects the Z option
/Prev/Restore/Save/Del/?/<World>: **Z** ↵

Rotate angle about Z axis <0>: **45** ↵   Sets the rotation angle

Command: **UCSICON** ↵

ON/OFF/All/Noorigin/ORigin <ON>: **OR** ↵ Set to origin

The grid, snap, and crosshair are now offset and rotated, with the UCS icon displayed at the new origin.

Move around the crosshairs, and watch the
coordinates to get a feel for the new UCS.

```
Command: ARC ↵
ARC Center/<Start point>: Pick 0,0.25
Center/End/<Second point>: Pick -0.25,0
End point: Pick 0,-0.25
Command: LINE ↵
From point: Press Enter
Length of line: 1.5 ↵                    Draws 1.5" along the new X axis,
                                         to coordinates 1.5<0
To point: Press Enter
Command: ARC ↵
Center/<Start point>: Press Enter
End point: Pick at 0.5<90
Command: LINE ↵
From point: Press Enter
Length of line: Pick at 1.5<180
To point: Press Enter
```

After you finish, the slot appears as shown in figure 3.10. You are now finished creating the slot.

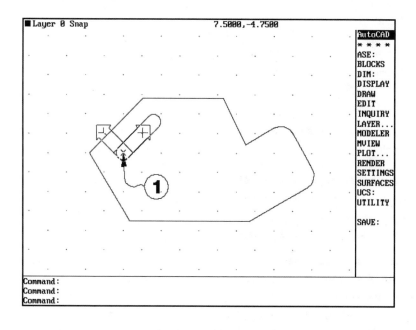

Figure 3.10:

Slot with rotated and offset UCS.

You can override the current UCS and make AutoCAD interpret points as relative to the WCS by prefacing them with an asterisk. For example, *3,2 specifies the point 3,2 in the WCS, not the current UCS.

In the next exercise, set the UCS back to the default WORLD and draw the two circles for the last part of the plate. First, try saving and restoring the UCS with a name.

Saving and Restoring UCSs

Continue from the previous exercise.

```
Command: UCS ⏎
Origin/ZAxis/3point/Entity/View/X/Y/Z      Selects the Save
/Prev/Restore/Save/Del/?/<World>: S ⏎     option
?/Desired UCS name: SLOT ⏎                 Specifies the name for the UCS
Command: UCS ⏎
Origin/ZAxis/3point/Entity/View/X/Y/Z      Restores the default
/Prev/Restore/Save/Del/?/<World>:          WCS
Press Enter
Command: UCS ⏎
Origin/ZAxis/3point/Entity/View/X/Y/Z      Lists all saved
/Prev/Restore/Save/Del/?/<World>: ?        UCSs
UCS names(s) to list <*>: Press Enter      Accepts the * wild card for all
                                           UCS names

Current UCS: *WORLD*

Saved coordinate systems:

SLOT

Origin = <3.7500,4.5000,0.0000>,
X Axis = <0.7071,0.7071,0.0000>

Y Axis = <-0.7071,0.7071,0.0000>,
Z Axis = <0.0000,0.0000,1.0000>

Restore/Save/Del/?/<World>: R ⏎
Origin/ZAxis/3point/Entity/View/        Selects the Restore option
X/Y/Z/Prev/
?/Name of the UCS to restore: SLOT ⏎   Restores SLOT
```

You can also set many UCS options by using dialog boxes, just as you do with the drawing modes.

Selecting Preset UCS Definitions

The DDUCSP command displays the UCS Orientation dialog box. This dialog box enables you to define a new UCS by selecting an icon. Figure 3.11 shows the UCS Orientation dialog box.

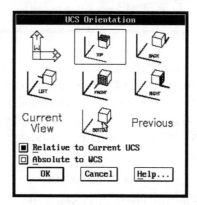

Figure 3.11:

Select an orientation by clicking on its icon.

DDUCSP. The DDUCSP command displays the UCS orientation dialog box. The dialog box displays six preset UCS definitions as icons, which you can use to help define a new UCS. You can also pick the WCS, current UCS, or the previous UCS.

Using the DDUCS Command To Select Named UCSs

The DDUCS command brings up the UCS Control dialog box for selected options of the UCS command. Figure 3.12 shows the UCS Control dialog box.

Figure 3.12:

UCS Control dialog box.

 **DDUCS.** The DDUCS (Dynamic Dialog User Coordinate System) command displays the UCS Control dialog box, which enables you to set the current UCS, rename, delete and list UCSs (User Coordinate Systems). The *WORLD* UCS, called the WCS, is the default coordinate system.

UCS Control Options

- **Current.** Click in this button to change the current UCS. *WORLD* sets the World Coordinate System (WCS). *PREVIOUS* returns to the previous coordinate system.

- **Rename.** With this option, you can rename a UCS. If the current UCS is unnamed, it is listed as *NO NAME*.

- **List.** Click in this button to display the origin and X,Y,Z axes direction of the UCS.

- **Delete.** The Delete option deletes selected named UCSs.

Use the UCS Control dialog box to get back to the WCS.

Using the DDUCS Command and Finishing with Circles

Continue in the SHEARPL2 drawing.

Command: **DDUCS** ⏎   Displays Dialog box

The dialog box appears, showing *WORLD*, *PREVIOUS*, and SLOT (current).

Click on *WORLD*	Selects *WORLD*, makes Current, Delete, List, and Rename to available
Click on Current	Makes the selected UCS (*WORLD*) current
Click on OK	

```
Command: CIRCLE ⏎

3P/2P/TTR/<Center point>:
```
Pick 4.5,2.5

```
Diameter/<Radius>: .25 ⏎          Specifies a radius distance

Command: CIRCLE ⏎

3P/2P/TTR/<Center point>:
```
Pick 8,2.5

```
Diameter/<Radius>: Pick a
```
point at coordinates 0.2500<0

```
Command: QSAVE/Pete ⏎          Saves the drawing to the same
                                name
```

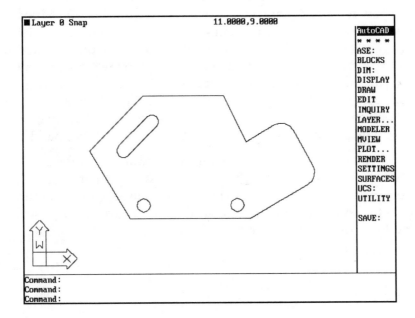

Figure 3.13:

Finished shear plate with circles.

After you finish the exercise, your shear plate is complete.

Because you used SNAP, GRID, ORTHO, and coordinates, your shear plate drawing is now accurate. You probably found that it was easier to draw with these tools than it was to estimate points, as you did in Chapter 2.

Of course, not everything you draw fits a reasonable snap grid. For this reason, do not forget to use typed coordinates, relative coordinates, and object snap modes.

When you pick a series of points with object snap modes, it might be more efficient to set the desired object snap modes once and then pick repeatedly without reentering the object snap modes. You can do this with running object snap modes.

Summary

You now have complete control over the accuracy of your drawings. You can combine snap and grid to lay out points accurately on a regular grid, using the coordinates to identify them. Drawing 90-degree angles is easy and quick if ortho is on when you draw. You can snap to existing points of objects in your drawing using object snap, whether they fall on the snap grid or somewhere else. For one-shot use, you use object snap overrides; for repeated picks, you can set running modes with the OSNAP command.

When you draw objects that are offset or rotated from the grid, you can use SNAP or UCS to relocate the snap grid or entire coordinate system. You learned to use individual commands and turns to control these settings, and to use dialog boxes when you find them more convenient.

Basic Drawing and Editing

It is a rare designer or drafter who can produce a drawing without an eraser or—in the case of the AutoCAD user—the ERASE command. But the AutoCAD user has much more than an electronic eraser. AutoCAD provides an assortment of commands for not only removing entities from the drawing, but moving them, modifying them in place, and duplicating them. If you have any doubt about the benefits of CAD, consider what it takes to enlarge a room, or change the style of lettering on a manually-prepared floor plan. For the AutoCAD user, such changes are a snap.

Indeed, AutoCAD's editing tools encourage methods of design that are not possible on the board. You can draw a component in an unused part of your drawing and move it to its final destination when you are satisfied. You can draw a component to approximate shape, and "stretch" it into shape. You can copy, mirror, and array a single component or a group of components to form regular patterns.

You have already discovered the ERASE command, which removes entities from the drawing, and the UNDO command, which enables you to backspace through the commands you have submitted to AutoCAD. These are the most basic editing commands. In this chapter, you will learn the commands that enable you to modify existing entities, rather than redraw them.

Using the OOPS Command

You know how to draw with AutoCAD, you know how to ERASE what you have drawn, and you know how to UNDO what you have done. But occasionally you erase something, do several useful things, and then realize that you now have to redraw what you erased earlier. You can undo the drawing to the way it was before the ERASE command, but you also undo all the useful things you did after the ERASE command.

The answer to this problem is the OOPS command.

OOPS. The OOPS command restores the objects that were erased with the last ERASE command. (The BLOCK command, covered in a later chapter, also performs an erase operation, and OOPS will restore those objects, as well.) OOPS restores the erased objects, even if other commands have been used after the ERASE command, but it only restores objects erased in the last erase operation. Objects erased in earlier erase operations cannot be restored.

You can use OOPS to simplify drawing and editing, not just to correct mistakes. If an existing entity interferes with the task at hand, erase it, complete the task, and then restore the erased entity with OOPS.

Using the OOPS Command

Start a new drawing called SAMPLE.

Command: *Turn snap on*

Command: *Draw a two inch square anywhere on the screen with LINE*

Next, change the size of the box to three inches wide and two inches high.

```
Command: ERASE ↵
Select objects: Pick the right vertical line
Select objects: Press Enter                    Ends ERASE command and
                                               erases selected objects

Command: LINE ↵
Draw three new lines to extend the box
one inch to the right
From point: END ↵                              Selects End point object snap
of Pick on the bottom line near the            Starts the new line at the end of
right end of the line                          the bottom line
To point: @1<0 ↵                               Draws a 1" line at angle 0
To point: @2<90 ↵                              Draws a 2" line at angle 90
To point: @1<100 ↵                             Draws a 1" line at angle 180
To point: Press Enter
```

Now, change the box back to its original size.

```
Command: OOPS ↵
Use the OOPS command to retrieve the
line you erased
Command: ERASE ↵
Erase the lines no longer needed
```

Modifying Existing Entities

Drafting is repetitive. Real world objects (and symbols on a drawing) occur in groups, often in regular patterns. At the board, you must draw each symbol individually; it takes just as long to draw the last item in a group as it does to draw the first item. AutoCAD provides commands that copy individual entities or groups of entities. AutoCAD also provides a command to move one or more entities. Some commands can copy or move entities. Although copying and moving seem to be dissimilar operations, there are many similarities.

AutoCAD also enables you to modify existing entities in other ways. In addition to moving or copying an entity or group of entities, you also can rotate, scale, mirror, array, and stretch entities. Before you learn how to use these commands, however, consider some concepts common to many editing commands.

Using Displacement

In a number of the commands that are described in the following sections, you encounter the term *displacement*, which refers to a distance in a specific direction—a vector. Whether you copy or move an entity, you must specify the distance between the old and the new entity, and you must specify the direction in which to measure that distance. Alternatively, you can indicate the original position and the new position, in which case AutoCAD calculates the displacement.

When AutoCAD needs a displacement, it asks for a Base point or displacement:. After you indicate a point by typing coordinates, or picking a point, AutoCAD asks for the Second point of displacement:. In response to the second prompt, you can enter another point or press Enter.

If you enter two points, AutoCAD calculates the distance and direction, measured from the first point to the second. If you enter only one point and press Enter at the second prompt, AutoCAD calculates the distance and direction from the origin (0,0) to the first, and only, point. Figure 4.1 illustrates the two methods.

Base Points

You encounter the term *base point* as part of the first prompt for a displacement vector. In the context of other commands, a base point is a point that is not affected by the operation—it can be any point on the entity or off it. When an entity is rotated, it is rotated about a base point. When an entity is scaled, the base point is the one point that does not move. In some cases (rotate and scale, for example), you must pick the base point exactly. In others (stretch, for example), the base point can be relative.

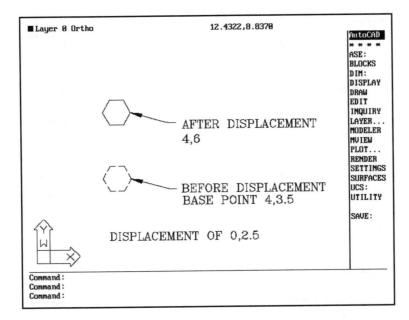

Figure 4.1:

Displacement can be specified with one point or two.

Selection Sets

CAD is notorious for assigning formal names to concepts that are intuitively obvious, and the discussion of such a concept often creates confusion. An example is that of AutoCAD's selection sets.

If you are going to use an eraser for any useful purpose, you must first have something to erase. Similarly, if you have a number of symbols on the paper, you must avoid some objects while erasing others. Manual drafters use erasing shields, AutoCAD uses a selection set.

All editing commands ask you to identify the entities to which the operation should be applied. The entities you identify form a *selection set*. The concept is analagous to marking up a print of a drawing and scratching out those lines that need to be erased. You have several ways to identify entities, and AutoCAD acknowledges the identification of entities for the selection set by highlighting them. In most video configurations, highlighted entities appear dashed as shown in figure 4.2. In AutoCAD terms, the highlighted entities have been added to the selection set.

Figure 4.2:

Highlighted entities of a selection set.

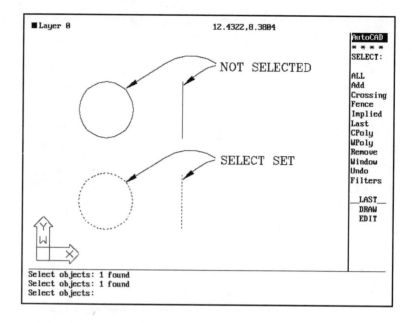

You can use four basic methods to select entities that form a selection set: pick, window, crossing box, and fence. When AutoCAD expects you to build a selection set, it displays the prompt, Select objects: and changes the crosshair pointer to a pick box, as shown in figure 4.3.

Picking an Entity

To pick an entity, you place the pick box so that it touches the entity you want to select, and press the *pick button* (data button) on your pointing device. AutoCAD acknowledges the pick by high-lighting the entity. You can continue to pick entities; each one will be added to the selection set. Use the pick button to select entities when the ones you want to edit are surrounded or overlapped by ones you do not want to edit.

Window and Crossing Box Selection

To *window* entities, place the pick box to the left of an imaginary rectangle that encloses or crosses all objects you want to select, pick, then move the cursor to the right, and pick again. As you move the cursor, AutoCAD draws a rectangle from the first point, extending in the direction you move the pointing device. (Neither the pick box nor the crosshair pointer are visible.) If you begin the window at the lower left corner and drag it up and to the right, AutoCAD selects the objects that fall entirely within the window. If you begin at the upper right corner and drag the window down and to the left, AutoCAD selects all the objects that cross the window. Figure 4.4 shows the two effects. Both windows and crossing boxes can be used to select a number of objects simultaneously. Again, like with pick, each window or crossing adds to the selection set until you press Enter.

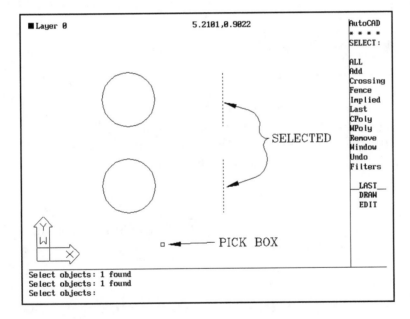

Figure 4.3:

The crosshair pointer replaced by a pick box.

Fence Selection

To fence select objects, you must first notify AutoCAD by typing **F** at the `Select objects:` prompt. AutoCAD then prompts you as follows:

```
First fence point:
Undo/<End point of line>:
Undo/<End point of line>:
```

Figure 4.4:

Window and crossing box selection.

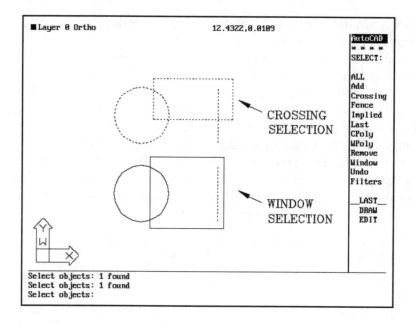

You draw a series of line segments, just as if you were using the line command, crossing the objects you want to edit. When you end the fence, by pressing Enter or the space bar, AutoCAD highlights all the objects crossed by the fence.

 You can build a selection set before entering a command with picks, windows, and crossing boxes, but not fences.

Using Grips Autoediting Modes

Think of *grips* in AutoCAD as being convenient locations on each entity to help control and manipulate that entity. Each entity has several grip points that you can choose accurately (without speci-fying object snap modes) by picking in the grip box. For instance, the grip points on a line are the endpoints and the midpoint (see fig. 4.5). If the GRIPS system variable is set to 1 (on, which is the default), the grips appear on an entity when that entity is selected at the Command: prompt.

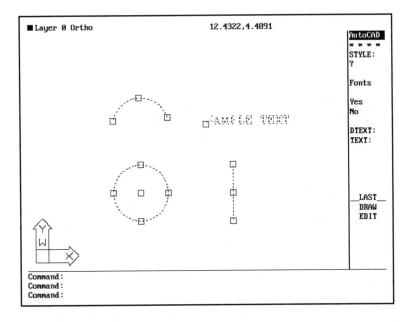

When you click on a visible grip, it becomes "hot" (selected) and displays highlighted. A hot grip becomes a base point for one of the autoediting modes by which you can manipulate the entity. Autoediting modes are a special group of common editing commands, which are available when a base grip is chosen. These modes are briefly explained in the following list.

- **Stretch.** The stretch mode enables you to modify entities by moving one or more grips to another location while leaving the other part of the entity in its original location. This can easily change the size or shape of an entity or a group of entities. In some cases the stretch mode moves an entity.

- **Move.** The move mode relocates entities from a base point to another specified location. The size and orientation does not change.

- **Rotate.** This mode enables you to rotate objects around a specified base point. The angle can be entered or specified by dragging.

- **Scale.** The scale mode enables you to scale entities up or down by a given scale factor about a specified base point.

Scale factors can be directly entered, dragged to size, or given by using the reference option.

- **Mirror.** Selected entities can be mirrored about a line formed by the base point grip and another selected point.

All of these autoediting modes have several things in common. First of all, when entities are selected and a base grip is chosen to issue the command, you can choose the proper mode by entering the first two letters of the mode (SC for scale, for example) or press Enter or the space bar to switch between the modes. If you want to make a copy while executing an autoediting mode, use the copy option or hold down the Shift key while making multiple second point picks. The Undo option undoes the last edit, and the eXit option exits the autoediting modes.

Stretch Mode

Stretching an object leaves one or more key points in place while the selected point is moved. Stretching a line makes it longer, shorter, or rotates it around the stationary endpoint. Stretching a circle makes it larger or smaller. Stretching an arc changes the angle it subtends and/or the radius of the arc.

In some cases, stretching an object actually moves it. For example, if you select a line segment at its midpoint grip, moving that grip moves the entire line. This effect is to be expected, because moving the midpoint without moving the endpoints transforms the line into an arc or into two separate line segments. Although stretching an object can change its shape, it cannot change its entity type.

The Copy option creates stretched copies of the original object. If you use the Copy option, you can create multiple stretched objects by picking several points in succession. Each new object passes through the point you pick to create it. You also can invoke the Copy option by holding the Shift key down as you pick points. AutoCAD uses the first point to define an offset. As long as you hold the Shift key down, each new object is offset from the previous object by the same distance. If you release the Shift key, you remain in the "stretch and copy" mode, but are not constrained by the offset distance. Again, the actual effect varies with the object. Figure 4.6 shows the effects you can achieve with the Stretch mode.

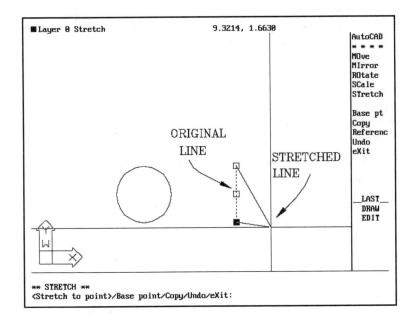

```
■Layer 0 Stretch                    9.3214, 1.6630
                                                          AutoCAD
                                                          * * * *
                                                          MOve
                                                          MIrror
                                                          ROtate
                                                          SCale
                                                          STretch

                                                          Base pt
                                                          Copy
                     ORIGINAL                             Referenc
                       LINE                               Undo
                                    STRETCHED             eXit
                                       LINE



                                                          _LAST_
                                                           DRAW
                                                           EDIT



** STRETCH **
<Stretch to point>/Base point/Copy/Undo/eXit:
```

Figure 4.6:

The Stretch autoediting mode.

Using Stretch Autoediting Mode

Start a new drawing called AUTOEDIT. Draw a line and a circle similar to figure 4.6.

Command: *Pick the line for autoediting by clicking on the line*
Shows grip points and high-lights the line

Command: *Pick the midpoint grip on the line*
Starts autoediting the selected set

Move the crosshairs around

Notice the line that is in the center of the crosshairs. The line will be moved to whatever point you specify, either by picking a point or with coordinates.

```
** STRETCH **
<Stretch to point>/Base point/Copy/
Undo/eXit: Pick a point @.5<180
```
Moves the line .5" to the left

Command: *Press Ctrl-C twice*
Deselects and removes the grips

Select the line again, but this time click with the pick button above and to the left of the line. Drag the window down and to the right to include the entire line. This action selects the line with a window.

Command: *Select the line with a window*

Command: *Pick the midpoint grip*   Makes the grip hot and starts
                                                     editing

** STRETCH **

<Stretch to point>/Base point/Copy/   Copies the line
Undo/eXit: *Press and hold the Shift key,*
pick a point 0.5000<0

Continue to hold the Shift key down and move
the crosshairs.

The crosshairs offset by the amount of the first copy.

Release the Shift key and move the crosshairs

The crosshairs move freely, you can copy the line anywhere.

<Stretch to point>/Base point/Copy/   Ends the Autoedit
Undo/eXit: *Press Enter*

Command: *Pick the bottom grip on the*   Makes the grip hot and starts
highlighted line   editing

** STRETCH **

<Stretch to point>/Base point/Copy/   Picks a new endpoint of the line
Undo/eXit: *Pick a point @0.5000<180*   .5" to the left

Command: *Press Ctrl-C twice*   Deselects the line and removes
                                                     grips

Command: *Pick the circle*   Adds the circle to the select set

Command: *Pick the center grip*   Makes grip hot

** STRETCH **

<Stretch to point>/Base point/Copy/   Moves the circle .5" to the right
Undo/eXit: *Pick a point @0.5000<0*

Command: *Pick one of the grips on the*   Makes grip hot
circumference

** STRETCH **

<Stretch to point>/Base point/Copy/   Stretches the radius .5"
Undo/eXit: *Pick a point .5" out from the*
hot grip

Command: *Press Ctrl-C twice*   Deselects the circle

Move Mode

In Move mode, you translate the selected object or objects. The objects retain their original orientation. All points on an object, or each object in a group of objects, are moved by the same displacement.

The Copy option enables you to create multiple copies of the original; the original remains in place. If you invoke the copy mode by holding the Shift key down as you pick new points, the first copy defines a virtual snap grid that is active as long as you hold the Shift key down. Figure 4.7 shows the effects you can achieve in Move mode.

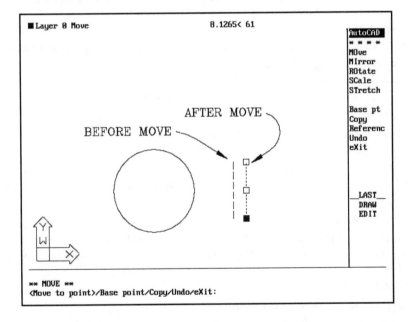

Figure 4.7:

The Move autoediting mode.

Using Move Autoediting Mode

Continue from the previous exercise.

Command: *Pick the slanted line*   Adds the line to the select set

Command: E ↵   Erases the select set

ERASE 1 found

Command: *Pick the remaining line*	Adds the line to the select set
Command: *Pick any grip*	Makes the grip hot
** STRETCH **	
<Stretch to point>/Base point/Copy/ Undo/eXit: *Press Enter*	Changes autoediting mode to move
** MOVE **	
<Move to point>/Base point/Copy/ Undo/eXit: *Pick a point @0.5000<0*	Moves the line .5" to the right
Command: *Pick the circle*	Adds the circle to the selection set
Command: *Pick a grip*	Makes the grip hot
** STRETCH **	
<Stretch to point>/Base point/Copy/ Undo/eXit: *Press Enter*	Changes autoediting mode to move
** MOVE **	
<Move to point>/Base point/Copy/ Undo/eXit: *Pick a point @0.5000<0*	Moves the selection set .5" to the right
Command: *Pick any grip*	Makes the grip hot and starts autoediting mode
** STRETCH **	
<Stretch to point>/Base point/Copy/ Undo/eXit: *Press Enter*	
** MOVE **	
<Move to point>Base point/Copy/ Undo/eXit: *C* ↵	Starts copy
** MOVE (multiple) **	
<Move to point>/Base point/Copy/ Undo/eXit: *Pick a point @0.5000<90, then pick a point @1.0000<90*	Copies the selection set up .5", then makes a second copy of the selection set
** MOVE (multiple) **	
<Move to point>Base point/Copy/ Undo/eXit: *Press Enter*	
Command: *U* ↵	Removes the copies
Command: *R* ↵	Issues REDRAW command

The difference between the Move and Stretch modes is that Move mode always moves; Stretch mode only moves an entity if you pick its center or midpoint grip. Move mode also moves every selected object, not just the last object or those objects added with the shift select method.

Using Rotate Mode

In Rotate mode, you can rotate the selected objects or group of objects around a hot grip. AutoCAD draws a rubber-band from the selected grip to the crosshair pointer, and as you move the crosshair pointer, you drag the selected objects. The rotation angle of the objects is the same as the angle between the positive X axis and the rubber-band cursor.

The rotate autoediting mode's Copy option creates copies of the original, rotated from the original; the original object remains in place. All copies use the hot grip as the rotation base point. Figure 4.8 shows the effects you can achieve in Rotate mode.

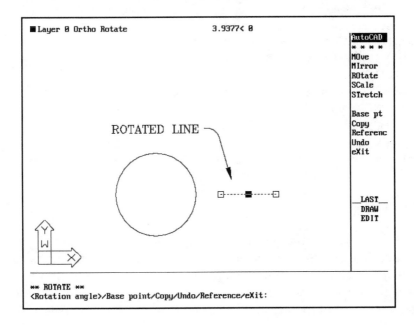

Figure 4.8:

The Rotate autoediting mode.

Using Rotate Autoediting Mode

Continue from the previous exercise.

Command: *Pick the line*	Adds the line to the selection set
Command: *Pick the midpoint grip*	Makes the grip hot
** STRETCH **	
<Stretch to point>/Base point/Copy/ Undo/eXit: *Press Enter twice*	Changes the autoediting mode to ROTATE
** ROTATE **	
<Rotation angle>/Base point/Copy/ Undo/eXit: 90 ↵	Rotates selection set 90 degrees
Command: *Pick the midpoint of the line and* *change to rotate mode*	Makes the grip hot
** ROTATE **	
<Rotate angle>/Base point/Copy/ Undo/eXit: C ↵	Specifies rotate mode copy
** ROTATE (multiple) **	
<Rotate angle>/Base point/Copy/ Undo/eXit: *Move the crosshairs around the* *midpoint grip, picking 3 points*	Makes three rotated copies
** ROTATE (multiple) **	
<Rotate angle>/Base point/Copy/ Undo/eXit: *Press Enter*	
Command: U ↵	
Command: R ↵	

Scale Mode

The Scale mode enlarges or shrinks an object or group of objects.
The selected grip—the one you select to start Autoedit—remains
fixed, and all other points are moved toward or away from the
selected grip by a scale factor. You can type a scale factor, or you
can pick a point to indicate the scale factor graphically. AutoCAD
uses the scalar distance from the selected grip to the pick point as
the scale factor. That is, you can pick a point anywhere on a 2.0
unit radius circle centered at the selected grip to indicate a scale
factor of 2.0.

The Copy option creates scaled copies of the original, leaving the original in place, and the Shift-pick option snaps to increments of the first scale factor. All copies pass through the selected grip. Figure 4.9 shows the effects you can obtain in the Scale mode.

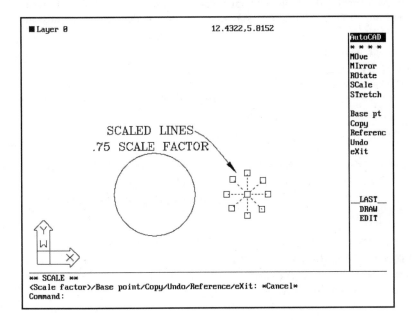

Figure 4.9:

The Scale autoediting mode.

Using Scale Autoediting Mode

Continue from the previous exercise.

Command: *Pick the unselected lines*   Adds all lines to the select set

Command: *Pick the midpoint grip cycle to*   Starts Autoedit
Scale mode

Because the midpoint grip is shared by all of the lines, they are selected for Autoedit.

Move the crosshairs to and away from the midpoint grip.

** SCALE **

<Scale factor>/Base point/Copy/Undo   Scales the select set by .75
/Reference/eXit: .75 ⏎

Command: *Pick an endpoint grip, cycle to Scale mode*

127

```
** SCALE **
<Scale factor>/Base point/Copy/Undo/          Start copy scale
Reference/eXit: C ↵
** SCALE (multiple) **
<Scale factor>/Base point/Copy/Undo/          Makes three copies of the select
Reference/eXit: Move the crosshairs           set, scaled from the endpoint
around and pick 3 points                      grip
** SCALE (multiple) **
<Scale factor>/Base point/Copy/
Undo/Reference/eXit: Press Enter
```

Mirror Mode

Mirror mode reverses, or *mirrors*, an object or group of objects about a line passing through the selected grip and the second point you pick. In normal Mirror mode, the original objects disappear.

The Copy option enables you to create multiple mirror images, while leaving the original in place. The Shift-pick option has no effect other than that of invoking the Copy option. Figure 4.10 shows the effects of mirroring objects.

Figure 4.10:

The Mirror autoediting mode.

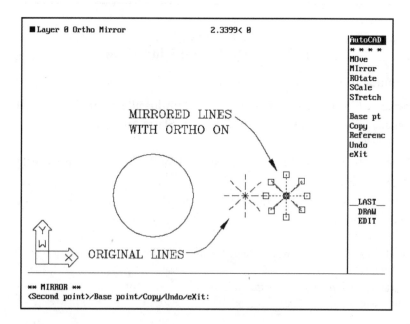

Using Mirror Autoediting Mode

Continue from previous exercise.

Command: *Pick all of the lines* — Adds lines to the selection set

Command: *Pick the right most grip and press Enter four times* — Makes the grip hot and changes to Mirror mode

```
** Mirror **
```

`<Second point>/Base point/Copy/ Undo/eXit:` *Move the crosshairs around, and press F8*

Notice the selected objects mirror on a line between the grip and the crosshair.

Pick a point at 90 or 270 degrees to mirror the selection set

Command: *Pick the left most grip and change to Mirror mode*

```
** MIRROR **
```

`<Second point>/Base point/Copy/ Undo/eXit:` C ↵ — Specifies the Copy option

```
** MIRROR (multiple) **
```

`<Second point>/Base point/Copy/ Undo/eXit:` *Pick a point to mirror the selection set back to its original location*

```
** MIRROR (multiple) **
```

`<Second point>/Base point/Copy/Undo/ eXit:` *Press Enter*

Command: *Press Ctrl-C twice*

The Base Point Option

Often the grip you use to begin autoediting may not be in the right place to achieve the effect you want. Each Autoedit mode has an option to handle this situation—the Base point option.

When you select the Base point option, AutoCAD removes the rubber-band cursor (from grip to crosshair pointer) and requests a base point. You can pick this point using any of the tools you have learned about: keyed-in coordinates, pointing, or object snaps. When you pick the base point, AutoCAD redisplays the rubber-band cursor, from the base point to the crosshair pointer. Figure 4.11 shows the effects you can achieve with the Base point option in the various modes.

Figure 4.11:

Autoediting modes Base point option.

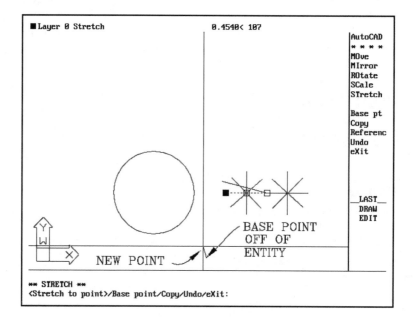

Using the Autoediting Modes Base Point Option

Continue from previous exercise.

Command: *Select one of the lines and pick any grip*

** STRETCH **

<Stretch to point>/Base point/Copy/   Specifies Base point option
Undo/eXit: B ↵

Base point: *Pick any point move*   Selects the new base point of
the cursor   displacement

Notice the rubber-banding of the selected line and displacement vector.

Command: *Press Ctrl-C three times*

Command: *Pick the circle, then pick any grip on the circle and change to Move mode*

```
** MOVE **
<Move to point>/Base point/Copy/
Undo/eXit: B ⏎
Base point: ENDP ⏎
```
Specifies the ENDPoint object snap

of Pick the endpoint of one of the lines
Specifies new base point at the end of the line

```
** MOVE **
<Move to point>/Base point/Copy/
Undo/eXit: @0.5000<90 ⏎
```
Moves circle .5" up from the end of the line

`Command:` *Pick a grip of the circle and change to Rotate mode*

```
** ROTATE **
<Rotation angle>/Base point/Copy/
Undo/Reference/eXit: B ⏎
```
Specifies Base point option

`Base point:` *Pick a point anywhere*
Picks the new base point

```
** ROTATE **
<Rotation angle>/Base point/Copy/
Undo/Reference/eXit: 30 ⏎
```
Rotates the circle 30 degrees counter-clockwise

`Command:` *Pick a grip on the edge of the circle, cycle to Scale mode*

```
** SCALE**
<Scale factor>/Base point/Copy/
Undo/Reference/eXit: B ⏎
```
`Base point:` *Pick a point off the circle*

```
** SCALE **
<Scale factor>/Base point/Copy/
Undo/Reference/eXit: .5 ⏎
```
Scales the circle by .5 from the new base point

`Command:` *Select a grip on the circle and change to Mirror mode*
Starts Autoedit

```
** MIRROR **
<Second point>/Base point/Copy/
Undo/eXit: B ⏎
```
`Base point:` *Pick a point off of the circle*

```
** MIRROR **
<Second point>/Base point/Copy/
Undo/eXit:
```
Pick another point off of the circle

`Command:` *Press Ctrl-C three times*

131

Selecting Grips

You can select a grip by moving the cursor into a grip box and pressing the pick button. You also can select multiple grip points by holding down the Shift key while picking grip boxes. To enter autoediting mode, release the Shift key and pick any grip. This grip becomes the base point for the various autoediting modes. If two or more entities have grips at the same point, you can select all of those grips by selecting all of the objects and then selecting the common grip box. Thus, you can stretch two lines that share an endpoint or enlarge a circle while stretching a line that ends at one of its quadrant points (0 degrees, 90 degrees, 180 degrees, or 270 degrees). Figure 4.12 shows two objects stretched simultaneously.

Figure 4.12:

Stretching two objects simultaneously.

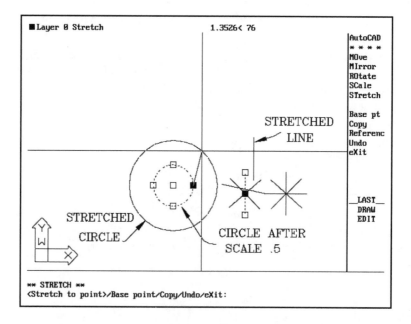

Stretching Two Objects Simultaneously

Continue from previous exercise.

Command: *Pick a line and the circle*

```
Command: Press and hold down the Shift key,
pick a  grip on the circle and one on the line,
and then release Shift and pick a grip on the circle

** STRETCH **
```

`<Stretch to point>/Base point/Copy` `/Undo/eXit:` *Pick a point anywhere*	Stretches both the line and the circle

```
Command: Pick a non-selected line

Command: Press and hold down the Shift
key, pick a grip on each selected line
```

`Command:` *Pick one of the grips*	Starts Autoedit

```
** STRETCH **
```

`<Stretch to point>/Base point/Copy` `/Undo/eXit:` *Pick a point anywhere*	Stretches both lines relative to each other

Controlling GRIPS and Object Selection Parameters

The GRIPS system variable must be set to 1 for the autoediting modes to function. The Grips dialog box can be displayed by the DDGRIP command or by choosing Grips from the Settings pull-down menu. Putting a check mark in the Enable Grips check box turns on the GRIPS system variable; clearing the box turns it off.

Controlling Entity Selection with DDSELECT

Two other settings, Use Shift to Add and Press and Drag, improve the versatility and interaction of editing with grips. They are found in the Entity Selection Settings dialog box (see fig. 4.13). The DDSELECT command brings up this dialog box, or you can choose Selection Settings from the Settings menu.

AutoCAD editing modes and commands operate on a *selection set* of entities that you select. The current selection is generally indicated by highlighting the entities. The Use Shift to Add setting controls how entities are added to the selection set (same as the

PICKADD system variable). When this is on, (1—the default), entities are added to the selection set as they are selected. When this is off (0), newly selected entities replace the existing selection set, unless you hold down the Shift key as you select them. Whether PICKADD is on or off, holding down Shift and selecting currently highlighted entities removes those entities from the selection set. To add entities when PICKADD is off, hold down the Shift key while you select entities.

Figure 4.13:

The Entity Selection Settings dialog box.

If the Noun/Verb Selection box is not checked, you must enter a command before you can select objects to build a selection set. If it is checked, you can select objects at the Command: prompt, and then enter a command to process the selection set.

The Press and Release box determines the way you draw a selection window. If the box is not checked, you pick two points to define a window—that is, two clicks of the left mouse button. If the box is checked, you must press the button at one corner and hold it down while you move the pointing device to size the window. While you hold down the button, the window is displayed; when you release it, objects are selected and the window disappears. This box must be checked to enable Autoedit to function.

The Grips Dialog Box

The Grips dialog box is displayed when you select Grips from the Settings pull-down menu. The settings in this dialog box determine whether or not grips appear when you select objects, and the ways that the grips are displayed. Figure 4.14 shows the Grips dialog box, with the correct settings for autoediting.

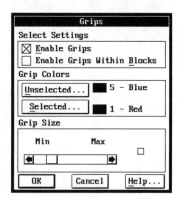

Figure 4.14:

The Grips dialog box.

In the Select Settings block, there are two check boxes. The first box, **E**nable Grips, enables Autoedit when checked. If Grips are enabled, grip boxes appear when you select an object at the Command: prompt. The second box, Enable Grips Within **B**locks, determines the way grips are displayed when you select a block. Blocks are covered later in the book—they are user-defined symbols composed of other entities, but which AutoCAD treats as single objects. If the second box is not checked, only one grip appears when you select a block: the grip at the block's insert point. If the box is checked, all the grips of all the entities that make up the block are displayed when you select a block.

In the Grip Colors block, there are two buttons, labeled **U**nselected and **S**elected. (The ellipsis following the label indicates that pushing the button displays another dialog box.) Both of these buttons display the same dialog box, the Select Color dialog box, shown in figure 4.15.

Unselected and **S**elected apply to the grip boxes that AutoCAD displays. Unselected grips are those grips that appear when you select an object—the default color is blue. The default color for hot grips is red.

The Grip Size block contains only one control, a slider bar to enlarge or shrink grip boxes (see fig. 4.16). The default size is appropriate for a VGA display. If you have a high-resolution display, you may want to use larger grip boxes.

Figure 4.15:

The Select Color dialog box.

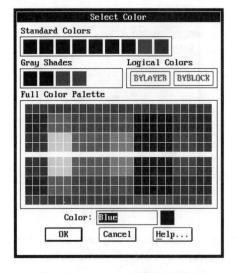

Figure 4.16:

Grip Size block.

Change Grip Size

Continue with the previous exercise.

Choose Settings, *then* Grips	Displays the Grips dialog box
Click on the left arrow *in the* Grip Size Box	Decreases the grip size
Click on the right arrow *in the* Grip Size Box	Increases the grip size

Click and hold the box *in the* Grip Size slide bar *with the pick button.*

Move the cursor left and right   Increases and decreases the grip
                                                                 size

Release the button when the grip size is   Accepts the dialog box
right for your display

Click on OK

Using DDMODIFY

Every entity that you can draw with AutoCAD is ultimately defined in terms of points, or points and distances. If you move a point, or change a distance, you modify the object. In some cases, you can look at the drawing on the screen and determine which objects need to be modified and how they should be modified. For example, it may be obvious that a line needs to be stretched so that its endpoint coincides with the endpoint of another line. In other cases, it may not be obvious from the display that an object needs to be changed, but you know that a change is required.

You can examine the entire definition of any object with the DDMODIFY command. To use DDMODIFY, you enter DDMODIFY at the command prompt. DDMODIFY is not a built-in command; it is an AutoLISP program that is furnished with AutoCAD. The first time you enter the command in any given drawing session, AutoCAD loads it automatically. For the remainder of that drawing session, the command works like a built-in command.

When you enter the DDMODIFY command, AutoCAD displays the following prompt:

`Select object to list:`

When you select an object, AutoCAD displays a dialog box that lists all the parameters that define the object, as well as the object's properties: color, linetype, layer, and thickness. Each entity type has its own dialog box, because each entity type has its own set of defining parameters. The dialog boxes for line, circle, arc, and text entities are shown in figures 4.17 through 4.21.

Figure 4.17:

The Modify Line dialog box.

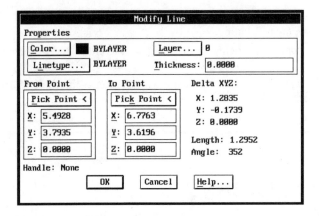

Figure 4.18:

The Modify Circle dialog box.

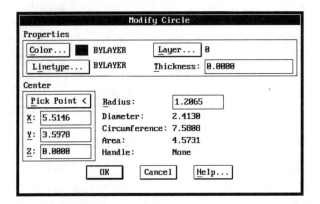

Figure 4.19:

The Modify Arc dialog box.

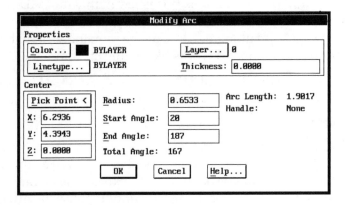

Examine the Modify Circle dialog box, shown in figure 4.18. It includes a point (Center) and a distance (Radius), which together define the circle, and display several geometric statistics of the circle. It also lists the properties of the circle. First, consider the lower portion of the dialog box.

```
┌─────────────────────────────────────────────────────────┐
│                      Modify Text                          │
│ Properties                                                │
│  ┌─────────┐  ███ BYLAYER      ┌─────────┐                │
│  │ Color...│                   │ Layer...│ 0              │
│  └─────────┘                   └─────────┘                │
│  ┌─────────┐     BYLAYER                   ┌──────────┐   │
│  │Linetype.│              Thickness:       │ 0.0000   │   │
│  └─────────┘                               └──────────┘   │
│  Text: ┌────────────────────────────────────────────┐    │
│        │ DD                                         │      │
│        └────────────────────────────────────────────┘    │
│  Origin                                                   │
│  ┌──────────────┐  Height:    ┌────────┐  Justify: ┌────────┐ │
│  │ Pick Point < │             │ 0.3000 │           │ Left  ▼│ │
│  └──────────────┘             └────────┘           └────────┘ │
│  X: ┌────────┐  Rotation:   ┌────────┐  Style:  ┌──────────┐  │
│     │ 5.6016 │              │ 0      │          │ STANDARD▼│  │
│     └────────┘              └────────┘          └──────────┘  │
│  Y: ┌────────┐  Width Factor:┌────────┐  ☐ Upside Down      │
│     │ 3.0761 │              │ 1.0000 │                       │
│     └────────┘              └────────┘                       │
│  Z: ┌────────┐  Obliquing:  ┌────────┐  ☐ Backward          │
│     │ 0.0000 │              │ 0      │                       │
│     └────────┘              └────────┘                       │
│  Handle: None                                             │
│        ┌──────┐    ┌────────┐   ┌────────┐                │
│        │  OK  │    │ Cancel │   │ Help...│                │
│        └──────┘    └────────┘   └────────┘                │
└─────────────────────────────────────────────────────────┘
```

Figure 4.20:

The Modify Text dialog box.

The Center block describes a point—the center of the circle. The X, Y, and Z coordinates are listed in edit boxes. You can specify a new center point by editing the X, Y, and Z values. If you click on the OK button after entering new coordinates, the entity is moved to the location defined by the new coordinates.

If you do not know the coordinates to which you want to move the circle, you can click on the **P**ick Point box. The angle bracket indicates that this selection enables you to point to a new value. AutoCAD clears the dialog box from the screen and prompts you for a new center point. You then can move the crosshair pointer to the desired location and pick the new center point, and you can use object snaps to locate the new point precisely. When you pick the new point, AutoCAD moves the circle, displays the circle in the new location, and then redisplays the dialog box. When the dialog box reappears, the new coordinates are shown in the Center block.

To the right of the Center block, several numerical values are displayed. The first is the **R**adius, which appears in an edit box. This means that you can edit the value. By changing the radius value, you change the size of the circle. The change takes effect when you exit the dialog box by clicking on the OK button or pressing Enter.

Below the **R**adius box the values for Diameter, Circumference, Area, and Handle are indicated. The Diameter value is twice the **R**adius value, as expected, but you cannot edit this value. If you want to change the diameter, you must edit the value in the **R**adius box. Similarly, the Circumference and Area values are calculated from the **R**adius value. To change them, you must change the **R**adius value.

Study the other three entity dialog boxes—they are similar. The Modify Text dialog box contains an Origin box, and several scalar value boxes that can be edited. The Modify Line dialog box contains two boxes for points—From Point and To Point—and calculated values for length in the X, Y, and Z directions, length, and angle relative to the 0 axis. Again, values in boxes can be edited, values not in boxes are calculated, display only values.

Now, use DDMODIFY to tune the drawing you made with earlier exercises. When you are through, your drawing should look like figure 4.21.

Figure 4.21:

Tuning the drawing with DDMODIFY.

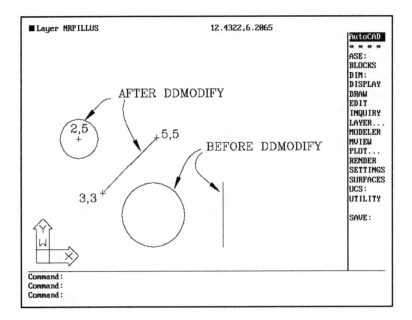

Tuning the Drawing with DDMODIFY

Command: *Choose* Modify, *then* Entity	Displays the Modify Entity dialog box
Select object to modify: *Pick a line*	Displays the Modify Line dialog box
Click on Pick Point *in the* From Point box	
From pt: *Pick a new from point*	Changes the first point of the line
Double click To Point X: **3** ↵	Changes the endpoint's X to 3
Double click To Point Y: **3** ↵	Changes the last point's Y to 3
Click on OK	Accepts the dialog box

Notice that the lines To point moves to 3,3.

Command: **DDMODIFY** ↵	
Select object to modify: *pick the circle*	Displays the Modify Circle dialog box
Click on Pick point	Changes the center point
Center point: **2,5** ↵	Changes the center point to 2,5
Double click on Radius: **.75** ↵	Changes the radius to .75
Click on OK	Accepts the dialog box

If you have used an earlier version of AutoCAD, you should appreciate the power of Release 12's Autoedit mode and DDMODIFY command. These two new tools replace a dozen editing and inquiry commands. (The commands are still available, of course.) If Release 12 is the first CAD system you have used, you can rest assured that you are learning CAD with one of the most efficient CAD interfaces available.

Summary

In this chapter, you learned how to edit your drawing—that is, to modify the geometry you entered with drawing commands. You learned the basic editing operations without having to learn any commands. Then, you learned a command, DDMODIFY, that enables you to examine the definition of an entity and modify it interactively.

Drawing Setup and Screen Control

The mechanics and concepts of drawing on a CAD system are different from drawing manually. With a paper drawing, you begin with a fixed size of paper and draw to a scale that fits on the paper. You can always see the entire drawing, at the scale you selected. In AutoCAD, you draw the object actual size, whether it is two inches by three inches or two miles by three miles, and scale the plot to fit the image on the paper. The bridge shown in figure 5.1 is 92 feet long. As you create the drawing, you must also display it on the screen, with an area even smaller than that of the plotter paper. Clearly, there are some fundamental differences between drawing on the board and on the screen.

In this chapter, you will learn how to draw full size on a small screen, in your choice of units of measure, and you will learn how to scale the limits of your drawing area to the paper sheet on which it will be plotted. You will learn how to define the size of your drawing world (your full-size electronic board), how to specify the units in which you measure distances, and how to verify your drawing setup.

In the first four chapters, you made full-size drawings, but they were small enough that they fit on the screen of your computer. The size of your "drawing board" was 12 units wide by 9 units high. The size of your monitor screen is approximately 12 inches wide by 9 inches high, so your display was approximately correct for a drawing measured in inches. Recall, however, that no units were attached to the dimensions you used in these exercises.

Figure 5.1:

A bridge profile.

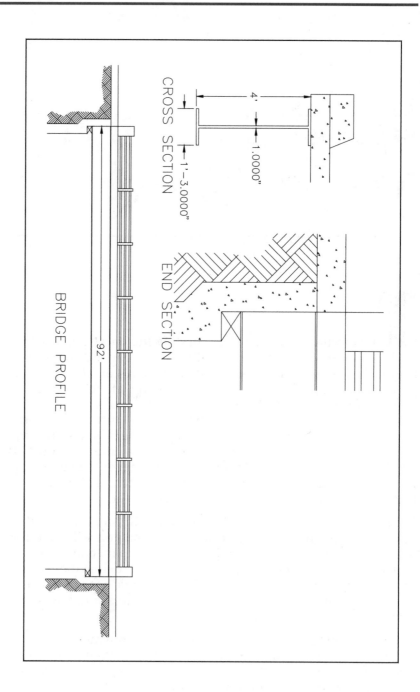

In order to draw large objects at full size, or to examine fine detail in any drawing, you need to use AutoCAD's display control commands. These commands include ZOOM, which controls what portion of the CAD drawing is visible on the screen and at what magnification; PAN, which slides the current screen view around different areas of the drawing; and VIEW, which you can use to save and restore the drawing views you define with PAN and ZOOM. These commands enable you to view and manipulate the drawing's image to your advantage.

You also learn to divide the drawing display area into one or more viewports. *Viewports* give you multiple views into your drawing so you can simultaneously see several portions at different magnifications. You can define tiled viewports for use as a drafting aid, and you can define multiple viewports in paper space as a drawing composition aid. You will learn about model space and paper space, and how to switch between the two.

In this chapter, you learn how to do the following:

- Set up your drawing environment

- Use AutoCAD's display commands

- Use extents, virtual screen, and regeneration

- Save and restore views

- Work with multiple views and viewports

Setting Up Your Drawing Environment

When you begin a new drawing, you must perform several preparatory tasks. You define the drawing's *limits*—the size of your drawing world. You specify the type of units you will be using, such as decimal, architectural, or fractional units. You create viewports to view your drawing. Each of these setup tasks contributes to your drawing efficiency and accuracy. You should develop the habit of doing as much of this setup as possible before you start to draw, but you can adjust these parameters at any time. The best place to begin a drawing setup is by setting units and limits; then set the snap interval, grid interval, text size, and other settings.

The two most essential setup tasks are setting the units and setting the drawing's limits. These tasks are interrelated and depend on the way the drawing will be scaled for plotting. Your first task is usually to set the drawing units, which may vary, depending on what you want AutoCAD to do.

Working with Units in AutoCAD

When you work on a drawing of a real-world object, you think in terms of the units used to measure the real world object—inches, feet, millimeters, and so on. AutoCAD, however, stores dimensions in terms of *drawing units*, which are numeric values that can be used to represent general distances and dimensions. It is your task to assign a meaning to AutoCAD's drawing units. If you are a surveyor, you may use feet or miles as your basic unit. If you are an industrial designer, you may use inches as your basic unit. But to AutoCAD, there is no fundamental difference between parsecs and Angstrom units.

To aid you in working with dimensions, AutoCAD enables you to set the format in which distances and dimensions are interpreted, when they are keyed in, and how they are displayed. AutoCAD includes several predefined formats, listed in table 5.1 and described below. To achieve a specific unit-display format, AutoCAD generates a text string that includes the numeric values in the correct format and a suffix to identify the specified system of units. The unit-display format saves you the effort of mentally translating from the meaning you have assigned to drawing units to the drawing units.

The type of unit formats you can use include scientific, decimal, engineering, architectural, and fractional formats. Most of these apply equally well to any system of measurement. Decimal, for example, works well for either metric or English decimal units. Architectural and engineering units, however, are useful only with the English system of measurement.

The units setting does not affect how AutoCAD works internally; the program still "thinks" in drawing units. Unit settings control the user interface and dimensioning that provide a frame of reference in which to work. For example, if you select architectural units, AutoCAD displays dimensions in feet and inches, but it interprets a number entered without a suffix as a value in inches. The units you set define the way distances and angles are displayed by the prompts, by the coordinate display on the status line, and by anything else in which AutoCAD presents units to you.

Unit settings determine the way AutoCAD interprets values you enter—that is, you can enter dimensions in a familiar format. The formats in which you can enter distances, points, and angles depend on the units you set. In its automatic dimensioning, AutoCAD formats dimension text according to the units you set.

In addition to specifying linear units of measure, unit settings define the way in which angles are displayed. You can choose to display angles in decimal degrees, degrees/minutes/seconds, grads, radians, or surveyors' units. By default, the zero degree-direction is oriented to the right (or east) on the display, and angles are measured counterclockwise from zero. You can change the zero-degree orientation and change the angular measure to clockwise instead of counterclockwise.

Some input formats differ from the display format. Fractions display with spaces between them and the preceding whole number: for example, 1'-3 1/2" or 15 1/2. But when you input fractions, you cannot include spaces, because AutoCAD interprets a space as Enter. Examples of the various display and input formats are shown in table 5.1.

Table 5.1

Units Formats Table

Linear Units	Display/Dimensioning	Input Format
Scientific	2.75E+01	Same as display
Decimal	27.50	Same as display
Engineering	2'-3.50"	Same as display
Architectural	2'-3 1/2"	2'3-1/2"
Fractional	25 1/2	25-1/2

continues

Table 5.1 Continued

Units Formats Table

Angular Units	Display/Dimensioning	Input Format
Decimal deg	60.0000	Same, or 60.0000
Deg/min/sec	60d0'0"	Same as display
Grads	66.6667g	Same as display
Radians	1.0472r	Same as display
Surveyors' units	N 30d0'0" E	N30d0'0"E

Controlling Units

You control AutoCAD's units with the Units Control dialog box, which is displayed when you select Units Control from the Settings pull-down menu. This dialog box is shown in figure 5.2.

Figure 5.2:

The AutoCAD Units Control dialog box.

The Units Control dialog box contains two blocks of controls—*Units* and *Angles*, and a button to display the direction control dialog box. The dialog box also has the standard OK, Cancel and Help options.

The Units block has radio buttons for selecting the desired unit of measure format and a **P**recision prompt, which displays a submenu of precision levels.

Values and Units

You can enter values in almost any manner, regardless of the units you set. Any units mode accepts distances in scientific or decimal linear units; and accepts angles in decimal degrees, grads, or radians. When angular units are set to grads or radians, you can omit the g or r from the input, but you must add a **d** to the end of decimal input in those modes. You can also omit the trailing inch or seconds mark (") from input in engineering, architectural, and deg/min/sec modes.

When you are working with architectural or engineering units, you can enter input in inches, feet, or both. If you enter a number without any indicator, AutoCAD treats it as inches. To indicate feet, include a foot mark ('). To enter feet and inches, enter the number of feet, a foot mark, and the number of inches. Do not put a space between a whole number and a fraction when inputting. AutoCAD interprets a space as Enter, so put a dash before any fraction that is input after a whole number (5-1/2").

The following are examples of feet and inch values you can enter in AutoCAD:

```
2           (2 inches)
2-1/2       (2 and one-half inches)
3'          (3 feet)
5'2-1/2     (5 feet, 2 and one-half inches)
```

The input and display formats for feet and inches differ. You can force AutoCAD to display feet and inches, angles, and fractions in the input format by setting the system variable UNITMODE to 1. To set it, type UNITMODE at the command prompt and press Enter.

The following exercise shows you how to use the UNITS command to set engineering units, with four fractional places for inches and angles. These engineering units are suitable for most civil and structural applications, although for survey work you set the angles to surveyor's units.

Setting Units with the UNITS Command

Start ACAD from the AB directory, and begin a NEW drawing named BRIDGE.

Choose Settings, *then* Units Control dialog box	Displays the Units Control
`Command: ddunits Initial load,` `please wait.DDUNITS loaded.`	

With the exception of Engineering and Architectural formats, these formats can be used with any basic unit of measurement. For example, Decimal mode is perfect for metric units, as well as for decimal English units.

Click on Engineering or the box to the left of Engineering	Sets units to Engineering
Click on the box under Precision for Angles	Displays the Precision pull-down menu
Choose 0.00	Sets the Angle precision to two decimal places
Click on OK	Accepts the dialog box
`Command: QSAVE ⏎`	Saves the drawing to the same name

Even if your application needs only two decimal places of precision, set it to four. If it needs four, set it to six. If it needs fractions no finer than 1/2 inch, set it to 1/64. This ensures precision. For example, if you set the precision to two decimals, everything drawn is rounded to hundredths when displayed, even if this is not accurate. Individual drawing errors are less likely to show up, but they may cause cumulative errors. If you set the precision to four places, drawing errors are more likely to show up. For instance, if a coordinate displays as 1.0023 inch when you know it should be 1.0000 inch, you know it is not drawn correctly. Units can be changed at any time. Before you dimension, change the units to two decimal places, so the dimension text shows only the two decimal places you want.

Now that you have units set, the next setup task is to figure your plot scale and set your limits and text height.

Specifying Drawing Limits

Although the size of the object you can draw in AutoCAD is almost unlimited, setting limits on the area in which you are going to draw verifies that the object you are drawing will fit at the desired scale on the sheet size on which you intend to plot it. Setting drawing limits also sets the extents of the default grid, giving you a boundary in which to work.

AutoCAD's limits are defined by the coordinates of the lower left and upper right corners of your planned drawing area. You set these coordinates with the LIMITS command.

LIMITS. The LIMITS command defines the drawing area by the coordinates of its lower left and upper right corners. This sets the extents of the grid in the WCS and defines the minimum area for ZOOM All. If LIMITS are set on (off is the default) and you pick a point outside the limits, AutoCAD gives an **Outside limits prompt and rejects the point.

LIMITS Options

- **ON.** Turn limits checking on to prevent points from being picked outside the limits.

- **OFF.** Turn limits checking off (the default) to enable you to pick points outside the limits.

- **Lower left corner.** Enter the coordinates for the lower left corner of the limits (default is 0,0).

- **Upper right corner.** Enter the coordinates for the upper right corner of the limits (default is 12,9).

If grid is on and you are in the WCS, grid dots are displayed only within the drawing limits. In a UCS, the grid extends to the edges of the screen or viewport. Although the default limits may define a drawing area as 12"-by-9", the actual area displayed depends on the proportions of your display screen.

Calculating Limits To Fit a Drawing and Sheet

To determine the limits to use for any particular object, you must know the size of the object and decide the sheet size on which you will plot the drawing. The sheet size is determined by the object size and the plot scale you use for the drawing, or the plot scale is determined by the sheet size and object size. The following are examples.

A Flat Pattern

Suppose you are drawing a flat pattern for a sheet metal part whose flat size is 48"-by-24". The company uses a standard B-size sheet (17"-by-22") for such parts. You need to calculate the plot scale to determine the limits (see fig. 5.3).

```
Size of part 48" x 24"
Sheet size   17" x 22"
```

Figure 5.3:

Limits of B-size sheet for 48" by 24" part.

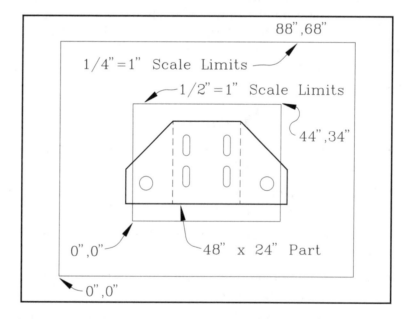

AutoCAD plot scaling is calculated as the ratio of plotted inches to drawing units. First, try a scale of 1/2"=1", or `1 plotted inch = 2 drawing units`, which gives a plot scale factor of 1/2. Divide the proposed sheet size by the plot scale factor to determine the required sheet size.

```
Width:      22" divided by 1/2 = 22" x 2 = 44"
Height:     17" divided by 1/2 = 17" x 2 = 34"
```

The resulting limits, 44" × 34", are not large enough to enclose the 48" × 24" part. If you make the limits approximately two times this size (plot scale 1/4"=1" or 1/4), you have plenty of room for the part and still have room around it for dimensions and a title block.

```
Width:      22" divided by 1/4 = 22" x 4 = 88"
Height:     17" divided by 1/4 = 17" x 4 = 68"
```

These limits, 88" x 68", leave plenty of room for the part, its dimensions, a title block, and any notes or other details that may be required.

Another important setting related to plot scale is the height of symbols (such as bubbles) and annotation text. Calculate these the same way you calculate the limits: divide the desired plotted height of the symbol by the plot scale factor to determine the height in drawing units. For example, to get 1/8" plotted text, set the text size to 1/2 (1/8 divided by 1/4 plot scale factor = 4/8 = 1/2).

A Small Bridge

Suppose you are drawing an elevation of a small bridge whose length is 92 feet. (Its height is comparatively small, so you can disregard height.) You draw it for plotting at 1/4"=1'-0" scale (1"=48", or 1/48 plot scale) to show enough detail. You need to calculate the sheet size to determine the limits (see fig. 5.4).

```
Length:  92' x 1/48 = 1104"/48 = 23"
```

The plotted object length, 23", is too long to fit a C-size sheet, so you have to use a 34" x 22" D-size sheet. Now calculate the limits:

```
Width:      34" x 48 = 1632" or 136'
Height:     22" x 48 = 1056" or 88'
```

Figure 5.4:

Limits of (and sheet size for) a 92-foot bridge.

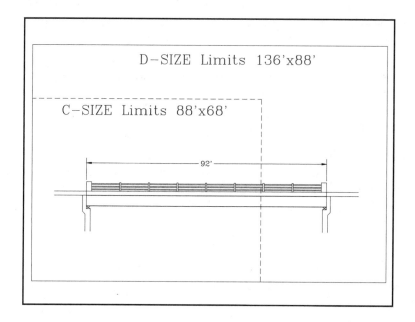

These limits, 136' × 88', leave plenty of room. With these limits and this plot scale, to get 1/8" plotted text, set text size to 6 (1/8 divided by 1/48 plot scale factor = 48/8 = 6). An initial snap of 6" and grid of 4' is appropriate for this drawing.

Setting Limits with the LIMITS Command

Continue from the previous UNITS exercise.

`Command:` *Press F7*	Turns on the drawing grid; the 1" grid covers the default 12 x 9 limits
Choose Settings, *then* Drawing Limits	
`Reset Model space limits:`	

`ON/OFF/<Lower left corner>`
`<0'-0.0000",`
`0'-0.0000">:` *Press Enter*
	Accepts the default setting

`Upper right corner`
`<1'-0.0000",0'-9.0000">:`
`136', 88'` ⏎
	Sets the upper right corner at 136' by 88'

Be sure to enter the foot marks, or AutoCAD will interpret the numbers as inches.

```
Command: QSAVE ↵                        Saves the drawing to the same
                                        name
```

Nothing appears to have changed. If you move the cursor, you see that the upper right corner is still somewhere near the coordinates of 12,9. AutoCAD has reset the drawing limits as requested, but it has not changed the area displayed. To use the limits, you have to zoom the drawing.

Zooming the Limits

The objects you draw in AutoCAD are sometimes much bigger than the size of the display. Therefore, you need to reposition the display to view all the drawing. Think of the display as a window through which you are looking at the drawing. You can move it closer to the object to view detail, move it farther away to view more of the object, or move it around to focus on different areas. AutoCAD has several commands for controlling the view of the drawing. This chapter covers viewing in detail later. The most important of these display controls is the ZOOM command.

For now, just preview the All option so you can zoom out to the drawing limits. In 2D, ZOOM All displays the drawing limits or the drawing extents, whichever is greater.

> **Note** The drawing *extents* is the area occupied by entities since the last regeneration. The extents may exceed the limits if you draw beyond the limits. If a ZOOM All zooms too far out, you may have drawn outside the limits. If so, look for an offending object to erase and then zoom again.

Use ZOOM All options to zoom out to the new limits. Set text size to 6 (1/8 plotted text size divided by 1/48 plot scale factor = 48/8 = 6), snap to 6" and grid to 4'.

Zooming to the Limits

Continue from the previous LIMITS exercise.

Choose View, *then* Zoom	Displays the ZOOM submenu
Choose All	Selects the All option

```
Regenerating drawing.
Grid too dense to display
```

You need to reset the grid to a usable size.

```
Command: GRID ↵
```
Set to 48 (4')

```
Command: SNAP ↵
```
Set to 6

Move the cursor around and watch the coordinates change. Check the coordinates of the upper right corner of the grid.

`Command: TEXTSIZE ↵` `New value for TEXTSIZE <0'-0.2000">6`	Sets the default text height to 6
`Command: QSAVE ↵`	Saves the drawing to the same name

The results should look like figure 5.5.

Figure 5.5:

The BRIDGE drawing zoomed to limits with four-foot grid.

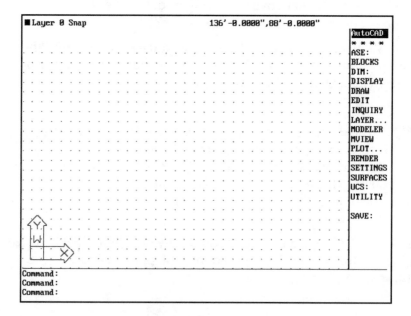

Now you can see the entire limits, from 0,0 to 136',88', and the 48"
grid covers the limits.

Using AutoCAD's Display Commands

AutoCAD enables you to create drawings of large objects with
fine detail. You can draw the solar system with details a few
inches in height, or you can draw more mundane objects with
microscopic detail. AutoCAD must display your drawings on
a screen that can subdivide the entire drawing into only a few
hundred steps in both the X and Y directions. Plotting is not much
better, with resolutions of a several thousand lines-per-inch, at
best. And even if your workstation were capable of displaying
objects at the resolution that AutoCAD can represent them, the
human eye would not be able do discern the details. You need to
move the display closer to the object to view detail, move it farther
away to see more of the object, and pan around to focus on different areas, with AutoCAD's display control commands.

Regeneration

When you changed the limits of your drawing and used the
ZOOM All command to display those limits, you saw the following message: Regenerating drawing. Regeneration can be disconcert-
ing if AutoCAD performs the operation when you are in a hurry.

As noted in Chapter 1, an AutoCAD drawing is a file on disk—it
is an electronic list of geometric shapes. This list cannot be viewed
directly, however. The drawing file defines drawing entities in
terms of key points and entity types, but an image on the screen
consists of dots. When AutoCAD loads a drawing for editing, it
reads through this file and creates a *display list*, which is a list of
images that can be displayed on the screen. Consider a line—
although the definition of a line in the drawing file contains only
the two endpoints, the corresponding display list entity contains a
series of points corresponding to the pixels that must be lighted
on the screen to display the image of the line.

The display list cannot contain the level of detail that the drawing file definition implies—the amount of memory required to hold the display list would be astronomical. Instead, the display list is an approximate image of the drawing file; the amount of detail that can be stored in the display list is limited by the amount of memory available to it. If you try to zoom in or out by too great a factor, AutoCAD must reread the drawing file to construct a new display list to display the image you request (it regenerates the drawing).

Release 12 regenerates less often than earlier versions, but certain commands still force it to regenerate. As you work with the exercises in this book, regeneration is not time-consuming because the drawings are not large. As you work with larger and larger drawings, however, regeneration becomes more and more time-consuming. There are occasions when you want to force a regeneration, but generally you should avoid it. As you study the display controls, bear in mind that there are often several ways to manipulate your display, some of which force regeneration; some of which do not.

Using the ZOOM Command

ZOOM. The ZOOM command controls the display in the current viewport, zooming in (magnifying the image) or out (shrinking the image). Zoom in for greater detail of a small part of the drawing or zoom out to view a larger part in less detail.

You have already used ZOOM's All option. ZOOM provides several other flexible and convenient options that specify what to display. All of its options act in the current viewport.

ZOOM Options

- **All.** In 2D (plan view), ZOOM All displays the larger of the drawing limits or extents. In a 3D view, All displays the Extents.

- **Center.** The Center option zooms to the center point and displays the height (in drawing units) or the magnification that you specify. Pick a new center and press Enter to *pan* (move the display without changing the zoom magnification). The center point picked becomes the viewport center. Press Enter at the new center-point prompt instead of specifying a new point—the center point remains unchanged as the display height or magnification changes.

- **Dynamic.** The Dynamic option graphically combines the PAN command with ZOOM All and Window. It displays an image of the entire generated portion of your drawing, and you indicate with your cursor where to zoom. Dynamic can zoom in or out, or it can pan the current viewport. Dynamic is explained in more detail later in this chapter.

- **Extents.** The Extents option displays all drawing entities as large as possible in the current viewport.

- **Left.** The Left option zooms to the lower left corner point and displays the height (in drawing units) or the magnification that you specify. The point you specify becomes the new lower left corner of the current viewport. In all other ways, Left works in the same way as Center.

- **Previous.** The Previous option restores a previous display for the current viewport, whether it was generated by the ZOOM, PAN, VIEW, or DVIEW commands. Up to ten previous views are stored for each viewport, so you can step back through them by repeatedly using ZOOM Previous.

- **Vmax.** The Vmax option zooms to the currently generated virtual screen to display the maximum drawing area possible without a regeneration.

- **Window.** The Window option zooms to the rectangular area you specify by picking two diagonally opposite corner points. Unless the X,Y proportions of the window you specify exactly match the proportions of the viewport, a little extra width or height of the image shows.

- **Scale(X/XP).** Enter a magnification factor to zoom by. This option is the default.

159

Several of these options are diagrammed in figure 5.6.

Figure 5.6:

ZOOM option examples.

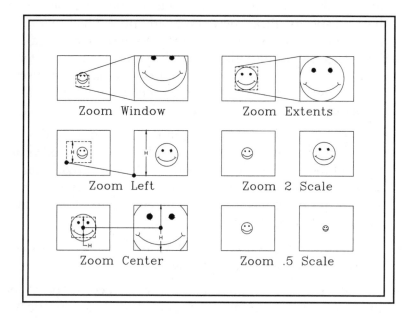

Zooming by Magnification or Scale Factor

The default Scale(X/XP) option enables you to enter a *magnification* or *scale factor*. The default, a simple scale factor of 1, displays the drawing limits; 2 displays approximately one-fourth of the drawing with twice the magnification; and .5 displays more than the entire limits with half the magnification of 1.

You can enter a relative scale by entering the magnification value followed by an X (times). If you do this, AutoCAD zooms relative to the current display of the current viewport. For example, ZOOM .5X zooms the current viewport's display to half of its current magnification and displays twice as much of the drawing.

The ScaleXP option scales the magnification of viewports in paper space. The Center and Left options also accept a magnification relative to the current display of the current viewport. If you enter a number at the magnification or height prompt, it becomes the new view height in the current viewport. If you enter a relative scale by entering a magnification value followed by an X, the viewport's current height is zoomed by that scale factor. For example, if a viewport displays 20 feet of the drawing in the Y axis and you enter a magnification of 2X, it zooms to display ten feet of the drawing.

Using the Zoom Options

You can see that the ZOOM command has many options. Until you master the more powerful Dynamic option, you will most often use the All, Window, and Previous options. The Center and Left options are also valuable for positioning specific views. No matter how you zoom, however, you are not changing the real scale of the drawing. You still draw full size. ZOOM changes only the display of your view of the drawing model.

You are already familiar with ZOOM All, so the discussion that follows covers the other options. The Window option of the ZOOM command enables you to pick two points to define a window; then it zooms the contents of the window to fill the current viewport. This procedure is useful when you want to zoom in on an area of the drawing to see it in more detail.

The Center and Left options work similarly. Each starts with a reference point and accepts a new view height, which can be specified as a magnification relative to the current view height. The only difference is that Center zooms around a new center point and Left sets the new point in the lower left corner of the viewport.

The Previous option restores the image that was displayed previously. For example, when you zoom in to an area and you want to restore the larger view you had before zooming in, use the ZOOM Previous command. AutoCAD keeps track of the last ten views, and each successive ZOOM Previous goes back one view.

Begin drawing a bridge. You use this drawing to zoom around in. Keep the bridge simple: ignore camber, deflection, the adjacent conditions, and use even inches for most dimensions. Even if you do not complete the bridge drawing, it amply demonstrates the use of the zoom. The bridge girders are 92' long, so zoom the top viewport to display a 104'-by-32' window in which to draw the elevation (see fig. 5.7). Because the exercise concentrates on display controls, instructions for previously covered commands, such as PLINE, are abbreviated.

Using Zoom To Draw a Bridge

Continue with the BRIDGE drawing from the previous exercise.

`Command: ZOOM ↵`	Selects the Window option
`All/Center/Dynamic/Extents/Left/` `Previous/Vmax/Window/<Scale(X/XP)>: W ↵`	
`First corner: 16',0 ↵`	Places the window's lower left corner
`Other corner: 120',32' ↵`	Places the window's upper right corner
`Command: LINE` *Draw the 48" deep by 92' long* *girder from point 20',24' to points* *@92'<0, @0,-4', @-92',0 and enter* *C to close*	

Notice that the line appears in all viewports as you draw.

`Command: UCS ↵` *Set the UCS to the top left of the girder*	
`Origin/ZAxis/3point/Entity/View/X/Y/Z` `/Prev/Restore/Save/Del/?/<World>: O ↵`	Selects the Origin option
`Origin point <0,0,0>:` *Pick point 20',24'*	
`Command: UCSICON ↵`	
`ON/OFF/All/Noorigin/ORigin/ <ON>: OR ↵`	Sets the UCSICON to display at 0,0,0
`Command: ZOOM ↵`	
`All/Center/Dynamic/Extents/Left/Previous/` `Vmax/Window/<Scale(X/XP)>: C ↵`	Selects the Center option
`Center point: 92',-2' ↵`	Sets the zoom's center point

Magnification or Height `<75'-2.6690">: 8' ↵`	Sets the height of the view
Command: `ZOOM ↵`	
`All/Center/Dynamic/Extents/Left/Previous/` `Vmax/Window/<Scale(X/XP)>: P ↵`	Selects the Previous option
Command: `ZOOM ↵`	
`All/Center/Dynamic/Extents/Left/Previous/` `Vmax/Window/<Scale(X/XP)>: L ↵`	Selects the Left option
Lower left corner point: `-6',-6' ↵`	Sets the zoom's lower left corner
Magnification or Height `<75'-2.6690">: 88' ↵`	Sets the height of the view
Command: `ZOOM`	
`All/Center/Dynamic/Extents/Left/` `Previous/Vmax/Window/<Scale(X/XP)>: L ↵`	Selects the Left option
Lower left corner point: *Press Enter*	
Magnification or Height `<88'-0.0000">: 11X ↵` 11 times	Magnifies the view
Command: `QSAVE ↵`	Saves the drawing to the same name

```
■ Layer 0 Snap              100'-0.0000",45'-6.0000"
                                                        AutoCAD
                                                        * * * *
                                                        ASE:
                                                        BLOCKS
                                                        DIM:
                                                        DISPLAY
                                                        DRAW
                                                        EDIT
                                                        INQUIRY
                                                        LAYER...
                                                        MODELER
          ┌─ RELOCATED UCS                              MVIEW
          │    NEW 0,0                                  PLOT...
      ◇                                                 RENDER
      ╱↑                                                SETTINGS
      └─┐                                               SURFACES
       ┌┼─×─────────────────────────────┐              UCS:
       └─┘                               │              UTILITY
                                          ╲
             92' BRIDGE GRIDER ──╲        ↗            SAVE:


   Command:
   Command:
   Command:
```

Figure 5.7:
A bridge girder.

Because the lower left viewport was zoomed to the height of 88 feet, the ZOOM L to a magnification of 11X (the current 88 feet divided by 11) ended up with the same magnification as the ZOOM C to a height of eight feet. The center and left corner points were specified to align the views in this example.

Zooming Transparently

Most zooms can be *transparent*, meaning that you can perform the zoom while AutoCAD is in the middle of another command. A transparent zoom interrupts the pending command and issues a zoom prompt. The prompt is prefixed with >> to indicate that it is a transparent command. When the zoom completes, the interrupted command resumes.

Prefix the ZOOM command with an apostrophe, like 'ZOOM, to issue a transparent zoom. Make sure the viewport you want to zoom is current before issuing the command. You cannot switch viewports in the middle of a zoom, whether the zoom is transparent or not.

Using Extents, Virtual Screen, and Regeneration

The ZOOM Extents option causes AutoCAD to display the drawing's *extents* as large as possible on the display. The extents is the rectangular area in which all of the drawing's entities (lines, arcs, and so on) reside. As you add new entities to the drawing or erase existing entities, the extents can change. If the extents are larger than the drawing's limits (you have been drawing outside the limits), ZOOM All also displays the extents as large as possible. ZOOM Extents and ZOOM All always regenerate the screen.

Controlling Regeneration

Sometimes you want AutoCAD to regenerate the drawing. For example, some AutoCAD commands do not show any visible effects until a regeneration has occurred. When you turn FILL off, for example, the change is not apparent until a regeneration occurs. To force AutoCAD to perform a regeneration, use the REGEN or REGENALL commands.

REGEN. The REGEN command regenerates the current viewport. Regeneration recalculates and redisplays all entities that are in the current viewport except those on frozen layers. To regenerate all viewports, use the REGENALL command. You can press Ctrl-C to stop a regeneration. An automatic regeneration may be caused by commands that require a regeneration before their effects become visible. To suppress automatic regenerations, use the REGENAUTO command and set it to off.

MOVING Around with PAN

Often, you need to move your drawing up, down, or sideways on the display to view a different part of it without changing the display magnification. The PAN command acts just like a camera pan: as you pan, the image in the display moves accordingly. Like zoom views, pan views can be recalled by ZOOM Previous.

PAN. The PAN command moves up, down, and sideways in the drawing without changing the current zoom magnification. You can pick points or enter a displacement in relative coordinates. 'PAN is a transparent command if it does not require a regeneration.

Pan displacement can be specified in two ways. You can enter a relative X,Y distance and press Enter at the second point prompt, or you can enter coordinates for both the displacement and the second point prompts. If you enter coordinates for both prompts, the displacement is the vector (distance and angle) from the first to the second point. Think of the drawing as a sheet of paper: you are "grabbing" the sheet at the first point and sliding under the window of the current viewport to the second point. PAN gives you a rubber-band line between your two points to indicate the direction you are panning.

Using the PAN Command

Continue from the previous exercise.

Command: **PAN** ↵

Displacement: *Pick one grid dot to the left of the Bridge span*
Specifies point from which to pan

Second point: *Pick one grid dot to the right*
Specifies the new on-screen location for the displacement point

Command: **QSAVE** ↵
Saves the drawing to the same name

The results are shown in figure 5.8.

Figure 5.8:

Panning across the drawing.

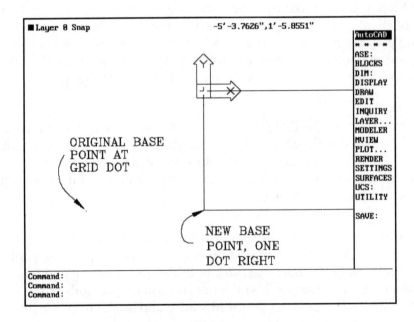

Zooming Dynamically

When your drawing is not complex, regeneration happens almost as quickly as a redraw. As the drawing becomes more complex, however, regeneration time increases, sometimes dramatically. Therefore, use other zoom options and avoid using ZOOM All whenever possible. One option that can perform any kind of zoom you desire is ZOOM Dynamic.

ZOOM Dynamic combines the PAN command with ZOOM All and Window. Dynamic displays an image of the virtual screen, along with boxes that indicate the current view, the extents, and the view to which you are zooming. The view box can be moved, without resizing, to pan the display. You can change the size of the view box to zoom the new view, or move and resize the view box to both pan and zoom.

A solid white or black box border indicates the current drawing extents. On a color monitor, a dashed green box indicates the current view of the current viewport, and four red corner lines indicate the currently generated virtual screen that can be displayed without requiring regeneration. If you specify a zoom or pan that requires a regeneration, an hourglass warning icon appears in the lower left corner of the viewport.

You can switch between panning and resizing the zoom box by clicking the pick button. When you are panning (the default), an x appears in the box. If you move the cursor at this time, it drags the box. When resizing (zooming) the zoom box, an arrow appears at the right side of the box. If you move the cursor, it changes the size of the box. Once the box size and location are satisfactory, press Enter.

 If the zoom box disappears, you probably resized it to a tiny dot. Move or click and move the cursor to the right, and it will reappear.

Try to zoom and pan the lower right viewport with ZOOM Dynamic (see fig. 5.9).

Using Zoom Dynamic To Pan and Zoom

Continue from the previous exercise.

`Command: ZOOM ↵`

`All/Center/Dynamic/Extents/Left/Previous/`　　Selects the Dynamic
`Vmax/Window/<Scale(X/XP)>: D ↵`　　　　　　option

The entire girder appears in the black or white drawing extents box, with red corners marking the virtual screen box and a small dashed green box indicating the current view. The cursor is in the small zoom box that has an X in it.

Move the cursor around.

Notice that the hourglass appears at the lower left when the zoom box exits the virtual screen area.

Click and the X in the zoom box changes to an arrow. Move the cursor to the right until the zoom box is about twice as large as the dashed green current view.

Click and the arrow in the zoom box changes to an X. Move the cursor (pan) to place the X over the top right corner of the girder, and press Enter to perform the zoom.

`Command: QSAVE ↵`　　　　　　　　　Saves the drawing to the
　　　　　　　　　　　　　　　　　　　same name

The top right corner of the girder should be centered, and the view height should be about 16 feet. ZOOM Dynamic is not as precise as other zoom options because you must pick points to indicate the zoom. You cannot type exact points because all input, except cursor picks, Enter, and Ctrl-C, are suppressed during ZOOM Dynamic. If you need to zoom or pan more precisely, either use other zoom options or use the PAN command.

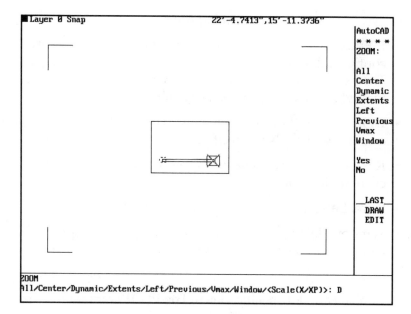

Figure 5.9:
Using ZOOM Dynamic in the lower left viewport.

Saving and Restoring Views

ZOOM Previous can step back through views, but it cannot switch back and forth between a standard set of views. You can create, save, and redisplay standard views, however, by using the VIEW command.

Using the VIEW Command

Use the VIEW command to save the current display so that you can return to it without having to use the PAN or ZOOM options to respecify the view.

VIEW. The VIEW command saves the current viewport's view or a user-specified window as a named view with a name (up to 31 characters long). Saved views can be restored with the VIEW Restore option. Enter 'VIEW to execute VIEW transparently (in another command).

VIEW Options

- **?.** Enter an asterisk to display a list of all saved viewport configurations or use wild cards to list a specific set of views. The list shows an M or P to show whether the view is defined in model space (M) or paper space (P).

- **Delete.** Enter the name of a view to delete. In Release 11, you can use wild cards to specify a group of views to delete.

- **Restore.** Enter the name of a saved view to display it in the current viewport.

- **Save.** Enter a name to save the current viewport's view.

- **Window.** Define a window to save as a view by specifying its corners, and then enter a name for the view.

 You can plot specific views. The PLOT command's View option prompts for the view name.

Use the VIEW command to save the view in the lower right viewport as the name RIGHTEND. Then save a windowed view of the left end in the upper viewport as LEFTEND, and restore it.

Saving and Restoring Views

Continue from the previous exercise.

```
Command: VIEW ↵
?/Delete/Restore/Save/Window: S ↵      Selects the Save option
View name to save: RIGHTEND ↵          Specifies a name for the saved
                                       view

Command: ZOOM ↵
Zoom Previous
Command: VIEW ↵
```

`?/Delete/Restore/Save/Window:` W ↵	Selects the Window option
`View name to save:` LEFTEND ↵	Specifies a name for the view that the window will contain
`First corner:` -4',-8' ↵	Sets the window's upper left corner
`Other corner:` *Drag and pick at 12',4'*	Sets the window's lower right corner and saves the view
`Command:` VIEW ↵ `?/Delete/Restore/Save/Window:` R ↵	Selects the Restore option
`View name to restore:` LEFTEND ↵	Displays the view named LEFTEND
`Command:` QSAVE ↵	Saves the drawing to the same name

Your results should look like figure 5.10.

Now, each end of the girder is saved as a named view. Whenever you need to work on a particular end, you can use the VIEW command to take you directly to it. These named views are always available in the current drawing, even if you end the drawing and come back to it.

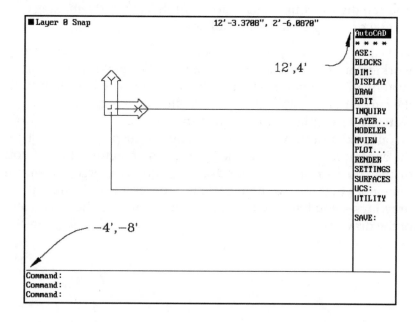

Figure 5.10:
LEFTEND view.

Working with Multiple Views and Viewports

Your screen's drawing area has adequate detail for most small drawings, such as those plotted on an A-size (11"-by-8.5") sheet. When you are working on larger drawings, such as the D-size example, you can zoom the display to view various portions and to work at varying degrees of detail. Zooming is only a partial solution, however. When you are working on a large paper drawing, you can view and check alignment of any portion at any time. AutoCAD enables you to view and work on more than one portion of the drawing at a time by creating and manipulating viewports.

Defining Tiled Viewports

A *viewport* is a rectangular area on the display that acts as a *window* into your drawing. By default, AutoCAD starts with a single viewport, which is what you have been working with up to now. You can divide your screen into multiple viewports, making several drawing areas instead of one.

You can work in only one viewport at a time—the one you are working on is called the *current* viewport. To make a viewport current, pick a point inside it with the cursor. The border around the current viewport widens to indicate that it is current. Use AutoCAD's display control commands to zoom these viewports in, out, and around your drawing. You can display any portion of the current drawing in any viewport at any magnification. If you display the same part of your drawing in two different viewports, remember that the two images do not represent two different drawings—you have two windows that open into the same view of the drawing.

Because all viewports look into the same drawing, you can draw from one viewport to another. If you need to draw a line from one end of an object to another (but any one view does not show sufficient detail), you can display each end of the object in a different view, and then draw between them. You can pick a point to start a line in one viewport, then make another viewport current and continue the line. AutoCAD rubber-bands the line across the entire object and shows it in each viewport.

You can subdivide the screen into *tiled* viewports by using the VPORTS command. The term *tiled* indicates that the viewports are square or rectangular in shape, they cannot overlap, and they must cover the graphics window, like tile on a floor. Tiled viewports are a drawing aid only—you cannot plot the tiled layout.

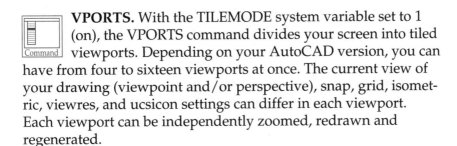

VPORTS. With the TILEMODE system variable set to 1 (on), the VPORTS command divides your screen into tiled viewports. Depending on your AutoCAD version, you can have from four to sixteen viewports at once. The current view of your drawing (viewpoint and/or perspective), snap, grid, isometric, viewres, and ucsicon settings can differ in each viewport. Each viewport can be independently zoomed, redrawn and regenerated.

VPORTS Options

- **Save.** The Save option saves and names (up to 31 characters) the current viewport configuration.

- **Restore.** The Restore option restores any saved viewport configuration. Enter a specific name to restore, enter an asterisk to see a listing of all saved viewport configurations, or use any wild cards to list a specific list of names.

- **Delete.** The Delete option deletes a saved viewport configuration.

- **Join.** The Join option combines the current viewport with a selected viewport. The two viewports must be adjacent and form a rectangle.

- **SIngle.** The SIngle option changes the screen to a single viewport, displaying the view of the current viewport.

- **?.** Enter an asterisk to list all named viewport configurations, or use wild cards to list a specific set of viewports.

- **2.** The 2 option divides the current viewport into a horizontal or vertical pair of viewports.

- **3.** The 3 option (the default) divides the current viewport into three viewports.

- **4.** The 4 option divides the current viewport into four viewports.

To experiment with tiled viewports, use VPORTS to create three tiled viewports in your SETUP drawing.

Creating Tiled Viewports with the VPORTS Command

Continue from the previous exercise.

Command: ZOOM ⏎
Zoom All

Choose View, *then* Layout	Displays the Layout submenu
Choose Tiled Vports	Displays the Tiled Viewport Layout dialog box
Choose Three: Above	Highlights the Three: Above icon
Click on OK	Accepts the dialog box
Command: QSAVE ⏎	Saves the drawing to the same name

The results should look like figure 5.11.

Figure 5.11:

Tiled Viewport Layout dialog box.

```
                   Tiled Viewport Layout

 Single
 Three:  Vertical
 Three:  Horizontal
 Four:   Equal
 Two:    Vertical
 Three:  Right
 Three:  Left
 Four:   Left
 Two:    Horizontal
 Three:  Above
 Three:  Below
 Four:   Right



     Previous     Next              OK      Cancel
```

The display is now filled with one large horizontal viewport above two smaller ones.

The Tiled Viewport Layout Dialog Box

If you select the VPORTS command from the pull-down menu, AutoCAD displays the Tiled Viewport Layout dialog box. You can select the viewport layout you want from this dialog box, shown in figure 5.11.

You can display the overall elevation of a bridge in the upper viewport while zooming in on various details in the lower viewports (see fig. 5.12). To try this, you need to use some other ZOOM options. The next section examines a handful of commands that you use frequently. Although none of them actually create drawing entities or add to the drawing in any way, they are indispensable AutoCAD view-manipulation commands. You will use these commands as you draw a bridge.

Saving and Restoring Viewports

The Save, Restore, and Delete options of the VPORTS command work exactly like those same options in the VIEW command.

Figure 5.12:

Three tiled viewports in the BRIDGE drawing.

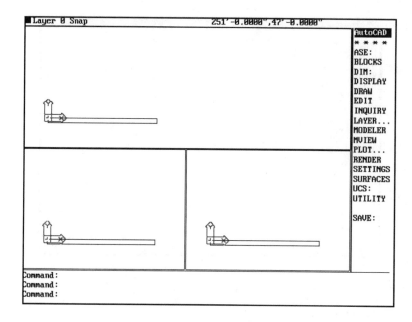

When you save a viewport configuration, VPORTS saves the current view, snap, grid, UCS icon, and viewres settings for each viewport. Although the VPORTS SIngle option restores a single viewport without its having been saved, you should save a single, named viewport to save the settings.

Try saving the current viewport configuration, change to a single viewport, change the view, and restore the saved viewport. Name it 3H because it is a horizontal setup with three viewports.

Saving and Restoring Viewports

Continue from the previous exercise.

Make sure the lower left viewport is current. If not, click in the viewport.

Choose View, *then* Set View, *then* Named View	Selects the View Control dialog box
Command: Initial load please wait... DDVIEW loaded	Loads and displays View Control dialog box
Click on LEFTEND, *then* Restore, *then* OK	Sets the view to LEFTEND

Set the right viewport to RIGHTEND

Make the lower left viewport current

You now have three viewports. The upper viewport contains the entire span, the lower left viewport has the LEFTEND view, and the lower right viewport has the RIGHTEND view. Save the viewport configuration so it can be recalled later. When you restore this viewport setting, the lower left viewport will be the current one.

From the screen menu, choose SETTINGS,
then next, *then* VPORTS

`Save/Restore/Delete/Join/SIngle/?/2` `/<3>/4:` *Choose* SAVE	Selects the Save option
`?/Name for new viewport` `configuration: 3H ↵`	Names the saved viewpoint
`Command: VPORTS ↵`	
`Save/Restore/Delete/Join/SIngle/?/2` `/<3>/4: SI ↵`	Selects the Single option
`Regenerating drawing.`	

The view from the lower left viewport regenerates in the single viewport.

`Command: VIEW ↵`	
`?/Delete/Restore/Save/Window: R ↵`	Selects the Restore option
`View name to restore: RIGHTEND ↵`	Displays the view named RIGHTEND

The view from the lower right viewport regenerates in the single viewport, but the grid and other settings remain unchanged.

`Command: VPORTS ↵`	
`Save/Restore/Delete/Join/SIngle/?/2` `/<3>/4: R ↵`	Selects the Restore option
`?/Name of viewport configuration to` `restore: 3H ↵`	Displays viewport settings called 3H
`Regenerating drawing.`	

The three viewports reappear, with the views and settings of each intact.

`Command: QSAVE ↵`	Saves the drawing to the same name

Now, try drawing between viewports. Draw the one-inch flange thickness of the girder, as shown in figure 5.13. To see better, try a transparent zoom during one of the LINE commands.

Figure 5.13:

Drawing a line from one viewport to another.

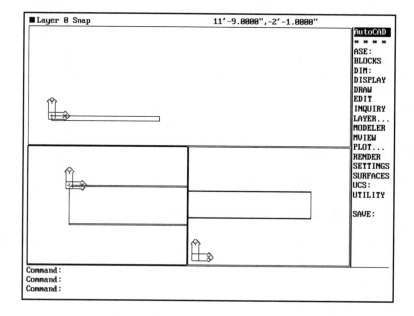

Drawing between Viewports and Zooming Transparently

Move the cursor to the lower left viewport, click in the viewport to make it current.

Command: **SNAP** ⏎
Set to 1

Command: **GRID** ⏎
Set to 6

Command: **LINE** ⏎

From point: **0,-1** ⏎   Specifies the line's start point.

Move the cursor and watch the line rubber-band in the lower left viewport.

Click in the lower right viewport to make it current.

Move the cursor and watch the line rubber-band in the lower right viewport.

To point: **PER** ⏎   Specifies the Perpendicular
                                         object snap mode

to *Pick vertical end line of girder*

`To point:` *Press Enter*

`Command: LINE` ⏎

`From point: @0,-46` ⏎   Specifies the line's start point

Click in the lower left viewport to make it current.

`To point: 'ZOOM` ⏎	Zooms in closer, transparently
`>>Center/Dynamic/Left/Previous/Vmax/` `Window/<Scale(X/XP)>: C` ⏎	Selects the Center option.
`>>Center point: MID` ⏎	Selects MIDpoint object snap
`>>of` *Pick the vertical end of the span*	Specifies the Center point

The >> prompt indicates a transparent command.

`>>Magnification or Height` `<8'-0.0000">` `: 4'6` ⏎	Sets the new viewing height
`Resuming LINE command.`	
`To point:` *Pick 92'<180*	
`To point:` *Press Enter*	Ends the LINE command
`Command: QSAVE` ⏎	Saves the drawing to the same name

You should now have a long girder drawn with both top and bottom flanges visible (see fig. 5.13).

Before continuing, try a ZOOM All and ZOOM Previous to get a sense of the size of the girder and its placement, relative to the limits you set for your plotted sheet size (see fig. 5.14). Remember, ZOOM All zooms either the limits or the extents, whichever is greater.

Zooming All and Previous

`Command: ZOOM` ⏎	
`All/Center/Dynamic/Extents/Left/Previous/` `Vmax/Window/<Scale(X/XP)>: A` ⏎	Selects the All option
`Regenerating drawing`	
`Grid too dense to display`	
`Command: ZOOM` ⏎	
`All/Center/Dynamic/Extents/Left/Previous/` `Vmax/Window/<Scale(X/XP)>: P` ⏎	Selects the Previous option

Figure 5.14:

The girder in lower left viewport, using ZOOM All.

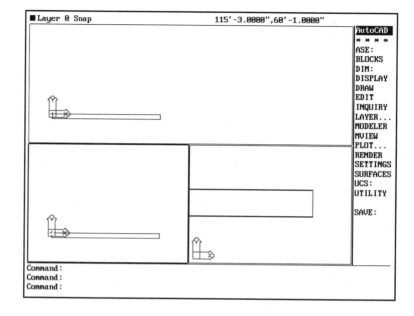

The previous zoomed-in view of the lower left viewport should now be restored. The ZOOM Previous command, when accessed repeatedly, steps back through the previous views used in the current drawing session in the current viewport, until it reaches the limit of ten views or it runs out of previous views. You then see the following prompt: No previous view saved.

Remember that tiled viewports are drawing aids, not entities in the drawing. To understand the difference between tiled viewports and the more general mview viewports, you must understand the two drawing worlds that AutoCAD provides: model space and paper space.

Model Space and Paper Space

The drawing environment that is visible through a tiled viewport is model space. *Model space* is the 3D drawing environment that you have worked in until now. It is a 3D drawing environment, whether you work in 2D or 3D. Model space was the only drawing environment available until Release 11.

Paper space is a two-dimensional drawing environment, independent of model space, (similar to the 2D drawing world of the early versions of AutoCAD). On a blank *paper space sheet*, you can add items such as a title block, notes, section cuts, and a sheet border. When you first display paper space, it is opaque—it obscures model space. You can, however, open viewports in this paper space sheet that look into model space.

The limits of paper space are independent of model space, so you can enter text and drawing reference symbology in paper space at actual plot size, rather than scale it up to match the drawing geometry. You set the limits of this sheet to the size of your intended plot sheet, instead of to a size that will accommodate the full-size model (as you do in model space).

Paper space is both a drawing aid and a drawing-composition tool. You can compose your drawing by arranging the viewports in paper space and then plotting from the paper-space environment.

Tiled and Mview Viewports

With tiled viewports, you plot from model space, so your border must be part of your model space drawing and scaled to the limits. In paper space, however, whatever you draw is separate from your model space drawing. Paper space works like a second drawing that overlays the model space drawing. The entities you draw in paper space appear over (not in) the viewports. You can draw a border to the size you want to plot it, and then arrange mview viewports within this border in the same way that you lay out a paper drawing.

Whether AutoCAD displays tiled or mview viewports depends on the TILEMODE system variable. If TILEMODE is set to 1 (on, the default) you can work in tiled viewports. If it is set to 0 (off), you can work in mview viewports. Tiled viewports can only subdivide the drawing screen; mview viewports can be any size, be located in any position, and can overlap.

When you begin a new drawing, TILEMODE is on (set to 1), and you have a single viewport. You can, however, create multiple viewports in which to view and manipulate your drawing.

Entering Paper Space with TILEMODE

When you turn off TILEMODE (set it to 0), AutoCAD enters paper space (or the current mview viewport in paper space). When you first enter paper space in a new drawing, you see a blank drawing area because you have not drawn anything on the paper space sheet. AutoCAD tells you that you are in paper space by displaying a triangular paper space icon in the lower left corner of the drawing area and a P on the status bar.

Try turning TILEMODE off in the BRIDGE drawing. Then, do some drawing setup in paper space and draw a simple rectangular border, as shown in figure 5.15.

Figure 5.15:

A fresh sheet of paper space, with a border.

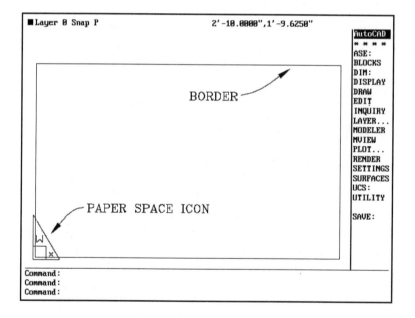

Entering Paper Space with TILEMODE Off

Continue from the preceding exercise.

```
Command: Vports ↵

Save/Restore/Delete/Join/SIngle/?/2
/<3>/4: R ↵
```

```
?/Name of viewport configuration to
restore: 3H ⏎
```

Choose Settings, *then* Tilemode, *then* Off

```
New value for TILEMODE <1>: 0 ⏎          Turns off TILEMODE
Regenerating drawing.
Command: LIMITS ⏎
ON/OFF/<Lower left corner> <0'-0.0000",
0'-0.0000">: ⏎
Upper right corner <1'-0.0000",0'-9.0000">: 34,22 ⏎
Command: SNAP ⏎
Snap spacing or ON/OFF/Aspect/Rotate/
Style <0'-1.0000">: .125 ⏎
Command: GRID ⏎
Grid spacing(X) or ON/OFF/Snap/Aspect <0'-6.0000">: 1 ⏎
Command: ZOOM ⏎
```
Select the Zoom All option
```
Command: LINE ⏎                          Draws a border
From point: 1.125,1.125 ⏎
```
*Pick end points at coordinates 2'7.75<0,
1'7.75<90 and 2'7.75<180, then enter* **C** *to close.*
```
Command: VIEW ⏎
?/Delete/Restore/Save/Window: S ⏎        Selects the Save option
View name to save: SHEET ⏎               Names the viewpoint SHEET
Command: QSAVE ⏎                         Saves the drawing
```

Using Paper Space

When you first entered paper space, you saw a blank drawing
area, except for the triangular paper space icon. Paper space
inherits the snap and grid settings of the current tilemode
viewport, but it maintains its settings independently. Paper space
limits default to 12 by 9. You typically set limits to the plot sheet
size, such as the 34 by 22 used previously.

When you enter paper space for the first time, you do not
see your model space drawing. Paper space is initially
blank and opaque.

Your existing girder drawing is not visible because you have no mview viewports opened into model space. You use the MVIEW command to create viewports in paper space.

Creating and Controlling Mview Viewports

The MVIEW command works much like the VPORTS command when creating viewports. The 2, 3, and 4 options of the MVIEW command divide the current display in the same manner. MVIEW has additional control features, but it lacks the ability to save and restore viewport configurations.

MVIEW. The MVIEW (Make VIEWport, Release 11 only) command creates mview model space viewports in paper space. MVIEW also controls the visibility of viewports and controls hidden line removal in paper space plots.

MVIEW offers a number of convenient ways to create viewports: you can fit a single viewport on the display; you can create 2, 3, or 4 viewports within a rectangular area or fit them to the display; or you can create a single viewport by picking the corners of a rectangular area. MVIEW also has options to turn mview viewports on and off. When a viewport is on, it is active and model space is visible through it. When a viewport is off, it is inactive and appears blank.

MVIEW Options

- **First point.** Specify two diagonally opposite corner points to define a new viewport, which becomes the current viewport.

- **ON.** The ON option makes all model space entities in the selected viewports visible.

- **OFF.** The OFF option makes all model space entities in the selected viewports invisible.

- **Hideplot.** Select the viewports from which 3D hidden lines are to be removed during plotting.

- **Fit.** The Fit option creates a single viewport the size of the current paper space view.

- **2/3/4.** This option creates two, three, or four viewports, like the similar option of the VPORTS command.

- **Restore.** The Restore option creates an arrangement of mview viewports that matches the appearance of a tiled viewport configuration that has been saved with the VPORTS command. MVIEW cannot save and restore mview viewport configurations.

After you create the viewports, you can edit them just like any other entity: you can stretch, move, erase, and copy them. The only feature lacking in mview viewports is a direct means of saving and restoring viewports configurations. If you use VIEW to save and restore a view in paper space, it will display any viewports that happen to be currently within the extents of that view. VIEW will not, however, restore the configuration of any viewports that have been changed.

The Mview > item on the Display pull-down menu turns TILEMODE off (if it was on) and issues the MVIEW command.

Use MVIEW to open three viewports: one for the full elevation, one for a partial cross-section, and one for a section or detail of the left end.

Each newly opened viewport initially displays the view of the current model space viewport, which is the lower left tilemode viewport, in this case.

Making Viewports with MVIEW

Continue from the previous exercise.

Choose View, *then* Mview, *then* Create Viewport

Create a new elevation view.

```
ON/OFF/Hideplot/Fit/2/3/4/Restore/
```

```
<First Point>: Pick 2,2
Other corner: Pick 2'8,8
Regenerating drawing.
Command: MVIEW ↵                          Creates a cross section view
ON/OFF/Hideplot/Fit/2/3/4/Restore/
<First Point>: Pick 2,9
Other corner: Pick 10,1'8
Regenerating drawing.
Command: MVIEW ↵                          Creates the end section
ON/OFF/Hideplot/Fit/2/3/4/Restore/
<First Point>: Pick 11,9
Other corner: Pick 1'7,1'8
Regenerating drawing.
Command: Press F7                         Turns off the grid
Command: QSAVE ↵                          Saves the drawing to the same
                                          name
```

Your results should look like figure 5.16.

If an mview viewport were the current model space viewport, its view would be the default.

To switch between paper space and model space, use the MSPACE and PSPACE commands.

Figure 5.16:

Mview viewports on a paper space sheet.

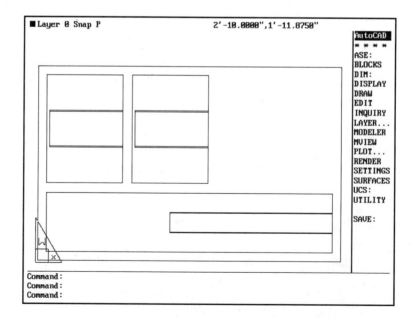

Switching between Paper and Model Space

After you have opened viewports in paper space, both paper space and model space are visible, but only one environment is active at any given time. You select the space you want to work in with the MSPACE and PSPACE commands. The MSPACE command switches to model space, and the PSPACE command switches to paper space.

Switching to Model Space with MSPACE

When you switch from paper space to model space in an mview viewport, the drawing's appearance does not change. Three indications, however, let you know that you have switched to model space.

The first indication is the ucsicon. In paper space, the ucsicon displays as a triangle; in model space, it changes back to the X-Y double-arrow.

The second indication is the crosshair pointer. In paper space, the crosshair is active over the entire drawing area. In model space, the crosshair pointer is active only in the current model space viewport. When you move the cursor outside the current viewport, the cursor changes to an arrow pointer, which you can use to pick a new current viewport.

The third indication is the disappearance of the P from the status line. A P on the status line indicates that paper space is current—there is no indicator for model space. You change from paper space to model space by using the MSPACE command.

MSPACE. The MSPACE (Model SPACE) command switches the current viewport from paper space to model space, if the TILEMODE system variable is off. Before using MSPACE, you must use the MVIEW command to create model space viewports to work in.

Most of your work will be done in model space. When you are initially setting up your drawing and when you are nearly done with your drawing, however, you probably will switch back and forth often between model space and paper space to annotate and prepare the plot.

Switching to Paper Space with PSPACE

If TILEMODE is off, the PSPACE command switches the drawing editor from model space to paper space.

 PSPACE. The PSPACE (Paper SPACE Release 11 only) command switches from model space to paper space, if TILEMODE is 0 (off). The letter P on the status line, and, if UCSICON is on, the triangular paper space icon in the lower left-hand corner of the screen indicate that paper space is current.

 Paper space must be active (TILEMODE O) before you can use MSPACE and PSPACE.

Note

Before you can use MSPACE, you must use MVIEW to open a viewport.

In paper space, you set up viewports, draw or insert a title block, add annotation, and prepare the plot. When you need to exit paper space and return to model space to work on your drawing model, use the MSPACE command.

Note

In paper space, you can use object snap overrides with model space points that are inside the viewports, as well as with points that are in paper space. You cannot, however, use object snap overrides with paper space points when you are in model space.

Drawing in Model Space and Paper Space

You already know how to draw in paper space. The drawing, editing, and display control commands you have learned up to this point work in paper space, as well as in model space. The few exceptions are a consequence of the two-dimensional nature of paper space.

You do have an entity to deal with in paper space that you do not have in model space—the viewport entity. Viewports are like lines, circles, and arcs in that you may have to edit them as your drawing evolves. You can stretch, move, scale, and copy viewports—you can even use the Autoedit mode to move, scale, and copy viewports.

Try a series of exercises that demonstrates the use of display controls, drawing commands, and editing commands by drawing a section of the bridge. Try zooming in paper space and panning in model space to draw a cross section of the girder. Align its start point with the end of the girder in the end section, using a point filter and an INT object snap mode.

Drawing in Model Space

Continue from the preceding exercise.

Command: **ZOOM** ↵
Zoom Window with corners 1,7 and 11,1'9

Choose View, *then* Model space   Enters model space

The UCS icon appears and crosshairs become active in the end section viewport.

Click in the section viewport on the left to make it current.

Command: **PAN** ↵

Displacement: **28',-2'** ↵   Slide model to the right and down a little

Second point: *Press Enter*

The viewport now shows an area about 20 to 28 feet left of the end of the girder.

```
Command: UCS ⏎
```
Aligns the UCS in cross section viewport with the girder in the end section

```
Origin/ZAxis/3point/Entity/View/X/Y/Z/Prev/
Restore/Save/Del/?/<World>: O ⏎
Origin point <0,0,0>: -24,0 ⏎
Command: ZOOM ⏎
```
Center point 0,-2' and height 6'
```
Command: LINE ⏎
```
Draws the girder in section
```
From point: 0,0 ⏎
```
With snap and ortho on, use snap, the grid, and the coordinate display to draw 15" W by 48" D girder, with 1" flanges and web, with upper left corner at 0,0 as in fig. 5.17
```
Command: QSAVE ⏎
```
Saves the drawing to the same name

The results of the exercise should look like figure 5.17.

Figure 5.17:

The section viewport zoomed in paper space.

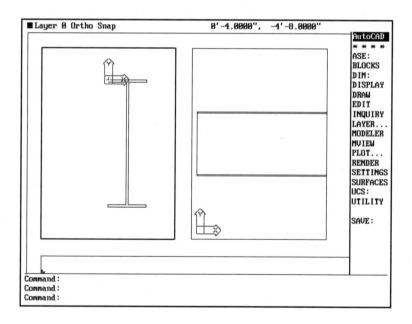

If you were to ZOOM All, you would see that the section and elevation are aligned in the full model space drawing, which shows that you can use point filters and object snaps any time to align objects between them.

The end section should be plotted at 1"=1'-0" (1:12 or .08333333), the cross section scaled 1-1/2"=1'-0" (1:8 or .125), and the elevation 1/4"=1'-0" (1:48 or .02083333). You need to scale each viewport on the paper space sheet.

Scaling Viewports to Paper Space

The ZOOM *scale*XP option scales mview viewports relative to paper space. You enter the magnification factor followed by XP, and AutoCAD zooms one unit in the viewport to align with the number you specify as the scale factor in paper space. If you enter .083333333XP (1/12), for example, you zoom the viewport so that 12" in the viewport appears to equal 1" on the paper space sheet (and plot).

Try scaling the three viewports. Then add an 8" concrete deck to the cross section, and check the dimensions in each space.

Scaling Viewports

Continue from the preceding exercise.

Command: ZOOM ↵   Zooms cross section
                                             viewport for 1-1/2"=1'-0"

All/Center/Dynamic/Extents/Left/Previous/
Vmax/Window/<Scale(X/XP)>: .125XP ↵

Click in the end section viewport to
make it current

Command: ZOOM ↵   Zooms end section
                                             viewport for 1"=1'-0"

All/Center/Dynamic/Extents/Left/Previous/   Selects the Center
Vmax/Window/<Scale(X/XP)>: C ↵   option

Center point: MID ↵

of *Pick the vertical line of the girder*

Magnification or Height <12'-0.0000"> :
.08333333XP ↵

Click in the elevation viewport (at the
bottom of the screen) to make it current

Command: ZOOM ⏎   Zooms elevation viewport
                                                    for 1/4"=1'-0"
All/Center/Dynamic/Extents/Left/Previous/   Specifies new zoom
Vmax/Window/<Scale(X/XP)>: .02083333XP ⏎   magnification
*Click in the cross section viewport
to make it current.*

Command: PLINE ⏎
*Draw the concrete deck from 2'6,0 to
points @3'<180, @8<90 and @3'<0*

Command: PLINE ⏎
*Draw the curb from -6,8 to points
@10<90, @1'6<0 and @4,-10*

Command: VIEW ⏎   Restore the view named SHEET

?/Delete/Restore/Save/Window: R ⏎

View name to restore: SHEET ⏎

Restoring Paper space view.

The view was saved in paper space.

Regenerating drawing.

Paper space remains active.

Command: MSPACE ⏎

Click in the lower viewport to make it current

Command: PAN ⏎

Pan to show the whole span

Displacement: *Pick point near left end of girder*

Second point: *Pick point near left end of viewport*

Command: PSPACE ⏎

Command: DIST ⏎
*Check height of girder in cross section
viewport from paper space*

First point: *Use INT object snap to pick
point just above upper left corner of girder*

Second point: *Use INT to pick just below
lower left corner of girder*

Delta X = 0'-0.0000", Delta Y =
-0'-6.0000",   Delta Z = 0'-0.0000"

These are paper space dimensions.

Command: QSAVE ⏎   Saves the drawing to the same
                                                    name

The results of the exercise appear in figure 5.18.

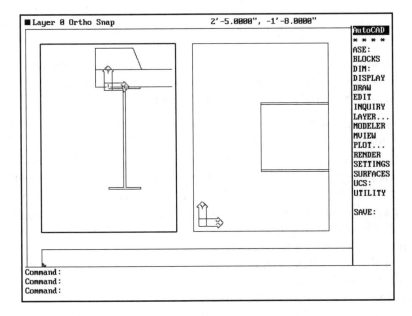

Figure 5.18:

Three viewports scaled to paper space.

If you check the height of the girder in each viewport, you find it to be 6", 4", and 1", exactly the same as if you had drawn it manually at the scales of 1-1/2"=1'-0", 1"=1'-0", and 1/4"=1'-0".

If you restore a paper-space view while working in model space, you are switched to paper space. If tilemode is on, you cannot restore a paper space view. If you restore a model space view while working in paper space, you are asked to select a viewport, which must be on (active). You then are switched to model space in that viewport.

This capability to scale and edit viewports on the paper space sheet makes composing plots easy and natural. The plot chapter covers plot composition and editing viewports in more detail. You also learn how to turn off the viewport borders so they do not plot.

Much of the paper space and viewport setup process can be automated by an AutoLISP routine, MVSETUP.LSP, that is included in the AutoCAD package.

Automating Setup with MVSETUP

You can use MVSETUP to set up a sheet, add a title block, open mview viewports, and set up the view orientation in each viewport, all with a few quick menu selections.

After you draw the sheet, MVSETUP gives you options for creating mview viewports on the sheet. You can choose a unique arrangement or select from a pre-defined set. MVSETUP then creates the viewports for you, arranging them to fit on the sheet. Finally, MVSETUP gives you the option of scaling each viewport to a specific plot scale. MVSETUP includes an option to create title block sheet drawing files so that MVSETUP can insert the title block much faster than MVSETUP initially draws it. You can edit these drawing files to customize or replace the title blocks for use with MVSETUP. MVSETUP will insert them as *blocks*, which are the main topic of the next chapter.

| Note | MVSETUP is a bonus AutoLISP program that is included as part of the regular AutoCAD installation. (AutoLISP is AutoCAD's programming language.) When you install |

AutoCAD, you have the option of installing the bonus files. If you did not install these files when you installed AutoCAD, simply run the installation program again, and install only the bonus files.

Take the time to create your own standard title blocks to use with MVSETUP, and make MVSETUP a part of your normal drawing setup routine. Also, take the time to experiment with its many options to see how they work. You will use MVSETUP in the next chapter to insert a title block.

Layers, Colors, and Linetypes

Each entity in a drawing has three *entity properties*: layer, color, and linetype. In previous chapters, you used the default entity

194

properties, white color on a dark background or black on a light background, and continuous linetype, and Layer 0.

In this section of the chapter, you learn to use layers, colors, and linetypes to enhance your drawings, make them more readable, and make it easier for you to locate information as you are drawing.

To begin with, consider AutoCAD's layers.

Using Drawing Layers

You may have used a manual drafting technique called *overlay drafting*, in which you use multiple sheets to draw different parts of a drawing and *overlay* the sheets for reference, or to print a composite drawing.

AutoCAD's layers are somewhat similar in concept, as illustrated in figure 5.19. They enable you to separate different parts of the drawing. In contrast to the Mylar overlays described earlier, a layer in an AutoCAD drawing is not a physical thing—it is simply a property that is assigned to each entity in your drawing. AutoCAD uses this property to sort entities for various purposes.

What benefit do you derive from using layers? Many objects you draw can be easily organized into layers: printed circuit boards have different layers of conductive patterns, and other objects can be broken up in a similar fashion. Architectural drawings for buildings may have different drawings for different floors or trades (electrical, plumbing, and so on). Layers give you a way to separate some data from other data on the same drawing. You can, for example, place a site plan on one layer, a floor plan on another, services on another, the roof plan on another, and so on. Layers also are used to differentiate and group entities by visibility, linetype, and color. Colors can be mapped to plotter pens, which enables you to control lineweights in a plot.

AutoCAD automatically creates a single layer when you begin a new drawing. The layer is given the name 0. Layer 0 uses the

CONTINUOUS linetype and the color white by default (more about color and linetype shortly). You can create as many additional layers as you need, assigning each one an English name as you create it. At any time, one layer is active, or current—anything you draw is assigned that layer name.

Figure 5.19:

Drawing layer organization.

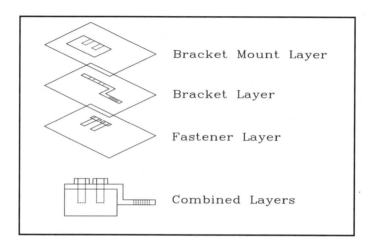

When you create, or define, a new layer, AutoCAD assigns it the color, White, and the linetype, CONTINUOUS. You can change layer colors and linetypes at any time with the Layer command, or the Ddlmodes dialog box. Assigning different colors makes it easier to keep track of entity layer assignments while you are drawing, and enables you to either plot in color, or plot with pens of different widths.

The primary command for manipulating layers in AutoCAD is the LAYER command.

LAYER. The LAYER command is used to create new layers, set the current layer, set layer color, and linetype, and control layer visibility.

The LAYER command offers a set of options for creating and working with layers.

LAYER Options

- **?.** Lists the names and properties of layers defined in the drawing. Use the default asterisk (*) for a sorted list of all layers.

- **Make.** Specify a name to create a new layer and make it current.

- **Set.** Specify a layer name to make the specified layer current (default 0).

- **New.** Specify name(s) to create new layer(s).

- **ON.** Specify layer name(s) to turn on.

- **OFF.** Specify layer name(s) to turn off.

- **Color.** Specify a color and layer name(s) to assign the color to the specified layer(s) (the default is 7, white).

- **Ltype.** Specify a linetype for one or more layers.

- **Freeze.** Specify layer(s) to freeze, to make the specified layer(s) invisible, and to prevent them from regenerating.

- **Lock.** Enables you to lock a specific layer and to make the specified layer's(') entities visible but unavailable for editing.

- **Thaw.** Specify layer name(s) to thaw.

Except for the New option, any of the layer options that can operate on more than one layer accepts a list of names separated by commas, and you can use wild cards in the name(s). If you use a list of names, you can apply an option to several layers at once

To try the LAYER command, set up a layering scheme to use for the cam housing and cam drawing. In this chapter, you redraw the cam and housing drawing, using layers, colors, and linetypes. Assign the colors and linetypes shown in the exercise, but do not worry about their implications, which are covered later in the chapter. Save a view named ALL, to avoid later ZOOM All regenerations.

Creating Layers with LAYER

Start ACAD from the AB directory, and begin a NEW drawing named BASEPL.

```
Command: LIMITS ↵
```
Set the limits to 0,0 to 10.5,9

```
Command: ZOOM ↵
```
Use ZOOM and zoom All

```
Command: SNAP ↵
```
Set SNAP to 0.0625

```
Command: GRID ↵
```
Set GRID to 0.25

```
Command: LAYER ↵

?/Make/Set/New/ON/OFF/Color/Ltype/Freeze
/Thaw/LOck/Unlock: N ↵

New layer names (s): DIVLINE,HLINE,CLINE ↵
```
Creates three new layers

```
?/Make/Set/New/ON/OFF/Color/Ltype/Freeze
/Thaw/LOck/Unlock: M ↵

New current layer <0>: PLATE ↵
```
Creates a new layer and sets it current

```
?/Make/Set/New/ON/OFF/Color/Ltype/Freeze
/Thaw/LOck/Unlock: L ↵
```
Sets a linetype

```
Linetype (or ?) <CONTINUOUS>: HIDDEN ↵

Layer name(s) for linetype HIDDEN <PLATE>: HLINE ↵
```

```
?/Make/Set/New/ON/OFF/Ltype/Freeze
/Thaw/LOck/Unlock: L ↵
```
Sets another linetype

```
Linetype (or ?) <CONTINUOUS>: CENTER ↵

Layer name(s) for linetype CENTER <PLATE>: CLINE ↵
```

```
?/Make/Set/New/ON/OFF/Color/Ltype/Freeze
/Thaw/LOck/Unlock: C ↵
```
Assigns a color

```
Color: 6 ↵

Layer name(s) for color 6 (magenta)
<PLATE>: ?LINE ↵
```
The ? wild card equals CLINE and HLINE

```
?/Make/Set/New/ON/OFF/Color/Ltype/Freeze
```
Lists the results

```
/Thaw/LOck/Unlock: ? ↵
Layer name(s) to list <*>: Press Enter              * wild card
                                                     lists
                                                     all layers

      Layer name      State       Color         Linetype
 ------------------- -------- ------------- ------------
0                     On        7 (white)     CONTINUOUS
DIVLINE               On        7 (white)     CONTINUOUS
CLINE                 On        6 (magenta)   CENTER
HLINE                 On        6 (magenta)   HIDDEN
PLATE                 On        7 (white)     CONTINUOUS

Current layer: PLATE
?/Make/Set/New/ON/OFF/Color/Ltype/Freeze        Ends the LAYER
/Thaw/LOck/Unlock: Press Enter                  command

Command: QSAVE ↵                                Saves the drawing
                                                BASEPL to the same name
```

The only visible change is on the status line, where the current layer, CAM, should now be listed.

You can make layer changes interactively with the Layer Control dialog box, displayed with the DDLMODES command.

DDLMODES. The DDLMODES (Dynamic Dialogue Layer modes) dialog box, like the Layer command, sets layer settings. It can create new layers, rename layers, and modify layer properties (linetype and color) and visibility (on/off and freeze/thaw). Enter 'DDLMODES to use it transparently (within another command).

DDLMODES includes the same options for creating and manipulating layers as the LAYER command. To use an option, move the cursor to highlight it, then take the action listed in the following DDLMODES option list.

DDLMODES Options

- **Current.** This option makes the selected layer the current layer.

- **On.** This option turns on the selected layer(s).

- **Off.** This option turns off the selected layer(s).

- **Freeze.** This option freezes the selected layer(s).

- **Thaw.** This option thaws the selected layer(s).

- **Unlock.** This option unlocks the selected layer(s).

- **Lock.** This option turns on the selected layer(s).

- **Cur VP Thw.** Use Cur VP Thw to thaw the selected layer(s) in the current mview viewport.

- **Cur Vp Frz.** This option freezes the selected layer(s) in the current mview viewport.

- **New VP Thw.** This option thaws the selected layer(s) for all new viewport entities.

- **New VP Frz.** This option freezes the selected layer(s) for all new viewport entities.

- **Set Color.** This option opens a Select Color dialog box to assign a color to the selected layer(s).

- **Set Linetype.** This option opens a Select Linetype dialog box to assign a linetype to the selected layer(s). Only linetypes that have previously been loaded can be assigned.

- **Filters Set.** This option displays the Set Layer Filters dialog box.

- **Filters On.** This option turns on layer name list filters.

- **Rename.** Use this option to rename the selected layer.

- **New.** Use New to make AutoCAD accept a typed layer name as a new layer.

- **Select All.** This option selects all layers for applying attributes.

- **Clear All.** This option deselects all layers.

| Note | Changes that require a regeneration will not be visible until the next regeneration. If you use DDLMODES transparently, changes may not take effect until completion of the current command. |

To compare DDLMODES to the LAYER command, set some more colors and create three more layers, as shown in figure 5.20.

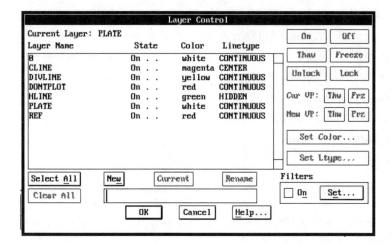

Figure 5.20:

Finished layer settings in the DDLMODES dialog box.

Setting Layers with the DDLMODES Dialog Box

Continue from the preceding exercise.

Command: **DDLMODES** ⏎   Displays the Layer Control
                                        dialog box

Enter **DONTPLOT** ⏎

Click on New   Accepts new name

Enter **REFERENCE** ⏎

Click on New   Accepts new name

Click on REFERENCE *in the layer name list*   Selects REFERENCE for
                                        edit

Click after the E in the entry box   Cursor appears after the E

Backspace to leave REF   Shortens the layer name

Click on Rename   Renames the layer

Click on REF   Unselects REF

Click on PLATE   Selects PLATE for edit

Click on Current

Click on the Current button to set the PLATE layer current

Current Layer says PLATE

Click on Clear All	Unselects all layers
Click on DONTPLOT	Selects DONTPLOT to edit
Click on REF	Selects REF to edit as well

Click on Set Color

Click on the Set Color buttom to open the Select Color dialog box

Enter RED ↵ *or Click on a RED box*	Sets color to red
Click on OK	Accepts the dialog box

Notice both layers are now red.

Set the following layers and colors:

LAYER	COLOR
DIVLINE	Yellow
HLINE	Green

Click on Set Ltype	Open the Select Linetype dialog box

Note that only CONTINUOUS and the linetypes previously loaded by the LAYER command are listed

Click on Cancel	Returns to main dialog box without making changes
Click on OK	Saves all of the changes and exits the dialog box
Command: QSAVE ↵	Saves the drawing BASEPL to the same name

You can see from the exercise that DDLMODES offers all of the options of the LAYER command in a more usable form. You will use the LAYER and DDLMODES commands again in upcoming exercises.

The purpose of most of these layers is obvious from their names. REF is for reference lines, and DONTPLOT is a layer for construction lines and other entities you would not want in a plot of the drawing. Freeze or turn off DONTPLOT before plotting.

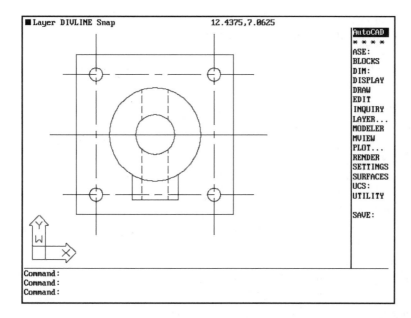

Drawing on Layers

Continue from the preceding exercise

Command: **LINE** ↵
Use LINE and draw the perimeter of the base plate from point 2,2 to @6,0, to @0,6, to @-6,0, to C to close the line

Command: **CIRCLE** ↵
Use CIRCLE and draw the shaft sleeve center at 5,5 radius .75

Click on the circle to select it

Click on the right grip   Start Autoedit

** STRETCH **

<Stretch to point>/Base point/Copy/Undo
/eXit: **C** ↵   Selects Copy

** STRETCH (multiple) **

<Stretch to point>/Base point/Copy/Undo
/eXit: **6.75,5** ↵

** STRETCH (multiple) **

<Stretch to point>/Base point/Copy/Undo   Ends Autoedit
/eXit: **X** ↵

Command: **^C**   Removes grips

```
Command: CIRCLE ↵
```
Use Circle and draw the lower left screw hole center at 2.75,2.75

Click on the new circle   Selects the circle

Click on the center grip   Starts Autoedit

```
** STRETCH **
<Stretch to point>/Base point/Copy/Undo
/eXit: Press Enter                                           Cycles to Move
** MOVE **
<Move to point>/Base point/Copy/Undo
/eXit: C ↵                                                   Selects Copy
** MOVE (multiple) **
<Move to point>/Base point/Copy/Undo
/eXit: 2.75,7.25 ↵                                           Selects Copy
** MOVE (multiple) **
<Move to point>/Base point/Copy/Undo
/eXit: Press Enter
```

Click on the upper circle to select it

Click on the center grip of the upper circle

```
** STRETCH **
<Stretch to point>/Base point/Copy/Undo
/eXit: Press Enter                                           Cycles to Move
** MOVE **
<Move to point>/Base point/Copy/Undo
/eXit: C ↵                                                   Selects Copy
** MOVE (multiple) **
<Move to point>/Base point/Copy/Undo
/eXit: 7.25,7.25 ↵                                           Selects Copy
** MOVE (multiple) **
<Move to point>/Base point/Copy/Undo
/eXit: Press Enter
Command: ^C                                                  Clears grips
Command: LINE ↵
```
Use line and draw the key mount from 4.125,3.5 to 4.125,2.5625 to 5.875,2.5625 to 5.875,3.5

```
Command: LAYER ↵
```
Set HLINE current to draw the key slot

```
?/Make/Set/New/ON/OFF/Color/Ltype/                          Selects the Set
Freeze/Thaw/LOck/Unlock: S ↵                                 option
```

`New current layer <PLATE>: ` **`HLINE`** ⏎	Specifies the new current layer
`?/Make/Set/New/ON/OFF/Color/Ltype/` `Freeze/Thaw/LOck/Unlock: ` *Press Enter*	Ends the LAYER command
`Command: ` **`LINE`** ⏎ *Draw the key slot lines from 4.5,6.6875* *to 4.5,5.5625 and from 4.5,4.4375 to* *4.5, 2.5625*	
Click on both hidden lines	Selects the lines
Click on the bottom grip	Starts Autoedit
`** STRETCH **`	
`<Stretch to point>/Base point/Copy/Undo` `/eXit: ` *Press Enter*	Cycles to Move
`** MOVE **`	
`<Move to point>/Base point/Copy/Undo` `/eXit: ` **`C`** ⏎	Selects Copy
`** MOVE (multiple) **`	
`<Move to point>/Base point/Copy/Undo` `/eXit: ` **`5.5,2.5625`** ⏎	Selects Copy
`** MOVE (multiple) **`	
`<Move to point>/Base point/Copy/Undo` `/eXit: ` *Press Enter*	
`Command: ` **`^C`**	Clears grips
`Command: ` **`LAYER`** ⏎ *Set CLINE current to draw the key slot.*	
`?/Make/Set/New/ON/OFF/Color/Ltype/` `Freeze/Thaw/LOck/Unlock: ` **`S`** ⏎	Selects the Set option
`New current layer <HLINE>: ` **`CLINE`** ⏎	Specifies the new current layer
`?/Make/Set/New/ON/OFF/Color/Ltype/` `Freeze/Thaw/LOck/Unlock: ` *Press Enter*	Ends the LAYER command
`Command: ` **`LINE`** ⏎ *Use line and draw the center lines from* *1.5,2.75 to 8.75,2.75* *1.5,7.25 to 8.75,7.25* *2.75,1.25 to 2.75,8.75* *7.25,1.25 to 7.25,8.75*	
Set the layer to DIVLINE and draw *the divide line from 1,5 to 9.25,5*	
`Command: ` **`QSAVE`** ⏎	Saves the BASEPL drawing to the same name

Controlling Layer Visibility

You can use layers to prevent the display or plotting of groups of objects. You might, for example, be working on a building plan. You can use layers to combine the architectural floor plan, reflected ceiling plan, structural framing plan, electrical plan, lighting plan, HVAC, and plumbing, all in a single drawing. This would make it easy to align and coordinate the various plans and would eliminate duplication. It also would be useless in the field. By displaying various combinations of layers, however, you could display the floor plan, structural framing plan, HVAC plan, electrical plan, and plumbing plan, all based on the same "base sheet," just as you would with manual overlay drafting.

Layers can be suppressed in two ways. They can be *frozen* or turned *off*. You can use the Freeze/Thaw and On/Off options of the LAYER command to control layer visibility. Both options cause the entities on the specified layer(s) to disappear from all viewports, and both options suppress redrawing and plotting them. AutoCAD regenerates layers that are turned off, but not those that are frozen. You should freeze layers that you do not need to display to make regenerations faster.

Try On/Off and Freeze/Thaw with the layers in the cam drawing shown in figure 5.22.

Turning Layers On and Off, Frozen and Thawed

Continue from preceding exercise

```
Command: LAYER ⏎
?/Make/Set/New/ON/OFF/Color/Ltype
/Freeze/Thaw/LOck/Unlock: OFF ⏎
Layer name(s) to turn Off: DIVLINE ⏎      Turns off the DIVLINE layer
Really want layer CAM (the CURRENT layer) off? <N> Y ⏎
?/Make/Set/New/ON/OFF/Color/Ltype
/Freeze/Thaw/LOck/Unlock: Press Enter
Command: LINE ⏎
Use LINE and draw a test line.
```

The line does not show up.

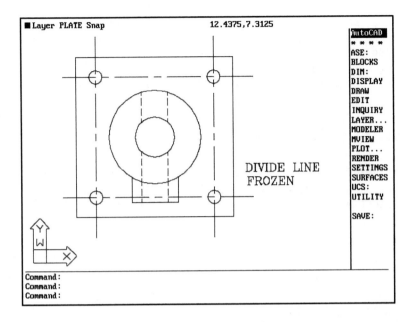

Figure 5.22:

Base plate drawing with divline layer off.

Command: **REDRAW** ⏎

The line is still invisible.

Command: **REGEN** ⏎

No effect on DIVLINE (but on a slow system, you may notice a slight delay as the invisible entities regenerate).

Command: **LAYER** ⏎

```
?/Make/Set/New/ON/OFF/Color/Ltype
/Freeze/Thaw/LOck/Unlock: F ⏎
```

Layer name(s) to Freeze: **DIVLINE** ⏎	Freezes the layer DIVLINE
Cannot freeze layer DIVLAYER.,, It is the CURRENT layer.	Refuses to freeze the layer
?/Make/Set/New/ON/OFF/Color/Ltype /Freeze/Thaw/LOck/Unlock: **S** ⏎	Sets a different layer current
New current layer <DIVLAYER>: **PLATE** ⏎	Names the current layer
?/Make/Set/New/ON/OFF/Color/Ltype /Freeze/Thaw/LOck/Unlock: **F** ⏎	Selects the Freeze option
Layer name(s) to Freeze: **DIVLINE** ⏎	Freezes the DIVLINE layer
?/Make/Set/New/ON/OFF/Color/Ltype /Freeze/Thaw/LOck/Unlock: *Press Enter*	Ends the LAYER command

```
Command: REGEN ↵
```
No effect on DIVLINE; it does not even regenerate

```
Command: LAYER ↵
?/Make/Set/New/ON/OFF/Color/Ltype
```
Selects the THAW /Freeze/Thaw/LOck/Unlock: T ↵ option

```
Layer name(s) to Thaw: * ↵
```
Thaws all layers

```
?/Make/Set/New/ON/OFF/Color/Ltype
/Freeze/Thaw/LOck/Unlock: ON ↵
```
Selects the ON option

```
Layer name(s) to turn On: * ↵
```
Turns on all layers

```
?/Make/Set/New/ON/OFF/Color/Ltype
/Freeze/Thaw/LOck/Unlock: Press Enter
```
Ends the LAYER command

```
Regenerating drawing.
Command: ERASE ↵
```

Exploring Entity Properties

When you draw an entity, AutoCAD assigns it three properties: layer name, color, and linetype. These properties are part of the entity's definition. The property assignments are determined by the current layer, color, and linetype settings.

Using COLOR and LINETYPE

You can override the layer color and linetype settings by assigning an *explicit* entity color and linetype. You do this with the COLOR and LINETYPE commands prior to creating the entity.

Both the COLOR and LINETYPE commands are *BYLAYER* by default. BYLAYER means an entity assumes the color and/or linetype of its layer. For example, you drew the ellipses on the CAM layer, which had a layer color of cyan. Because entity color was still the default BYLAYER, the ellipses were cyan. If you change the color of the CAM layer, all entities created with the color property set to BYLAYER will change accordingly.

COLOR. The COLOR command controls the color of new entities. The default is BYLAYER, which displays in the color of the entity's layer. To set a new color that overrides the layer color default, enter a color number or name. You also can set entity color with the 'DDEMODES dialogue box. Layer color defaults are controlled by the LAYER and DDLMODES commands. The colors of existing entities can be changed with the CHPROP command.

The COLOR command has only one prompt. You enter a new color, BYLAYER or BYBLOCK. Enter BYLAYER to make new entities take on the color of their layer. Enter BYBLOCK to defer color until entities are inserted as a block. New entities are white. However, when they are saved as a block and the block is inserted, the entities receive the entity color setting current at the time of insertion.

You can specify the current entity color for new entities, by name or number. AutoCAD uses up to 255 colors, depending on your system's video graphics card. The seven standard assignments are the following:

```
1 = Red       5 = Blue
2 = Yellow    6 = Magenta
3 = Green     7 = White
4 = Cyan
```

You can abbreviate color names to their first letter, and use BYB and BYL for BYBLOCK and BYLAYER.

LINETYPE. The LINETYPE command controls the appearance of lines, circles, arcs, and 2D polyline segments.

AutoCAD's standard linetypes are shown in Figure 5.23. Except for CONTINUOUS, these linetypes are defined in the ACAD.LIN file. CONTINUOUS, is AutoCAD's "built-in" linetype.

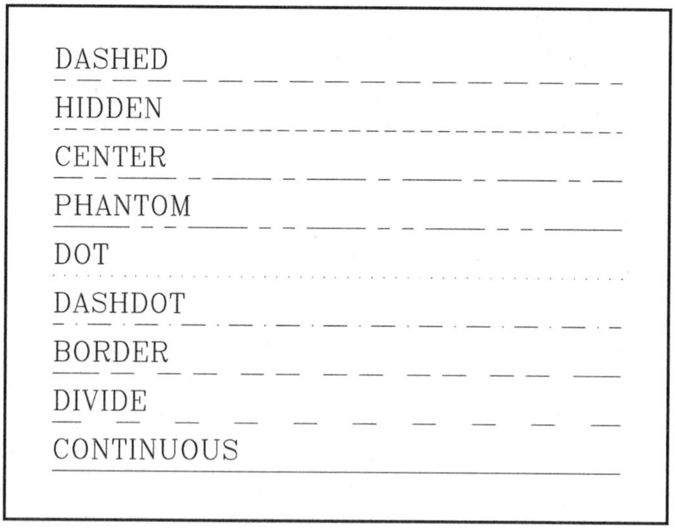

Figure 5.23:

AutoCAD's standard linetypes.

| DASHED |
| HIDDEN |
| CENTER |
| PHANTOM |
| DOT |
| DASHDOT |
| BORDER |
| DIVIDE |
| CONTINUOUS |

LINETYPE Options

- **?.** This option lists linetypes from a linetype file. You can use wild-card characters to create a specific set of linetype names.

- **Create.** The Create option creates new linetypes. See the *AutoCAD Reference Manual* or *Inside AutoCAD* or *Maximizing AutoCAD Volume I* from New Riders Publishing for more details on creating linetypes.

- **Load.** Specify linetypes to load from a file. You can use wild cards to load multiple linetypes.

- **Set.** Specify the current entity linetype to use for new entities.

Changing Many Property Settings at Once

You can set color, linetype, current layer, text style, and other entity properties interactively with the Entity Creation Modes dialog box.

DDEMODES. For new entities, the DDEMODES (Dynamic Dialogue Entity creation MODES) dialog box (see fig. 5.24) changes the current default settings for the layer, color, linetype, text style, elevation, and thickness.

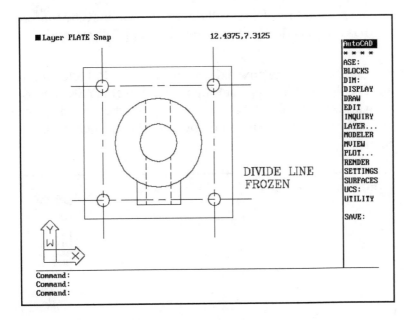

Figure 5.24:

Entity Creation Modes dialog box.

DDEMODES Options

- **Color.** Click on current color to open a Select Color dialog box. (The default is BYLAYER.)

- **Layer.** Click on current layer to open a Select Layer dialog box. (The default is 0.)

- **Linetype.** Click on current linetype to open a Select Linetype dialog box. Only currently loaded linetypes are available. (The default is BYLAYER.)

- **Text style.** Click on current style to open a Select Text Style dialog box. (The default is STANDARD.)

- **Elevation.** Enter new elevation value. (The default is 0.)

- **Thickness.** Enter new thickness value. (The default is 0.)

Enter 'DDEMODES to use the dialog box transparently within another command; however, many changes do not take effect until the current command is completed.

You cannot use DDEMODES to select a linetype that has not been loaded with the LINETYPE command.

Use DDEMODES in the next exercise to set layer to HOUSING and to set color and linetype settings back to BYLAYER. Try drawing and inserting bolts and mounting brackets for the housing to see how layers, colors, linetypes, and blocks behave (see fig. 5.25).

Figure 5.25:

Base plate with key.

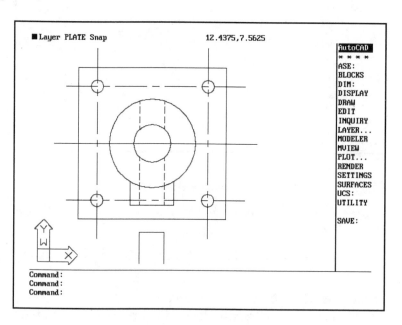

Setting Color and Linetype Using DDEMODES

Continue from the preceding exercise.

```
Command: LINETYPE ↵
?/Create/Load/Set: L ↵                     Loads a linetype
```

`Linetype(s) to load: PHANTOM`	Displays the Select Linetype File dialog box
Click on OK	Uses the ACAD.LIN linetype file
`Linetype PHANTOM loaded`	
`?/Create/Load/Set:` *Press Enter*	
Choose Settings, *then* Entity Modes	Displays the Entity Creation Modes dialog box
Click on Color	Displays the Select Color dialog box
Set the color to red by typing it or clicking on a red box	
Click on OK	Accepts the dialog box
Click on Linetype	Displays the Select Linetype dialog box
Click on the line left of PHANTOM	Selects PHANTOM as the linetype
Click on OK	Accepts the dialog box
Click on OK	Accepts the dialog box
`Command: LINE` ↵	
Use LINE to draw the key from 4.5,2.5 to 4.5,1.5 to 5.5,1.5 to 5.5,.25	

Notice that the key is drawn with red lines, even though the PLATE layer is set to white continuous lines. The lines also are phantom, but they are too short to show in phantom. You will fix this in the next exercise by resetting the linetype scale.

Controlling Linetype Dash-Dot Spacing

Linetypes other than CONTINUOUS should have a dash-dot spacing that complies with your firm's drafting standard. You can control this spacing somewhat by choosing the *name*2 or *name*X2 linetype variations. However, when you plot at a scale smaller than 1/2, or larger than 2X, the dash-dot spacing will not look right.

Just as you scale symbols and text, you need to scale linetypes. Do this with the LTSCALE command.

LTSCALE. The LTSCALE (LineType SCALE) command controls the scale for all linetypes by setting a global scale factor (default 1.0).

The LTSCALE command changes the dash length and the dash-dot spacing of all linetypes in the drawing. Entering a value larger than 1.0 increases the lengths of the dashes and spaces; entering a value smaller than 1.0 decreases the lengths of the dashes and spaces. Entering too high or too low a value will make all linetypes look continuous.

To display and plot dash-dot lines correctly, set the LTSCALE.

To estimate an LTSCALE setting that will plot well, divide 0.375 by the drawing plot scale factor. For example, for a drawing to be plotted at 1/8"=1'0" (1/96), divide 0.375 by 1/96 to obtain a LTSCALE setting of 36. This "rule of thumb" yields a plotted appearance that works well with most drafting standards. Remember that all linetypes are affected, so the "best" setting is usually a compromise.

You will not see a change in the on-screen linetype scale until the drawing regenerates if REGENAUTO is set to OFF.

Try two variations of the CENTER linetype to compare their scales. Then change the linetype scale (see fig. 5.26).

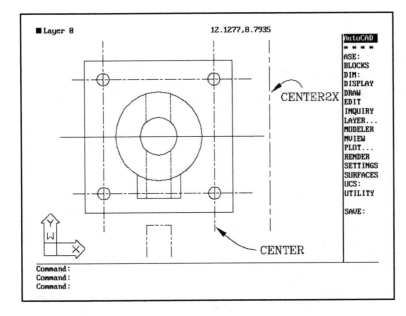

Figure 5.26:

Base plate with two center linetypes and a 0.375 LTSCALE.

Comparing Linetype Variations and Changing Linetype Scale

Continue from the preceding exercise.

Command: **LINETYPE** ↵
Use LINETYPE and reload CENTER and load the CENTER2 and CENTERX2 linetypes, using the wild-card name C*

Click on OK   Selects the ACAD.LIN linetype
                                                               file

Linetype CENTER is already loaded.   Reloads CENTER
Reload it? <Y> *Press Enter*

Linetype CENTER reloaded
Linetype CENTER2 loaded
Linetype CENTER2X loaded

?/Create/Load/Set: **S** ↵   Sets the current linetype

New entity linetype (or ?)   Sets CENTERX2
<PHANTOM>: **CENTERX2** ↵   current

?/Create/Load/Set: *Press Enter*

Command: **LINE** ↵
Use LINE and draw a line from 9.5,8.75 to 9.5,1.25

215

Notice the difference between the CENTER and CENTERX2 linetypes.

```
Command: LINETYPE ↵                    Set BYLAYER current
Command: LTSCALE ↵
New scale factor <1.0000> .75 ↵
Regenerating drawing
```

The hidden and center lines look good but the phantom lines still do not show and this will plot too loose.

```
Command: LTSCALE ↵
New scale factor <0.7500>: .375 ↵
Regenerating drawing.
```

This is perfect for plotting and the phantom lines now show. The hidden line dashes are much smaller and you can turn off the grid by pressing F7 to see them.

```
Command: END ↵                         Saves the drawing and exits
                                       ACAD
```

An LTSCALE setting that plots correctly may not look right on the screen. You can temporarily change the LTSCALE setting for convenience in editing, but reset it before plotting.

Summary

In this chapter, you learned the differences between the process of setting up and getting around in a CAD drawing and the process of manual drawing. You set up in AutoCAD to draw objects at their actual size, whether they are inches or miles across. You do not worry about scale except for scaling to the plotted paper size. You set up your drawing units and limits to correspond to the type of drawing and size of the paper sheet on which it will be plotted.

You used AutoCAD's display control commands to draw full size on a small screen. You used PAN, ZOOM, and VIEW to control the magnification and portion of the CAD drawing visible on the screen; REGEN to recalculate the image; and REGENAUTO and VIEWRES to control the speed and behavior of PAN, ZOOM, VIEW, and REGEN.

You divided the display into multiple viewports to view several portions of the drawing simultaneously, controlling tiled viewports with the VPORTS command. You created mview viewports in paper space, the electronic sheet on which you place viewports and compose images so that what you see is what you get when you plot the drawing.

For simplicity, not every exercise in the book takes advantage of all of these setup and display control features. Bear in mind, however, that you will want to use these features for maximum efficiency in your real work.

In the next chapter, you learn to use one of AutoCAD's most powerful features, the capability to group a number of objects and then copy, rotate, scale, and manipulate the group as a single object.

More Drawing Commands

In Chapter 2, you created a simple drawing by using only the basic geometric entities; in Chapter 3, you learned several techniques for drawing precisely. Although you can make drawings using only the commands you have learned up to this point, you encounter many awkward situations if you use only those tools and techniques.

Consider the situation in which you must draw a circle with its center located midway between two existing points. With the commands you have learned, you can construct this circle in much the same way you do with a compass on the board—you draw a line between the two points, enter the CIRCLE command, snap the center point to the midpoint of the line, and snap the radius point to one endpoint of the line.

AutoCAD offers an alternative, however, in one of the CIRCLE command's options. You indicate that you want to enter a diameter instead of a radius vector, pick the two points, and AutoCAD then draws the circle.

Many of AutoCAD's drawing commands include options that automate constructions like the one described previously. The CIRCLE command includes five options for drawing circles. The ARC command provides twelve ways to draw arcs. The PLINE command enables you to draw a complex shape rapidly as a single entity called a *polyline*.

In this chapter, you will learn how some of the commands and command options can improve your efficiency. The first sections explore the options available for the CIRCLE and ARC commands and introduce the PLINE command and the polyline entity. Then you will investigate more options of the TEXT command and try the efficient DTEXT command.

AutoCAD has a variety of *text fonts* (collections of character styles). You will learn to use the STYLE command to modify the appearance of these fonts. For example, you can create a style that squeezes the characters, creating condensed text that fits in tight places.

Several commands automatically create regular geometric shapes from polylines (ELLIPSE, POLYGON, and DONUT are three of these commands). You can create polylines and donuts that have wide lines instead of thin lines (single-pixel lines on the screen or the pen-width lines in a plot). To speed up redraws, you use the FILL command to display these wide lines as boundaries instead of filled-in areas. The SOLID command also creates a filled-in area, which you use to create a solid key on a shaft. A drawing created by using all these commands is shown in figure 6.1.

In this chapter, you learn the following:

- Using circle and arc options
- Using polylines
- Annotating with DTEXT
- Drawing special shapes

- Drawing solids
- Constructing circles and polylines

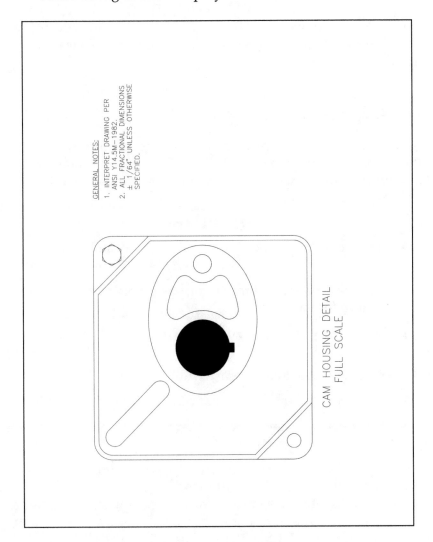

Figure 6.1:

A dimensioned cam housing drawing.

Using Circle and Arc Options

Chapters 2 and 3 introduced you to the CIRCLE and ARC commands. You used one of the five methods for drawing circles (the default center point and radius) and two of the twelve ways of drawing arcs.

Drawing Circles

AutoCAD draws circles by using almost any geometric method. If you enter a point at the initial CIRCLE command prompt, it prompts you for the diameter or radius. The complete set of options is listed as follows:

CIRCLE Options

- **Center point.** Type or pick the center point, and CIRCLE prompts for a diameter or radius. This option is the default.

- **Diameter.** Enter a distance or pick two points to show a distance for the diameter.

- **Radius.** Enter a distance or pick two points to show a distance for the radius.

- **3P.** Specify the circumference with three points.

- **2P.** Specify two diameter points on the circumference.

- **TTR.** Select two lines, circles, or arcs that form tangents to the circle, and then specify a radius.

To illustrate the difference between these two methods and the two-point option, begin a new drawing and use the CIRCLE command to create a few circles. Use the drawing shown in figure 6.2 and begin the cam housing with two bolt holes and the center shaft. You draw in a UCS with its origin at 2,2 of the WCS, so that you can easily specify points relative to the lower left corner of the housing. If points fall on the snap grid, you can type the input points and distances shown in the exercises or use snap and the coordinate display to pick the points.

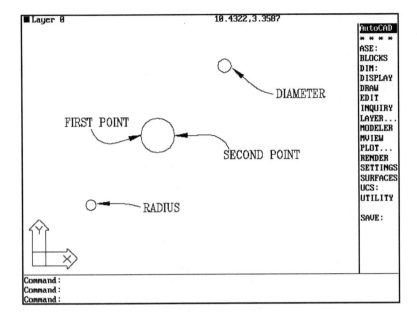

Figure 6.2:

Cam housing holes and shaft.

Cam Housing Holes and Shaft

Start ACAD from the AB directory and begin a NEW drawing named CAMHSE.

```
Command: UCS ↵
```
Starts the UCS command

```
Origin/ZAxis/3point/Entity/View/X/Y/Z
/Prev/Restore/Save/Del/?/<World>: O
```

```
Origin point <0,0,0>: 2,2
```
Sets the origin at 2,2, where the housing will be

```
Command: SNAP ↵
```
Set the snap increment to .0625

```
Command: GRID ↵
```
Set the grid spacing to .25

```
Command: CIRCLE ↵
```
or C, use the radius option

```
3P/2P/TTR/<Center point>: .5,.5
```

```
Command: Press F6 twice
```
Turns the coordinate display to polar

```
Diameter/<Radius>:
```
Drag cursor and pick 0.1875<0

```
Command: CIRCLE ↵
```
Use the Diameter option

```
3P/2P/TTR/<Center point>: 5.5,5.5 ↵        Selects the diameter option
```

```
Diameter/<Radius>: D
Diameter: Drag the cursor and
```
pick 0.375<0

```
Command: CIRCLE ↵
```
Use the 2-point option

```
3P/2P/TTR/<Center point>: 2P            Selects the two-point option
```

```
First point on diameter: 2.375,3
```

```
Second point on diameter: 3.625,3
```

```
Command: QSAVE ↵                        Saves the CAMHSE drawing
                                        to the same name
```

Note If you want to take a break between sections or exercises, end your drawing where the exercise shows the SAVE command. Then reload the drawing when you continue.

The perimeter of the cam housing consists of lines and arcs. Use lines and arcs to draw the outer profile, and use polylines to draw the inner profile. This provides an opportunity to try some of the other options of the ARC command before you learn what polylines are and how to draw them.

Drawing Arcs

Combining the eight options of the ARC command with four options for continuing an arc tangent to the last arc yields twelve ways to draw an arc. You can specify the arc by virtually any combination of Start point, Second point, Endpoint, Center, Angle, Length of chord, Radius, and Direction. You have used the default 3-point arc (start, second, and endpoints), and the tangent-to-last-line method, which prompts only for the endpoint. ARC options include the following:

ARC Options

- **Start point.** Pick the beginning point of the arc. This option is the default.

- **Center point.** Specify the center of the arc.

- **Endpoint.** Specify the endpoint, or last point, of the arc.

- **Angle.** Specify the included angle of the arc from the start point.

- **Length.** Specify the arc chord length from start point to ending point.

- **Radius.** Specify the radius of the arc.

- **Direction.** Specify the tangent direction from the start point.

- **Press Enter.** Press Enter at the start point prompt to begin an arc that is tangent to the previous line or arc drawn. You can do the same thing by selecting the CONTIN: item on the screen menu.

There is no need to memorize all of these options, because you can display the cascading Arc menu and compare the options with the points you can specify.

ARC is on the DRAW screen menu and the Draw pull-down menu. The pull-down menu spells out the options, but the screen menu abbreviates them with their first letters, as in S,C,E:, S,E,A:, and C,S,A:. (The twelfth method—Start, End, Center—is not on the menu, but it uses the same points as S,C,E:.) If you enter options at the command line, prompts appear in steps, but the context-sensitive screen menu appears, listing the various combinations. Enter the first letter of the option you want or enter a point to supply the default shown in angle brackets in one of the sequences listed in the screen menu.

Experiment with a few of the options by drawing the outer perimeter of the cam housing with ARC and LINE (see fig. 6.3). The following exercises use as many options as possible, although they may not always use the most efficient option. The exercises also use object snaps for some points that are actually on the snap grid so that you can practice using object snaps and point filters.

Figure 6.3:

Cam housing perimeter.

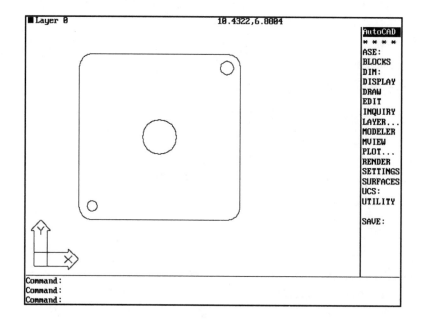

Cam Housing Perimeter with ARC Options

Continue from previous exercise.

```
Command: LINE ↵
From point: .5,0 ↵
To point: 5.5,0 ↵
To point: Press Enter
Command: ARC ↵
Center/<Start point>: @ ↵          Specifies the last point drawn
                                    as the arc's start point

Center/End/<Second point>: c ↵     Specifies the Center option
Center: 5.5,0.5 ↵
Angle/Length of chord/<Endpoint>: A ↵   Specifies Angle option
Include angle: Drag cursor straight up
to indicate 90 degree angle, then pick
(or just type 90)
```

```
Command: LINE ↵
From point: Press Enter               Starts line tangent to arc
Length of line: 5 ↵                   Specifies the line length
To point: Press Enter                 Ends the line command
Command: ARC ↵
Center/<Start point>: C ↵
Center: CEN ↵                         Specifies the CEN object snap
                                      mode

of Pick the top right circle
Start point: ENDP ↵                   Specifies the ENDP object
                                      snap mode

of Pick the top end of the last line
Angle/Length of chord/<Endpoint>:     Draws arc to picked endpoint
Drag straight up 90° and pick         with radius centered to start
                                      point

Command: LINE ↵
From point: Press Enter
Length of line: 5 ↵
To point: Press Enter
Command: ARC ↵
Center/<Start point>: C ↵             specifies the Center option
Center: .5,5.5 ↵                      Specifies the center of the arc
Start point: ENDP ↵
of Pick the end of the last line
Angle/Length of chord/<Endpoint>: L ↵
Length of chord: Drag the cursor
diagonally and pick 0.7071 at any
angle on the coordinate display
or type it
Command: LINE ↵
From point: Press Enter
Length of line: 5 ↵
To point: Press Enter
```

```
Command: ARC ⏎
SER—Start, End, Radius
Center/<Start point>: @ ⏎          Specifies the last point drawn as
                                   the arc's start point

Center/End/<Second point>: E ⏎
Endpoint: ENDP ⏎                   Uses the ENDP object snap
                                   point

of  Pick end of other line at the
lower left
Angle/Direction/Radius/
<Center point>: R ⏎

Radius .5 ⏎
Command: QSAVE ⏎                   Saves the CAMHSE drawing to
                                   the same name
```

Each of the different arc options used in the previous exercise produced the same result: a 90-degree, .5"-radius arc. Only the type of information you entered for each arc or the order in which you entered it was different. Most AutoCAD commands offer many ways to achieve the same effect.

AutoCAD angles are specified counterclockwise. To specify a clockwise included angle, enter it as a negative angle.

You can draw a single entity consisting of a sequence of separate lines and arcs by using a single command: PLINE.

Using Polylines

In AutoCAD, you can use the LINE command to draw a continuous series of lines from point-to-point. Each line, however, exists as a separate entity. Although adjacent segments connect at common endpoints, AutoCAD does not recognize them as being related to one another.

Usually this does not pose a problem. Sometimes, however, you want AutoCAD to recognize that those line segments are associated with each other; for example, if you need to move, copy, or erase a complex shape made up of line and arc segments. If you draw them with the PLINE command, you can pick a single segment; AutoCAD automatically picks all the other segments.

PLINE. The PLINE command creates two-dimensional polylines. A *polyline* is a series of vertices that defines contiguous line and arc segments as a single entity. The default line mode includes the Arc, Close, Halfwidth, Length, Undo, Width, and Endpoint options. If you enter Arc for arc mode, AutoCAD presents the additional Angle, CEnter, Direction, Line, Radius, and Second pt options. You can edit polylines by using PEDIT or the regular editing commands.

Using Polyline Options

A polyline is a series of vertex points connected by line and arc segments. Each segment is associated with and controlled by the preceding vertex, and all segments are joined without interruption as one contiguous entity. This makes it possible to select all segments of a polyline with a single entity selection.

Unlike lines and arcs, polylines are not limited to a single width. You can assign a starting and ending width to each segment. AutoCAD draws both edges of a wide polyline and fills in the space between the edges. This is a good way to draw wide lines without requiring a wide pen tip and to have line widths visible on the screen.

When you are drawing a series of lines and arcs with PLINE, you can simply alternate between the Line and Arc options instead of reentering repeated line and arc commands.

The PLINE command has numerous options, but you do not need to remember them all because the command prompts you for them as you draw. These options are discussed in the following sections.

Polyline Line Options

- **Arc.** The Arc option switches from drawing polylines to drawing polyarcs and issues the polyarc options prompt.

- **CLose.** The CLose option closes the polyline by drawing a segment from the last endpoint, to the initial start point, to the last endpoint, and then by exiting the PLINE command.

- **Halfwidth.** Enter the distance from the center to the polyline's edges (half the actual width).

- **Length.** Enter the length of a new polyline segment at the same angle as the last polyline segment or tangent to the last polyarc segment.

- **Undo.** The Undo option undoes the last drawn segment.

- **Width.** Enter a width (default is 0) for the next segment to create polylines. To taper a segment, define different starting and ending widths. After AutoCAD draws the tapered segment, it draws the next segment with the ending width of the tapered segment.

- **Endpoint of line.** Specify the endpoint of the current line segment. This option is the default.

Polyline Arc Options

- **Angle.** Enter the included angle (a negative angle draws the arc clockwise).

- **CEnter.** Specify the arc's center.

- **CLose.** The CLose option closes the polyline by connecting the initial start point to the last endpoint with an arc segment, and then exits the PLINE command.

- **Direction.** Specify a tangent direction for the segment.

- **Halfwidth.** Specify a halfwidth, the same as for Line options.

- **Line.** The Line option switches back to Line mode.

- **Radius.** Specify the arc's radius.

- **Second pt.** Select the second point of a three-point arc.

- **Undo.** The Undo option undoes the last segment drawn.

- **Width.** Enter a width, the same way as for Line mode.

- **Endpoint of arc.** Specify the endpoint of the current arc segment. This option is the default.

To understand how the PLINE command works and to experiment with some of its options, draw the inner boundary of the cam housing by using a single polyline (see fig. 6.4).

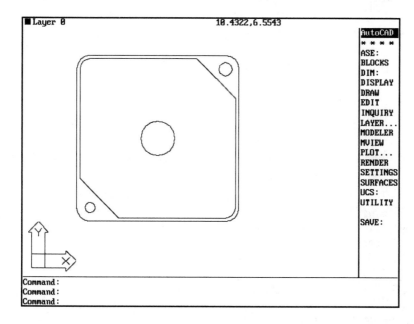

Figure 6.4:

Polyline for cam inner housing.

Adding a Polyline to the Cam Housing

Continue from the previous exercise.

Command: **PLINE** ↵	Starts a polyline
From point: **1.5625,.125** ↵	Specifies the polyline's start point
Current line-width is 0.0000	
Arc/Close/Halfwidth/Length/Undo/Width/ <Endpoint of line>: *Pick 3.9375<0*	Specifies the polyline's endpoint
Arc/Close/Halfwidth/Length/Undo/Width/ <Endpoint of line>: **A** ↵	Selects the Arc option

```
Angle/CEnter/CLose/Direction/
Halfwidth/Line/Radius/Second pt/
Undo/Width/<Endpoint of arc>:
```
Align horizontal crosshair with center
of lower left center of lower left circle
and vertical crosshair on snap point .125
to left of rightmost vertical line,
then pick 0.5303<45

```
Angle/CEnter/CLose/Direction/          Selects the Line option
Halfwidth/Line/Radius/Second pt/
Undo/Width/<Endpoint of arc>: L ↵
```

```
Arc/Close/Halfwidth/Length/Undo/       Selects the Length option
Width/<Endpoint of line>: L ↵
```

```
Length of line: 3.9375 ↵
```

```
Arc/Close/Halfwidth/Length/Undo/
Width/<Endpoint of line>:
4.4375,5.875 ↵
```

```
Arc/Close/Halfwidth/Length/Undo/
Width/<Endpoint of lines>:
```
Pick 3.9375<180, aligned with lower
left circle

```
Arc/Close/Halfwidth/Length/Undo/       Selects the Arc option
Width/<Endpoint of line>: A ↵
```

```
Angle/CEnter/CLose/Direction/          Selects the arc's endpoint
Halfwidth/Line/Radius/Second pt/
Undo/Width/<Endpoint of arc>:
@-.375,-.375 or pick 0.5303<225,
aligned with upper right circle
```

```
Angle/CEnter/CLose/Direction/          Selects the Line option
Halfwidth/Line/Radius/Second pt/
Undo/Width/<Endpoint of arc>: L ↵
```

```
Arc/Close/Halfwidth/Length/
Undo/Width/<Endpoint of line>:
```
Pick 3.9375<270

```
Arc/Close/Halfwidth/Length/Undo/       Closes to the point
Width/start<Endpoint of line>: C ↵
```

```
Command: QSAVE ↵                       Saves the CAMHSE drawing
                                       to the same name
```

The polyline does not look much different from the lines and arcs that you used to draw the outer perimeter of the cam housing. If you pick one of the segments during object selection, however, you see that AutoCAD selects all the segments as a single polyline. To see this, erase the polyline, and then use Undo to bring it back.

Selecting and Restoring the Polyline

Continue from the previous exercise.

```
Command: ERASE ↵
Select objects: Select any of the poly-
line segments
1 select, 1 found
Select objects: Press Enter          Erases the entire polyline
Command: U ↵
ERASE                                Restores the polyline
```

Because the entire polyline is a single entity, a U command used after a PLINE command undoes the entire polyline, not just the last segment of it. Both the PLINE command line and arc prompts include an Undo option that will undo the previous segment and take you back to the previous point (type U and press Enter).

Finish the cam housing by adding the slot for the cam follower, as shown in figure 6.5. First, use ID and object snap to reset the last point to the upper left. Because the points do not fall on the snap grid, use the @ sign to enter them as relative coordinates. These options are not necessarily the most efficient ones, but they give you an opportunity to try different polyline options.

Figure 6.5:

Drawing the cam follower slot.

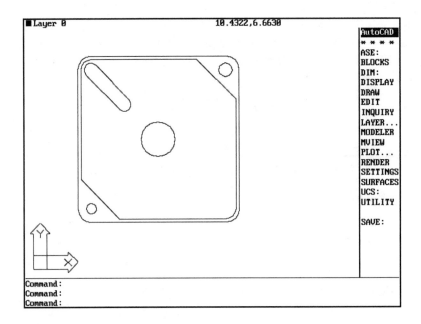

Adding the CAM Follower Slot

Continue from previous exercise.

Command: `ID` ↵	Resets last point
Point: `CEN` ↵	Specifies the CEN object snap mode
of *Pick either arc at upper left*	
Command: `PLINE` ↵	
From point: `@.25<225` ↵	Specifies the polylines's end-point
Current line width is `0.0000`	
Arc/Close/Halfwidth/Length/Undo/ Width/<Endpoint of line>:	Specifies the polyline's endpoint
`@1.25,-1.25` ↵	
Arc/Close/Halfwidth/Length/Undo/ Width/<Endpoint of line>: `A` ↵	Selects the Arc option
Angle/CEnter/CLose/Direction/ Halfwidth/Line/Radius/Second pt/ Undo/Width/<Endpoint of arc>: `R` ↵	Selects the Radius option
Radius: `.25` ↵	Sets the arc's radius at .25 units

`Angle/<Endpoint>: @.5<45 ↵`	Sets the arc's endpoint in relation to the line's endpoint

`Angle/CEnter/Close/Direction/`
`Halfwidth/Line/Radius/`
`Second pt/Undo/Width/<Endpoint of`
`arc>: L ↵`
	Selects the Line option

`Arc/Close/Halfwidth/Length/Undo/`
`Width/<endpoint of line>:`
`@-1.25,1.25 ↵`
	Specifies the line's endpoint in relation to its start point

`Arc/Close/Halfwidth/Length/Undo/` `Width/Arc<Endpoint of line>: A ↵`	Selects the option

`Angle/CEnter/CLose/Direction/`
`Halfwidth/Line/Radius/Second pt/`
`Undo/Width/<Endpoint of arc>: CL ↵`
	Closes the polyline

`Command: QSAVE ↵`	Saves the CAMHSE drawing to the same name

The cam housing is now complete except for one minor detail—you need to draw two lines for the diagonal corners of the outer housing. This procedure is tricky because the lines need to be parallel to and exactly .125 inches from the inner housing corner lines.

To draw the corner lines (illustrated in fig. 6.6), align the UCS with the lower left existing diagonal corner. Then draw construction lines .125 inches from the corners. After using object snap to draw the final lines to the intersections of the construction lines and the outer boundary lines, erase the construction lines. First, use the three-point option to define the origin and X axis of a UCS.

Drawing Cam Corner Lines

Continue from the previous exercise.

`Command: UCS ↵`	

`Origin/ZAxis/3point/Entity/View/`
`X/Y/Z//Prev/Restore/Save/Del/?/`
`<World>: 3 ↵`
	Selects the 3-point option to set a three-point UCS

`Origin point <0,0,0>: INT ↵`	Specifies the INT object snap mode

of Pick the upper left end of the lower left diagonal, at ① (see figure 6.6)

Figure 6.6:

Drawing corner lines in a UCS.

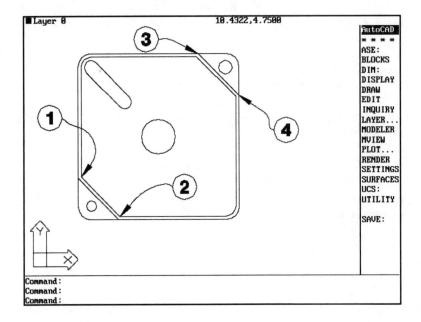

Point on positive portion of the
X-axis<1.1250,1.5625,0.0000>: INT ⏎

of *Pick the lower right end of lower left diagonal, at* ②

Point on positive-Y portion of the
UCS XY plane <0.8321,2.2696,0.0000>:
Press Enter

Commamd: LINE ⏎

From point: *Pick -.5,-.125*

To point: *Pick 3<0*

To point: *Press Enter*

Command: ID ⏎
Reset the last point to the upper left end of the upper right diagonal

Point: INT ⏎   Uses the INT object snap mode

of *Pick the upper left end of upper right diagonal*

X = 0.0000   Y = 6.0988   Z = 0.0000

Command: LINE ⏎

From point: @-.5,.125 ⏎

To point: @3<0 ⏎

```
To point: Press Enter
Command: LINE ↵
From point: INT ↵
```
of *Pick one intersection of the new*
upper right diagonal, with perimeter, at ③
```
To point: INT ↵
```
of *Pick other intersection of the new*
upper right diagonal, at ④
```
To point: INT ↵
Command: LINE ↵
From point: INT ↵
```
of *Pick one intersection of the new*
lower left diagonal
```
To point: INT ↵
```
of *Pick the other intersection of new*
lower left diagonal
```
To point: Press Enter
Command: ERASE ↵
Select objects: Select both construction
```
lines to erase
```
Command: REDRAW ↵
Command: UCS ↵
Origin/ZAxis/3point/Entity/          Restores the previous UCS
View/X/Y/Z/Prev/Restore/Save/Del/
?/<World>: P ↵
Command: QSAVE ↵                      Saves the drawing to the same
                                     name
```

This exercise completes the housing. Next, explore text options to add some text to the drawing. Instead of using the TEXT command, however, try the DTEXT (Dynamic TEXT) command.

Annotating with the DTEXT Command

You used the TEXT command in Chapter 2 to place single lines of text in your drawings. You also pressed Enter at the TEXT command's start point prompt to continue entering multiple lines of text just below the previous line. The TEXT command has two limitations: you must reenter the TEXT command each time you want to place another line of text, and you cannot see the text on the drawing screen until you complete the TEXT command. To enable you to see text as you type it, and for convenience in entering multiple lines of text, AutoCAD includes the DTEXT command.

DTEXT. The DTEXT (Dynamic TEXT) command provides more control and flexibility than the TEXT command because the screen dynamically shows the text as you type it. At any time during DTEXT, you can pick a point to relocate the cursor and then enter more text without exiting the command. Press Enter once to enter another line below the current line of text; press Enter on a blank line to exit DTEXT.

Using TEXT and DTEXT

TEXT and DTEXT share the same options, and both offer many ways to justify text. *Justification* is the alignment of the text string with control points at the left, middle, right, top, bottom, and so forth. The following section lists the TEXT and DTEXT options.

Primary TEXT and DTEXT Options

- **Justify.** The Justify option issues the prompt for text justification.

- **Style.** Specify a text style to change the current style default. The style must already have been created with the STYLE command.

- **Start point.** Pick a point for the default bottom left justification.

- *Press Enter.* When you press Enter at the start point prompt, AutoCAD highlights the last text entered and prompts for a new text string. It places the new text directly below the highlighted text, using the same style, height, and rotation. With DTEXT, you can also pick a new point before entering the text.

- **Height.** Enter the text height (the default is 0.2). You are not prompted for height when using the Align justification or any text style with a predefined height.

- **Rotation angle.** Specify the text angle (the default is 0).

- **Text.** Enter the text string.

Although the text commands have many options, these options are easy to use. Just break the options down into the following categories: justification or start point or both, text height, text rotation angle, font style, and the actual text string. You enter text with as few as four items of information: start point, height, rotation, and text string. When you enter a J at the primary text prompt, AutoCAD issues a prompt for the justification options:

```
Align/Fit/Center/Middle/Right/TL/TC/TR/ML/MC/MR/BL/BC/BR:
```

You need not enter a J to use any of these options; the Justify option is just a reminder. You can enter any of these options directly at the primary text prompt.

Text Justification Options

- **Align.** Specify the beginning and ending points of the text baseline. The text height is scaled to fit the text between these points without distortion.

- **Fit.** Specify the beginning and ending points of the text baseline. The text width is distorted to fit the text between these points without changing the height.

- **Center.** Specify a point for the horizontal center and the vertical baseline of the text string to the point you enter.

- **Middle.** Specify a point for the horizontal and vertical mid-point of the text string.

- **Right.** Specify a point for the bottom right baseline of the text string.

- **TL.** Specify a point for the left of the text string, aligned with the top of the tallest character.

- **TC.** Specify a point for the center of the text string, aligned with the top of the tallest character.

- **TR.** Specify a point for the right side of the text string, aligned with the top of the tallest character.

- **ML.** Specify a point for the left side of the text string, aligned halfway between the top of the tallest character and the bottom of the lowest descender.

- **MC.** Specify a point for the center of the text string, aligned halfway between the top of the tallest character and the bottom of the lowest descender.

- **MR.** Specify a point for the right side, between the top of the tallest character and the bottom of the lowest descender.

- **BL.** Specify a point for the left side of the text string, aligned at the bottom of the lowest descender.

- **BC.** Specify a point for the center of the text string, aligned at the bottom of the lowest descender.

- **BR.** Specify a point for the right side of the lowest descender.

The primary advantage of DTEXT over TEXT is that you can pick a new start point for additional text strings whenever you want; you do not even need to press Enter to terminate the previous string. When you pick a new point, the box cursor, which DTEXT displays to show the current text entry position, moves to that new point.

The secondary advantage of DTEXT is that it enables you to see the text in the drawing as you type it. This lets you easily find and correct errors (by backspacing). You can even backspace through multiple lines of text, if they were entered in the current DTEXT command. Notice, however, that each line of text that is entered with a single DTEXT command is a separate text entity—you cannot select an entire paragraph with a single pick.

You can edit existing text strings with the DDEDIT or DDMODIFY dialog box or the CHANGE command.

Use the DTEXT command to add the text shown in figure 6.7. Press Enter after typing each line of text shown. If you make a mistake in text entry, backspace and correct it. You can even backspace into a previous line.

Using DTEXT To Add Detail Descriptions

Continue from the Previous exercise.

```
Command: DTEXT ↵
Justify/Style/<Start point>: J ↵          Selects the Justify option
Align/Fit/Center/Middle/Right/TL/         Specifies the Center option
TC/TR/ML/MC/MR/BL/BC/BR: C ↵
Center point: 3,-.5 ↵
Height <0.2000>: Press Enter
Rotation angle <0>: Press Enter
Text: CAM HOUSING ↵
```

As you type, the text appears temporarily left-justified.

```
Text: FULL SCALE ↵
Text: Press Enter                         Redraws the text center
                                          justified

Command: QSAVE ↵                          Saves the CAMHSE drawing
                                          to the same name
```

 You can shut grid off temporarily by pressing Ctrl-G or F7 to see the text more clearly.

Figure 6.7:

*Annotated cam
housing drawing.*

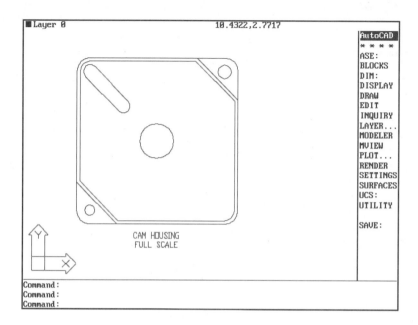

AutoCAD also provides you with several special text characters.

Using Special Character Codes

You can enter the special character codes shown in Table 6.1 in
your text string to draw special characters.

As you enter text in DTEXT, these control characters appear in
the text string on the drawing screen. When you end the DTEXT
command, the appropriate characters or effects replace the control
codes. Figure 6.8 shows text that was added using special characters.

In addition to the commonly used drafting character codes shown
in Table 6.1, you can enter any ASCII character that is available on
your system (and defined in the font being used) by entering %%
followed by the character's ASCII value. For example, the code

%%168 draws an inverted question mark character (¿), which is ASCII character 168. Refer to your printer manual, operating system manual, or to the *AutoCAD Reference Manual* for additional ASCII codes.

Table 6.1

Special Text Characters

Character	Function
%%o	Turn overscore mode on/off
%%u	Turn underscore mode on/off
%%d	Draw degrees symbol
%%p	Draw plus/minus tolerance symbol
%%c	Draw diameter symbol
%%%	Draw a single percent symbol

In the following exercise, use the %%u code to underline the first line of text and the %%p plus/minus code to put a +/- sign in the next-to-last line of text.

Annotating with Special Characters

Continues from the previous exercise.

Command: DTEXT ↵

Justify/Style/<Start point>: TL ↵
Use Top-Left to align with top of the housing's right side

Top/left point: 7,6 ↵

Height <0.2000>: .125 ↵

Rotation angle <0>: *Press Enter*

Text: %%uGENERAL NOTES:%%u ↵

Text temporarily appears above point, nested in %%u codes. The %%u codes underline the nested text.

Text: *Press Enter*

Command: **DTEXT** ⏎
Relocate following text by picking a
new point at 7,5.6875, and accept default
height and rotation

Text: **1. INTERPRET DRAWING PER** ⏎

Text: **ANSI Y14.5M-1982.** ⏎

Text: **2. ALL FRACTIONAL DIMENSIONS** ⏎

Text: **%%p 1/64" UNLESS OTHERWISE** ⏎

Text: **SPECIFIED.** ⏎

Text: *Press Enter*   The text redraws, properly
                                                     justified

The %%p code converts to a plus minus mark.

Command: **QSAVE** ⏎   Saves the CAMHSE drawing to
                                                     the same name

---

Figure 6.8:

*Detail of text added
with special
characters.*

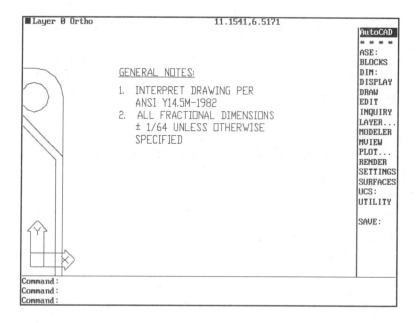

The new text is small and hard to read on the screen. In the next
chapter, you learn how to enlarge portions of the screen to see
them better. Regardless of how it looks to you now, the text is
properly sized for plotting and will be legible in a plot.

Base your text height on the scale at which you plan to plot the drawing. The text height you specify in AutoCAD should be the height of plotted text, divided by the plot-scale ratio. For example, a car drawn as 16 feet (192 inches) long, on a 220"×170" electronic sheet plots at 1:20 (plot scale 0.05) to fit on an 11"×8.5" sheet. You set your text height to .125/0.05=2.5" to make it plot .125" high.

The text font used in the preceding example is a bit crude and boxy. AutoCAD provides a number of other fonts that can be used.

Character Sets, Fonts, and Styles

A *character set* is a group of symbols that your computer can display, your printer can print, and your plotter can plot. Character sets are often associated with written and spoken languages, such as English, French, and German. They may also be associated with special tasks: mathematics, line drawing, and so on.

A *text font* is a description of the characters of a character set in terms of pen strokes. AutoCAD's default font is a single stroke font. Each character is drawn strictly with single stroke, straight-line segments, which accounts for its angular appearance. Characters drawn in a font like Old English are drawn with many strokes, arcs, and straight line segments, which yield complex characters. A font definition does not include information about the sizes, proportions, or slant of characters.

A *style* is based on a particular font. A style adds information about the proportions of characters, slant, and (optionally) size.

Adding Style to Your Text with the STYLE Command

The default text that AutoCAD uses is quick and efficient, but many drawings need a different text style. For example, architectural drawings often use a hand-lettered style, and some companies and government agencies require a font style similar to a

Leroy lettering template. AutoCAD provides you with a variety of fonts to use in your drawings. You can also create your own fonts or purchase fonts from third-party vendors.

To use a different font in AutoCAD, whether it is one included with AutoCAD or one you have acquired from another source, use the STYLE command.

STYLE. The STYLE command lists, creates, and modifies text styles. You specify a style name (up to 31 characters long), its height, width, factor, obliquing angle, and whether it is backward, upside-down, or vertical. The text style loads and references a font character set, as defined in a font file. Source font files have an SHP extension. They must be compiled with main menu item 7 to create a working font file with an SHX extension. The fonts shipped with AutoCAD are already compiled.

Font-definition files, as designated by an SHX extension, are separate from the drawing file. If you use a third-party font file, anyone who wants to edit or plot the drawing also needs the font file.

Use the STYLE command to define a character style by name and to modify one of AutoCAD's existing styles or define new ones. The following list includes all STYLE options.

Style Options

- **Style name.** Name a new style to create or an existing style to edit. This style becomes the current default style.

- **?** The ? option lists named styles defined in the current drawing. In Release 11, you can enter an asterisk (the default) to list all named styles or use wild cards to list a specific set of styles.

- **Font.** Enter a font file name for the style to reference. The default <TXT> references the TXT.SHX file.

- **Height.** Enter text height for a fixed height style or enter0 (the default) for a variable height style. Text commands do not prompt for height unless you use a variable height style.

- **Width factor.** Enter a width factor to expand or condense text (default 1 = normal).

- **Obliquing angle.** Enter a number to slant the text characters, italicizing them (default 0 = vertical). To slant toward the right, use a positive number; to slant toward the left, use a negative number. Use small angles; a little slant is adequate.

- **Backwards.** Enter**Yes** to mirror-reverse text horizontally (the default is No).

- **Upside-down.** Enter**Yes** to mirror-reverse text vertically (the default is No).

- **Vertical.** Enter**Yes** to style text vertically, one character above another (the default is No). Vertical only works with fonts that define the necessary alignment points.

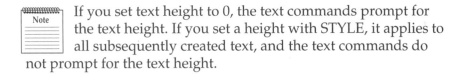

If you set text height to 0, the text commands prompt for the text height. If you set a height with STYLE, it applies to all subsequently created text, and the text commands do not prompt for the text height.

Speed is the trade-off between fancy, curvaceous fonts with serifs, such as ROMANT (ROMAN Triplex), and crude fonts, such as the default TXT. Fancy fonts take longer to redraw.

In the following exercise, you will create a somewhat narrower (condensed) style with the ROMANS font, which is illustrated in figure 6.9. ROMANS is similar to the default TXT font, but it has smooth curves instead of boxy corners. ROMANS is a good compromise font; it looks good and redraws reasonably fast.

To make it easy to select fonts and to define any of AutoCAD's standard styles, AutoCAD includes several pages of icon menus.

The first two pages are illustrated in figures 6.10 and 6.11, showing some of the fonts shipped with AutoCAD. The third page includes several symbol fonts.

You can create a new style by selecting a font from the icon menus (this will have the same style name as the font). To get to these icon menus, select Draw–Text> Set Style from the Options pulldown menu, then select Text Font.

Figure 6.9:

Text in the ROMANS font.

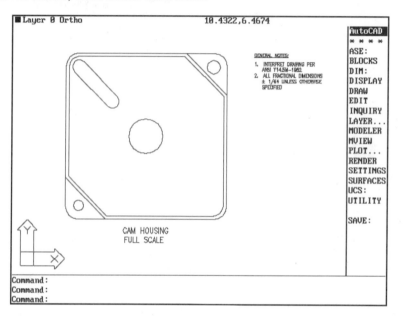

The default style is STANDARD, which uses the TXT font file. Use the STYLE command to redefine it.

Redefining the Annotation Text's Font

Continue from previous exercise.

```
Command: STYLE ↵
```

`Text style name (or ?) <STANDARD>:` *Press Enter*	Redefines the STANDARD font style
`Existing style: ROMANS ↵`	Selects the ROMANS.SHX font file

`Height <0.000>:` *Press Enter*	Leaves the text variable height
`Width factor <1.00> .8 ↵`	Condenses the style by 20 percent
`Obliquing angle <0>:` *Press Enter*	Adds No slant
`Backwards? <N>` *Press Enter*	
`Upside-down? <N>` *Press Enter*	
`Vertical? <N>` *Press Enter*	Regenerates with the new style

STANDARD is now the current text style.

`Regenerating drawing`

The new narrower style replaces the boxy text.

`Command: QSAVE ↵`	Saves the CAMHSE drawing to the same name

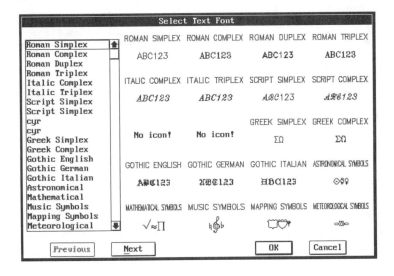

Figure 6.10:

First icon menu for creating text styles.

The new style looks a little more refined than the original. If you add more text, it defaults to this new style.

 When you turn on the Quick TEXT mode with the QTEXT command, outline boxes display in place of subsequently created or regenerated text strings and attributes. This saves time when you are redrawing or regenerating drawings that have a lot of text. The box approximates the height and length of the text, depending on the font and style.

Figure 6.11:

Second icon menu for creating text styles.

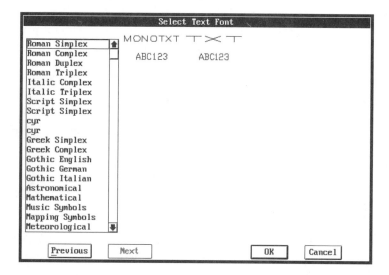

Occasionally, you will make a mistake when entering text and not notice it until later. Or you may have to revise a drawing, which requires an annotation change.

Editing Text with the DDEDIT Command

The DDEDIT command enables you to change selected text without having to erase and retype the entire string. If you need to change a single character in a long line of text, for example, DDEDIT provides the only direct means to do so without having to retype the entire line.

DDEDIT. The DDEDIT (Dynamic Dialogue EDIT) dialog box edits text strings and the tag, prompt, and default values of attribute definitions. Use DDATTE to edit attributes after they have been blocked and inserted. DDEDIT repeats for additional selections until you press Ctrl-C or Enter at its selection prompt.

DDEDIT Options

- **Select a TEXT or ATTDEF object.** Select text or an attribute definition to edit. You can edit a text string or modify the tag, prompt, and default values of attribute definitions. After you edit one object, the DDEDIT command repeats for additional selections.

- **Undo.** The Undo option undoes the last edit(s) of the current DDEDIT command.

The DDEDIT command prompts you to select a line of text or an attribute definition; then it displays a dialog box containing the text (see fig. 6.12). If you place the cursor over the line and begin to type, the entire line is replaced by the new text. This is called *replace mode*. If you place the cursor over the line you want to modify and press the pick button, the cursor highlights the character you pick. New text is inserted at that point as you type. This is called *insert mode*.

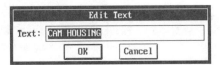

Figure 6.12:
DDEDIT'S dialog box.

Use the DDEDIT command to change the detail description under the cam housing, as shown in figure 6.13.

Editing the Detail Description

Continue from the previous exercise.

From the screen menu, choose EDIT, *then* DDEDIT
Displays the Edit Text dialog box

```
<Select a TEXT of ATTDEF
object>/Undo:
```
Select the CAM Housing text string

Press and hold the pick button. Move the arrow cursor back and forth over the text string in the dialog box and see the small text cursor highlight different characters. When you start typing, the highlighted text will be replaced.

Click on a single character to position the cursor on a single letter	Nothing is highlighted, you are in insert mode
Click at the end of the line to place the text cursor after HOUSING.	

No letters should be highlighted. The cursor should be after the G.

Type a space, then the word **DETAIL**

The line should read: CAM HOUSING DETAIL.

Click on OK

```
<Select a TEXT or ATTDEF object>/Undo:
```
Press Enter

Command: **QSAVE** ↵	Saves the CAMHSE drawing to the same name

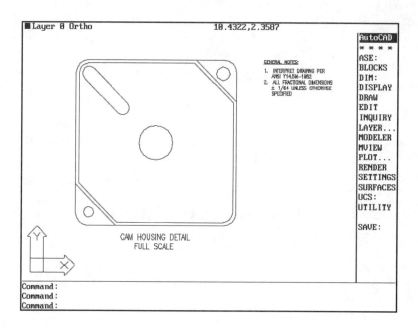

Finish the cam housing with several commands that automate the creation of polylines.

Drawing Special Shapes

The handful of drawing commands you have used so far—Line, Circle, Arc, Text and Pline—can create most of the graphic entities you find in a typical drawing. A few shapes, however, are too time-consuming to draw using these commands. These shapes include ellipses, regular polygons, and donuts (which can create washers, pipe cross-sections, and filled dots). AutoCAD gives you drawing tools to create these shapes.

Drawing Ellipses

You can draw an ellipse by using polylines or arc segments, but it is time-consuming and difficult to lay out. The ELLIPSE command creates ellipses easily, accurately, and efficiently.

ELLIPSE. The ELLIPSE command constructs ellipses by combining axis endpoints, center points, and axis distances. The ELLIPSE default is to specify the endpoints of the major and minor axes. If snap is set to isometric mode, the ELLIPSE Isocircle option draws an isometric circle in the current isometric plane.

The ELLIPSE prompts are simpler than they look. An ellipse can be defined by four points it passes through—the endpoints of its two axes. The first axis can be defined either by its center point and one endpoint or by two endpoints. The second axis is always perpendicular to the first axis. Therefore, the second axis can be defined by its distance from the center or by its rotation around the first axis. Think of the rotation as viewing a circle in 3D: the rotation is the angle that the axis endpoint rotates out of the coordinate system's plane.

Ellipse Options

- **Axis endpoint *n*.** Pick the endpoint to define the axis.
- **Center.** Enter a center point and ELLIPSE prompts for one endpoint of the axis.

253

- **Rotation.** Enter the rotation angle (0 to 89.4 degrees) or enter a point to indicate the angle of rotation around the major axis.

- **Other axis distance.** Enter a distance for the axis.

- **Isocircle.** The Isocircle prompt appears only if snap is set to Isometric mode. Isocircle prompts for the center point and for the radius or diameter; then it draws an isometric circle in the current isoplane.

You do not need to remember each of the options for the ELLIPSE command. Instead, remember that you can construct an ellipse, based on a number of different parameters and rely on the menu or prompts to apply them to any particular ellipse. Regardless of how you create them, ellipses are actually closed polyline entities made of short arc segments.

 To construct an elliptical arc, draw an ellipse and use the BREAK or TRIM EDIT commands.

Draw an elliptical cam inside the cam housing, as illustrated in figure 6.14.

Drawing an Elliptical Cam with ELLIPSE

Continue from previous exercise.

```
Command: ELLIPSE ⏎
<Axis endpoint 1>/Center: 3.75,1.5 ⏎
Axis endpoint 2: @0,3 ⏎                  Defines an ellipse 3" in height
<Other axis distance>/Rotation: 2 ⏎     Sets the distance from the ellipse
                                         center, defining an ellipse that is
                                         4" in overall width
Command: ELLIPSE ⏎
<Axis endpoint 1>/Center: C ⏎            Selects the Center option
Center of ellipse: 3.75,3 ⏎             Specifies the ellipse's center
                                         point
```

Axis endpoint: **@1.5<0** ↵	Defines an ellipse 3" in width
<Other axis distance>/Rotation: **R** ↵	Selects the Rotation option
Rotation around major axis: **48** ↵	Rotates the ellipse
Command: **QSAVE** ↵	Saves the CAMHSE drawing to the same name

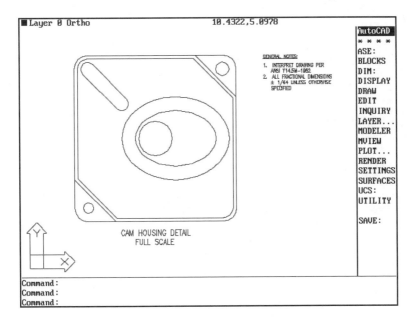

Figure 6.14:

An elliptical cam.

You can see that the ELLIPSE command provides an easy way to lay out an ellipse. To be precisely two inches high, the second ellipse should be specified with a distance of one for the second axis. To demonstrate the use of the rotation option, however, the ellipse is approximate with a rotation angle of 48 degrees. This inner ellipse needs to be trimmed, but leave it for now. You will use it as a construction entity later in the chapter.

Drawing Regular Polygons

Like the ELLIPSE command, POLYGON provides a means to draw quickly common shapes by using polylines. The POLYGON command draws regular polygons with a specified number of sides. The minimum number of sides is three (you cannot have a closed shape with fewer than three sides), and the maximum number of sides is 1,024.

POLYGON. The POLYGON command draws two-dimensional regular polygons as closed polylines. You specify the center point and whether to inscribe it within or circumscribe it about a circle, or you specify a single side. Then, you specify the number of sides (from 3 to 1,024).

POLYGON Options

- **Edge.** Size the polygon and define the location of one edge by specifying the endpoints of that edge.

- **Center of polygon.** Specify the center point of the polygon, and POLYGON prompts for the following options:

- **Inscribed in circle.** This option draws the polygon within an imaginary circle with each vertex touching the circumference.

- **Circumscribed about circle.** This option draws the polygon outside an imaginary circle, with each edge touching the circumference at its midpoint.

- **Radius of circle.** Enter the radius for the imaginary circle.

POLYGON creates a polyline entity with 0 width. You can use the PEDIT command, however, to assign a width to an existing polygon. See Chapter 8 for more information about the PEDIT command.

You can draw a polygon by using one of three methods: an edge method and two center methods. The *edge method* draws a polygon counterclockwise from an edge defined by two points that you specify. A rubber-band polygon stretches along the cursor as you move it to pick the second point of the edge.

One center method draws the polygon *inscribed* (within) or *circumscribed* (around) a circle. After picking a center point, specify inscribed or circumscribed, then specify the radius of the imaginary circle. Inscribed is sometimes referred to as drawing *across corners* because the radius is half the distance across opposite corners for a polygon with an even number of sides. Circumscribed is sometimes referred to as drawing *across flats* because the radius is one-half the distance across two opposite (flat) sides; sizing a hex bolt head involves drawing across flats.

Use the Circumscribe option of the POLYGON command to draw a hex-head bolt to the upper cam housing mounting hole. Then, erase the bolt-hole circle and replace it with another circle representing the top of the bolt. Figure 6.15 shows the result.

Using POLYGON To Draw a Hex Bolt

Continue from previous exercise.

Command: **POLYGON** ↵	
Number of sides: **6** ↵	Specifies a six-sided polygon
Edge/<Center of polygon>: **5.5,5.5** ↵	Picks the center of the bolt hole
Inscribed in circle/Circumscribed about circle (I/C): **C** ↵	Draws the polygon around an imaginary circle
Radius of circle: **.25** ↵	Gives the imaginary circle a radius of .25 units
Command: **ERASE** ↵	
Select and erase the bolt hole.	
Command: **CIRCLE** ↵	
3P/2P/TTR/<Center point>: **5.5,5.5** ↵	
Diameter/<Radius>: **.25** ↵	
Command: **QSAVE** ↵	Saves the CAMHSE drawing to the same name

---

Figure 6.15:

Adding a hex bolt head with POLY-GON.

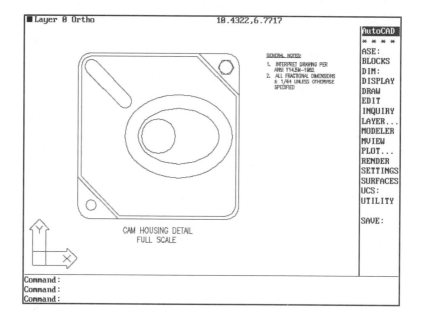

Like ELLIPSE and POLYGON, the DONUT command also creates polylines.

Drawing Donuts and Dots

Unlike ELLIPSE and POLYGON, the DONUT command draws wide polylines. Specifically, it draws a 180-degree arc segment and closes it with a second 180-degree arc segment to create a circle. The advantage of DONUT over CIRCLE is that it can draw a circle with any width of circumference line; it can look like a donut, pipe section, or washer. To make the DONUT command easy to use, you specify the inner and outer diameters of the donut, instead of having to calculate the centerline diameter of the circumference. If the inner diameter is zero, the circle appears as a filled dot.

DONUT. The DONUT or DOUGHNUT command (AutoCAD accepts both spellings) draws filled circles or rings by using a closed wide polyline arc. You specify the inside (default 0.5) and outside (default 1.0) diameters by entering a value or picking two points for each. A zero inside diameter creates a filled dot. DONUT repeats the center prompt until you cancel it or press Enter.

Although donuts can be used any time you need a filled ring or circle, they are particularly useful in printed circuit board drawings for component mounting pads and ground holes. In the next exercise, however, you use the DONUT command to draw a shaft in the middle of the cam, as illustrated in figure 6.16. First draw it hollow, then undo it and redraw it solid.

Using DONUT To Draw a Cam Shaft

Continue from the previous exercise.

```
Command:  DONUT ↵
Inside diameter <0.5000>:  1 ↵              Sets the "hole's"
                                           diameter

Outside diameter <1.0000>:  1.5 ↵          Sets the outer diameter
Center of doughnut:  3,3 ↵                 Places the donut in the drawing
Center of doughnut: Press Ctrl-C
*CANCEL*                                    Cancels the DONUT command
Command:  U ↵                              Undoes the donut you just drew
Command:  DONUT ↵
Inside diameter <1.0000>:  0 ↵
```

A radius of 0 creates a filled circle.

```
Outside diameter <1.0000>:  1.5 ↵          Sets the outer diameter
Center of doughnut:  3,3 ↵                 Places the donut in the drawing
Center of doughnut: Press Enter            Ends the DONUT command
Command:  QSAVE ↵                          Saves the CAMHSE drawing to
                                           the same name
```

By default, donuts and other wide polylines are automatically filled.

Figure 6.16:

Adding a shaft to the cam.

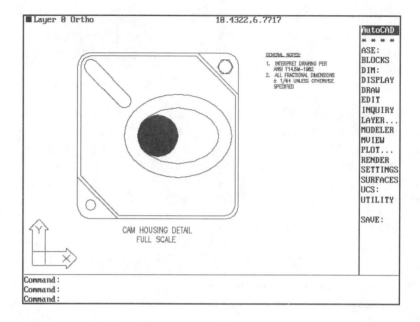

Controlling FILL

By using the FILL command, you can control whether the donut will be filled. If you have many wide polylines or filled objects in a drawing, redraw and regeneration time increases noticeably. Turning off FILL saves redraw and regeneration time.

FILL. The FILL command controls the way solids, traces, and wide polylines are displayed and plotted, filled in (the default, fill on), or as outlines only. The FILL command controls whether wide polylines, solids, and traces are displayed and plotted as filled in or as outlines. The default is On (filled in).

> **Note**
> When you change the fill setting, you do not see the change in existing entities until the drawing is regenerated.

Turn off FILL and regenerate the drawing to see how this affects the donut. The outline of the donut displays, along with radial lines indicating that the two circles are a polyline, not separate circles. Figure 6.17 shows the drawing.

Turning Off FILL with the FILL Command

Continue from the previous exercise.

```
Command: FILL ↵
ON/OFF <On>: OFF ↵                    Turns off FILL
Command: REGEN ↵
Regenerating drawing                  Displays the donut without
                                      the fill

Command: FILL ↵
ON/OFF <Off>: ON ↵                    Turns FILL back on
Command: REGEN ↵
Regenerating drawing                  Displays the donut with the fill
```

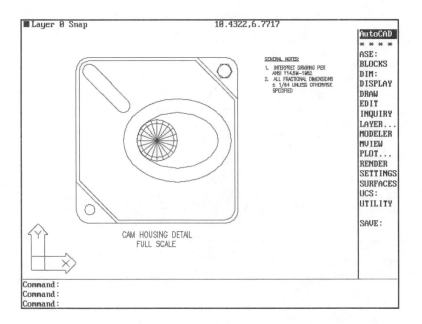

Figure 6.17:

The cam housing with FILL turned off.

Now you can add the keyway and key by using another filled entity, the solid.

Drawing Solids

The solid entity, created by the SOLID command, should not be confused with 3D solids modeling. A *solid* is a two-dimensional, three- or four-sided, filled entity.

SOLID. The SOLID command draws triangular or quadri-lateral filled areas (not AME solids). You enter points in a bow-tie fashion. Enter the first corner point; then enter two adjacent corners as points two and three. Press Enter to create a triangular solid or to specify the opposite corner as point four. If you press Enter to create a triangular solid, the fourth point is created, coincident with point three. SOLID repeats, using the previous points three and four as new points one and two, and prompts for additional points three and four to draw another contiguous solid. To exit, press Enter at the third point prompt. If FILL is on, solids are filled.

Solids are a quick way to create a filled triangle or rectangle. If you want to create a complex solid shape, use consecutive commands to attach one solid to another.

Add the key to the shaft, as shown in figure 6.18, by using the SOLID command.

Using SOLID to Add a Key to the Cam Shaft

Continue from the previous exercise.

```
Command: SOLID ⏎
First point: 2.875,2.375 ⏎          Defines the solid's first corner
Second point: @.25<0 ⏎             Defines the solid's second
                                    corner
Third point: @-.25,-.25 ⏎          Defines the solid's third corner
```

Fourth point: `@.25<0` ↵	Defines the solid's fourth corner
Third point: *Press Enter*	Ends the SOLID command
Command: **QSAVE** ↵	Saves the CAMHSE drawing to the same name

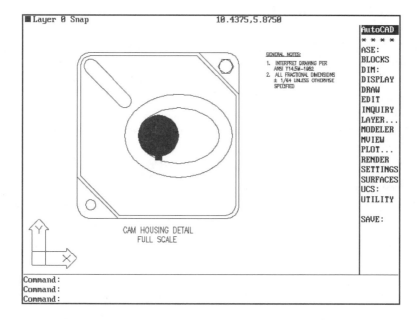

Figure 6.18:

Adding a solid key.

The TRACE command creates four-cornered, filled linear entities that have width (the width default is .05). A series of traces looks similar to straight polyline segments. Traces are individual, not continuous, entities, however. Trace entities are actually identical to solid entities, differing only in name and method of creation.

TRACE does not display each segment until after the endpoint of the next segment is entered; it needs the next endpoint to calculate the miter between adjacent segments. If FILL is on, traces are displayed as filled. Polylines are much more flexible and versatile than traces are. You can use the ENDP object snap mode to snap to the corner points and use MID to snap to the midpoints of trace edges.

Constructing Circles and Polylines

To finish the cam housing drawing, you need to add the final circle and cutout to the cam. This involves repeating the CIRCLE command. You can automate the repeating of a command with the MULTIPLE command.

MULTIPLE. The multiple command causes the next command to repeat. Just enter **MULTIPLE**, followed by a space or Enter. Then enter any other command. MULTIPLE repeats the command, but it does not repeat input, command parameters, or options. Press Ctrl-C to end a repeating command.

The inside ellipse forms part of the cutout. Finish the drawing by adding construction circles, as shown in figures 6.19 and 6.20. Use the circles as construction entities to draw a polyline around the perimeter of the cutout.

Creating Multiple Construction Circles

Continue from the previous exercise.

```
Command: MULTIPLE CIRCLE ⏎
3P/2P/TTR/<Center point>: 5.25,3 ⏎        Specifies the first circle's center
Diameter/<Radius>: .25 ⏎                   Draws a circle with a .25-unit
                                           radius
CIRCLE 3P/2P/TTR/<Center point>: 3,3 ⏎ Repeats CIRCLE
Diameter/<Radius>: 1 ⏎
CIRCLE 3P/2P/TTR/<Center point>:
5.25,3 ⏎
Diameter/<Radius>: .5 ⏎
CIRCLE 3P/2P/TTR/<Center point>: TTR ⏎ Choose Tangent-To-Radius
                                           option
Enter Tangent spec: Pick at point
① (see fig. 6.19)
Enter second Tangent spec: Pick at
point ②
```

Radius: .25 ↵

CIRCLE 3P/2P/TTR/<Center point:
TTR ↵

Enter Tangent spec: *Pick at point* ③

Enter second Tangent spec: *Pick at point* ④

Radius: .25 ↵

CIRCLE 3P/2P/TTR/<Center point>:
TTR ↵

Enter Tangent spec: *Pick at point* ⑤

Enter second Tangent spec: *Pick at point* ⑥

Radius: .25 ↵

CIRCLE 3P/2P/TTR/<Center point>:
TTR ↵

Enter Tangent spec: *Pick at point* ⑦

Enter second Tangent spec: *Pick at point* ⑧

Radius: .25 ↵

CIRCLE 3P/2P/TTR/<Center point>:
Press Ctrl-C *Cancel*

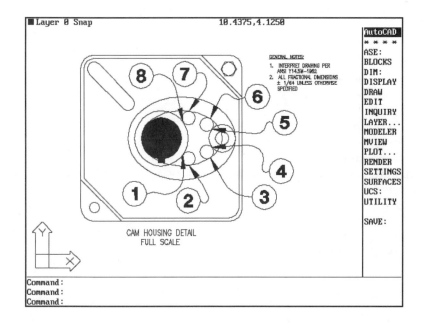

Figure 6.19:

Cutout construction circles.

Now, you have all the construction points you need to draw the cutout. Snap to the circles and inner ellipse with object snap to draw a polyline arc series around the inside perimeter of the cutout. Set a radius for the first arc segment. The rest of the arcs need only endpoints because they will be a continuous series of tangents. If you pick the right points, you do not see the polyline as you draw it because it overlays the construction entities exactly. When you erase the construction circles and the inside ellipse, you see the polyline cutout.

Tracing the Construction Circles with a Polyline

Command: **OSNAP** ⏎ | Sets a running mode
Object snap modes: **INT** ⏎ | Specifies the INTersection object snap

Command: **PLINE** ⏎
From point: *Pick point* ①
(see fig. 6.20)
Current line-width is 0.0000
Arc/Close/Halfwidth/Length/Undo/ | Selects the Arc option
Width/<Endpoint of line>: **A** ⏎
Angle/CEnter/CLose/Direction/ | Selects the Radius option
Halfwidth/Line/Radius/Second pt/
Undo/Width/<Endpoint of arc>: **R** ⏎
Radius: **.25** ⏎
Angle/<Endpoint>: *Pick point* ②
Angle/CEnter/CLose/Direction/
Halfwidth/Line/Radius/Second pt/
Undo/Width/<Endpoint of arc>:
Pick point ③
Angle/CEnter/CLose/Direction/
Halfwidth/Line/Radius/Second pt/
Undo/Width/<Endpoint of arc>:
Pick point ④
Angle/CEnter/CLose/Direction/
Halfwidth/Line/Radius/Second pt/
Undo/Width/<Endpoint of arc>:
Pick point ⑤

```
Angle/CEnter/CLose/Direction/
Halfwidth/Line/Radius/Second pt
/Undo/Width/<Endpoint of arc>:
```
Pick point ⑥
```
Angle/CEnter/CLose/Direction/
Halfwidth/Line/Radius/Second pt/
Undo/Width/<Endpoint of arc>:
```
Pick point ⑦
```
Angle/CEnter/CLose/Direction/
Halfwidth/Line/Radius/Second pt/
Undo/Width/<Endpoint of arc>:
```
Pick point ⑧

```
Angle/CEnter/CLose/Direction/          Closes the polyline
Halfwidth/Line/Radius/Second pt/
Undo/Width/<Endpoint of arc>: CL ⏎
```

Command: **ERASE** ⏎

Select objects: *Select all the*
construction entities

Select objects: *Press Enter*

Command: **REDRAW** ⏎

Command: **END** ⏎   Saves the drawing and exits
                                          AutoCAD

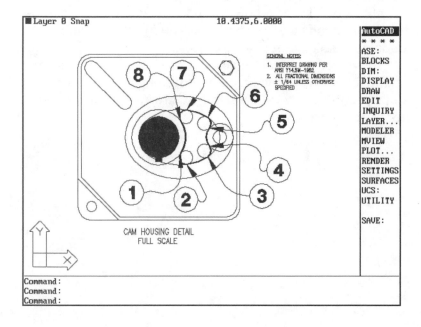

Figure 6.20:

Polyline construction.

Your cam housing drawing is now complete.

Summary

You now know how to use all of AutoCAD's primary drawing commands. You know several ways to draw circles and even more ways to specify arcs. You can choose efficiently from a wide range of tools and use the options that suit your particular application. You can rapidly draw a complex shape as a single polyline entity by using PLINE, ELLIPSE, POLYGON, and DONUT, and you can now control the filling of wide polylines and solid objects to speed up redraws.

You can annotate your drawing quickly and efficiently by using the DTEXT command, and you can control the placement and justification of the text with a multitude of text options. You can edit text with the Ddedit dialog box. When you need text that is fancier than the default, you can use the STYLE command to choose from a variety of text fonts and to modify them to suit your own style.

You can now draw just about anything, but you can still work more efficiently. In the following chapters, you will learn to use editing commands to correct mistakes and to make changes without undoing and replacing objects. You will see that editing can also be used for creating objects. You will also learn to annotate drawings with automated dimensioning and to work with groups of entities, symbols, or entire drawings as blocks and external references.

Enhancing and Correcting Your Work

In this chapter, you learn to set up and organize your drawing and to make changes and corrections without redrawing. This chapter teaches you how to do the following operations:

- Add color and linetypes to objects, using colors to indicate different lineweights for plotter pens

- Organize objects, colors, and linetypes in layers, much like manual overlay drafting

- Change the layer, color, and linetype of entities

- Create selection sets using a variety of selective and efficient methods

- Undo and redo any number of commands to try out alternatives and to correct mistakes

- Break and trim portions of entities; extend, shorten, and move entities; and change the rotation angle and size of entities

- Edit drawing text

- Explode polylines and blocks into individual entities

- Change construction lines into finished objects

Overview

The previous chapters are somewhat unrealistic. For the most part, they assume that you do not make mistakes, that you never need to modify your drawings, and that your drawings are so simple you do not need to use different linetypes or lineweights. In the real world, however, you do have to modify your drawings, and cosmetics are extremely important.

In Chapter 4, you learned about AutoCAD's new Autoedit feature, which enables you to stretch, move, rotate, scale, mirror, and copy objects without entering commands. You also learned about DDMODIFY, which lets you make changes in geometry and in the properties of entities using a dialog box. Autoedit and DDMODIFY suffice for most of your changes in geometry and properties, but they do not handle all editing tasks. This chapter presents the traditional editing commands for those occasions when Autoedit and DDMODIFY will not fill the bill.

Most editing commands modify the entities in a selection set, as you discovered when you used the ERASE command. In this chapter, you learn a bit more about selection sets, including additional ways you can create them.

You also learn to use layers, colors, and linetypes to enhance your drawings and make them convey more information. Figure 7.1 shows the enhanced drawing you can complete by the chapter's end.

Before you begin editing, draw a cam housing using commands you learned in earlier chapters.

Drawing the Cam Housing

Launch AutoCAD from the AB directory, and begin a NEW drawing named CAMHS2.

Command: **ZOOM** ↵
*Use Window and draw a window
from 1.5,1.5 to 10.5,8.5
Set UCS Origin at 2,2*

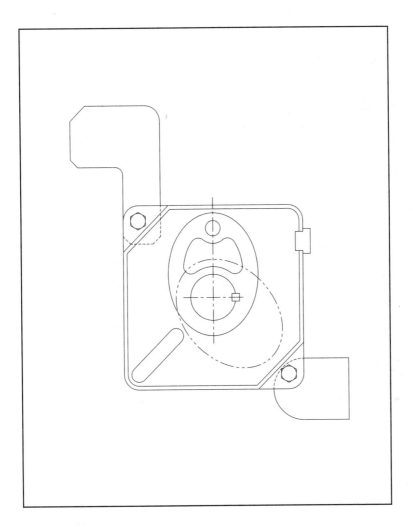

Figure 7.1:
The cam housing.

Command: **UCSICON** ⏎

Set to ORigin

Command: **SNAP** ⏎

Set snap to 0.0625

Command: **GRID**

Set grid to 0.5

*Use PLINE and draw the
outer perimeter from point
.5,0 to @5,0 then use option
and points: Arc to @.5,.5 Line*

to @0,5 Arc to @-.5,.5 Line to
@-5,0 Arc to @-.5,-.5 Line to
@0,-5 and Arc to Close.

Use PLINE and draw the inner
wall from point 1.5625,.125 to
@3.9375,0 then Arc to @.375,.375
Line to @0,3.9375 to @-1.4375,1.4375
to @-3.9375,0 Arc to @-.375,-.375
Line to @0,-3.9375 and Close

Next, draw a cam follower slot.

Use CIRCLE and draw a circle at
1.75,4.25 with radius 0.25

Use CIRCLE and draw a circle at
0.5,5.5 with radius 0.25

Command: OSNAP ⏎

Set the running snap mode to TAN

Use LINE and draw a line tangent
from the lower left of top circle
to lower left of bottom circle

Use LINE and draw a line tangent
from the upper right of top circle
to upper right of bottom circle

Command: OSNAP ⏎

Set OSNAP back to NON

Use CIRCLE and draw a circle that
has a center point of 3,3 and a
radius of 0.75

Command: ELLIPSE ⏎

<Axis endpoint 1>/Center: *Pick 3.75,1.5*

Axis endpoint 2: *Pick at 3<90*

<Other axis distance>/Rotation: 2 ⏎

Command: ELLIPSE ⏎

<Axis endpoint 1>/Center: C ⏎   Selects the Center option

Center of ellipse: *Pick 3.75,3*

Axis endpoint: *Pick at 1.5<0*

<Other axis distance>/Rotation: 1 ⏎

Command: QSAVE ⏎   Saves the drawing to the same
name

Selecting Entities for Editing

You learned a little about selection sets when you learned to use the ERASE command. Most AutoCAD editing commands generate the same `Select objects:` prompt. Recall that a selection set is a group of entities that you select. As you build a selection set, AutoCAD highlights the selected entities. After you finish building a selection set, tell AutoCAD to act on the set by pressing Enter. In the case of the ERASE command, AutoCAD then erases all the entities in the set. Most editing commands work this way—you identify entities, then direct AutoCAD to perform some action on those entities.

Options for Selecting Entities

So far, you have only selected entities by picking them using a small square cursor called the pick box. You might have noticed, however, that the screen menu for commands that use selection sets includes additional options.

Selection Set Options

- **(Pick with pick box).** This option selects a single object using the pick box (the default).

- **ALL.** This option selects all objects in the drawing.

- **Add.** The Add option enters Add mode (the default). Subsequently selected objects are added to the selection set.

- **Crossing.** Specify two corner points to select all objects within or touching a window specified by two corner points.

- **Fence.** Draw an open polyline, or *fence*, through the objects you want to select. AutoCAD selects the objects the fence crosses. The fence can cross itself.

- **Implied.** Same as Box option.

- **Last.** The Last option selects the last object created.

- **Cpoly.** Draws a closed, irregular polygon. AutoCAD selects all objects entirely or partially enclosed by the polygon. Similar to the Crossing option.

- **Wpoly.** Draws a closed, irregular polygon. AutoCAD selects only those objects entirely enclosed by the polygon. Similar to the Window option.

- **Multiple.** The Multiple option enables you to select multiple entities without finding the same entity twice. It does not highlight the entities until you press Enter at a `Select objects:` prompt.

- **Previous.** The Previous option selects all objects from the previous selection set.

- **Window.** Specify two corner points so that you can select all objects completely contained within a window.

- **BOX.** This option combines Window and Crossing. Pick the second corner point to the right of the first for Window; pick it to the left for Crossing. This option is used primarily in menu items.

- **AUto.** The AUto option combines the default (pick using pick box) with BOX. It picks a single entity and returns to the `Select objects:` prompt, or it acts like the BOX option if the first pick misses all entities. The AUto option is primarily used in menu items.

- **SIngle.** The SIngle option enters single mode and repeats the `Select objects:` prompt. SIngle mode places AutoCAD into a mode in which the first successful object selection closes the selection set and continues the command. It exits object selection as soon as any object or group of objects is selected. The SIngle option is primarily used in menu items.

- **Remove.** The Remove option enters Remove mode. Remove enables you to remove selected objects from the selection set currently being created.

- **Undo.** The Undo option removes the last selection that added (or removed) entities to the selection set.

- **Press Enter.** Press Enter to complete and exit object selection.

- **Filters.** Filters objects from the selection set based on entity type, location, and properties.

You can build a selection set by using any and all of these options interactively. For example, to select all but one entity in an area, you could select all entities in a window by using the Window option, then pick the entity to exclude by using the Remove mode.

Set the PICKBOX system variable to change the pick box's size if it is too large or too small.

Except for Previous, object selections consider only those entities visible in the current viewport. You can, however, zoom transparently and switch viewports during object selection.

You might have noticed that the BOX, AUto, Multiple, and SIngle options do not show up in any of AutoCAD's menus, nor do any options appear in the Select objects: prompt. If you enter an incorrect response to the Select objects: prompt, however, you see a list of all available options, such as in the following example:

```
Select objects: ABC ↵
Invalid selection*
Expects a point or Window/Last/Crossing/BOX/Add/Remove/Multiple/
Previous/Undo/AUto/SIngle
```

Preparing Some Circles for Editing

In the following exercise, you create some construction circles that you can use to experiment with some editing commands. Later, you can edit these circles into the cam's cutout. Then you add the shaft key using a polyline.

Drawing TTR Circles for the Cam Cutout

Continue from the previous exercise.

Command: ZOOM ↵
Set ZOOM Center point at 4,3
with height 3.5

Command: MULTIPLE CIRCLE ↵

3P/2P/TTR/<Center point>:
Draw at 3,3 with radius 1

CIRCLE 3P/2P/TTR/<Center point>:
Draw at 5.25,3 with radius 0.25

CIRCLE 3P/2P/TTR/<Center point>: @   Draws at same point,
                                          with radius 0.5

CIRCLE 3P/2P/TTR/<Center point>: .5,.5
with radius 0.1875

CIRCLE 3P/2P/TTR/<Center point>: 5.5,5.5
with radius 0.1875

CIRCLE 3P/2P/TTR/<Center point>: TTR ↵
Use Tangent-To-Radius *to pick* ①
and ② *(see fig. 7.2), radius 0.25*

CIRCLE 3P/2P/TTR/<Center point>: TTR ↵
Pick TTR points ③ *and* ④*, radius 0.25*

CIRCLE 3P/2P/TTR/<Center point>: TTR ↵
Pick TTR points ⑤ *and* ⑥*, radius 0.25*

CIRCLE 3P/2P/TTR/<Center point>: TTR ↵
Pick TTR points ⑦ *and* ⑧*, radius 0.25*

CIRCLE 3P/2P/TTR/<Center point>: *Press*   Exits CIRCLE
*Ctrl-C *Cancel**   command

Command: ZOOM ↵
Use Previous *option*

Command: QSAVE ↵   Saves the drawing to
                                             the same name

You now are ready to edit your drawing by using the SELECT command.

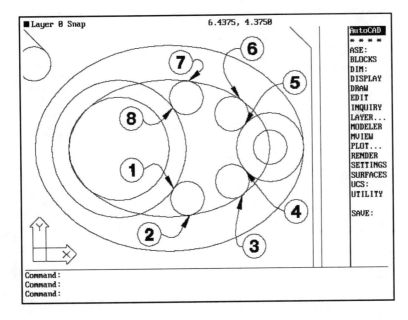

Figure 7.2:
Circle pick points.

Using SELECT for Selection Sets

When you use an editing command such as ERASE, COPY, or MOVE, AutoCAD prompts you for a selection set. You can, however, create a selection set without using an editing command.

SELECT. The SELECT command creates a selection set that you can later recall by using the Previous object-selection option.

Using Window and Crossing Object Selection

If you select the Window or the Crossing options, AutoCAD prompts you to identify two corner points of a box, which AutoCAD rubber-bands as you select the points. The Window option places all entities that are *completely* inside the box into the selection set. The Crossing option places all entities that are inside or *cross* (touch) the box in the selection set (see fig. 7.3).

Figure 7.3:

A window and crossing box and the entities they select.

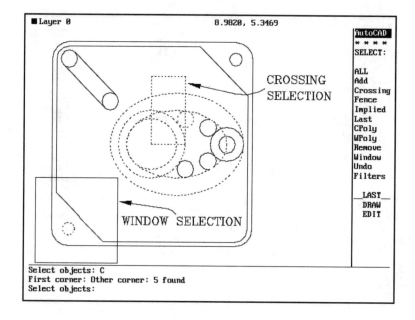

Using the SELECT Command with Window and Crossing Options

Continue from the preceding exercise.

From the screen menu, choose EDIT,
then NEXT, then SELECT

Select objects: *Pick at point -0.5,-0.5*

Other corner: *Pick at point 2,2*

1 found   Highlights bolt hole

By selecting a window from left to right, you used the window option. Only objects that fit entirely within the window were selected.

Select objects: *Pick at point 4,5*

Other corner: *Pick at point 3,3*

5 found   Highlights ellipses, center
                                                 circles, and one small circle

By selecting a window from right to left, you used the crossing option. Every object inside or crossing the box is selected.

Continue object selection in the next exercise.

The AUto and BOX options combine both Window and Crossing.

Using AUto and BOX Object Selection

The BOX option combines the Window and Crossing options; the AUto option combines the pick, Window, and Crossing options. (see fig. 7.4).

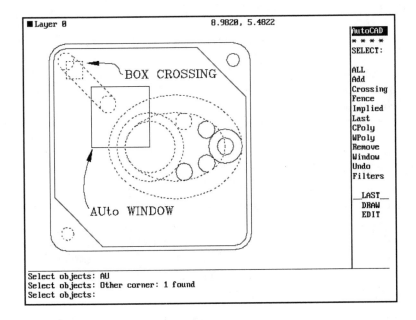

Figure 7.4:

A crossing BOX and AUto window and selected objects.

Selecting Using AUto and BOX

Continue object selection from the preceding exercise.

`Select objects:` **BOX** ⏎   Specifies the Box object selection
                                mode

`First corner:` *Pick at point 1,5*

`Other corner:` *Move cursor to right and notice solid window box. Move cursor to left and notice dashed crossing box. Pick crossing style at point 0.5,5.5*

```
3 found                              Selects upper circle and two
                                     lines of cam follower slot

Select objects: AU ↵                 Selects Auto
Select objects: Pick at 1.25,4.75
```

Notice the pick box. If you pick an object, it is selected. Otherwise, you get an `Other corner:` prompt.

`Other corner:` *Move cursor to left and right and notice dashed crossing and solid window boxes. Then, pick window-style at 3,3*

```
1 found                              Highlights lower circle of cam
                                     follower slot

Select objects: Press Enter          Completes object selection and
                                     exits
```

Continue to the next exercise without ending.

Using Previous Object Selection

You can have only one selection set at a time. When you create a new set, it replaces the previous set. You still can use the previous set while you are selecting entities for the new one, however. When you use the Previous option, AutoCAD takes the entire contents of the previous selection set and adds it to the current set.

Selecting Using Previous

Continue from the preceding exercise, in which you completed an object selection.

```
Command: LINE ↵
```
Draw a line from 0.0,-0.375 to @8<0, for later use
```
Command: SELECT ↵
Select objects: P ↵                  Reselects the Previous selection set
10 found                             Highlights all the objects from
                                     the previous Select exercise series
```

Continue object selection in the next exercise.

Now add the line you just drew to the set.

Using Last Object Selection

The Last option is similar to Previous, but it selects the *last visible entity* created, not the previous selection set. No matter how many other commands you have used in the meantime, even if you end and reopen the drawing, Last recalls the last visible entity created.

Selecting Using Last

Continue from the preceding exercise, in which you selected Previous.

`Select objects: L ⏎`	Specifies the Last object selection mode
`1 found`	Highlights the line from previous exercise

Continue object selection in the next exercise.

In the next section, remove the bolt head and base line of the bracket from the selection set.

Adding to and Removing Entities from a Selection Set

As you build a selection set, you might pick an entity that you do not want in the selection set. Or, you might want to select part of the previous selection set. You can use the Remove option to remove the unwanted entities from the set you are building.

The two modes available when selecting entities are Add and Remove. You begin building a set in the Add mode—each entity or group of entities you select is added to the set. You enter the Remove option to delete one or more entities from the set. AutoCAD stays in Remove mode until you enter the Add option, to return to the Add mode.

Adding and Removing Entities

Select objects: R ↵	Selects the Remove option
Remove objects: *Pick the lower left bolt hole*	
1 found, 1 removed	Removes the bolt hole from the select set
Remove objects: *Pick the bolt hole again*	
1 found	

If it does not say 1 removed, it is already removed

Remove objects: *Pick the base line of the bracket at 0,-0.375*	
1 found, 1 removed	
Remove objects: A ↵	Returns to the default Add mode prompt
Select objects: *Pick the lower left bolt hole*	Adds the bolt hole back again
1 found	

Continue object selection in the next exercise.

Figure 7.5:

Bolt head removed from previous set.

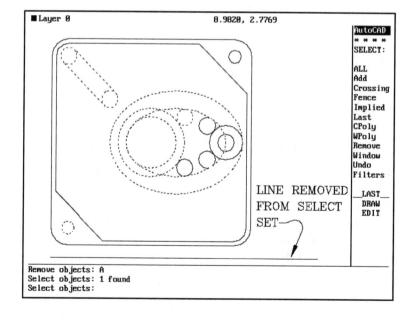

Using Multiple Object Selection

Object selection using the pick box always finds the most recently created entity in the pick box. In the preceding exercise, the new line was found instead of the bracket base line "under" it.

The Multiple option enables you to pick any number of entities, one after the other. Multiple does not find the same object twice or reprompt. At each pick point, it finds the most recent, next most recent, and so on. It does not highlight the selected objects until you press Enter to exit Multiple mode and return to the `Select objects:` prompt.

You cannot use other options in Multiple mode. AutoCAD will exit Multiple if you try to use it with another option and have not yet picked anything.

Selecting Multiple Objects

Continue from the preceding exercise using its open selection set.

`Select objects: R ↵`	Selects the Remove option
`Remove objects: M ↵`	Selects the Multiple option
`Remove objects:` *Pick the new line at 0,-.375, the lower left circle twice, and press Enter*	
`2 selected, 1 found`	

The line cannot be removed because it is not selected.

`Remove objects: A ↵`	Selects the Add option
`Select objects: L ↵`	Selects the Last option
`1 found`	Adds the newer line back to the set
`Select objects:` *Press Enter*	Ends object selection
`Command: ERASE ↵`	
Erase the new line at 0,-.375	

Note that the Select command options are common to all editing commands that present the `Select objects:` prompt.

Shift to Add

If you are accustomed to using Macintosh computers or Microsoft Windows, you can configure AutoCAD to select objects in a similar manner—using Shift to Add as explained in Chapter 4. The Remove option works if Shift to Add is active, but you can add objects to the selection set only by pressing and holding the Shift key while you use any one of the selection options.

Click and Drag

Windows and crossing boxes are entered with two picks—one at each end of a diagonal—or by holding down the pick button and dragging the window. The first mode is the normal mode, and the second mode is the Click and Drag Mode. Both the Shift to Add and Click and Drag modes are controlled by the Entity Selection Settings dialog box described in Chapter 4.

Modifying a Drawing Using Editing Commands

The rest of this chapter deals with editing commands: commands that help you correct errors, complete change orders and revisions, and simplify laying out and creating drawings.

Using TRIM To Shorten Entities

The TRIM command enables you to use entities, such as lines, arcs, circles, and polylines, as cutting edges to trim off portions of other entities.

TRIM. The TRIM command removes portions of lines, arcs, circles, and 2D polylines that cross a cutting edge. You can use lines, circles, arcs, and polylines as cutting edges. An entity can act as a cutting edge *and* be an entity to trim.

Use normal object selection to create the selection set of cutting edges. Then use the pick box to select the part of each entity you want to trim off. The Undo option restores the last entity trimmed.

 If an entity crosses two or more cutting edges, you can trim one end in steps. The first pick trims the entity to the first edge; a second pick trims it to the next cutting edge.

Trim the circles' inner parts to finish making the cam follower slot. Then create the housing's lower-left outer wall diagonal by drawing it long and trimming it to fit between the housing perimeter's outer polyline.

Using the TRIM Command

Continue from the preceding exercise.

```
Command: LINE ↵
```
Draw a line from 0,1.5 to @3<315

Choose Modify, *then* Trim

```
Select cutting edge(s)...
```
Select outer polyline and two lines of cam follower slot with a Crossing window from ① to ② (see fig. 7.6)

```
4 found
```
The extra polyline does not hurt.

```
Select objects: Return Enter
<Select object to trim>/Undo:
```
Pick lower right side of upper left circle

```
<Select object to trim>/Undo: Pick
```
upper left side of lower right circle

285

```
<Select object to trim>/Undo: Pick
lower right end of new line
<Select object to trim>/Undo: Press Enter      Ends the TRIM command
Command: QSAVE ⏎                                Saves the drawing to the
                                                same name
```

Figure 7.6:

Relocated UCS and crossing window selection for TRIM.

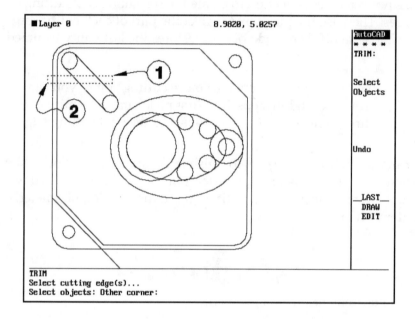

Figure 7.7:

Cam follower slot and diagonal of housing after TRIM.

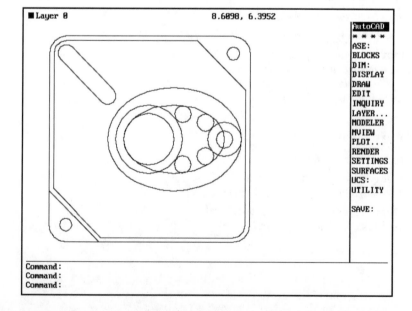

You can use the TRIM command to trim construction geometry so that it is a part of the finished drawing. The circles and line in this case act as construction geometry for the arcs and finished line that result from the TRIM command. TRIM also is great for cleaning up wall intersections.

Try some more trims to turn the construction circles of the cam cutout into the finished cutout. Then trim the center shaft circle at the key.

Trimming Circles To Make a Cam Cutout

Use ZOOM and zoom at Center point 4,3 with height 3

Choose Modify, *then* Trim

Select cutting edge(s)...

Select objects:
Select Crossing window from 5,4 to 3,2

Select objects: *Press Enter*

<Select object to trim>/Undo: *Pick circle at ① (see fig. 7.8)*

<Select object to trim>/Undo: *Pick circle at ②*

<Select object to trim>/Undo: *Pick circle at ③*

<Select object to trim>/Undo: *Pick circle at ④*

<Select object to trim>/Undo: *Pick circle at ⑤*

<Select object to trim>/Undo: *Pick arc remaining from last circle at ⑥*

<Select object to trim>/Undo: *Pick other end of arc at ⑦*

<Select object to trim>/Undo: *Pick circle at ⑧*

<Select object to trim>/Undo: *Pick arc remaining from last circle at ⑨*

<Select object to trim>/Undo: *Pick other end of arc at ⑩*

```
<Select object to trim>/Undo: Press Enter
Command: ZOOM ↵
Use the Previous option
Command: QSAVE ↵
```
Saves the drawing to the same name

Figure 7.8:

Pick points for trimming cam cutout circles.

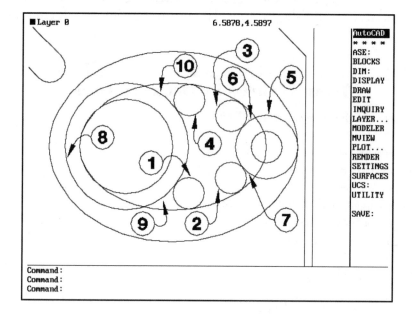

The results should look like figure 7.9.

Using EXTEND

EXTEND lets you lengthen lines, arcs, and open polylines to meet *boundary edges*. Like TRIM, you can use EXTEND to turn construction lines into finished geometry. EXTEND is great for stretching a line while maintaining its original angle or extending an arc that does not sweep as far as needed.

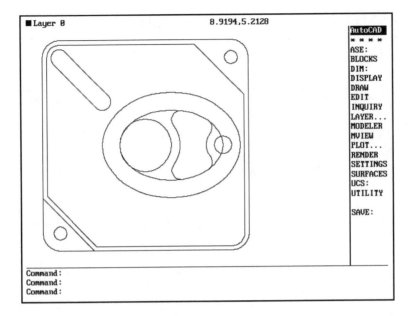

EXTEND. The EXTEND command lengthens selected lines, arcs, and open polylines to meet a selected boundary edge. You can use lines, arcs, circles, and polylines as boundary edges. You can select an entity as both a boundary edge and as an entity to extend.

Use normal object selection to create the selection set of boundary edges. Then use the pick box to select the part of each entity you want to extend. The Undo option restores the last entity extended to its original length.

If an entity crosses two or more boundary edges, you can extend it in steps. The first pick extends the entity to the first edge. A second pick extends it to the next boundary edge.

Wide polylines are extended on their centerlines; they have square ends even if diagonal to the boundary edge.

Use EXTEND to help create the upper-right diagonal line of the housing's outer wall by drawing it short and extending it to the housing perimeter's outer polyline (see fig. 7.10).

Figure 7.10:

Line after EXTEND.

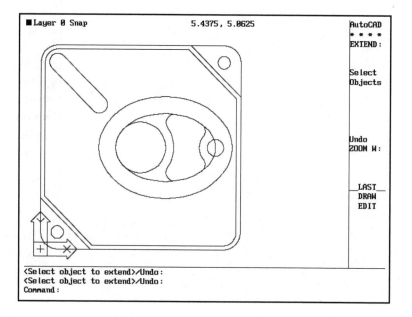

Using the EXTEND Command

Command: `LINE` ↵

Draw a line from 5,5.5 to 5.5,5

Choose Modify, *then* Extend

`Select objects:` *Pick the outer*
polyline perimeter

`1 selected, 1 found`

`Select objects:` *Press Enter*   Ends object selection

`<Select object to extend>/Undo:` *Pick one*
end of the new line

`<Select object to extend>/Undo:` *Pick*
other end of the new line

`<Select object to extend>/Undo:` *Press Enter*   Ends the EXTEND
                                                        command

Command: `QSAVE` ↵   Saves the drawing to the
                                                        same name

EXTEND is useful when laying out drawing geometry and when making changes. Another useful editing command for changes and layout is the BREAK command.

Using BREAK

Like TRIM, you use the BREAK command to remove a portion of an entity. Instead of using other entities as a cutting edge, however, you pick points on the entity to break out a portion. You can remove a portion of an open entity from the interior or from one end. Removing an interior portion of one open entity leaves two separate entities in the drawing. Removing part of a circle transforms it into an arc.

BREAK. The BREAK command erases portions of entities between two specified points. You can break lines, circles, arcs, traces, and 2D polylines. The point you pick to select an object to break becomes the default first break point, but you can use the F option to respecify the first point.

BREAK Options

- **Select object.** Select the object to break. AutoCAD assumes that the pick point of your object selection is the first break point unless you enter **F** (first point) and respecify the first break point. If you use other object selection modes, AutoCAD breaks the most recent entity found. You are prompted for the first break point.

- **F.** Enter an **F**, and AutoCAD prompts for the first break point. If you repick the first point off the entity, it acts like an object snap (NEArest).

- **Enter second point.** Specify the break's second point. If you pick off the entity, Break acts like an object snap (NEArest). If you pick beyond the end of an entity, the entire end is removed.

Note | Circles break counterclockwise from first to second point. If you reverse the points, you end up with the opposite section of the circle. You cannot break closed polylines across the first vertex. If you try, you end up with the opposite part of the polyline.

Use the BREAK command to help draw an oil drain plug in the housing wall. Use the F option when you issue the second BREAK command, and pick points that demonstrate that they need not be on the entity. (Do not bother with the detail of threads on the plug or hole.)

Breaking Polylines

Continue from the preceding exercise.

Choose Modify, *then* Break,
then Select Object, 2nd Point

`Select object:` *Pick point 4.5,0
on the outer polyline*

`Enter second point (or F for first point):` *Pick point 5.125,0*

Choose Modify, *then* Break, *then* Select Objects, Two Point

`Select object:` *Pick anywhere on the inner polyline*

`Enter second point (or F for first point):` *First*

`Enter first point:` *Pick 4.5,0 again*

`Enter second point:` *Pick point 5.125,0 again*

`Command:` `PLINE` ⏎

*Draw the plug from 4.5,.25 to
points @.25<270, @-.09375,0, @.25<270,
@.8125,0, @.25<90, @-.09375,0, @.25<90 and* Close

The results of the exercise are shown in figure 7.11.

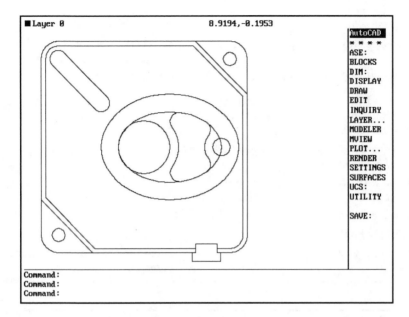

Figure 7.11:

Drain hole and plug.

Now use the BREAK command to remove the excess of the inner polyline ellipse. Take care to snap to the ellipse itself using object snap mode, or it might find a vertex instead of the desired point. If you pick the second point beyond the end, you break off the end of an entity. You do not need to pick the exact end point.

Breaking an Ellipse

Command: ZOOM ↲

Zoom to center point 4,3 with height 3.5

Command: BREAK ↲

Select object: *Pick inner ellipse anywhere*

Enter second point
(or F for first point): F

Reprompts for first point

Enter first point: *Use the* ENDP *object snap mode to pick upper left arc of cutout at ① (see fig. 7.12), avoiding ellipse*

Enter second point: *Use the* ENDP *object snap mode to pick lower left arc of cutout at ②, avoiding ellipse*

Command: *Press Enter*   Repeats command

BREAK Select object: L ↵   Selects the polyline created by
                                   the previous ellipse break

Notice that the former ellipse is now two entities.

Enter first point: *Use the* ENDP
*object snap mode to pick arc of cutout
at* ③, *near highlighted entity*

Enter second point: *Pick anywhere beyond
end of highlighted entity*

Repeat BREAK *for other end of former
ellipse at* ④

Command: ZOOM ↵

Select the Previous option

Command: QSAVE ↵   Saves the drawing to the same
                                   name

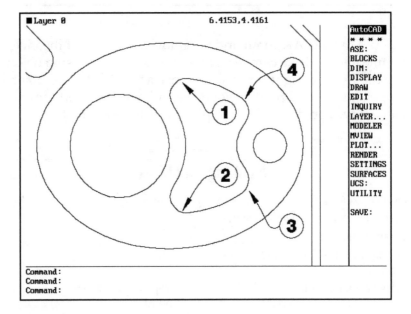

 Enter @ (last point) for the second break point to break an
entity in two at a single point.

Most of your drawing is now roughed out. Assume, however, that you must make some changes to the drawing. For example, you must shorten the cam follower slot by one-half inch, rotate the cam to check clearance, and make the bracket larger. To do these edits, you use AutoCAD's STRETCH, ROTATE, and SCALE commands.

Working with STRETCH

In Chapter 2, you drew a shear plate without regard to accuracy, and then you learned techniques to draw the same part accurately. You often know the general shape of a component early in the design phase, but cannot determine the exact dimensions until later. With AutoCAD, you can draw the component approximately, and then "stretch" it to the correct dimensions. You can stretch the cam follower slot, for example, using the STRETCH command.

STRETCH. The STRETCH command stretches entities that cross a crossing window. You can stretch lines, arcs, solids, traces, polylines (including all polyline and polyface meshes), and 3Dfaces. For stretchable entities, end points that lie inside the crossing window are moved while end points outside the window remain fixed. All entities entirely in the window move, and text, blocks, shapes, and circles move if their insert or center points are in the window.

STRETCH Options

- **Select objects.** Select the objects to stretch by using a crossing window. If you use Window, the items selected are moved, not stretched. Only the last Window or Crossing selection is recognized if you select more than one. Other forms of object selection highlight, but they are ignored.

- **Base point.** Specify the stretch displacement's *from* point.

- **New point.** Specify the stretch displacement's *to* point. You can specify a relative displacement by using any point as the base point and entering *@dist<angle* or *@X,Y* at the new point prompt.

To stretch an object, you use a Crossing window to select the end point or entity reference points you want to move (centers of circles and arcs or block and text insert points, for example). If an entity extends outside the box, the points outside the box remain fixed as the entity is stretched. Any entities completely inside the box are moved, rather than stretched (all points are moved the same distance).

> **Note** If you select Stretch from the screen or pull-down menu, it automatically uses the Crossing option. If you enter the command from the keyboard, you have to enter the C manually.

Use the STRETCH command to stretch the cam follower slot. You also set a Mark using the UNDO command, for later use and explanation.

Stretching the Cam Follower Slot

Continue from the preceding exercise.

Command: **UNDO** ⏎

Auto/Back/Control/End/Group
/Mark/<number>: **M** ⏎

Choose Modify, *then* Stretch.
*Stretch the follower slot 1/2",
reducing its length*

Select objects: **-C**   Selects Crossing

First corner: *Pick at point*
① *(see fig. 7.13)*

Other corner: *Pick at point* ②

3 found

Select objects: *Press Enter*

Base point or displacement: *Pick a point near
the arc's center*

Move the cursor and see how the
entities stretch on the screen

New point: @.5<135 ↵

Command: QSAVE ↵   Saves the drawing to the same
                                     name

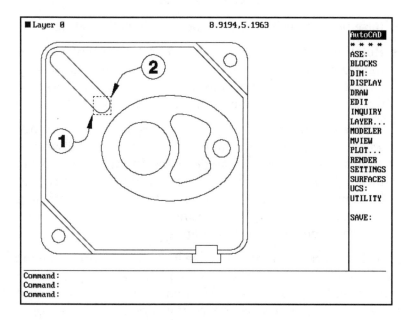

Figure 7.13:

Pick points for
stretching the cam
follower slot.

The stretch caught the phantom ellipse, but it was unaffected
because it was a block. A block cannot be stretched, it can only be
moved. And it is moved only if its insertion point is inside the
Crossing box.

Now, rotate the cam to see its clearance and alignment with the
slot.

Using the ROTATE Command

See how far the cam extends along the cam follower shaft by
lining up the elliptical cam's longitudinal centerline with the
follower slot. To do so, use the ROTATE command to rotate the
cam 135° counterclockwise.

ROTATE. The ROTATE command rotates entities in the X,Y plane around a specified base point using a relative rotation angle that you enter or a reference angle that you indicate by picking points.

ROTATE Options

- **Base point.** Specify the point about which the entities rotate.

- **Rotation angle.** Specify the angle to rotate the entities from their current orientation. You can enter an angle or specify two points to show the angle. A positive angle rotates counterclockwise and a negative angle rotates clockwise.

- **Reference.** Enter an **R** to get a `Reference angle <0>:` prompt, so you can specify the rotation as the difference between two angles. You can enter an angle or specify two points to show the angle. Then, you get a `New angle:` prompt with a rubber-band line anchored to the base point. You can enter an angle or specify a point to show the angle. The objects rotate by the difference between the two angles.

ROTATE is an easy command to use in its simple form. You build a selection set of entities to be rotated, pick a base point, and specify a rotation angle. AutoCAD then rotates the entities accordingly. The more elaborate reference angle method is good for aligning the rotated entities at a specific angle from existing geometry.

Try rotating the cam around the slot as shown in figure 7.14.

Using the ROTATE Command To Rotate the Cam

Continue from the preceding exercise.

Choose Modify, *then* Rotate

`Select objects:` *Pick from 1.5,1.5*
to 6,4.5

`Select objects:` *Press Enter*

`Base point:` `CEN` ⏎
Pick the shaft circle

<Rotation angle>/Reference: *Drag the cursor and see the image rotate, then enter* 135

Command: QSAVE ↵   Saves the drawing to the same name

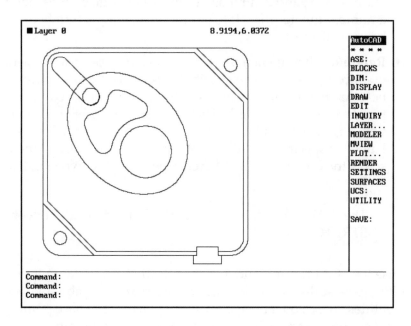

Figure 7.14:
Rotating the cam.

Rotating the cam is that easy. You rotate the cam back into its original position a little later. Next, change the bracket's size.

Resizing Entities Using SCALE

The last revision is to increase the bracket size by 25 percent. You could erase and redraw it, but you can enlarge the existing geometry using the SCALE command.

SCALE. The SCALE command changes the size of existing entities relative to a specified base point, by a specified scale factor, or relative to a specified reference distance.

SCALE Options

- **Base point.** Specify the point that remains fixed as the entities shrink or expand around it.

- **Scale factor.** Specify a positive value to multiply the selected entities' X, Y, and Z dimensions by. To enlarge entities, enter a number greater than 1; to shrink them, enter a number between 0 and 1.

- **Reference.** If you enter an R, Scale returns a Reference length <1>: prompt, so you can specify the scale as the difference between two lengths. You can enter a length or specify two points to show the length. Then you get a New length: prompt with a rubber-band line anchored to the base point. Enter a length or specify a point to show the length, AutoCAD then scales the objects by the difference between the two lengths.

 Note The X, Y, or Z values cannot be scaled independently—use STRETCH instead.

To use the SCALE command, build a selection set containing the entities to be scaled up or down, specify a base point about which the entities are scaled, and specify a scale factor. The base point is an *anchor* point—it remains fixed. All other points are moved away from or toward the base point.

Use SCALE to change the bracket size.

Scaling Entities Using SCALE

Continue from the preceding exercise.

Choose Modify, *then* Scale

Select objects: *Pick -0.5,1.5
to 4.5,6.5*

Other corner: 15 found

Select objects: *Press Enter*

Base point: CEN ↵

of *Pick the shaft circle*

`<Scale factor>/Reference:` *Move the cursor, watching the entities change size, then enter* `.9`

`Command: `**`UNDO`** `↵`

Undo Back

`Command: `**`QSAVE`** `↵`   Saves the drawing to the same name

By picking the base point at the arcs' center (the corner of the housing), you maintain the arcs' position relative to the housing. If you pick the base at the corner of the lower right bracket, the bracket grows from that corner and the hidden line arc peeks out from behind the housing. Remember that the base point does not move. If you do pick the wrong base point, you can move the previous selection set to correct the problem, or undo and repeat the SCALE command.

Changing Existing Entities

The CHANGE and CHPROP commands can modify several types of entities. By using the CHANGE command, you can edit a text string and its parameters, extend a line, reorient or relocate a block, and resize a circle. You can use it to change the location, size, and other physical characteristics of many types of entities.

Using CHANGE

Although CHANGE and CHPROP seem similar, they are two different commands. CHANGE is used to modify the geometry of existing entities. CHPROP edits the properties, such as color, linetype, and so on, of existing entities.

CHANGE. The CHANGE command modifies the geometry and properties of existing entities. Its default is Change point, which specifies a new primary point for most entities. The effect varies with the entity type.

301

In addition to the properties options, which work like those of the CHPROP command (discussed next), the CHANGE command responds to the following options.

CHANGE Effects

- **Change point**. The point you pick at the default Change point prompt becomes the *change point*. Moving the change point redefines the location or size of entities as listed. The prompts you see vary with the type of entity selected.

- **Lines.** The change point relocates the end points of selected lines. The end points closest to the new point you specify are stretched to that point. If several lines are selected, they converge at the new point. If ORTHO is on, the lines are extended parallel to the current snap grid orientation.

- **Circle.** The change point changes the radius to the distance from the existing center to the specified point.

- **Block.** The change point relocates the insertion point and prompts for a new rotation angle.

- **Text.** The change point relocates the text insertion point to the specified point. It also prompts for a new style, height, rotation angle, and text string. Press Enter at the change point or any other prompt to keep the original value at that prompt.

- **Attribute Definition.** This option works the same as Text, but also changes the attribute tag, prompt, and the attribute's default value. If you modify an attribute definition, existing attributes do not inherit the changes.

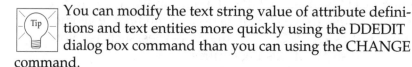 You can modify the text string value of attribute definitions and text entities more quickly using the DDEDIT dialog box command than you can using the CHANGE command.

You should not use CHANGE to modify entity properties because it does not always accept all entity selections when working in 3D. Use CHPROP instead.

If you select several entities to change, the CHANGE prompts repeat for each in turn. The change point is only applied to line entities, however; it is ignored for the others. CHANGE reprompts for points for each entity other than lines.

Changing Existing Entities

Continue from the preceding exercise.

```
Command: CHANGE ↵
Select objects: Select a crossing
window from 3,3 to 1,5
5 found
Select objects: Press Enter
Properties/<Change point>: Pick
point 2,4
Change point ignored
Enter circle radius: .8125 ↵
```

The lines are stretched to converge at the change point first specified. The circle gets a new radius.

```
Command: U ↵
CHANGE                          Undoes the changes
```

To change the entity properties of existing objects, instead of their geometry, use the CHPROP command.

Using CHPROP

The command you use to change the properties of existing drawing entities is CHPROP. The CHPROP command is designed specifically to change the color, linetype, layer, and thickness of entity properties.

Figure 7.15:

The changed lines and circle.

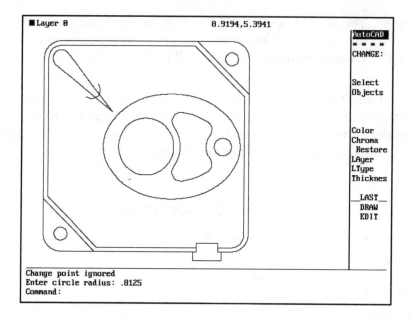

```
■Layer 0                                8.9194,5.3941        ┌─────────┐
                                                            │ AutoCAD │
                                                            │ * * * * │
                                                            │CHANGE:  │
                                                            │         │
                                                            │Select   │
                                                            │Objects  │
                                                            │         │
                                                            │         │
                                                            │Color    │
                                                            │Chroma   │
                                                            │ Restore │
                                                            │LAyer    │
                                                            │LType    │
                                                            │Thicknes │
                                                            │         │
                                                            │__LAST__ │
                                                            │  DRAW   │
                                                            │  EDIT   │
                                                            │         │
Change point ignored
Enter circle radius: .8125
Command:
```

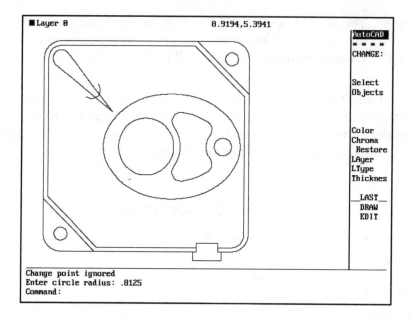
CHPROP. The CHPROP command redefines the color, layer, linetype, and thickness properties of one or more existing entities. CHPROP does *not* include point and text options. Use the CHANGE command to change geometry and text, and use CHPROP to change the properties of entities.

CHPROP Options

- **Color.** The Color option assigns an explicit entity color (or BYLAYER or BYBLOCK) to entities, regardless of the entities' layer(s).

- **LType.** Specify a new linetype name to assign BYLAYER or BYBLOCK to the selected entities, regardless of the entities' layer(s).

- **LAyer.** Specify a layer name to change entities from their current layers to the specified layer.

- **Thickness.** The Thickness option assigns extrusion thickness entities for 3D.

To create entities on a different layer or with an entity color or linetype different from the current default, use the current layer and defaults, then use CHPROP to change the entities after creation.

CHPROP uses a selection set. After you have completed the set, CHPROP prompts you to select a property to change. It then assigns the newly specified property to the selected entities. CHPROP continues to prompt you to change additional properties until you exit the command by pressing Enter or Ctrl-C.

Draw two lines through the cam shaft's center and try CHPROP to change them. For comparison, change one to the CLINE layer and the other to the entity color magenta and entity linetype CENTER.

Using CHPROP To Change Entity Properties

Continue from the preceding exercise.

```
Command: LAYER ↵

?/Make/Set/New/ON/OFF/Color
/Ltype/Freeze/Thaw/LOck/Unlock:
N ↵

New layer name(s): CLINE ↵

?/Make/Set/New/ON/OFF/Color
/Ltype/Freeze/Thaw/LOck/Unlock:
L ↵

Linetype (or ?) <CONTINUOUS>:
CENTER ↵

Layer name(s) for linetype CENTER
<0>: CLINE ↵

?/Make/Set/New/ON/OFF/Color
/Ltype/Freeze/Thaw/LOck/Unlock:
Press Enter

Regenerating drawing

Command: LINE ↵
```
Draw a line from point 1.5,3 to 6.25,3
```
Command: LINE ↵
```

Draw a line from point 3,4 to 3,2

```
Command: CHPROP ⏎
Select objects: L ⏎                           Selects the last line
Select objects: Press Enter
Change what property (Color/LAyer/           Changes Layer
LType/Thickness) ? LA ⏎
New layer <0>: CLINE ⏎
Change what property (Color/LAyer/
LType/Thickness) ? Press Enter
Command: CHPROP ⏎
Select objects: Select the other new line
Select objects: Press Enter
Change what property (Color/LAyer/
LType/Thickness) ? LT ⏎
New linetype <BYLAYER>: CENTER ⏎
Change what property (Color/LAyer/           Selects Color
LType/ Thickness) ? C ⏎
New color <BYLAYER>: M ⏎                      Sets color to Magenta (color 6)
Change what property (Color
/LAyer/LType/Thickness) ? Press Enter
Command: QSAVE ⏎                              Saves the drawing to the same
                                             name
```

The drawing is shown in figure 7.16.

Both lines now appear the same. One is on the CLINE layer with color and linetype BYLAYER, however, and the other is on the HOUSING layer with entity color Magenta and entity linetype CENTER. This setup is an example of how *not* to mix layer settings and entity settings—it creates inconsistent drawing organization that can make later changes confusing.

Using Autoedit and DDMODIFY

You can accomplish most of the effects illustrated in this chapter using Autoedit and DDMODIFY, as described in Chapter 4. The commands presented in this chapter comprise AutoCAD's traditional editing tool set—Autoedit and DDMODIFY are new tools. Use the tools you like best.

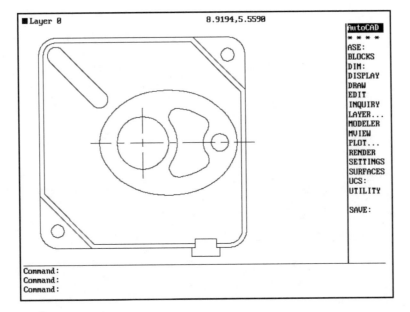

Figure 7.16:

Completed cam housing.

Summary

In this chapter, you learned to correct mistakes and make changes by using editing commands. You also learned to use AutoCAD's layers and entity properties to organize your drawings and differentiate objects with linetypes or lineweights.

You learned many ways to select entities, to quickly create specific selection sets of entities to edit. You learned to use editing commands to make changes and revisions, such as removing portions of entities, lengthening, shortening, and moving entities, changing the angle and size of entities, editing text, changing the layer, color, and linetype of entities, and erasing objects.

Editing
Constructively

In this chapter, you learn advanced editing commands that constructively create new objects and duplicate existing objects. This chapter teaches you how to do the following:

- Copy and move entities

- Create fillet arcs, chamfer lines, and simple intersections between entities

- Create parallel offset copies of lines, arcs, circles, and polylines

- Create multiple copies of entities, arrayed in a rectangular grid or circular pattern

- Create mirror images of entities

- Divide and measure distances on lines, arcs, circles, and polylines, and insert point entities or blocks along them

- Convert lines and arcs to polylines and edit existing polylines

Overview

In Chapters 2 through 6, you learned to use AutoCAD's drawing commands to create geometry (lines, circles, and polylines) and text. In Chapter 7, you learned to modify existing entities with editing commands. In this chapter, you learn about editing commands that create new entities. Some of these commands duplicate functions of the Autoedit Copy options, but occasions arise when you will prefer the traditional commands to Autoedit.

All of the commands in this chapter (except MOVE) create new entities that are guided by existing geometry. The COPY command, for example, does just what its name implies—it copies geometry that you select. The FILLET and CHAMFER commands modify intersections of entities, creating new fillet arcs, or chamfer lines. The OFFSET command copies geometry differently—it creates a new entity that lies parallel to an existing one. ARRAY performs a multiple copy, in a rectangular grid or circular pattern, and MIRROR creates a mirror image of most entities. DIVIDE and MEASURE insert multiple point entities or blocks along existing entities. The most complex editing command discussed in this chapter is PEDIT, which converts lines and arcs to polylines and enables you to modify every aspect of existing polylines. You will use all of these commands in this chapter to create the mount plate shown in figure 8.1.

To practice using these editing commands, you need existing entities that you can edit. Before you begin with the COPY and MOVE commands, use the following exercise and figure 8.2 to lay out a mount plate drawing.

Laying Out the Mount Plate

Start ACAD from the AB-ACAD directory, and begin a NEW drawing named MTPLATE.

Command: SNAP ↵

Set snap to 0.125

Command: GRID ↵

Set grid to 0.5

Command: *Press F8*   Turns on ortho

Command: *Press F6 twice*   Turns on the coordinate display

Command: PLINE ↵

Draw a polyline from 0,0 to @4<0,
@1<90, @2.5<0, @3<90, @2.5<180,
@1<90, @4<180, @2<270, @3<0,
@1<270, @3<180, and Close

Command: CIRCLE ↵

Draw a circle with a center point
of 0.75,1 and a Radius of 0.25

Command: QSAVE ↵   Saves the drawing to the same
                                        name

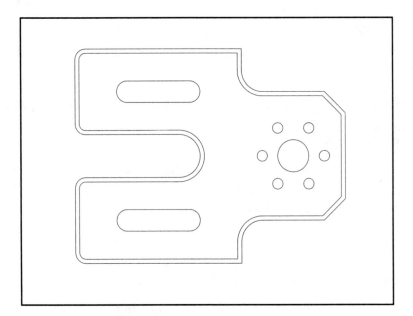

Figure 8.1:

The finished mount
plate drawing.

The new mount plate should resemble the mount plate in
figure 8.2.

Figure 8.2:

*Beginning the
mount plate
drawing.*

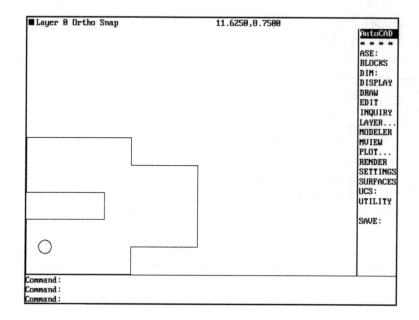

Displacing and Duplicating Entities with MOVE and COPY

The COPY and MOVE commands are two of the most commonly used editing commands. You can use the COPY command to duplicate one or more drawing entities, and the MOVE command moves one or more entities to a new location.

Using COPY to Duplicate Drawing Entities

To use COPY, you select the objects to copy and then specify the displacement between the original and the new objects.

COPY. The COPY command copies one or more entities. You select the entities with normal object selection and specify a displacement. The selected entities are not modified.

If you enter an M (Multiple) at the `<Base point or displacement>/`
`Multiple:` prompt, COPY repeats the prompt for the base point,
then repeatedly prompts for the second point. To make multiple
copies, specify as many second points as you want, then press
Enter to end the command.

With the TRIM and COPY commands, you can quickly build two
slots on the mount plate drawing from the existing circle and a
new line. First copy the circle, then draw one line of the slot across
the tops of the circles. After copying the line to the other side of
the slot, trim the circles and copy the entire slot to make a second
one.

Using the COPY Command

Continue from the preceding exercise.

From the screen menu, choose Edit,
then Copy

Select objects: L ↵   Selects the circle

1 found

Select objects: *Press Enter*

<Base point or displacement>
/Multiple: *Pick center of circle at 0.75,1*

Second point of displacement:
Drag and pick point with snap on at
1.5<0 using snap and looking at the
coordinate display

Use the LINE command and draw the
upper line of slot across top of
circles with snap on

Command: <Ortho off>   Turns off ortho

Command: COPY ↵

Select objects: L ↵   Selects the line

1 found

Select objects: *Press Enter*

<Base point or displacement>   Selects the Base
/Multiple: *Pick .75,1.25*   point

Second point of displacement:*.75,.75*

```
Command: TRIM ↵
```
*Select the two lines as cutting edges,
then select each circle inside the slot
as objects to trim*
```
Command: COPY ↵
```
```
Select objects: Pick the slot with a
window or cross box
```
Uses a window to
select the entire slot
```
Other corner: 4 found
```
```
Select objects: Press Enter
```
```
<Base point or displacement>
/Multiple: Pick any point in the drawing
```
Picks the Base point
of displacement
```
Second point of displacement: @0,3 ↵
```
Specifies a second
point 3 inches above the first
```
Command: REDRAW ↵
```
```
Command: QSAVE ↵
```
Saves the drawing to the same
name

The results are shown in figure 8.3.

Figure 8.3:

Two finished slots.

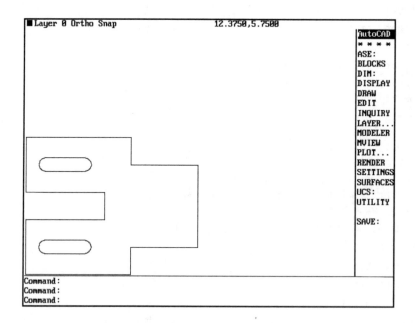

Although you could have drawn the second circle and line as quickly as you copied them, copying the slot was much faster than drawing the second slot. When you work with larger objects that contain more entities, COPY saves even more time.

Try the Multiple option in the following exercise. Make several copies of the Previous selection set (the bottom slot), then undo them.

Copying Objects Multiple Times

```
Command: COPY ↵

Select objects: P ↵                 Selects Previous

4 found

Select objects: Press Enter

<Base point or displacement>        Selects Multiple
/Multiple: M ↵                       option

Base point: Pick the center of the left arc

Second point of displacement:
Pick any point

Second point of displacement:
Pick any point

Second point of displacement:
Pick any point

Second point of displacement:
Press Enter

Command: U ↵                         Undoes the multiple copies
```

Moving Objects with the MOVE Command

MOVE is simpler than COPY because it has no Multiple option. MOVE works just like the COPY command except that MOVE moves the selection set instead of duplicating it.

 MOVE. The MOVE command relocates selected entities by the 2D or 3D displacement you specify.

Use the MOVE command to move both slots .5" to the right in the mount plate drawing. Then relocate the UCS and plate toward the center of the drawing area (see fig. 8.4 and the following exercise).

Figure 8.4:

Slots, plate, and UCS after using MOVE.

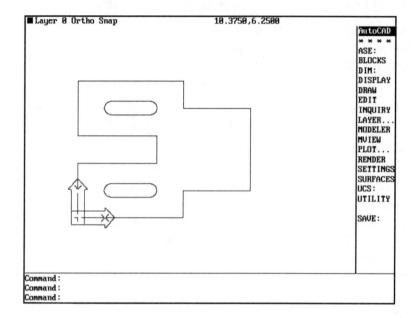

Using the MOVE Command

Continue from either of the two previous exercises.

From the screen menu, choose EDIT, *then* NEXT, *then* MOVE

`Select objects:` *Use a window to select both slots*

`Other corner: 8 found`

`Select objects:` *Press Enter*

`Base point or displacement:` *Pick any point*

`Second point of displacement: @0.5,0 ↵`

Use UCS and set the Origin to 2,2

Use UCS and save to name PLATE

Use UCSICON and set it to ORigin

```
Command: MOVE ↵
```
Move everything to the new UCS origin.

`Select objects: P ↵`	Selects the previously selected slots
`Select objects:` *Pick the polyline*	
`Select objects:` *Press Enter*	
`Base point or displacement: *0,0 ↵`	Specifies the WCS origin
`Second point of displacement: 0,0 ↵`	Specifies the UCS origin
`Command: QSAVE ↵`	Saves the drawing to the same name

See figure 8.4 for the new position of the mount plate

MOVE and COPY are relatively simple editing commands that you use extensively when you construct objects. The polyline editing command, PEDIT, is more complex.

Editing Polylines with PEDIT

When you edit a polyline with any of the commands you have encountered thus far, the change applies to the entire polyline because AutoCAD recognizes a polyline as a single entity. The PEDIT command enables you to edit the individual segments of a polyline and properties that are unique to polylines. The PEDIT command enables you to change the width of a polyline; join new segments to it; curve the polyline; add, delete, and move vertices.

PEDIT. The PEDIT (Polyline *EDIT*) command modifies 2D or 3D polylines and 3D polygon meshes, and converts lines and arcs into polylines. The option prompts vary, depending on the type of polyline selected. PEDIT has two main levels of editing functions. The first level modifies the entire polyline with options such as Close/Open, Join (to another polyline), Width, Fit curve, Spline curve, Decurve, Undo, and Edit vertex. Choose Edit vertex to access the second level for editing individual vertices. The edit vertex options include Break, Insert, Move, Regen, Straighten, Tangent, and Width.

You can use any of the normal object selection methods to select a polyline, but only the most recent entity found in the selection set is selected. A more predictable approach is to use Last or a point pick for selection. PEDIT does not highlight the entity to confirm selection. If the selected entity is a line or arc, you are asked if you want to turn it into a polyline. Otherwise, if the selected entity is not a polyline, the Select polyline: prompt repeats.

You use the options in the Close/Join/Width...: prompt to edit the entire polyline. Use the options in the second prompt, Next/Previous/Break...: (the edit vertex prompt), to edit individual vertices and their associated segments.

Editing an Entire Polyline

The first level of PEDIT options modify the entire polyline. You can open or close a polyline; join other lines, arcs, or polylines to it; alter its width; curve it; or decurve it. PEDIT repeats its option prompts until you exit. Enter X for eXit or press Ctrl-C to exit the PEDIT command and return to the Command: prompt. Even if you cancel, the completed edits remain.

The PEDIT Close and Open Options

PEDIT provides an Open or Close option, whichever is appropriate for modifying the selected polyline. Even if a polyline appears closed, it is open unless the last segment was created by the PLINE or PEDIT Close option. If a polyline is open, Close closes it by creating a segment from the endpoint of the last polyline segment to the first point of the first polyline segment. If it is closed, Open removes the closing segment. If the last segment is an arc, Close creates an arc segment; otherwise it closes with a straight segment.

You used the Close option in the PLINE command to draw the plate as a closed polyline. Use the Open option in the next exercise to open the polyline again, then use the Close option to close it again. The open polyline appears as in figure 8.5.

```
■Layer 0 Ortho Snap              10.3750,-1.3750                    AutoCAD
                                                                   * * * *
                                                                   PEDIT:

                                                                   Close
                                                                   Open
                                                                   Join
                                                                   Width
                                                                   Ed Urtx
                                                                   Fit Curv
                                                                   Spline
                                                                   Decurve
                                                                   Undo
                                                                   eXit

                                                                   PolyVars
                                                                   LT Updt
                                                                   _LAST_
                                                                   DRAW
                                                                   EDIT


 Open/Join/Width/Edit vertex/Fit/Spline/Decurve/Ltype gen/Undo/eXit <X>:
 Open/Join/Width/Edit vertex/Fit/Spline/Decurve/Ltype gen/Undo/eXit <X>: O
 Close/Join/Width/Edit vertex/Fit/Spline/Decurve/Ltype gen/Undo/eXit <X>:
```

Figure 8.5:

Plate with open polyline.

Opening and Closing a Polyline

Continue from the preceding exercise.

Choose Modify, *then* PolyEdit	Starts the PEDIT command
`Select polyline:` *Select the mount plate polyline.*	
`Open/Join/Width/Edit vertex/Fit curve/Spline curve/Decurve/Ltype gen/Undo/eXit <X>:` O ↵	Opens the polyline
`Close/Join/Width/Edit vertex/Fit curve/Spline curve/Decurve/ Ltype gen/Undo/eXit <X>:` C ↵	Closes the polyline again
`Open/Join/Width/Edit vertex/Fit curve/Spline curve/Decurve/Ltype gen/Undo/eXit <X>:` *Press Enter*	

319

The PEDIT Join Option

The PEDIT Join option joins individual 2D polylines, lines, and arcs and combines them into one 2D polyline. You can join two polylines to make one polyline, or add lines and arcs to a polyline. Join uses normal object selection to select the entities to join to the current polyline. The current polyline must be open. You can select as many entities as you want, but only 2D polylines, lines, and arcs that form a contiguous series with the original polyline will be joined. Join ignores other types of entities and entities with endpoints that do not match exactly.

 When you create entities that will be joined, use the ENDpoint object snap override.

You can create a new polyline from a contiguous series of lines and arcs. Select one of the entities at the PEDIT `Select polyline:` prompt, and press Y to turn it into a polyline. Then use Join and select the other entities.

If the entities form a closed shape, Join creates a closed polyline. The entity you select last becomes the closing entity. If you select by using Window or Crossing, the oldest entity selected becomes the closing entity.

To see how the Join option works, select one of the arcs of the lower slot and perform the following steps to turn it into a polyline. Then use the PEDIT Join option to add the arc and other lines of the slot. After joining the lines and arcs, test the new polyline by opening and closing it.

Converting and Joining Entities to Polylines

Continue from the preceding exercise.

Command: **PEDIT** ↵

Join the lower slot entities into a polyline.

Select polyline: *Pick the left arc of the lower slot.*

```
Entity selected is not a polyline
```
Do you want to turn it into one? <Y> *Press Enter*
```
Close/Join/Width/Edit vertex/ Fit curve/
Spline curve/Decurve/Ltype gen/Undo
/eXit <X>: J ↵
```
Select objects: *Use Crossing or Window*
to select the rest of the slot

Any selected objects that cannot be joined are ignored.

Select objects: *Press Enter*
```
3 segments added to polyline
```

Open/Join/Width/Edit vertex/Fit curve/Spline curve/Decurve/Ltype gen /Undo/eXit <X>: O ↵	Opens the right arc
Close/Join/Width/Edit vertex/Fit curve/Spline curve/Decurve/Ltype gen /Undo/eXit <X>: C ↵	Closes it with a line, as shown in figure 8.6

Continue to the next exercise without exiting the PEDIT command.

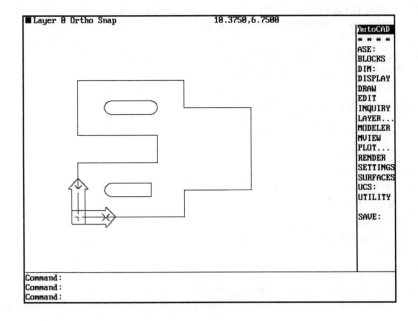

Figure 8.6:

The slot after Join, Open, and Close.

The Join option is useful for adding segments to an existing polyline, and it is the only way you can turn existing lines and arcs into a polyline.

Opening and closing the polyline in the previous steps replaced
the right arc with a straight segment. You need to undo the open
and close steps to fix the slot.

The PEDIT Undo Option

The Undo option steps back, one PEDIT option at a time, as many
times as you like within the PEDIT command. If you use the U or
UNDO commands after you use PEDIT, the entire PEDIT operation is undone.

Use Undo in the following exercise to fix the slot.

Undoing PEDIT Options

Continue from the preceding exercise. The prompt is still in the PEDIT
command.

```
Open/Join/Width/Edit vertex/Fit          Undoes Close
curve/Spline curve/Decurve/Ltype gen
/Undo/eXit <X>: U ⏎
Close/Join/Width/Edit vertex/Fit         Undoes Open
curve/Spline curve/Decurve/Ltype gen
/Undo/eXit <X>: U ⏎
Open/Join/Width/Edit vertex/Fit
curve/Spline curve/Decurve/Ltype
gen/Undo/eXit <X>: Press Enter
```

Command: PEDIT ⏎

Repeat the PEDIT Join from
the previous exercise on the upper slot

Command: SELECT ⏎

Select the polyline slot with Last
to show that it highlights as a single
new object.

Command: QSAVE ⏎

The fixed slot is illustrated in figure 8.7.

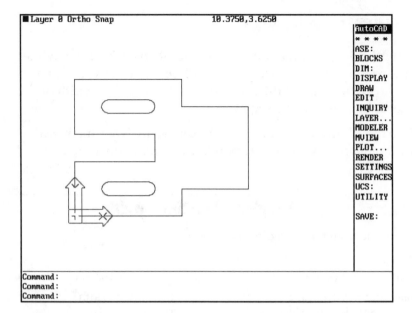

Figure 8.7:
The slot after Undo.

Controlling Polyline Width

Polylines have a width property. (Lines, circles, and arcs do not have a width property.) Changing a polyline's width makes it possible for you to control the line weight of the polyline. Polyline width is a good alternative to using color-to-plotter-pen assignments for controlling line weight, particularly when using a single pen plotter or laser printer. Unlike color-to-pen assignments, you can see polyline width on-screen.

A polyline with a width of 0 (the default) looks the same as lines and arcs. You can draw the polyline with varying widths for different segments. Each segment can have a different starting and ending width from the next segment. When you use PLINE, you can change the default starting and ending widths at any time, before you draw each segment.

The Width option of the PEDIT command enables you to assign a width to all segments in the polyline.

The PEDIT Width Option

The Width option redefines the width of an entire 2D polyline. If the existing segment widths vary, PEDIT Width overrides these widths. The PEDIT Edit vertex option has another width option that affects individual segments.

Use the Width option in the next exercise to experiment with different widths on the last polyline slot that you joined.

Changing a Polyline's Width

Continue from the preceding exercise.

Command: **PEDIT** ↵	
Select polyline: **L** ↵	Selects the last slot
Open/Join/Width/Edit vertex/Fit curve/Spline curve/Decurve/Ltype gen/Undo/eXit <X>: **W** ↵	Selects the Width option
Enter new width for all segments: **.05** ↵	Makes a heavy line (see fig. 8.8)
Open/Join/Width/Edit vertex/Fit curve/Spline curve/Decurve/Ltype gen/Undo/eXit <X>: **W** ↵	
Enter new width for all segments: **.5** ↵	Makes a solid slot
Open/Join/Width/Edit vertex/Fit curve/Spline curve/Decurve/Ltype gen/Undo/eXit <X>: **W** ↵	
Enter new width for all segments: **0** ↵	Restores the default width
Open/Join/Width/Edit vertex/Fit curve/Spline curve/Decurve/Ltype gen/Undo/eXit <X>: *Press Enter*	

As you change the width of a polyline, AutoCAD adjusts the polyline intersections so that they are correctly mitered. Two other options that affect the whole polyline add curvature to its segments.

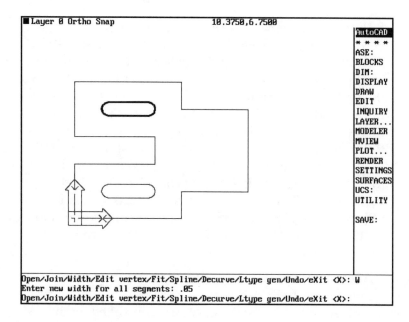

Figure 8.8:
*Polyline slot with
0.05 width.*

Applying Curves to Polylines

The PEDIT command includes two options that enable you to fit a curve to a polyline, transforming it from straight segments into a curve. The Fit Curve and Spline Curve options each apply a different type of curve to a polyline. The Decurve option enables you to change curved polylines back to straight segments.

PEDIT Curve Options

- **Fit.** Fit replaces all existing segments with tangential arc segments. The definitions of any existing arc segments are lost, unless you undo the Fit curve. If you explode a fit-curved polyline, AutoCAD creates a series of arc entities.

- **Decurve.** Decurve regenerates a polyline with straight line segments between all vertices. If a polyline is fit-curved or spline-curved and then is edited with the BREAK, EXPLODE, or TRIM commands, you cannot restore the original polyline by decurving it.

- **Spline**. Spline replaces any arc segments with line segments and uses the polyline as the control frame of a spline. By default, the polyline is not displayed, but the resulting spline is displayed. If the polyline is open, the spline passes through the first and last points only. The spline curve does not pass through other vertices, but is pulled toward (controlled by) them. If the polyline is closed, the spline does not pass through any vertices. To view the frame of the spline (the original polyline), set the SPLFRAME system variable to 1 (on). The spline type is set by the SPLINETYPE system variable; the default is 6, which is a cubic B-spline. If SPLINETYPE is set to 5, a quadratic B-spline curve is formed. Both curves are named for the formulas that are used to calculate them.

AutoCAD's splines are not smooth curves, but approximations consisting of straight line segments. The lengths of the straight segments that approximate the curve are controlled by the SPLINESEGS system variable. Each original segment is divided into the number of segments specified by SPLINESEGS. The higher the SPLINESEGS value, the smoother the curve, but the slower it regenerates. If SPLINESEGS is positive, it uses straight line segments to approximate the curve. If you set a negative number, it uses arc segments, which can create a smoother curve with a lower SPLINESEGS setting. A negative SPLINESEGS setting does not generate arc segments for 3D polylines.

The original vertices (the frame) are preserved and can be restored by using Decurve (except that original arc segments are straightened). If you edit a spline-curved polyline with BREAK, EXPLODE, or TRIM, however, the original vertices are lost and each segment of the spline is converted to a line segment.

Use the Fit Curve and Spline Curve options in the next exercise to apply different types of curves to polylines. Before you start, set an UNDO Mark, so you can easily undo the curve experiments. After you apply a fit curve to one slot and a cubic B-spline to the other slot and perimeter, the plate should match figure 8.9.

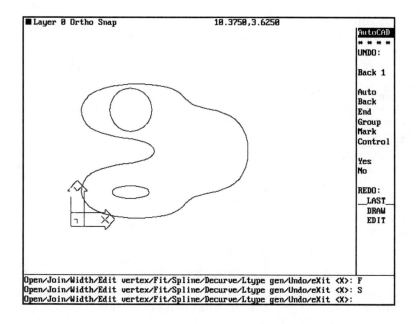

Figure 8.9:
Fit curved and cubic B-Spline slots, and cubic B-Spline plate.

Applying Curves to Polylines

Continue from either the previous exercise or from the Slot After Undo exercise.

Command: UNDO ↵

Auto/Back/Control/End/Group/Mark   Sets a mark to undo
/<number>: M ↵   back to

Command: PEDIT ↵

Select polyline: L ↵   Selects the upper slot

Open/Join/Width/Edit vertex/Fit   Draws a Fit curve
curve/Spline curve/Decurve/Ltype gen
/Undo/eXit <X>: F ↵

Open/Join/Width/Edit vertex/Fit
curve/Spline curve/Decurve/Ltype gen
/Undo/eXit <X>: *Press Enter*

Command: *Press Enter*   Repeats the command

PEDIT Select polyline: *Pick the lower slot*

Open/Join/Width/Edit vertex/Fit   Draws a Cubic B-spline
curve/Spline curve/Decurve/Ltype gen
/Undo/eXit <X>: S ↵

```
Open/Join/Width/Edit vertex/Fit
curve/Spline curve/Decurve/Ltype
gen/Undo/eXit <X>: Press Enter
```

Command: *Press Enter*   Repeats the command

`PEDIT Select polyline:` *Pick the plate.*

```
Open/Join/Width/Edit vertex/Fit              Draws a Fit curve
curve/Spline curve/Decurve/Ltype gen
/Undo/eXit <X>: F ↵
```

```
Open/Join/Width/Edit vertex/Fit              Draws a Cubic B-spline
curve/Spline curve/Decurve/Ltype
gen/Undo/eXit <X>: S ↵
```

```
Open/Join/Width/Edit vertex/Fit
curve/Spline curve/Decurve/Ltype
gen/Undo/eXit <X>: Press Enter
```

The plate now should match figure 8.9.

`Command: SPLINETYPE ↵`

`New value for SPLINETYPE <6>: 5 ↵`   Selects the Quadratic B-spline
                                              type

`Command: PEDIT ↵`

Select the plate and use the Spline   Redraws the plate with a
curve option again   Quadratic B-spline

The plate should now match figure 8.10

`Command: PEDIT ↵`

Select the upper slot and use the Spline
curve option again

`Command: SPLFRAME ↵`

Set SPLFRAME to 1 (on)

`Command: REGEN ↵`   Displays the polyline frames

`Command: ZOOM ↵`

Zoom Window from 1,3 to 3,5.

It looks pretty smooth with the default of 8 straight spline segments
between each vertex.

`Command: SPLINESEGS ↵`

Set SPLINESEGS to 4

`Command: PEDIT ↵`

Select the slot and use the Spline curve option

You can see the straight segments.

Command: **SPLINESEGS** ↵

Set SPLINESEGS to -4

Command: **PEDIT** ↵

Select the slot and use the Spline curve option

The arc segments look smoother.

Command: **UNDO** ↵

Auto/Back/Control/End/Group/Mark   Undoes the changes
/<number>: **B** ↵   back to the mark

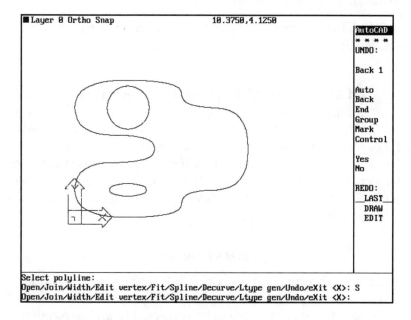

Figure 8.10:

Quadratic and cubic B-Spline slots, and a quadratic B-Spline plate.

A trial-and-error method may be the only way to find the curve you want because so many possibilities exist when you apply a curve to a complex polyline. If these curve options do not create the curve you want, you can add or move individual frame vertices.

Modifying Objects with FILLET and CHAMFER

Two other editing commands you will use often when you lay out a drawing are FILLET and CHAMFER. Both work similarly, creating or modifying intersections of existing entities.

Rounding Corners with FILLET

The FILLET command smooths the intersection of two entities with a radius.

FILLET. The FILLET command creates an arc between any combination of two lines, circles, or arcs. You also can use FILLET to create an arc between two adjacent segments of a 2D polyline, or at all vertices of a single 2D polyline. If the selected entities do not intersect, or if they extend past their intersection, FILLET extends or trims them as needed. You also can use FILLET to set a default fillet radius (initially 0) that is used by subsequent FILLET commands.

FILLET Options

- **Select two objects.** This option fillets two selected entities, or two adjacent segments of a single 2D polyline. The entities must intersect or be able to be projected to an intersection.

- **Polyline.** Polyline fillets all the intersections of a selected 2D polyline.

- **Radius.** Radius sets the default fillet radius. A radius of 0 creates an intersection with no arc by trimming or extending the entities to a corner instead of creating a new arc at the corner.

Tip The new arc is created with the layer, color, and linetype properties of the selected entities if they are both the same. If the entities are not the same, the arc is created with the current layer, color, and linetype settings.

Follow the steps in the next exercise to create a 0-radius fillet and use it to clean up some new line intersections. The next exercise also shows you how to set the fillet radius to 0.5 to fillet a line and circle and how to use the Polyline option to fillet the entire plate polyline. The last part of the exercise shows you how to undo these changes. After trying these fillets, undo the changes.

Using FILLET

Continue from the preceding exercise.

Command: **UNDO** ↵
Set a Mark to undo back to

Command: **LINE** ↵
Draw a line from 8,0 to @3<90

Command: **LINE** ↵
Draw a line from 8.25,.25 to @2<180

Command: **LINE** ↵
Draw a line from 8.5,3.5 to @1<0

Command: **CIRCLE** ↵
Draw a circle at 5,0 with radius 0.75

Command: **MULTIPLE FILLET** ↵   Repeats the FILLET command

Polyline/Radius/<Select first object>:
Pick the lower horizontal line to the left intersection with vertical line

Select second object: *Pick the vertical line above the intersection with horizontal line to clean up the intersection with a 0 radius*

FILLET Polyline/Radius/<Select first object>: *Pick the upper horizontal line*

Select second object: *Pick the vertical line*

```
FILLET Polyline/Radius              Selects the Radius
/<Select first object>: R ↵         option

Enter fillet radius <0.0000>: .5 ↵

FILLET Polyline/Radius/<Select first
object>: Pick the lower horizontal line

Select second object: Pick the circle,
near the top

FILLET Polyline/Radius              Selects the Polyline
/<Select first object>: P ↵         option

Select 2D polyline: Select the mount
plate polyline

10 lines were filleted 3 were too short
```

The drawing should look similar to figure 8.11.

```
FILLET Polyline/Radius/<Select first    Cancels command
object>: Press Ctrl-C
*Cancel*
```

Use UNDO Back to undo the FILLET exercise

Figure 8.11:

Line intersections, filleted circle, and filleted polyline.

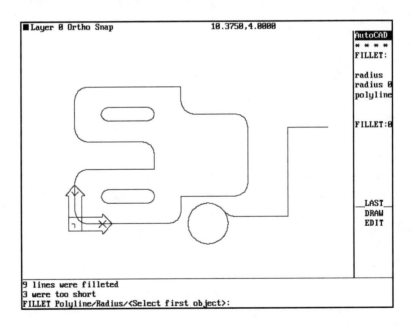

If you use FILLET with a radius of 0, you can extend entities to touch each other in situations where EXTEND will not work.

The 0.5 radius fillet used in the preceding exercise was too large to fillet both of the inside corners of the 1" slot cut into the left edge of the plate. Filleting the first inside corner left a 0.5" straight segment. The entire segment would need to be deleted to fillet the other inside corner, but fillet cannot delete an entire segment or entity.

The trick to filleting this slot is to use a radius that is almost 0.5"—use 0.4999999999. This time, select the specific segments to fillet as shown in figure 8.12.

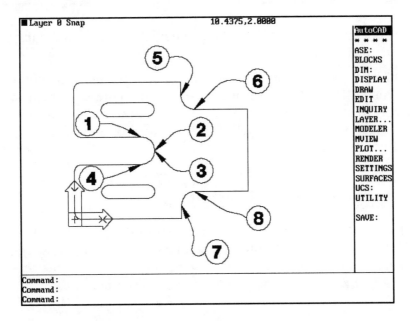

Figure 8.12:

Filleted polyline segments.

Filleting Individual Vertices

Continue from either of the previous two exercises.

```
Command: MULTIPLE FILLET ↵
Polyline/Radius/<Select first object>: R ↵
Enter fillet radius<0.0000>: .4999999999 ↵
FILLET Polyline/Radius/<Select first object>:
```
Pick at ① (see fig. 8.12)

```
Select second object: Pick at ②
```
Continue filleting at ③ and ④,
at ⑤ and ⑥, and at ⑦ and ⑧

Then, set the radius to 0.25 and fillet
the four corners at the left edge of the plate

```
FILLET Polyline/Radius                    Cancels the command
/<Select first object>: Press Ctrl-C
*Cancel*
Command: QSAVE ↵
```

The polyline segments should now be filleted as illustrated in figure 8.12.

FILLET is ideal for rounding the corner of two lines or polyline segments. Using FILLET is much simpler than drawing an arc and trying to make the line lengths match—you can rough out the geometry with straight lines, then fillet each corner with a quick entity selection.

Cutting Corners with CHAMFER

The CHAMFER command is similar to FILLET. Like FILLET, CHAMFER acts on the intersection of two lines or adjacent segments of a polyline. Instead of drawing an arc at the intersection, CHAMFER draws a diagonal line across the corner.

CHAMFER. The CHAMFER command creates a beveled line connecting two intersecting lines, or between adjacent segments of a single 2D polyline. You can preset two distances (default 0) from the real or projected intersection of the lines. CHAMFER extends or trims the lines to those distances from their intersection and then joins them with a new line or segment. The first line you select is modified by the first chamfer distance, the second line by the second distance.

CHAMFER Options

- **Polyline.** The Polyline option chamfers all vertices of a selected 2D polyline.

- **Distance.** The Distance option sets the default first and second chamfer distances. If you use a distance of 0, CHAMFER trims or extends the existing lines to their intersection instead of creating a new line at the corner.

- **Select two objects.** This option chamfers two selected lines or two adjacent segments of a single 2D polyline. The lines must intersect or be able to be projected to an intersection.

> **Note**
> The new chamfer line segment is created with the layer, color, and linetype properties of the selected entities if they are both the same. If the selected entities are not the same, the line is created with the current layer, color, and linetype settings.

Use CHAMFER in the following exercise to chamfer the corners on the right side of the drawing. In addition, follow the next exercise to draw a polyline profile of the edge of the plate and chamfer it. The pick points and results are shown in figure 8.13.

Using CHAMFER to Chamfer a Corner

Continue from the preceding exercise.

Choose Construct, *then* Chamfer

```
Polyline/Distances/<Select first
line>: D ↵
```
Selects Distance option

```
Enter first chamfer distance
<0.0000>: .5 ↵
```

```
Enter second chamfer distance
<0.5000>: Press Enter
```

Command: *Press Enter*   Repeats the command

```
CHAMFER Polyline/Distances/
<Select first line>:
```
Pick at ① *(see fig. 8.13)*

```
Select second line: Pick at ②
```

Command: *Press Enter*   Repeats the command

CHAMFER Polyline/Distances/<Select
first line>:

Pick at ③ (see fig. 8.13)

Select second line: *Pick at ④*

Command: **PLINE** ↵

Draw a polyline from 7.5,2.25 to @2<0,
@.5<90 and @2<180 (leave open)

Command: **CHAMFER** ↵

Set both distances to 0.1

Command: *Press Enter*   Repeats the command

CHAMFER Polyline/Distances/   Selects Polyline
<Select first line>: P ↵   option

Select 2D polyline: L ↵   Selects last object

2 lines were chamfered

Command: **QSAVE** ↵

Figure 8.13:

Plate with cham-
fered corner.

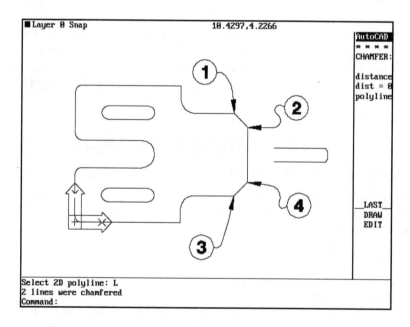

You can see the working similarities between FILLET and CHAMFER. The main difference is that FILLET creates a rounded corner and CHAMFER cuts the corner with a straight line.

If the edge of the plate is beveled, the bevel should show in the top view of the plate.

Creating Parallel Entities Using OFFSET

Showing the chamfer in the top view requires a polyline that is parallel to the plate perimeter and is 0.1" inside the existing polyline. You can draw the second polyline by using the OFFSET command.

OFFSET. The OFFSET command creates a parallel copy of a selected line, circle, arc, or 2D polyline. The copy is offset by a specified distance or drawn through a pick point (the default).

OFFSET Options

- **Offset distance.** Use this option to specify the offset distance by entering a distance, a value, or by picking two points to show the distance. Then you select an object to offset and pick a point to show which side of the object to offset to. You can pick as many objects and points as you like because OFFSET repeats the prompts Select object to offset: and Side to offset: until you press Enter or Ctrl-C to exit. Each object is copied parallel to itself at the specified distance on the side you pick. The specified distance becomes the new default for the offset, instead of the <Through> option.

- **Through.** For this option, press Enter if the default shows <Through>, or enter T to tell OFFSET you want to specify a point through which to offset existing entities. You can pick as many objects to offset and points as you like because OFFSET repeats the prompts Select object to offset: and

`Through point:` until you press Enter or Ctrl-C to exit. Each object is copied parallel to itself at a distance that makes it pass through the point picked.

You can offset only one entity per entity selection. If that entity is a polyline, the entire polyline is offset.

Try the OFFSET command on the plate, creating all of the chamfer lines with one quick command.

Creating Entities with OFFSET

Choose Construct, *then* Offset

`Offset distance or Through`   Specifies the
`<Through>: .1` ↵   distance

`Select object to offset:` *Pick the perimeter polyline of the plate*

`Side to offset?` *Pick any point inside the polyline*

`Select object to offset:` *Press Enter*

`Command:` **QSAVE** ↵

The resulting polyline is shown in figure 8.14.

In the preceding exercise, OFFSET saved you several minutes of work.

> **Note** If you offset complex polylines, the results may not be exactly what you want. You often may have more than one possible parallel to a polyline that has segments that intersect or pass close to one another. Or, the offset copy may not be the same shape. Offset makes its best attempt at a reasonable possibility; if you dislike it, you can edit the results.

OFFSET is one of AutoCAD's most useful commands for laying out drawing geometry. You can take a simple shape and quickly make larger or smaller versions of it, or lay out a line or arc a specific distance from an existing line or arc. If you need to create a series of parallel lines, you can select each newly created line as the next object to offset. OFFSET also is great for creating concentric circles.

Another command that makes copies of objects is ARRAY.

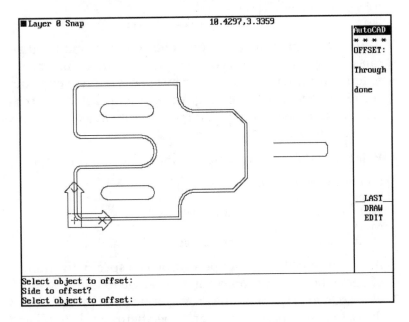

Figure 8.14:

A shape made by using the OFFSET command.

Making Multiple Copies with ARRAY

You used the Multiple option of the COPY command in the beginning of this chapter, and the Copy option of AUTOEDIT to place multiple copies at non-uniform locations. You also can use OFFSET to make multiple copies, such as a row of parallel lines. The ARRAY command is used to create a uniform pattern with a single command.

ARRAY. The ARRAY command makes multiple copies of entities, creating a rectangular array (copies arranged in an X,Y grid) or a polar array (copies arranged in a circle). Objects in polar arrays can be rotated about the array's center point or copied with their original orientation.

ARRAY Options

- **Rectangular.** The Rectangular option displays the following prompts:

```
Number of rows (---) <1>:
Number of columns (¦¦¦) <1>:
Unit cell or distance between rows (---):
```

You specify the number of rows and columns, and the distance between rows and columns. The distances may be entered as individual values, or by specifying two opposite corners of a *unit cell* (showing AutoCAD the X,Y distances with a rubber-band box). You must specify at least two rows or two columns.

- **Polar.** The Polar option displays the following prompts:

```
Center point of array:
Number of items:
Angle to fill (+=ccw, -=cw) <360>:
Angle between items:
Rotate objects as they are copied? <Y>
```

After you specify a center point, you can specify the number of items (how many copies) and the angle to fill (how much of a circle to cover with the array), or you can press Enter at the `Number of items:` prompt and specify the angle to fill and the angle between items. If you specify the number of items, the prompt for the angle between items will not appear. If you answer Y at the `Rotate objects as they are copied? <Y>` prompt, each copied object is rotated to have the same orientation relative to the base point as the selection set. If you answer N, the selection set is copied around the circle but not rotated.

The selection set of a rectangular array becomes the base item at the lower left corner of the array. Use negative distances to make it any other corner. You can create a rotated rectangular array by changing the UCS or the snap grid rotation.

Try the ARRAY command in the mount plate drawing. First, create a rectangular grid of bolt hole circles on the plate and use a unit cell to show the distances. The bolt grid is shown in figure 8.15. Then erase all but one circle and array it into a radial mounting hole pattern using a polar array.

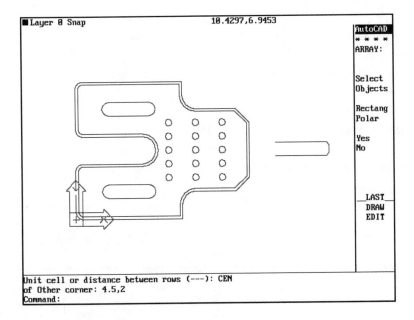

Figure 8.15:

A rectangular hole array.

Making Multiple Copies with ARRAY

Continue from the preceding exercise.

Command: **CIRCLE** ↵

Draw a circle with a center point of 3.5,1.5 and a radius of 0.125.

Choose Construct, *then* Array

Select objects: **L** ↵   Selects last entity

Select objects: *Press Enter*

Rectangular or Polar array   Selects Rectangular
(R/P) <R>: *Press Enter*   option

Number of rows (- - -) <1>: **5** ↵

Number of columns (| | |) <1>: **3** ↵

Unit cell or distance between
rows (- - -): *Pick the center of the circle*

Other corner: *Pick at 4.5,2*

The circles should appear as in figure 8.15.

Command: **ERASE** ↵

Erase all the circles except the one at the center (at 4.5,2.5)

```
Command: ARRAY ↵
Select objects: L ↵
Select objects: Press Enter
Rectangular or Polar array (R/P) <R>: P ↵
Center point of array: 5.25,2.5 ↵
Number of items: 6 ↵
Angle to fill (+=ccw, -=cw)<360>: Press Enter
Rotate objects as they are copied? <Y>: Press Enter
For circles, rotation is irrelevant.

Command: QSAVE ↵
```

The completed polar array should appear as shown in figure 8.16.

Figure 8.16:

A radial hole array.

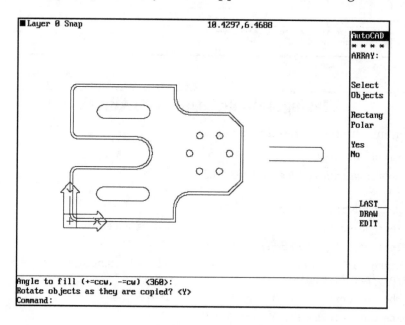

Like OFFSET, the ARRAY command is a real time-saver. It would have taken you much longer to locate and lay out the bolt patterns by drawing the circles individually.

In the last array, you could not see the effect of rotating objects as they were copied. In the next exercise, create two more arrays to see the difference between rotating and not rotating objects. Fill an

angle of only 180 degrees and specify the angle between items
instead of the number of items. Use 45 degrees between items to
copy one array counterclockwise, and -45 degrees to copy the
other array clockwise. Finally, compare the two arrays.

Rotating Entities During an Array

Continue from the preceding exercise.

Command: **UNDO** ⏎

Set a Mark to undo back to

Command: **ZOOM** ⏎

Use Center and zoom to point 12,3 with height 9

Command: **ARRAY** ⏎

Select objects: *Select the chamfered
polyline you drew for the edge profile*

Select objects: *Press Enter*

Rectangular or Polar array (R/P) <P>:
Press Enter

Center point of array: *Pick at 11,2.5*

Number of items: *Press Enter*

By not specifying the number of copies, you force AutoCAD to ask for
the angle between items.

Angle to fill (+=ccw, -=cw) <360>: **180** ⏎

Angle between items: **45** ⏎

A positive angle copies counterclockwise.

Rotate objects as they are copied?
<Y>: *Press Enter*

Command: *Press Enter*   Repeats the command

Select objects: **P** ⏎   Selects previous object

Select objects: *Press Enter*

Rectangular or Polar array (R/P) <P>:
Press Enter

Center point of array: **@** ⏎   Uses the same center point

Number of items: *Press Enter*

Angle to fill (+=ccw, -=cw) <360>: **180** ⏎

Angle between items: **-45** ⏎

A negative angle copies clockwise.

```
Rotate objects as they are copied? <Y> N ⏎
```
Arrays without rotating

The complete array should appear as shown in figure 8.17.

```
Command: UNDO ⏎
```
*Use the Back option to undo these changes
and return to the previous view*

```
Command: ERASE ⏎
```
Erase the chamfered edge profile polyline

```
Command: CIRCLE ⏎
```
*Add a shaft hole at point 5.25,2.5 with
radius 0.375*

```
Command: QSAVE ⏎
```

Figure 8.17:

*Rotated versus
non-rotated
objects in arrays.*

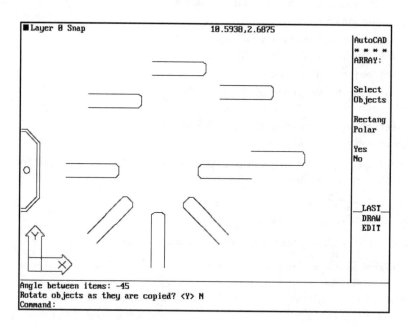

The last editing command that copies existing entities makes
mirror images of objects.

Making Mirror Images with MIRROR

Many objects, such as the mount plate, are symmetrical. When you draw symmetrical objects, you need to draw only one half. You then can use the MIRROR command to *mirror* copy the first half to create the second half. When you mirror an object (or any number of entities), you "flip" a copy of the object to the other side of a *mirror line*, creating a mirror image of the selected object.

MIRROR. The MIRROR command creates a mirror image of selected entities. The selected entities can be retained (the default) or deleted. The MIRRTEXT system variable controls whether text is mirrored or copied without being reversed. The default is 1, which mirrors text in reverse.

MIRROR Prompts

- **First point of mirror line:** At this prompt, you must specify the first point of an axis about which the selection set is to be mirrored.

- **Second point:** At this prompt, you must specify the second point of an axis about which the selection set is to be mirrored.

- **Delete old objects? <N>:** At this prompt, you must answer Y to keep the original in place and make a mirror copy, or N to mirror the object and delete the original.

To use MIRROR, you build a selection set, and then specify a mirror line by using two points. The mirror line is the line around which the object is "flipped." To make a mirror copy of an entity at a specific distance from the original, specify the mirror line exactly halfway between the original and the location of the copy.

You could have drawn only half the perimeter polyline of the plate, mirrored it, and used PEDIT to join the two halves. To see how MIRROR works, use BREAK in the next exercise to delete half of the perimeter polyline, then mirror the other half and join the two halves. The mirror line is shown in figure 8.18.

Figure 8.18:

*Half-perimeter
before MIRROR,
and mirror line
points.*

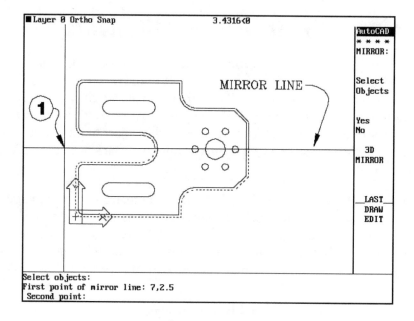

```
■Layer 8 Ortho Snap                    3.4316<8
                                                        AutoCAD
                                                        * * * *
                                                        MIRROR:

                                                        Select
                    MIRROR LINE                         Objects

                                                        Yes
                                                        No

                                                          3D
                                                        MIRROR


                                                        _LAST_
                                                        DRAW
                                                        EDIT



Select objects:
First point of mirror line: 7,2.5
Second point:
```

Using MIRROR to Create a Mirror Image

Continue from the preceding exercise.

Choose Modify, *then* Break, *then* Select
Object, 2nd Point

`Select object:` *Pick the outer perimeter
polyline at 6.625,2.5*

`Enter second point (or F for first point):`
Pick at 2.875,2.5

`Command:` **MIRROR** ↵

`Select objects:` **L** ↵

Last selects only part of the remaining half of the polyline because
breaking it splits it into two pieces at the first vertex.

`Select objects:` *Select the other part of
the polyline*

`Select objects:` *Press Enter*

`First point of mirror line:` *Pick at 7,2.5*

`Second point:` *Pick any point straight to
the left, such as ① (see fig. 8.18)*

346

```
Delete old objects? <N> Press Enter
Command: PEDIT ↵
```
Join the perimeter, which is now four polylines
```
Select polyline: L ↵                    Selects last object
Close/Join/Width/Edit vertex/Fit
curve/Spline curve/Decurve/Ltype gen
/Undo/eXit <X>: J ↵
Select objects: Pick each of the four
```
polylines that now form the plate's outer perimeter
```
Select objects: Press Enter
16 segments added to polyline
Open/Join/Width/Edit vertex/Fit
curve/Spline curve/Decurve/Ltype
gen/Undo/eXit <X>: Press Enter
Command: END ↵
```

Note

Text in a block is reversed when you mirror it, regardless of the MIRRTEXT setting. Mirrored blocks cannot be exploded.

Summary

Now you know how to use AutoCAD's editing commands to modify existing entities and to edit drawings constructively, to create new entities. You can use COPY to duplicate existing entities, FILLET and CHAMFER to modify intersections with new fillet arcs or chamfer lines, or OFFSET to create parallel copies. In addition, ARRAY makes multiple copies in a rectangular grid or circular pattern and MIRROR creates mirror images. In this chapter, you also learned how to use PEDIT, which is the most complex editing command in AutoCAD. With PEDIT, you can convert lines and arcs to polylines; change the width and curvature of polylines; and break, open, or close polylines.

Drawing Power: Blocks and Xrefs

Much of the work you do in a typical drawing duplicates something you have already done. Most drawings use standard parts and symbols that appear on other drawings. You use standard title blocks over and over again. An entire drawing, such as a shop drawing, may be similar to other drawings. If you have to redraw each part, symbol, title block, and drawing from scratch, AutoCAD does not save much time over manual drawing.

AutoCAD uses blocks to help you make use of standard parts and symbols from drawing to drawing. A *block* is a collection of entities grouped into a single entity. In this chapter, you learn to use blocks to copy repetitive items in your drawings; work with libraries of standard symbols, parts, and details; and insert standard title blocks into any drawing. You use the BLOCK command to define blocks; the INSERT command to place, scale, and rotate blocks; the WBLOCK command to write a block to a separate drawing file on disk; and the MINSERT command to insert rectangular arrays of blocks.

You also learn about *external references (xrefs)*, which are similar to blocks. Xrefs enable you to attach other drawing files to your current drawing, for display only. Xrefs enable you to save disk space and share drawings among designers.

In this chapter, you will learn to do the following:

- Define selections of entities as blocks
- Insert blocks any number of times, at any scale and rotation
- Use blocks to quickly copy repetitive items in your drawings
- Create and use libraries of standard symbols, parts, and details
- Insert multiple images of a block in a rectangular array
- Insert standard title blocks into any drawing
- Use any existing drawing as an inserted block
- Attach an existing drawing to the current drawing as an external reference (xref) for standardization, efficiency, and automatic updating

Explaining Blocks

Each line, circle, arc, or polyline is an individual entity. As individual entities, they have little meaning. Organized into patterns, they represent walls, desks, chairs, bolts, and brackets; and they form drawing reference symbols.

Parts and symbols are often frequently repeated throughout an individual drawing or in many different drawings. You can repeat symbols and parts within a drawing by using AutoCAD's COPY command, but using it has disadvantages. Copying entities is inefficient, because each copy is a new collection of individual entities. The more entities a drawing contains, the more disk space it takes. You can only copy entities within a single drawing, not from one drawing to another.

Blocks, however, are an easy, efficient way to repeat frequently used symbols and parts. A *block definition* (or *block*) is a group of entities that have been collected, given a name, and stored in memory. You can access a stored block and insert it into the drawing whenever you need it. An inserted block, called a *block reference* (or *insert*), is a single entity. A block definition may contain a thousand lines, circles, and arcs, but a block insert has only one entity. You can move, erase, or otherwise manipulate the block insert as a whole.

You create a block by drawing it with the drawing and editing commands you have already learned. You can define a block within a drawing, or insert any other drawing file into the current drawing as a block. Before you learn how to group entities to form a block, try inserting one drawing into another. First, you need a drawing to insert.

Inserting a Title Block

The AutoCAD package includes a standard title block called ADESK_B that you can insert into another drawing. Use the INSERT command to insert the title block drawing into a new drawing (see fig. 9.1).

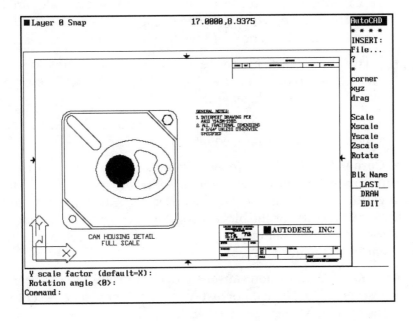

Figure 9.1:

Inserting a title block and a drawing.

To insert an existing drawing into another one, use the INSERT command.

INSERT. The INSERT command inserts a block or other drawing file into the current drawing. You specify an insertion point; X,Y,Z scale values; and a rotation angle. The insertion base point defined in the block or other drawing is placed at the insertion point. The default scales are X = 1 and Y = X; the default rotation angle is 0. To insert the entities in the block or drawing as individual entities, not as a block insert, preface the name with an asterisk. Otherwise, the insertion creates a single entity called an *insert* (also called a block reference).

To insert a block reference or another drawing into your current drawing, enter the name of the block or drawing, the coordinates where you want it located, and the block's scale and rotation. The INSERT options are as follows:

INSERT Options

- **Block name**. Enter the block or drawing name. Preface the name with an asterisk (*) to make the block insert as individual entities. If you use an asterisk, the Y and Z scales are set to the X scale, which must be positive. Enter a tilde (~) to display a file dialog box for selecting a drawing file to insert.

- **?**. The ? option lists blocks defined in the current drawing. Enter an asterisk for a sorted list of all named blocks, or use other wild cards to list specific sets of blocks.

- **X scale factor**. Specify the X scale. (You can also enter preset scales, which are discussed later in this chapter.)

- **Corner**. Specify the scale by forming a rubber-band box from the insertion point to a diagonally opposite corner point. The width (X) and height (Y) of the box specify the block's X- and Y-scale factors for the block. (You can accomplish the same results without using this option by picking the opposite corner at the initial X scale prompt).

- **XYZ**. The XYZ option causes INSERT to prompt for X, Y, and Z scale factors, instead of just X and Y (otherwise, Z is set to the scale of X).

- **Y scale factor**. Specify the X scale or press Enter to default it to the X scale.

- **Rotation angle.** Enter an angle for the block insertion or pick a point to indicate the angle from the insertion point to the point picked.

When you insert a block, AutoCAD copies the entities from the block definition in memory to your drawing. If you insert another drawing, AutoCAD first creates a block definition in memory (unless you preface the name with an asterisk), then inserts the block. After you insert a drawing from disk, it is available as a block in the current drawing whenever you want to insert it again.

Next, begin a new drawing called PART9, and use the INSERT command to insert the ADESK_B title block and CAMHSE drawings. The results should look identical to figure 9.2.

Using the INSERT Command To Insert a Drawing

Start ACAD from the AB directory and begin a NEW drawing named PART9.

```
Command: INSERT ↵
Block name (or ?): \ACAD\SAMPLE\ADESK_B ↵
```
Move the cursor slowly and watch the title block image drag.

```
Insertion point: 0,0 ↵
```
Move the cursor slowly near 0,0 and watch the scale drag.

```
X scale factor <1> / Corner / XYZ:
```
Press Enter
```
Y scale factor (default=X):
```
Press Enter

Move the cursor slowly and watch the drag angle.

```
Rotation angle <0>:
```
Press Enter
```
Command: ZOOM ↵
```
Zoom All to be sure you can see everything inserted.

```
Command: LIMITS ↵
```
Set limits from 0,0 to 17,11
```
Command: GRID ↵
```
Set to .5
```
Command: SNAP ↵
```
Set to 0.0625

The drawing is read from disk, defined as a block, and inserted as an insert entity. As you move the cursor, the block's image drags along with it.

After you pick or enter an insertion point, INSERT prompts you for the X-scale factor for the block. You can use the cursor to stretch the block, enter a scale factor using the keyboard, or accept the default X-scale factor of 1, which inserted the ADESK_B drawing at the same X scale as it was drawn.

Next, INSERT prompts you for the Y-scale factor. Again, you can drag with the cursor or enter a value. Press Enter to set the Y scale equal to the X scale. This setting gives you a drawing proportional to the original, regardless of the X scale you enter. Finally, you drag and pick or enter the rotation angle for the block.

Notice that inserting the ADESK_B drawing inserts a block of its drawing entities, but it does not affect zoom and the other settings in the new drawing.

 Enter negative values at the scale prompts to insert the block reference as a mirror image of the block definition.

 To update a drawing file with a revised block definition, insert a new drawing to redefine the block. To do so, enter the block name in the form *blockname=newdrawingname*. This format tells AutoCAD to look for a file on the disk first, then for existing block definitions in the current drawing. If you redefine a block, the drawing must regenerate before you can see the changes.

Comparing Blocks and Entities

A block insert is a single entity that contains only a reference to the block definition. Experiment with the block you just inserted to see the way AutoCAD really recognizes it as a single entity, rather than as individual lines and text.

If you want to edit the entities displayed by a block insert, you must replace the insert with the actual entities. The EXPLODE command replaces an insert entity with a copy of the block definition—that is, with the enitities used to create the block definition. When a block insert is exploded, AutoCAD removes the insert entity from the drawing. Other block inserts that refer to the same definition are not affected.

Listing and Exploding a Block

Continue from the previous exercise.

```
Command: LIST ↵
```

```
Select objects:
```
Select any entity on the title block

```
1 found
```
Selects the entire block, not just a single line

```
Select objects: Press Enter
```

The following message appears:

```
BLOCK REFERENCE Layer: 0
Space: Model space
ADESK_B
at point, X= 0.0000 Y= 0.0000 Z= 0.0000
X scale factor 1.0000
Y scale factor 1.0000
rotation angle 0
Z scale factor 1.0000
```
```
Command: EXPLODE ↵
```

```
Select objects: Select any entity
```
on the title block and on the cam housing

```
Command: LIST ↵
```

```
Select objects: Select the lower
```
border line

```
1 found
```
Selects the circle only

```
Select objects: Press Enter
```
Ends object selection

```
        LINE       Layer: 0
                   Space: Model space
```

```
    from point, X=   0.6200  Y=   0.3800  Z=   0.0000
      to point, X=  16.3800  Y=   0.3800  Z=   0.0000
Length =  15.7600,   Angle in XY Plane =      0
       Delta X =  15.7600, Delta Y =    0.0000, Delta Z =   0.0000
```

The previous exercise illustrates one of the main benefits of using blocks: they are easy to manipulate. You can move, copy, erase, and edit large portions of the drawing with a single entity selection.

Two simple utility commands help to control block insertions: DRAGMODE and BASE.

Controlling Block Insertions

You saw how the block insertion drags its image with the cursor movement. When inserting large, complex blocks, this dragging can cause jerky and awkward cursor motion. You can suppress dragging by using the DRAGMODE command.

DRAG and **DRAGMODE.** If DRAGMODE is set to Auto (the default) or to on, you can dynamically drag images of arcs, circles, blocks, and polylines on-screen as you draw and edit them. Auto automatically drags whenever possible. If DRAGMODE is off, AutoCAD suppresses all dragging to speed up editing and inserting complex objects. If DRAGMODE is on, AutoCAD drags the current operation only when you enter **DRAG** at an appropriate prompt.

Note

In multiple viewports, the entities drag only in the viewport from which they are selected.

Leave DRAGMODE set to its Auto default, unless you are inserting or editing a complex part that takes a long time to update. When editing such a part, temporarily turn off dragging before the operation.

The other insertion-control command that helps you control block insertions is the BASE command, which enables you to specify the point at which a drawing will be inserted into another drawing. A drawing's *base point* is placed at the insertion point when the drawing is inserted into another drawing. Every drawing has a default insertion base point of 0,0,0, which you can change with the BASE command.

BASE. The BASE command redefines the insertion base point of a drawing. This point is the point in the drawing that is placed at the insertion point if you use the INSERT or XREF commands to place it in another drawing. The insertion base point can be set to any 2D or 3D point.

BASE is particularly useful for changing the insertion point of a drawing without moving the drawing entities themselves. To change the insertion base point of an existing drawing, edit the drawing, change its base point by using BASE, and end it.

Using blocks involves more than just inserting title blocks or other existing drawings. Before you start creating blocks, you need to understand parts and symbols.

Creating and Using Parts and Symbols

As you use additional standard parts, symbols, and details, your drawing efficiency increases because you can insert a part or symbol into your drawing much more quickly than you can draw it. You can also replace a block by selecting it with a single pick.

If you use several parts (bolts, fittings, and so on) frequently, use AutoCAD to develop a block library of common parts and symbols. This section of the chapter teaches you how to do that. First, consider how to size parts and symbols.

Sizing Parts, Symbols, and Symbolic Parts

When defining blocks or drawings to be inserted as block references representing *parts* (groups of entities that represent real objects), you can either create them at full size or at a one-unit scale. Most objects are a specific size, with specific proportions and internal details. These objects should be drawn as full-size block definitions and inserted at an X and Y scale of 1. Some objects, however, such as a rectangular desk, table, bookcase, or a hex bolt head, appear in plan view in simple rectangular or hexagonal outlines. Objects such as these may be created at a one-unit scale and scaled when inserted to their real-world size.

How does one-unit scale work? For example, assume that you have a block definition or drawing containing only a one-inch square. It can represent a one-unit scale table. When you insert it, you can easily scale it to whatever size you need. If you need a table that is 60"×30", insert it with a scale of 60 in the X and 30 in the Y. The resulting block insertion appears as a 60"×30" rectangle representing a 60"×30" table.

Symbols (groups of entities that symbolize or carry information about real objects) should be scaled similarly to text, relative to the size you want them to appear in a plot. The easiest method is to draw symbols at the size they should appear when plotted, and then scale them by the inverse of the plot-scale ratio when you insert them. Take the example of a weld symbol that must plot 3/8" high. You use this symbol on many drawings with different plot scales. Draw the symbol 3/8" high. Assume that your drawing scale is 1/2"=1'-0", which is a plot scale of 1/24. To get the weld symbol to plot 3/8" high, insert it with a scale of 24.

Using BLOCK To Create Parts and Symbols

You create a full-scale part, a one-unit symbol, or a symbol that has no specific size by using the same methods and commands. As you did with the title block, you can create a drawing as you do any other, and then insert it into other drawings as a block.

If you want to save a group of entities from your current drawing as a separate drawing file on disk (to later insert as a block), use the WBLOCK (Write BLOCK) command. If you want to define a block only in your current drawing, you can do so with the BLOCK command. The BLOCK command uses entities selected from the current drawing, rather than entities stored on disk in a drawing file, to create a block definition.

BLOCK. The BLOCK command defines blocks in the current drawing. A *block* is a single object containing one or more entities. You define a block by specifying a name and insertion point and selecting entities from the current drawing. The selected entities are then erased and stored in the drawing as a block definition. You can insert defined blocks into a drawing by using the INSERT command.

Blocks can include entities on any layers, with any color or linetype. The relationship of blocks, colors, linetypes, and layers is explored in the next chapter.

Block Options

- **Block name.** Name the block definition with up to 31 characters.

- **?.** The ? option lists the currently defined blocks in the current drawing. In Release 11, enter an asterisk to display a sorted listing of all named blocks. You can use other wild cards for a more specific list.

- **Insertion base point.** Select the point to be placed at the insertion point when the block is inserted.

- **Select objects.** Select the objects to group in the block definition. They will be erased and copied into an invisible block definition in the current drawing.

The first item of information AutoCAD requests is the block's name. The name under which AutoCAD creates the block definition is the name you use later to insert visible block references to the block in your drawing.

Next, AutoCAD prompts you for an insertion base point. This point is the reference point by which the block will be inserted. The title block and border you inserted was created as a separate file, so it used the default 0,0 base point. If you dragged it with your cursor when you inserted it, you saw it move as if attached to the cursor at the bottom left corner of the sheet border. That was the block's insertion base point.

The location of a block's insertion point is important because it determines where the block will be located, in relation to the rest of the drawing. It also is the point about which the block is scaled if you specify scale factors other than 1, and about which it rotates if you specify a non-zero rotation. If you have two parts that must fit together when they are inserted, create them with coordinated insertion base points. Then, both parts can be inserted at the same coordinates and will fit together properly. In general, endpoints, centers, midpoints, or other object snap points are good insertion base points.

After you specify the insertion base point, AutoCAD prompts you to select entities. As it does with any command that generates the object selection prompt, AutoCAD is building a selection set. The *selection set* is the group of entities that will be placed in the block definition. When you finish selecting entities, press Enter. The entities disappear as AutoCAD places them in the block definition.

 The block is created relative to the current UCS, so be sure the correct UCS is current, particularly if you are using 0,0 as the insertion base point.

To see how easy it is to create blocks, draw a one-unit part—a 1-inch (across the flats) hex bolt head—and create a block, as shown in figure 9.2. Then, insert it at different scales to represent different bolt sizes, as shown in figure 9.3.

Creating Blocks

Continue from the previous exercise.

```
Command: CIRCLE ↵
3P/2P/TTR/<Center point>: Pick a point
in the clear area above the cam housing
Diameter/<Radius>: .5 ↵
Command: POLYGON ↵
Number of sides <4>: 6 ↵
Edge/<Center of polygon>: @ ↵
Inscribed in circle/Circumscribed about circle (I/C) <I>: C ↵
Radius of circle: .5 ↵
Command: BLOCK ↵
```

Block name (or ?) : **HEXHEAD** ↵	Names the new block
Insertion base point: @ ↵	Specifies the center point

```
Select objects: Pick the polygon
1 found
Select objects: Pick the circle
1 found
Select objects: Press Enter
```

The objects disappear into the block definition.

Command: **QSAVE** ↵	Saves the drawing to the same name

You can see that the bolt has been erased and moved into a block definition in memory. Next, insert the block at different scales to represent different sizes of bolts, as shown in figure 9.3.

Inserting and Scaling a One-Unit Block

```
Command: Erase the bolt head and bolt hole on the cam housing
Command: INSERT ↵
```

Block name (or ?) <CAMHSE>: **HEXHEAD** ↵	Specifies the described block
Insertion point: 7.5,7.5 ↵	Sets the location for the block

`X scale factor <1> / Corner / XYZ: .5 ↵`	Creates a .375-inch bolt
`Scale factor (default=X): ` *Press Enter*	
`Rotation angle <0>: ` *Press Enter*	Accepts the default
`Command: INSERT ↵`	
`Block name (or ?) <HEXHEAD>: ` *Press Enter*	Accepts the default
`Insertion point: 2.5,2.5 ↵`	Sets the location for the block
`X scale factor <1> / Corner / XYZ: .5 ↵`	Creates a .375 inch bolt
`Y scale factor (default=X): ` *Press Enter*	
`Rotation angle <0>: 30 ↵`	Rotates the block
`Command: QSAVE ↵`	Saves the drawing to the same name

Figure 9.2:

Defining a hex head block.

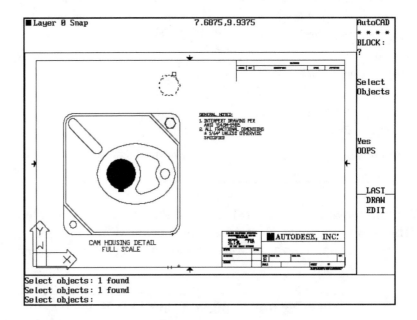

Create unit-scale blocks so that the dimension by which you scale them is one inch (in this case, two times the .5 inch radius equals one inch across the flats). Then you insert them with a scale that, in inches, equals the size you want that dimension to become.

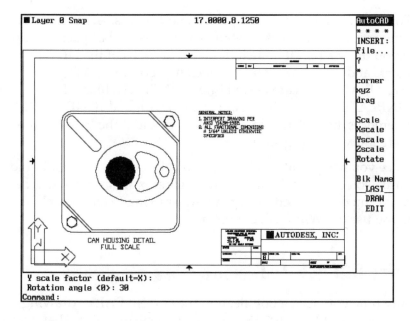

Using Blocks for Efficiency

When you create a block from entities in the drawing or insert a drawing as a block, AutoCAD builds a block definition in memory. The *block definition* is a list of all the entities that are included in the block, along with other information AutoCAD needs to draw the block. It takes roughly the same amount of memory to store the block definition as it does to store the entities that make up the block.

When you insert a copy of the block, its entities are not duplicated. Instead, AutoCAD inserts a *block reference*, which references the block definition. Each block reference requires only a small amount of memory—much less than the entities it represents. For example, if a block consists of 100 lines and you insert it 12 times, you end up with 112 entities (one entity for each of the 100 lines in the block definition, and one for each of the 12 block references). If you copy the same data 12 times, instead of inserting the data as blocks, you get 1200 lines. Thus, using blocks is not only more efficient for drawing time but more efficient for memory and disk usage.

For even greater efficiency, you can nest blocks. An inserted block reference is an entity. Any entity can be selected as part of a block. If you draw a part that includes ten insertions of the HEXHEAD block, and then make it into a block named TINPLATE, the HEXHEAD blocks are nested in the TINPLATE block. If you insert TINPLATE 20 times, it still only has the original 10 HEXHEAD references, not 200 (10 times 20), as it would if the HEXHEADs were individually inserted.

Once you have created a library of blocks to use as symbols and parts, you can quickly insert any number of them to build drawings. You do not need to start a new drawing to create each block if you use the WBLOCK command.

Using WBLOCK To Create a Library of Blocks

Any time you need a bolt head in the current PART9 drawing, you can insert the HEXHEAD block you created. But what if you want to use the bolt head in another drawing? Rather than take the time to re-create it in another drawing, you can use the WBLOCK (Write BLOCK) command to write the existing block definition to disk as a separate drawing file. Then you can insert the resulting drawing file into any drawing as a block.

WBLOCK. The WBLOCK (Write BLOCK) command writes selected entities, an existing block, or the entire drawing to a new drawing file. You can edit the new drawing file from or insert it into other drawings with the INSERT command.

The WBLOCK command works like the BLOCK command, with some additional options.

WBLOCK Options

- **File name.** Enter a file name (up to eight characters on DOS systems), including a drive and path specification if needed. WBLOCK automatically applies the DWG file extension.

- **Block name.** Either specify the name of an existing block in the current drawing to write it to disk as a drawing file; enter an equal sign or asterisk; or press Enter, as follows:

- **=.** Enter an equal sign at the block name prompt to write an existing block to the file. The file name you specified must match an existing block definition name in the current drawing. The block name must not contain more letters than the maximum allowable file name on your system.

- ***.** Enter an asterisk at the block name prompt to write the entire drawing (except any unreferenced symbols, such as unused layers, linetypes, blocks, text styles, UCSs, named views, or viewport configurations) to the file on disk.

- *Press Enter.* Press Enter at the block name prompt if you want to select the entities on which you will use the WBLOCK command. They will be erased and copied to the named drawing file. This works like the BLOCK command, except that no block definition is saved in the current drawing.

- **Insertion base point.** Select the point that will be placed at the insertion point when the block is inserted. This prompt appears only if you use the Enter option.

WBLOCK enables you to write a portion of the drawing, whether it is a block or separate entities, to disk as a drawing file. The drawing file created by WBLOCK is like any other drawing file. You can load it from the main menu and edit it, insert it as a block with INSERT, or attach it to a drawing with XREF.

WBLOCK prompts you to supply a file name for the drawing file to be created by WBLOCK. If the drawing file already exists, WBLOCK asks you if you want to replace it. If you answer Y, WBLOCK continues. If you answer N, the WBLOCK command aborts.

Next, WBLOCK prompts you for a block name. If you supply a name, WBLOCK checks for an existing block definition by that name. If you enter an equal sign, it looks for a block name matching the file name. If it finds one, WBLOCK creates or overwrites the file name you supply and copies into it all the entities in the named block. If WBLOCK does not find a block with the name you specify, it prompts you to enter the block name again.

Note   WBLOCK does not create a block definition, either in the current drawing or the new file. The file it creates contains the individual entities that you select or that come from the block name you specify. The file is not a block definition. There is no entity or thing called a "wblock." However, the file that WBLOCK creates can be inserted as a block.

Try using WBLOCK to create a file called HEXHEAD.DWG, which contains the data that makes up your one-unit bolt head.

Using WBLOCK To Write a Block to Disk

Continue from the previous exercise.

Command: WBLOCK ⏎	Displays the Create Drawing File dialog box
In the File: *text box, enter* HEXHEAD	
Block name: = ⏎	Looks for a block name matching the file name
Command: QSAVE ⏎	Saves the drawing to the same name

You can see that the WBLOCK command is easy to use—supply the name of the file and the name of the block, and WBLOCK does the rest.

In addition to writing blocks to disk as drawing files, WBLOCK enables you to select entities from the drawing to write to disk as a separate drawing file. Instead of entering a block name when prompted to do so, press Enter. WBLOCK prompts you to select objects to be placed in the new drawing file. As with the BLOCK command, the entities disappear as WBLOCK moves them to disk.

By drawing each part or symbol, and then using WBLOCK to write each part to a new file, you can quickly create a library of parts and symbols. As you do, consider how you want to organize them in subdirectories so that you can keep track of them. You can specify a directory path or enter a tilde at the file-name prompt to organize your files as you create them.

Use WBLOCK to create a few more files: a full-scale part and a symbol. The full-scale part is a mounting plate, shown in figure 9.4. The symbol is a surface quality symbol drawn for a 1/8" plotted text height, shown in figure 9.5. You can insert these into the previous PART9 drawing's title block to experiment with additional INSERT scaling options and to see how easy it is to build drawings with blocks.

This time, use WBLOCK to write some entities that are not part of a block out to disk as a drawing file.

Using WBLOCK To Create a Drawing File

Start a NEW drawing named TEMP.

Command: **SNAP** ↵
Set to 0.0625

Command: **GRID** ↵
Set to 0.5

Use lines and arcs to draw the plate shown in figure 9.4.

Command: **BLOCK** ↵

Block name (or ?): **MTPLATE** ↵   Specifies the desired block

Insertion base point: *Pick at ①*
(see fig. 9.5)

Select objects: *Select all lines and arcs*

Select objects: *Press Enter*

The selected objects disappear into the block definition.

Command: **WBLOCK** ↵

This time, write the block to a different file name.

In the File: *edit box enter* **PLATE** ↵

Block name: `MTPLATE` ⏎	Copies the entities in the MTPLATE block definition to the PLATE.DWG file

Draw three lines for a surface quality symbol.

Command: `LINE` ⏎
*From 3,3.125 to @.1443<300, to @.4330<60,
to @.5<0*

Command: `WBLOCK` ⏎

In the `File:` *edit box enter* `SURF` ⏎

Block name: *Press Enter*	Selects the desired entities

Insertion base point: *Object snap to
INTersection* ① *(see fig. 9.5)*

Select objects: *Select all three lines
of symbol with a window*

Select objects: *Press Enter*

The lines disappear as it is written to the SURF.DWG file. Continue to
the next exercise without ending the drawing.

Figure 9.4:

Creating a plate.

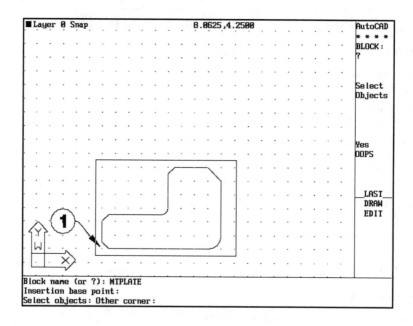

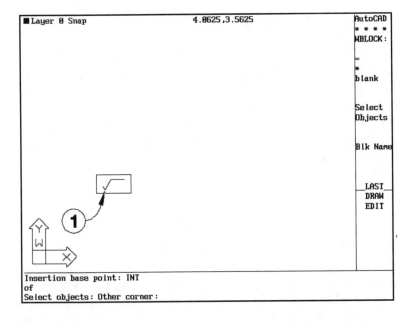

Figure 9.5:
Creating a surface symbol.

In this way, WBLOCK enables you to extract parts of your drawing and to save them as separate drawing files.

When you used WBLOCK on the MTPLATE block, you renamed it to the PLATE drawing file. It is still named MTPLATE within the current drawing, however. You can use the RENAME utility command to rename blocks and other named things within your current drawing.

RENAME. The RENAME command renames layers, linetypes, text styles, blocks, views, UCSs, and viewport configurations.

Enter **B, D, LA, LT, S, U, VI,** or **VP** (see the corresponding option names in the command definition) to indicate the type of named thing you want to rename, and the RENAME command prompts you for the current and new names.

Another useful utility command for working with blocks is the OOPS command.

Recovering Data with OOPS

When you create a block or write a file with WBLOCK, the entities you select disappear from your drawing. If you do not want the entities to disappear after using them so you can create a block for use elsewhere, use OOPS after BLOCK or WBLOCK. Remember that OOPS recalls only the last erase operation—if you use the ERASE command after the BLOCK command, you cannot recall the entities you used to create the block.

 OOPS. The OOPS command restores the selection set deleted by the last ERASE, BLOCK, or WBLOCK command in the current drawing session.

You can draw a part, use the BLOCK command to place the entities in a block definition or use WBLOCK to write them to a file. Then use the OOPS command to bring the entities back as they were before you used the BLOCK or WBLOCK command. After you use the OOPS command, the entities exist individually as part of the drawing and in the block definition in the current drawing or a separate drawing file.

Try using the OOPS command to bring back some entities.

Bringing Parts Back with OOPS

Continue from the previous exercise.

Command: **OOPS**↵   Redraws the surface symbol

The OOPS command is particularly useful if you are using a part as a template to create more than one block. You can create a block, bring the entities back, modify them, and create a new block. You can use OOPS over and over, bringing the entities back as many times as necessary to revise them and to create new blocks.

Now you have an empty PART9 drawing with only a title block, a hex bolt head, a plate, and a surface symbol. Try using INSERT to assemble these into a drawing.

Inserting Parts with Preset Scale and Rotation

Start a NEW drawing named ASSEMBLY.

```
Command: ZOOM ↵
```
Zoom Left, lower left corner 1,3 and default the magnification

```
Command: LIMITS ↵
```
0,0 to 30,30

```
Command: SNAP ↵
```
Set to 0.0625

```
Command: GRID ↵
```
Set to 0.5

```
Command: INSERT ↵

Block name (or ?): PLATE ↵

Insertion point: 3,9 ↵

X scale factor <1>/Corner/XYZ:
```
Press Enter

```
Y scale factor (default=X):
```
Press Enter

```
Rotation angle <0>: -90 ↵

Command: LINE ↵
```
Draw a bar from 4.25,8.5 at ① to @6<0 (see fig. 9.6)

```
Command: LINE ↵
```
Draw from 4.25,7 at ② to @ 6<0

```
Command: INSERT ↵

Block name (or ?) <PLATE>: Press Enter

Insertion point: 11.5,9 ↵

X scale factor: -1 ↵                    Mirrors the block

Y scale factor (default=X): 1 ↵         Sets the Y axis without rotation

Rotation angle: 90 ↵

Command: LIST ↵
```
Select the last insert

```
BLOCK REFERENCE Layer: 0
Space: Model space
PLATE
at point, X= 11.5000 Y= 9.0000 Z= 0.0000
X scale factor -1.0000
Y scale factor 1.0000
rotation angle 90
Z scale factor 1.0000
```

Figure 9.6

Two inserted plates.

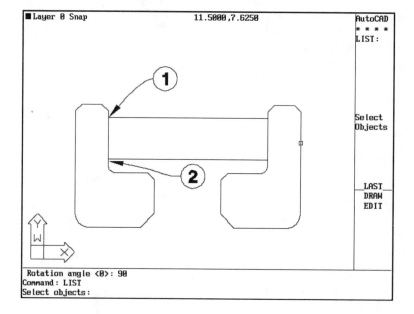

By inserting a common part at different scales, you have represented two mirror-imaged parts without duplicating any data. Your drawing contains two lines and two block references, plus the PLATE block definition. The entities that make up the block are not duplicated in each block reference's data. As the LIST command shows, the inserted block only contains a reference to the block definition and information on the insertion point, scale, rotation, and other data unique to the insertion.

Continue by inserting the one-unit scaled HEXHEAD and SURF symbol, which was sized for plot scale. Since this drawing would be plotted at 1:1 scale, SURF should be inserted at a scale of 1. The results are shown in figure 9.7.

Inserting Symbols and One-Unit Parts

Continue from the previous exercise.

```
Command: INSERT ↵
```
Insert the unit-scaled bolt head

```
Block name (or ?) <PLATE>: HEXHEAD ↵          Specifies the desired
                                               block

Insertion point: S ↵                           Selects XYZ scale option

Scale factor: .75 ↵

Insertion point: Drag and pick 3.75,5.5

Rotation angle <0>: Press Enter  Accepts the default of no
      rotation
```

Repeat for insertion points 5.25,5.5, 9.25,5.5 and 10.75,5.5.

Insert two more HEXHEAD blocks at 3.625,7.875 and 10.875,7.875, with default scale and rotation.

```
Command: INSERT ↵

Block name (or ?) <HEXHEAD>: SURF ↵

Insertion point: 8,8.5 ↵

X scale factor <1> / Corner / XYZ:
Press Enter

Y scale factor (default=X):
Press Enter

Rotation angle <0>: Press Enter

Command: ZOOM ↵
Zoom Center, press Enter to default the
center point, and enter height 6

Command: DTEXT ↵
```

Add a value for maximum waviness height.

```
Justify/Style/<Start point>:
8.25,8.9375 ↵

Height <0.2000>: .125 ↵

Rotation angle <0>:

Text: 0.005 ↵

Text: Press Enter

Command: ZOOM ↵
Select the Previous option

Command: QSAVE ↵                                Saves the drawing to the
                                               same name
```

Figure 9.7:

Plates with bolts and surface symbol added.

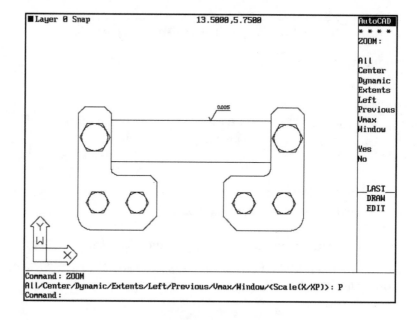

If you drew this for plotting at a scale other than 1:1, you have scaled the SURF symbol and sized the text for the plot scale. For example, if you are plotting at 1:4 (plot scale factor 0.25), you insert the SURF symbol with a preset scale of 4 and make the text 0.5 inches high.

When using symbols and parts with associated text, you can use attributes to make the text a part of the block.

Adding Information to the Drawing with Attributes

Another type of entity that is often used with blocks is the attribute. Essentially, an *attribute* is a string of text that is part of a block. If you incorporate ordinary text in a block, its value (the text string itself) is fixed and unchangeable. An attribute, however, can have its height, style, and position set in the block definition and yet leave its value undefined until you insert the block.

Because the value of an attribute is a string of text, attributes have the same properties as text. These properties include justification, an insertion point, height, and rotation. The font style that is active when you define the attribute is used when the attribute is filled in during block insertion.

When you insert a block containing an attribute, it prompts you to enter a text value. Unlike text, the text value, position, height, angle, style, layer, and color of variable attributes can even be changed after the block has been inserted. You can also define fixed attributes, whose values never change, and preset variable attributes, whose contents can be changed. Both fixed and preset attributes insert without prompting.

Attributes give you a way to attach information to items in a drawing. They are particularly useful for generating bills of materials and parts schedules. For example, assume that you are drawing a floor plan, and you associate three attributes with each door symbol in your drawing. The attributes store the door size, type, and manufacturer. You can later extract that information to generate a door schedule. The information can be exported and processed with other programs, such as a spreadsheet or database program.

The ATTDEF (ATTribute DEFinition) command is used to create attributes. It builds an attribute out of many information items. The attribute includes a tag to identify the attribute and a prompt that appears on the command line each time the attribute is inserted into the drawing. The prompt is an informational message that you define; it tells the user what action to take or what type of information to enter into the attribute. In addition, the attribute includes an optional default value that you assign. If you do not enter a value for the attribute when you insert it, it assumes the default value.

After you have defined and inserted attributes, you can edit them by using the ATTEDIT (ATTribute EDIT) command. Even though attributes contain text, their special nature means that you cannot edit them with the same commands you use to edit text. In addition to the value of the attribute, ATTEDIT enables you to edit other properties of the attribute, relocate them, and make other changes.

To extract the information stored in your drawing's attributes, display the drawing on-screen, or send it to a printer, use the ATTEXT (ATTribute EXTract) command. ATTEXT pulls the information out of the attributes in the drawing and creates a database file in Comma-Delimited Format (CDF) or Space-Delimited Format (SDF). You can then use the database file directly or import it into a program, such as dBASE, to perform tasks such as estimating costs and generating material orders. In order to extract a CDF or SDF file, you must create an ASCII template file. The template file specifies the type and order of data to be extracted. Each data item is listed on its own line, specifying field name, character width, and precision for numeric fields.

If you want to learn more about the attribute commands and tracking data in your drawings, see the *AutoCAD Reference Manual* or *Inside AutoCAD* (from New Riders Publishing).

If you are creating a regular rectangular block array, you can take the efficiency of blocks one step further with MINSERT.

Inserting Arrays of Blocks with MINSERT

The MINSERT command is similar to the INSERT command, except that it creates multiple copies of a block, not just a single copy.

MINSERT. The MINSERT (Multiple INSERT) command is like combining the INSERT and rectangular ARRAY commands. You specify the insertion point, X,Y scaling, and rotation angle, as for the INSERT command. MINSERT creates multiple copies of a specified block in a rectangular array as a single entity.

When you use MINSERT, you are asked to specify the number of rows and columns and the distance between them.

Note All the blocks making up a MINSERT array must remain intact. You cannot explode the array, nor can you use the MINSERT command to insert the block with an asterisk preceding the block name.

When you use MINSERT, each instance of the block is recognized as being part of the entire MINSERT, not as a block of its own. Think of it as a block of blocks. You cannot change any of the block instances. Instead, you must redefine the block itself or create a new MINSERT.

Using External References

An *external reference*, or *xref*, is like a block. There is one major difference, however—xrefs do not become a permanent part of the drawing, as blocks do. When you create a block or insert a drawing as a block, AutoCAD stores the block definition in the drawing. When you insert a block, AutoCAD creates an insert entity, a block reference.

Xrefs are attached, not inserted. *Attaching* an xref creates a link from the current drawing to another drawing file: the *source file*. Like a block insertion, an xref attachment creates a block reference. The xref definition is only loaded into the drawing's memory during the drawing session, however, and is not stored with the drawing file. Each time you reload your drawing, the xref source file is reloaded. Any changes that have been made in the source drawing file are automatically updated in the loaded drawing that references it.

Using the XREF Command

Xrefs are used for inserting common parts that may be revised at some time during the project. They always reflect the most current state of the drawing that they reference, and they help to reduce errors.

Xrefs are not inserted into a drawing as blocks are. Instead, xrefs are attached to the drawing. If you want to remove the reference from your drawing, you detach it. The primary command you use to work with xrefs is the XREF command.

XREF. The XREF command attaches external drawing files to the current drawing. After the external drawing is attached, AutoCAD prompts for an insertion point, scale factors, and rotation angle.

Before exploring the other XREF options, try the default Attach option. Use the XREF command to attach the ASSEMBLY title block to a new BASEPL drawing (see fig. 9.8). Then end the BASEPL drawing, edit the source ASSEMBLY drawing, and then edit BASEPL again, to see how it updates the xref in BASEPL when you reload it.

Attaching an Xref with XREF Attach

Start AutoCAD from the AB directory and OPEN an existing drawing named BASEPL.

```
Command: XREF ↵

?/Bind/Detach/Path/Reload/<Attach>:
Press Enter

Xref to Attach: ASSEMBLY ↵          Specifies the desired xref

Attach Xref ASSEMBLY: assembly

ASSEMBLY loaded.

Insertion point: -2.25,-5.125 ↵     Specifies the xref's location

X scale factor <1> / Corner / XYZ:
Press Enter

Y scale factor (default=X):
Press Enter

Rotation angle <0>:
Press Enter

Command: ZOOM ↵
Select the Zoom All option

Command: QSAVE ↵                     Saves the drawing to the same
                                     name
```

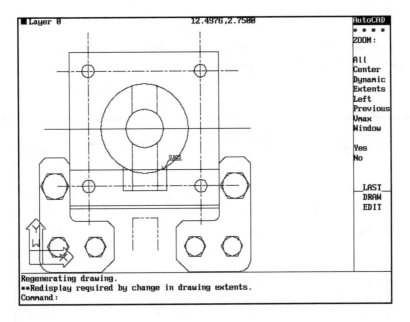

Figure 9.8:

ASSEMBLY externally referenced in BASEPL drawing.

No difference is apparent between this xref and the title block you inserted as a block in the previous PART9 drawing. They are considerably different, however. The block became a permanent part of the drawing, but the xref did not. If you make a change to the source drawing and reload the current drawing, you see the change take effect.

Save the current drawing as **BASEPL**. Then, reload the ASSEMBLY drawing and make a change to it. Finally, reload BASEPL to see if the change you made to ASSEMBLY appears in BASEPL.

Changing an Xref's Source Drawing

OPEN an existing drawing named ASSEMBLY.

Command: **ERASE** ↵
Erase the text and SURF block

Command: **CHPROP** ↵
Change the top bar line that connects the two plates to a hidden line

Command: **QSAVE** ↵ · · · · · · · · · · · Saves the drawing to the same name

OPEN an existing drawing named BASEPL.

```
Resolve Xref ASSEMBLY: assembly          Reloads the xref
```
Notice the SURF block and text are gone.

```
Command: QSAVE ↵                         Saves the drawing to the same
                                         name
```

Figure 9.9

The updated XREF.

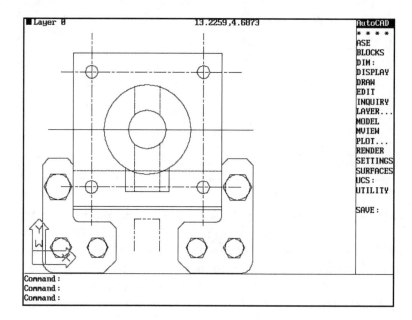

You can see that after the source drawing (ASSEMBLY) was updated, its external reference in BASEPL was automatically updated when loaded next. This simple example of changing a single piece of text illustrates that you can make changes to any drawing by changing the drawings that are referenced in it as xrefs.

Attach is not the only option of the XREF command. The following list discusses the other XREF options.

XREF Options

- **?.** The ? option lists the xrefs in the current drawing. Press Enter to accept the default asterisk for a complete list or use wild-card characters to specify a specific set of names.

- **Bind.** Use Bind to make one or more xrefs permanent in the current drawing file by converting them to blocks. Connect a single xref name, several xref names separated by commas, or use wild cards.

- **Detach.** This option removes xrefs from the drawing. Enter a single xref name, several xref names separated by commas, or use wild card.

- **Path.** This option changes the directory path of attached xrefs. Enter a single xref name, several xref names separated by commas, or use wild cards.

- **Reload.** Use Reload to update xrefs to the latest version of their referenced files without exiting the current drawing. Enter a single xref name, enter several xref names separated by commas, or use wild cards .

- **Attach.** This option enables you to enter a drawing file name to attach it to the current drawing as an xref.

Binding an xref copies the source drawing file into the current drawing as a block definition and a block insert, and it removes the link between the current drawing and the xref source drawing. Editing the source file no longer affects the block in the current drawing.

Like blocks, external references can be nested. In other words, one reference file can reference another. You can assign another name to referenced drawings with the following format: *xref name=file name*. The newly assigned xref name is the name for the xref, only within the current drawing. The actual file name remains unchanged. You may want to do this when you are attaching references that have the same name but are located in different directories, or when an item exceeds the 31-character limit. You can request the File dialog box by using the following format: *xref name=~*.

External references cannot be circular. That is, XREF cannot be used to attach a file to itself or to attach any sequence of files that references the current drawing.

Xrefs have a few limitations. Changes to the color, linetype, or visibility of xrefs affect only the current session. To make permanent changes, change the source file. You cannot explode xrefs. Only model-space entities can be referenced, and paper-space entities are ignored.

Note

A *log file* is maintained each time you use the Attach, Detach, and Reload options. This file contains a log of actions for those commands. The file (in ASCII format) has the same name as the current drawing, and it has the file extension XLG. You may want to periodically print and/or erase these files.

Although the primary benefit of xrefs is the fact that they do not become a part of the drawing in which they are referenced, sometimes you must permanently attach the xref to the drawing. For example, if you are archiving a drawing or sending it to someone else, and that drawing contains xrefs, you have two options: send the source file for each xref, or use the Bind option to make them all a permanent part of the drawing by converting them to blocks.

You can also use the XBIND command to bind individually named items from within an xref without binding the entire xref.

Command

XBIND. The XBIND command makes specified data (such as named blocks, layers, linetypes, and styles in externally referenced files) permanent in the current drawing. (The XREF command's Bind option makes the entire external reference file a permanent part of the current drawing.)

Whichever option you select, XBIND prompts for the names of specific items, such as blocks or text styles, and makes them permanent in the current drawing. XBIND renames the items in the same way as the XREF Bind option does.

Summary

Although AutoCAD's blocks and xrefs are not completely foreign to the manual drafting concepts of templates, transparent stick-ons, and overlays, they provide far more power and flexibility. You have used the BLOCK, INSERT, and WBLOCK commands to quickly copy repetitive items, to scale and rotate them, to work with libraries of standard symbols, parts, and details, and to insert standard title blocks. You have used the MINSERT command to create multiple images in a rectangular array.

You also learned how xrefs are stored as separate files to save disk space and to update the current drawing automatically when you change their source drawing. You should use blocks and xrefs to save time and maintain consistency when your drawings use standard parts and symbols, when they use standard title blocks, or when they are similar to other drawings. You should use xrefs for standardization and control in workgroup design.

You have also learned how redefining blocks or updating xrefs can quickly make wholesale changes to the drawing when you must make revisions.

Dimensioning Drawings

In this chapter, you learn to use AutoCAD's dimensioning commands to generate accurate dimensions from a drawing almost automatically. This chapter teaches you how to perform the following operations:

- Measure distances and areas defined by objects and points in your drawings

- Control accuracy so AutoCAD can calculate dimensions for you

- Dimension linear distances, diameters, radii, and angles by picking points or selecting entities

- Dimension successive linear distances with baseline or ordinate (datum) dimensions, or continuous strings of dimensions

- Draw center marks and leader lines with text notes

- Use associative dimensions to automatically update measurements when associated entities are edited

- Edit dimensions, use dimensioning variables, and create named dimension styles to make the appearance of dimensions meet your drafting standards

Overview

The geometry of a design is only a small part of an AutoCAD drawing. After you draw the object, you usually add notes, symbols, and dimensions to the drawing. In Chapters 6 and 9, you learned to add notes and symbols. In this chapter, you learn to use AutoCAD's dimensioning tools to add dimensions like those shown in figure 10.1. This procedure is done in AutoCAD's dimensioning mode, which has its own collection of commands. Dimensioning commands fall into the following four categories:

- Creating dimensions
- Editing dimensions
- Controlling dimension appearance
- Utility

You also use the regular AutoCAD commands DIST and AREA to measure distances and areas defined by objects and points in your drawings.

Dimensioning Accurately

Chapter 3 emphasized the importance of drawing accurately and presented the techniques you need to do so: snap, object snap, typed coordinate values, distances, and angles. AutoCAD calculates dimensions exactly. Accurate geometry produces accurate dimensions. AutoCAD can calculate the dimensions for you; you do not have to measure objects and enter values.

Measuring Areas and Distances

Although AutoCAD automatically calculates dimensions and places them, you occasionally need to measure distances and areas without adding the dimension text to the drawing. AutoCAD's AREA command measures the area of an object, and computes its perimeter length. The DIST command measures the distance between points.

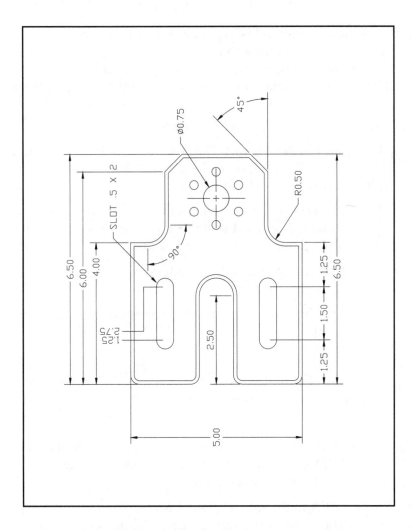

Using the AREA Command

You can measure the area and circumference of a circle or polyline simply by selecting it. If the polyline is not closed, AREA calculates its area as if it were closed from beginning point to end point. To measure areas not bounded by circles and polylines, you define the area to measure by picking its boundary points.

AREA. The AREA command calculates and displays the area and perimeter distance defined by a selected circle or polyline or by a series of three or more points that you pick. The default method is to pick points to define the area. AREA calculates the area and perimeter of open polylines as if they were closed between their beginning and endpoints. To calculate a running total, use AREA's Add and Subtract options.

AREA Options

- **First point** or **Next point.** Pick a series of points to define a closed area. (This option is the default.) Press Enter to complete the area and calculate it.

- **Entity.** Select polylines or circles to calculate their areas and perimeters. If you select more than one entity when in Entity mode, only the most recent one is found.

- **Add.** This option enters Add mode, which accumulates a running total of areas.

- **Subtract.** This option enters Subtract mode, which accumulates a running total of areas.

The entities and sets of points used by AREA must be parallel to the current UCS's X,Y plane.

The last values calculated by Area are saved in the AREA and PERIMETER system variables. You can later use SETVAR to redisplay them.

Try using AREA in the mount plate drawing you created in Chapter 8. The mount plate outline is a polyline, so you can use the Entity option to easily measure its area.

Measuring Area with the AREA Command

Start AutoCAD from the AB directory and edit an existing drawing named MTPLATE.

```
Command: AREA ↵
<First point>/Entity/Add/Subtract: E ↵ Starts Entity mode
Select circle or polyline: Select
the outer polyline
Area = 24.4110, Length = 27.1266
```

You now have the outer polyline's area, which represents the outer surface of the mount plate. The area displayed, however, includes the two slots and the mounting holes. To measure the area of the mount plate's top surface, measure the area of the inner polyline minus the slots and mounting holes.

In Add or Subtract mode, you can repeatedly enter sets of points, use the Entity option to select an entity, or use the Add or Subtract option. If you use Add or Subtract and the Entity option, AREA remains in Entity mode and reprompts until you press Enter at the circle or polyline selection prompt. In Add or Subtract mode, AREA accumulates the total of the areas and reprompts until you press Enter at the <First point>/Entity/Add: (or .../Subtract:) prompt.

Use the Add and Subtract options to find the area of the mount plate's top surface (see fig. 10.2).

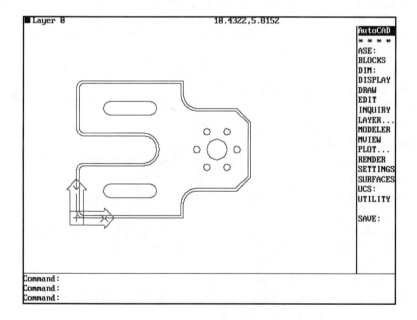

Figure 10.2:

The mount plate drawing.

Using Add and Subtract Mode with AREA

Continue from the previous exercise or edit an existing drawing named MTPLATE.

Command: `AREA` ⏎

`<First point>/Entity/Add/Subtract: A` ⏎   Selects Add mode

`<First point>/Entity/Subtract: E` ⏎   Selects Entity mode

`(ADD mode) Select circle or polyline:`
Select the inner polyline

`Area = 21.7349, Perimeter = 26.3952`

`Total area = 21.7349`

`(ADD mode) Select circle or`   Ends Add mode
`polyline:` *Press Enter*

`<First point>/Entity/Subtract: S` ⏎   Starts Subtract mode

`<First point>/Entity/Add: E` ⏎   Starts Entity mode

`(SUBTRACT mode) Select circle or polyline:`
Select the bottom slot

`Area = 0.9463, Perimeter = 4.5708`

`Total area = 20.7885`

`(SUBTRACT mode) Select circle or polyline:`
Select the top slot, then select the seven holes,
one at a time.

`Area = 0.0491, Circumference = 0.7854`

`Total area = 19.1058`

Your Area and Circumference may vary depending on which circle you picked last.

`(SUBTRACT mode) Select circle or`   Ends Subtract mode
`polyline:` *Press Enter*

`<First point>/Entity/Add:` *Press Enter*   Ends the AREA command

You can see that, as you add and subtract entities, AREA maintains a running total. The area of the mount plate's top surface, minus the slots and mounting holes, is 19.1058 square inches.

Measuring Distances with DIST

AutoCAD also includes the DIST command for measuring distances.

DIST. The DIST command calculates and displays the distance between any two points that you specify. It displays the X,Y,Z point-to-point distance, the angle in the X-Y plane between the first point and second point, the angle from the X-Y plane, and the X, Y, and Z distances between the points.

When you pick two points, DIST displays information about the points. The first item of information is the 3D distance between the two points. The second item is the bearing angle in the X-Y plane from the first point to the second point. The next item is the angle of inclination from the X-Y plane. The final item is the X, Y, and Z distances between the two points. A single DIST command provides the same information as several dimensioning commands, but does not create a dimension entity in the drawing.

AutoCAD saves the last distance measured in the DISTANCE system variable. You can later use SETVAR to redisplay it.

Measure the length of a slot in your mount plate drawing. Use a quadrant object snap to snap the points to the existing arcs.

Using DIST To Measure Distances

Continue from the previous exercise, or edit an existing drawing named MTPLATE.

```
Command: DIST ↵

First point: QUA ↵
of Pick the left arc of slot

Second point: QUA ↵
of Pick the right arc

Distance = 2.0000, Angle in XY Plane = 0,
Angle from XY Plane = 0

Delta X = 2.0000, Delta Y = 0.0000,
Delta Z = 0.0000
```

Dimensioning Drawings

The AutoCAD dimensioning commands construct dimensions with dimension lines, extension lines, leader lines, arrows or tick marks, and text. The *dimensioning mode* is separate from the normal AutoCAD command mode. In dimensioning mode, you can use only dimensioning commands, plus a few transparent commands, such as ZOOM. You use the DIM or DIM1 commands to enter dimensioning mode from the Command: prompt.

DIM, DIM1. The DIM command enters dimensioning mode, which displays the Dim: command prompt. In dimensioning mode, you can use only dimensioning commands and a few transparent commands. Use Exit or Ctrl-C to exit dimensioning mode.

The DIM1 command enters dimensioning mode to execute only one dimensioning command, and then returns to the Command: prompt.

The Elements of Dimensions

AutoCAD's dimensions are composite entities that consist of lines, circles, arcs, and text. Like blocks, you select them as single entities, but you can explode them into the separate entities.

Dimensions are located by definition points, which are usually obscured by the dimensioned geometry. *Witness lines* extend away from the definition points, and, therefore, away from the geometry. A *dimension line* drawn between witness lines indicates the direction in which the dimension measures a distance, angle, or location. A dimension line ends in an arrowhead, tick mark, or other symbol. *Dimension text*, positioned near or embedded in the dimension line, indicates the size of the dimension, along with optional prefixes and suffixes.

The appearance of AutoCAD's dimensions is controlled by *dimensioning variables*. You can tailor dimensions to meet any drafting standard or personal preference.

Dimensioning Commands and Prompts

The following list identifies the four dimensioning command categories and the commands that apply to each one:

- **Creating Dimensions.** ANgular; Leader; *ORdinate*; the linear dimensioning commands: ALigned, Baseline, COntinue, HORizontal, ROtated, and VErtical; and the radial dimensioning commands: CEnter, DIameter, and RAdius

- **Editing Dimensions.** HOMetext, Newtext, *OBlique*, *TEdit*, *TRotate*, and UPdate

- **Controlling Dimension Appearance.** *OVerride*, *REStore*, *SAve*, and *VAriables*

- **Utility.** Exit, REDraw, STAtus, STYle, and Undo

 You can abbreviate dimensioning commands by entering the least number of characters unique to a command. The shortest usable abbreviation for each command is shown in upper-case in the previous dimensioning command list and in the boxed command reference note for each dimensioning command. Otherwise, dimensioning commands are shown in this book's text in upper-case letters and are abbreviated to three characters in exercises (except U for Undo).

Although you can abbreviate some dimensioning commands to one or two characters, they are easier to remember if you use three-character abbreviations.

Dimensioning Command Prompts

Many of the dimensioning commands share common prompts and options. After you understand what is expected by each prompt, you can use any one of the dimensioning commands as easily as another.

Try the following example with the HORizontal dimensioning command, which is explained in detail later. Explanations of the command prompts follow the exercise.

Exploring Common Dimensioning Prompts

Continue from the previous exercise, or edit an existing drawing named MTPLATE.

The first dimension is for practice, so it is off of the mount plate.

Command: **DIM** ↵

Dim: **HOR** ↵

First extension line origin or
RETURN to select: *Pick at 5,5*

Second extension line origin: *Pick at 8,5*

Dimension line location (Text/Angle):
Pick at 6,6

Dimension text <**3.0000**>: *Press Enter*   Accepts the default text for
                                                    this dimension

Dim: **HOR** ↵

First extension line origin or RETURN   Enters entity select
to select: *Press Enter*   mode

Select line, arc, or circle: *Pick top
line of top slot at ① (see fig. 10.3)*

Dimension line location (Text/Angle):
Pick at 2,6

Dimension text <**1.5000**>: *Press Enter*   Accepts the default text for
                                                    this dimension

Dim: *Press Ctrl-C* ***Cancel***   Exits dimensioning mode

Command: **U** ↵   Undoes everything

The following list explains each of the dimension command prompts with descriptions of the possible actions AutoCAD expects.

- First extension line origin or RETURN to select: You can use one of two methods to dimension: select points to define the dimension (the default), or press Enter to select an entity to dimension. If you pick a point in response to the prompt, AutoCAD uses it as the first point for the dimension—the point you are dimensioning *from*.

- Second extension line origin: If you pick a point in response to the first prompt, AutoCAD asks for the point to dimension *to*.

- Select line, arc, or circle: If you press Enter at the first prompt, AutoCAD asks you to select an entity, which it uses to determine the dimension points. You can select polyline segments as well as line, arc, and circle entities. A wide polyline is dimensioned from its centerline.

- Dimension line location (Text/Angle): Specify a point through which you want the dimension line to pass.

- Dimension text <default>: AutoCAD calculates the exact dimension for the entity or points you specify and offers it as a default. You can enter a different dimension text string, or you can press Enter to use the calculated default value for the dimension. If you want blank dimension text, press the space bar and then press Enter.

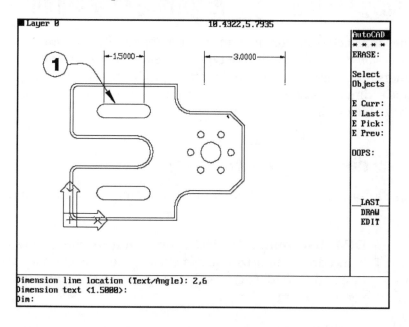

Figure 10.3:

Two horizontal dimensions.

You also can precede or follow the calculated default dimension value with a notation or other text. Enter a pair of brackets to indicate the location of the calculated text, preceded and/or followed by the text to add. For example, to get `This is 2.50 the added text.`, enter:

`Dimension text <2.50>: This is <> the added text.`

In the previous exercise, you exited the DIM command by pressing Ctrl-C. You also can use EXIT; there is essentially no difference in the effects of EXIT or Ctrl-C at the `Dim:` prompt.

 DIM Exit. The Exit dimensioning command returns you to the `Command:` prompt.

With this background on the dimensioning mode and prompts, you can begin dimensioning your mount plate drawing.

Using Linear Dimensioning Commands

The largest class of dimensioning commands is that of *linear dimensions*. HORizontal is one type of linear dimension, and the others are ALigned, Baseline, COntinue, ROtated, and VErtical. Linear dimension commands dimension a straight-line distance. They all work in much the same way.

Using HORizontal Dimensioning

Take a closer look at the HORizontal command you used earlier.

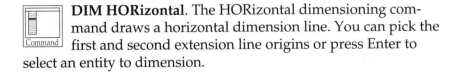 **DIM HORizontal**. The HORizontal dimensioning command draws a horizontal dimension line. You can pick the first and second extension line origins or press Enter to select an entity to dimension.

If you select a circle, its diameter is dimensioned using the 0- and 180-degree quadrant points as the extension line endpoints. If you select other entities, the horizontal projection of their endpoints is dimensioned.

Dimension the mount plate's overall width with a horizontal dimension. This time, use DIM1 to execute only a single dimensioning command. Use object snaps for precision.

Placing Horizontal Dimensions

Continue from the previous exercise, or edit an existing drawing named MTPLATE.

Command: **UCS** ↵ *Set back to World.*

Command: **DIM1** ↵

Dim: **HOR** ↵

First extension line origin or RETURN
to select: **ENDP** ↵
of *Pick point ① (see fig. 10.4)*

Second extension line origin: **ENDP** ↵
of *Pick point ②*

Dimension line location (Text/Angle):
Pick point at 4,1

Dimension text <6.5000>: *Press Enter*   Accepts the default text

Command: DIM1 returns to the
      Command: prompt.

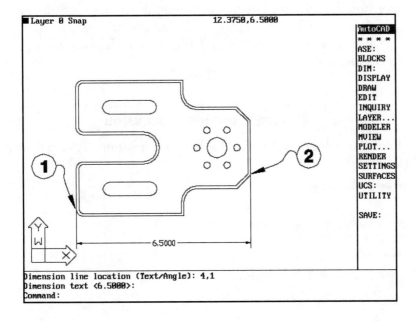

Figure 10.4:

Horizontal dimension.

Although this dimension might not appear exactly the way your dimensioning standards dictate, later in this chapter you see how to control its appearance. You can change many things, including text style, spacing between the dimension and object, the number of decimal places, or the units that AutoCAD uses to measure (decimal inches, millimeters, fractions, and so on).

Using VErtical Dimensioning

You place a vertical linear dimension in exactly the same way as a horizontal one. The only difference between horizontal and vertical dimensioning is the dimension's orientation.

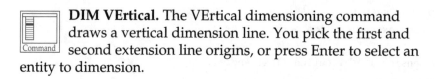 **DIM VErtical.** The VErtical dimensioning command draws a vertical dimension line. You pick the first and second extension line origins, or press Enter to select an entity to dimension.

If you select a circle, its diameter is dimensioned using the 90- and 270-degree quadrant points. If you select other entities, the vertical projection of their endpoints is dimensioned.

Dimension the mount plate's overall height using a vertical dimension. Place the dimension to the far-left side, as shown in figure 10.5. Leave room between it and the part for some later dimensions.

Placing a Vertical Dimension

Continue from the previous exercise, or edit an existing drawing named MTPLATE.

```
Command: DIM ↵

Dim: VER ↵

First extension line origin or
RETURN to select: ENDP ↵

of Pick at ① (see fig. 10.5)

Second extension line origin: ENDP ↵
```

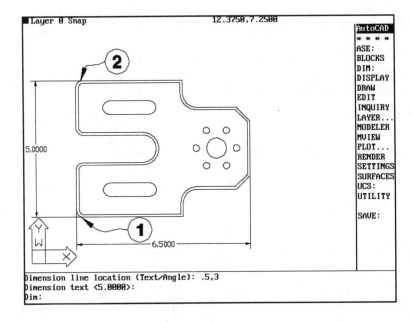

of *Pick at* ②

Dimension line location (Text/Angle):
Pick point .5,3

Dimension text <5.0000>: *Press Enter*   Accepts the default text

Dim: *Press Ctrl-C* *Cancel*   Exits from dimensioning mode

Command: **QSAVE** ↵   Saves the drawing to the same name

You see that the steps for placing a vertical dimension are virtually identical to the steps for horizontal dimensions. The default orientation for dimension text is horizontal, regardless of the dimension's orientation. As you see later in the chapter, you also can set the text orientation to align with the dimension line.

If you inadvertently enter the VErtical dimensioning command, and then enter the points for a horizontal dimension, AutoCAD draws the vertical dimension. If the points are aligned vertically, the result is a zero-length dimension. If the resulting dimension surprises you, double-check your command.

Dimensioning a Series with COntinue and Baseline

Often, you need to dimension a series of features. To avoid repeatedly respecifying the original or previous extension line origin, you can use the COntinue or Baseline dimensioning commands.

Baseline draws baseline dimensions, or dimension stacks. *Baseline dimensions* are multiple dimensions, all beginning at the same start point: the baseline. You first create or select a linear dimension, and then use Baseline to add other dimensions that use the same first extension line origin. Each dimension in the stack is a separate dimension entity.

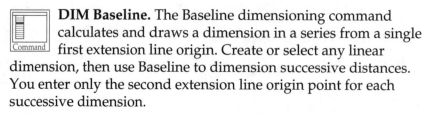

DIM Baseline. The Baseline dimensioning command calculates and draws a dimension in a series from a single first extension line origin. Create or select any linear dimension, then use Baseline to dimension successive distances. You enter only the second extension line origin point for each successive dimension.

Each dimension is offset from, and parallel to, the previous or selected dimension and shares the same first extension line origin. In Release 11, if the previous dimensioning command in the current drawing session is not a linear dimension, you are prompted to select a linear dimension.

Try Baseline to dimension across the top of the plate.

Creating Baseline Dimensions

Continue from the previous exercise

```
Command: DIM ↵
Dim: HOR ↵
First extension line origin or
RETURN to select: ENDP ↵
of Pick point ① (see fig. 10.6)
```

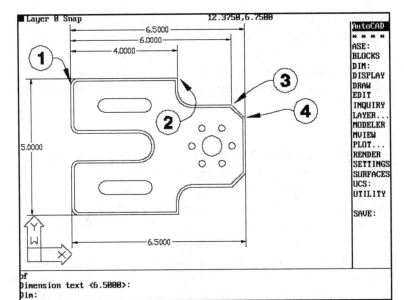

Figure 10.6:
Baseline dimension.

Second extension line origin: **ENDP** ↵

of *Pick point* ②

Dimension line location (Text/Angle):
Pick point 4,8

Dimension text <**4.0000**>: *Press Enter*   Accepts the default text

Dim: **BAS** ↵

Second extension line origin or
RETURN to select: **ENDP** ↵

of *Pick point* ③

Dimension text <**6.0000**>: *Press Enter*   Accepts the default text

Dim: **BAS** ↵

Second extension line origin or
RETURN to select: **ENDP** ↵

of *Pick point* ④

Dimension text <**6.5000**>: *Press Enter*   Accepts the default text

Dim: *Press Ctrl-C* *Cancel*   Exits from dimensioning mode

Command: **QSAVE** ↵   Saves the drawing to the same
name

The COntinue dimensioning command works in much the same way as Baseline. COntinue, however, draws *chained dimensions*, or dimension strings, rather than baseline dimensions. Each new chained dimension starts at the second extension line of the previous or selected linear dimension. The dimension lines are aligned.

DIM COntinue. The COntinue dimensioning command dimensions multiple distances, each measured from the previous or selected second extension-line origin. You create or select any linear dimension, and then use COntinue to dimension successive distances. AutoCAD aligns each dimension with the previous or selected dimension and uses its second extension line as the new first extension line. You enter only the second extension-line origin point for each successive dimension. In Release 11, if the previous dimensioning command in the current drawing session is not a linear dimension, you are prompted to select a linear dimension. In Release 10, you can only use the previous linear dimension, not select dimensions.

Dimension some features near the bottom of the mount plate using continued dimensions, as shown in figure 10.7. Before you place the dimensions, change UNITS to use two decimal places, to enable the dimension values to fit within the dimension lines.

Using COntinue To Place Chained Dimensions

Continue from the previous exercise, or edit an existing drawing named MTPLATE.

```
Command: UNITS ↵
Enter choice, 1 to 5 <2>: Press Enter        Leaves the type of units set to
                                             decimal
Number of digits to right of
decimal point (0 to 8) <4>: 2 ↵
Enter choice, 1 to 5 <1>:                    Ends the UNITS command
Press Ctrl-C *Cancel*
Command: DIM ↵
Dim: HOR ↵
```

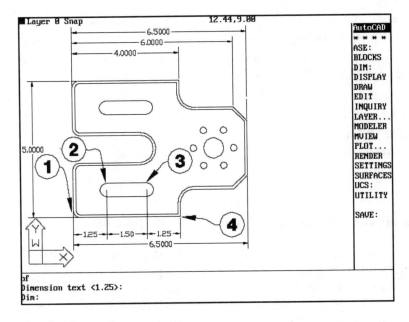

Figure 10.7:
Chained dimensions.

First extension line origin or RETURN
to select: **INT** ⏎
of *Pick point* ① *(see fig. 10.7)*

Second extension line origin: **CEN** ⏎
of *Pick point* ②

Dimension line location (Text/Angle):
Pick at coordinate display 3,1.38

Dimension text <1.25>: *Press Enter*   Accepts the default text

Dim: **CON** ⏎

Second extension line origin or

RETURN to select: **CEN** ⏎
of *Pick point* ③

Dimension text <1.50>: *Press Enter*   Accepts the default text

Dim: **CON** ⏎

Second extension line origin or

RETURN to select: **ENDP** ⏎
of *Pick point* ④

Dimension text <1.25>: *Press Enter*   Accepts the default text

Dim: *Press Ctrl-C* *Cancel*   Exits from dimensioning mode

Command: **QSAVE** ⏎   Saves the drawing to the same
                                                      name

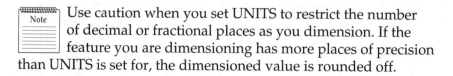 Use caution when you set UNITS to restrict the number of decimal or fractional places as you dimension. If the feature you are dimensioning has more places of precision than UNITS is set for, the dimensioned value is rounded off.

COntinue and Baseline align their dimensions to any angle established by the previous or selected dimension. The next two types of linear dimensions are not restricted to horizontal or vertical dimension lines.

Aligning and Rotating Linear Dimensions

Sometimes you need to draw a dimension parallel to the line of the points being dimensioned. For example, you can dimension the center-to-center distance between the two holes at the lower-right of the plate by using the ALigned dimensioning command. At other times, you need to draw a dimension where the dimension line is set to some other reference angle. For example, you can dimension the projected distance between the same two holes, projected to a 45-degree angle, by using the ROtated dimensioning command.

The difference between the ROtated command and the HORizontal or VErtical commands is that ROtated enables you to specify any angle to align the dimension line. This command is very useful for dimensioning features at an angle not parallel to the dimension line.

DIM ROtated. The ROtated dimensioning command calculates the dimension and draws the dimension line at any specified angle. You can pick the first and second extension line origins, or press Enter to select a line, circle, arc, or polyline to dimension. ROtated draws the extension lines perpendicular to the dimension line.

Except for the `Dimension line angle <0>:` prompt, the prompts for the ROtated command are the same as for the HORizontal or VErtical dimensioning commands. You can enter a specific angle for the dimension line, or pick two points to align it with other objects in the drawing.

Dimension the projected distance between the two holes at the lower-right of the plate, with the dimension line at 45 degrees. The results are compared to the results of an ALigned dimensioning command in figure 10.8.

Placing a Rotated Dimension

Continue from the previous exercise, or edit an existing drawing named MTPLATE.

Command: **DIM** ⏎

Dim: **ROT** ⏎

Dimension line angle <0>: **CEN** ⏎   Sets the dimension line's angle

First extension line origin or

RETURN to select: **CEN** ⏎

of *Pick at hole at ① (see fig. 10.8)*

Second extension line origin: **CEN** ⏎

of *Pick at hole at ②*

Dimension line location (Text/Angle):
 Pick at 9,2.5

Dimension text <0.72>: *Press Enter*   Accepts the default text

Continue to the next exercise without exiting dimensioning mode.

You see that ROtated calculated the projected distance between the two points, using 45 degrees as a reference. ALigned, by comparison, dimensions from point to point.

DIM ALigned. The ALigned dimensioning command calculates the point-to-point dimension between the two extension line origin points you specify and aligns the dimension line parallel to an imaginary line between the points. If you press Enter to select a line, circle, arc, or 2D polyline to dimension, the dimension line aligns with the entity.

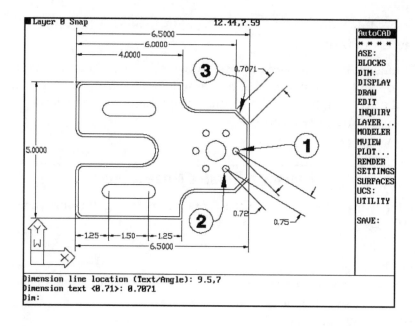

The ALigned dimensioning command's prompts are identical to
those of HORizontal and VErtical.

Try dimensioning the same two holes to compare ALigned to
ROtated. Then dimension the upper-right chamfered corner, using
entity selection to see how it aligns with the polyline segment.
This time, enter your own dimension text to override the default.

Placing an Aligned Dimension

Continue from the previous exercise.

```
Dim: ALI ↵

First extension line origin or
RETURN to select: CEN ↵

of Pick at hole at ① (see fig. 10.8)

Second extension line origin: CEN ↵

of Pick at hole at ②

Dimension line location (Text/Angle):
Pick point 10,1.5
```

```
Dimension text <0.75>: Press Enter        Accepts the default text
Dim: ALI ↵
First extension line origin or
RETURN to select: Press Enter
Select line, arc, or circle:
Pick polyline at ③
Dimension line location
(Text/Angle): Pick at 9.5,7
Dimension text <0.71>: 0.7071 ↵          Enters a more precise value
```
Continue to the next exercise without exiting dimensioning mode.

Compare the results of ALigned to ROT in figure 10.8.

After you use the entity selection option with ALigned, the resulting alignment depends on the type of entity selected. The dimension line aligns to the points derived from the entity. ALigned uses the endpoints of arcs and lines (or polyline segments). If you select a circle, it uses the pick point and the diameter point on the opposite side.

Undoing Dimensions

You might not always dimension perfectly, but if you make an error, you can fix it. You can undo dimensions in three ways. After you exit dimension mode, you can use ERASE to erase specific dimensions. You also can use the U or Undo command after exiting dimension mode. These two commands, however, undo the entire dimensioning mode session. If you need to undo a specific dimensioning command, you can use the dimensioning mode Undo command.

DIM Undo. The Undo dimensioning command cancels the latest dimensioning command, including any dimension variable settings made since the previous command. You can repeat Undo to step back to the beginning of the current dimensioning session. After you exit dimensioning mode, however, AutoCAD treats the entire dimensioning session as a single step.

Try undoing the previous rotated and aligned dimensions. Use the dimensioning mode Undo, and then exit and use the regular AutoCAD Undo.

Undoing Dimensions

Continue from the previous exercise.

`Dim: U ↵`
The aligned chamfer dimension disappears

`Dim: Press Ctrl-C *Cancel*`   Exits from dimensioning mode

`Command: U ↵`

`DIM`
The aligned and rotated hole dimensions disappear

`Command: QSAVE ↵`   Saves the drawing to the same name

 Be careful when you undo dimensions. You cannot reverse the dimension mode Undo; dimension mode REDO does not exist. Also be careful with the regular AutoCAD Undo after exiting DIM mode, because it undoes the entire dimensioning session.

Placing Ordinate Dimensions, Leaders, and Text

Ordinate (datum) dimensions indicate the positions of points or features relative to the current UCS's origin. You can use ordinate dimensions to indicate the elevations of floors in a building section, to mark increments along the X and Y axes of a graph, or to dimension a large number of holes in a part. Like Baseline, a set of ordinate dimensions typically uses a common base point (*datum point*). Ordinate dimensions use only leader lines and dimension text—they do not include dimension lines or extension lines. When dimensioning a large number of features from a common base, using ordinate dimensions makes a neater drawing than the individual dimensions Baseline creates. Ordinate dimensions also facilitate NC programming for parts that must be machined.

Using the DIM ORdinate Command

The ORdinate dimensioning command draws ordinate dimensions.

DIM ORdinate. The DIM ORdinate command draws a leader line and dimension text for ordinate or datum dimensions. The text aligns with the leader line. You pick the *feature* (the leader's first point) to dimension and the leader endpoint. Calculate the distance along the X or Y axis from 0,0 to the feature point, depending on the first (feature) and second leader points.

DIM ORdinate Options

- **Select Feature.** Pick the leader's first point.

- **Leader endpoint.** Pick the second point.

- **Xdatum/Ydatum.** Enter an X or Y to force an X-datum or Y-datum dimension, regardless of leader line points. ORdinate asks for the second leader endpoint.

Because ORdinate calculates the dimensions from 0,0, you generally change the UCS base point when you use it.

Dimension the upper slot's center points with ordinate dimensions. For the second arc center point, use the Xdatum option and make a stair-stepped leader. Set the UCS to the plate's upper-left corner, as shown in figure 10.9.

Figure 10.9:

A series of two ordinate dimensions.

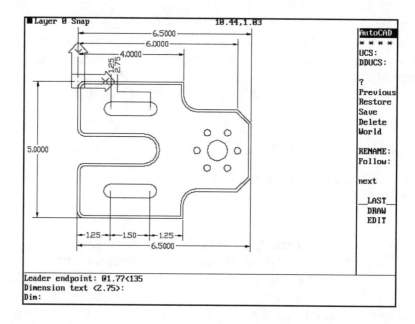

Drawing Ordinate Dimensions

Continue from the previous exercise, or edit an existing drawing named MTPLATE

```
Command: UCS ↵ Set Origin to 2,7
Command: DIM ↵
Dim: ORD ↵
Select Feature: CEN ↵
of Pick the upper slot's left arc
Leader endpoint (Xdatum/Ydatum): Pick at 1.25<90
Dimension text <1.25>: Press Enter
Dim: ORD ↵
Select Feature: CEN ↵
of Pick the right arc
Leader endpoint (Xdatum/Ydatum): X ↵    Forces an X datum
Leader endpoint: Pick at 1.77<135
Dimension text <2.75>: Press Enter        Accepts the default text
Dim: Press Ctrl-C *Cancel*                Exits from dimensioning mode
Command: UCS ↵                            Set to World
Command: QSAVE ↵                          Saves the drawing to the same
                                          name
```

Placing Leaders and Text

In addition to dimensions, drawings usually contain a number of leaders. *Leaders* consist of one or more line segments terminated by an arrowhead, and generally point from a text note to some other feature.

Command

DIM Leader. The Leader dimensioning command draws an arrowhead, one or more leader lines at any angle, and horizontal text.

Leader Options

- **Leader start.** Pick the point for the arrowhead.

- **To point.** Pick as many points as you like, like the LINE command. If the angle of the last two points is not horizontal, Leader adds a short horizontal line.

- **Dimension text <default>.** Press Enter to accept the default text (the text from the most recently calculated dimension) or enter your own text.

Add a leader and note to call out the upper slot in the mount plate drawing.

Placing Leaders

Continue from the previous exercise, or edit an existing drawing named MTPLATE and set UCS back to World.

Command: **LINE** ⏎

Draw a construction line, so the Leader points to the center

From point: **CEN** ⏎ *Pick the CENTER of the right arc on the upper slot*

To point: **6.25,6** ⏎

Command: **DIM1** ⏎

Dim: **LEA** ⏎

Leader start: **INT** ⏎ *Pick the INTersection at ① (see fig. 10.10)*

411

```
To point: INT ⌐ Pick the ENDpoint      at ②
To point: Press Enter                  Ends leader placement
Dimension text <2.75>: SLOT .5 X 2 ⌐   Replaces the default text
Command: INT ⌐ Erase the construction
line
Command: QSAVE ⌐                       Saves the drawing
```

Figure 10.10:

A leader and text call out.

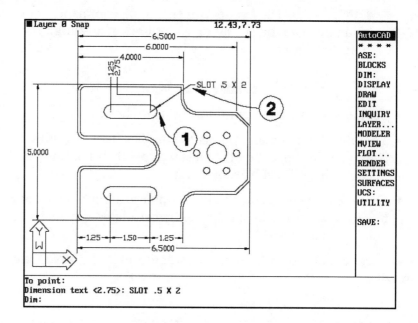

If you continued from the ordinate dimensioning exercise, the default leader text was the 2.75 from the last ORdinate command. The default is useful for calling out another type of dimension in which the text does not fit. Just enter a space for the original dimension text, then use Leader to place the text elsewhere, pointing to the original dimension line.

Tip: To draw a leader with no text, enter only a space as text. To enter additional lines of text, use the DTEXT command, pick the leader text as the start point with the INS object snap mode, and then enter a space and press Enter to step down for the next line of text.

Controlling Dimension Appearance

Many different dimensioning standards exist. You have learned how to change dimensioning by setting different units and text styles. You also can control the appearance and other characteristics of dimensions by changing the settings of dimension variables.

Dimension Styles and Variables

AutoCAD includes several dozen dimension variables. Each one controls some aspect of a dimension or its appearance. You can change many variables or just a few, depending upon the effects you want to achieve. A specific configuration of dimension variables produces a dimension style. Creating a new dimension style can be tedious, but AutoCAD enables you to save the variable settings under a dimension style name. From then on in that drawing, you can set the dimension style by its name.

The Dimension Styles and Variables Dialog Box

Using a series of dialog boxes, you can control all the dimension variables. You can display the top level dialog box, Dimension Styles and Variables, from the Dimension Style. . . option of the Settings pull-down menu, or using the DDIM command. From the top-level dialog box, you can assign new dimension style names, recall named styles, and display the Dimension Variables dialog boxes. Figure 10.11 shows the Dimension Styles and Variables dialog box.

When you display the Dimension Styles and Variables dialog box for the first time, the Dimension Styles box lists one dimension style, *UNNAMED. This style is defined by AutoCAD's default dimension variable settings. This style is suitable for full-size drawings in a variety of fields and disciplines.

Figure 10.11:

The Dimension Styles and Variables dialog box.

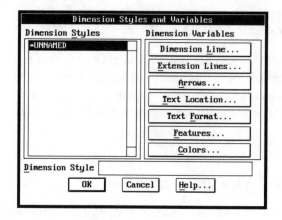

After you have changed one or more dimension variables, you can name the new style by entering a name in the **D**imension Style box. The new name appears in the Dimension **S**tyles list box. The first name you enter replaces the *UNNAMED style, and additional names are appended to the list. After you enter a new name, it is highlighted. If you exit the dialog box with OK, it becomes the current style. You can select a new style from the list by picking the name—it appears in the **D**imension Style box—and clicking on OK.

To change dimension variables, click on the appropriate Dimension Variables button. You do not need to know the variables' names, only the aspect of the dimension that you want to change.

All the dialog boxes show the current style name and include boxes to set the dimension element's color and the dimension scale relative to its plot size.

The Dimension Line Dialog Box

The Dimension Line dialog box controls the variables that affect how the dimension line is drawn. You can force AutoCAD to draw interior dimension lines even when the dimension text does not fit between the extension lines. You also can control how much of the line AutoCAD removes to embed dimension text, and set the distance AutoCAD moves when creating baseline dimensions. Figure 10.12 shows the Dimension Line dialog box.

```
                Dimension Line
Style: *UNNAMED
Feature Scaling          1.00000
[ ] Use Paper Space Scaling
Dimension Line Color  BYBLOCK  [ ]
Dimension Line
   [ ] Force Interior Lines
   [X] Reference Dimension
   Text Gap              0.09
   Baseline Increment    0.38
   [  OK  ]  [ Cancel ]  [ Help... ]
```

Figure 10.12:

The Dimension Line dialog box.

The Extension Lines Dialog Box

The Extension Lines dialog box (fig. 10.13) controls the variables that affect how AutoCAD draws extension lines (witness lines). You use the Extension Above Line box to set the distance by which the extension line continues past the dimension line. The Feature Offset box sets the distance between the definition point and the point where AutoCAD begins drawing the extension line. This setting enables you to have a gap between the object you select to define the extension line, and the extension line itself. The Visibility box enables you to suppress one or both extension lines which you might want to do when a dimension line ends on the dimensioned object. The Center Mark Size box defines the size of the cross AutoCAD draws at the center of an arc or circle after you enter the DIAMETER, RADIUS, or CENTER dimensioning commands. (These commands are discussed later.)

The Arrows Dialog Box

The Arrows dialog box controls the dimension variables that determine how AutoCAD terminates dimension lines (see fig. 10.14). The row of radio buttons enables you to select an arrowhead (the default), a tick mark (diagonal slash), a dot, or a user-defined symbol. The Arrow Size box enables you to enter the size of the arrow, tick mark, dot, or user symbol. If you select a user-defined arrow, the User Arrow box darkens, and you enter the name of the block to use. If you select a user-defined arrow, you also can check Separate Arrows and specify a different block for each end of the dimension line. The Tick Extension box darkens after you select Tic**k**, so you can specify that the dimension line extends through the tick marks and past the extension lines.

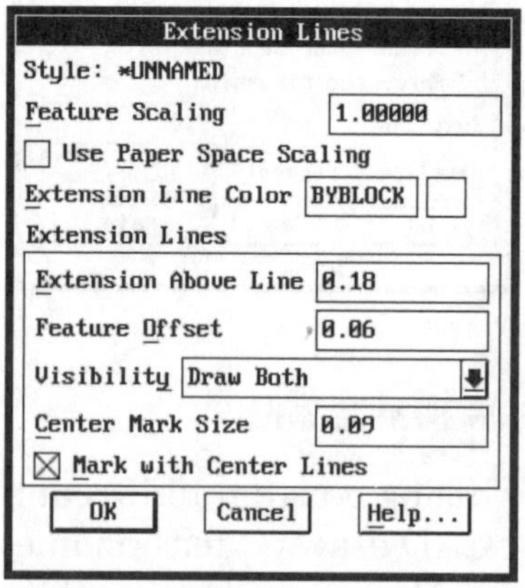

Figure 10.13:

The Extension Lines dialog box.

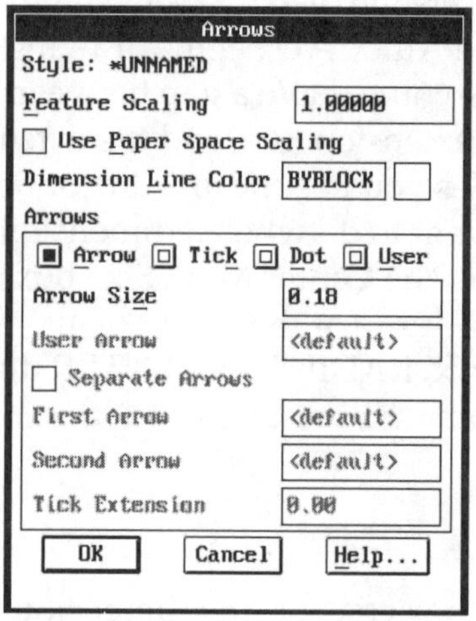

Figure 10.14:

The Arrows dialog box.

The Text Location Dialog Box

The Text Location dialog box controls the dimension variables that determine the size of dimension text and where AutoCAD locates it relative to the dimension line (see fig. 10.15). The Text **H**eight box controls the height of dimension text and **T**olerance

Height controls the height of dimension tolerances if they are drawn. The Text Placement boxes, **H**orizontal and **V**ertical, enable you to locate text embedded in the dimension line, above it or below it, centered along its length, at either end, and inside or outside the extension lines. The A**l**ignment box enables you to control whether dimension text is always horizontal, aligned with the dimension line, or varied. The setting depends upon whether the dimension text is inside or outside the extension lines.

```
┌─────────────────────────────────────┐
│          Text Location              │
│ Style: *UNNAMED                     │
│ Feature Scaling      │ 1.00000 │    │
│ ☐ Use Paper Space Scaling           │
│ Dimension Text Color │BYBLOCK│  □   │
│ Text Position                       │
│ ┌─────────────────────────────────┐ │
│ │ Text Height        │ 0.18 │     │ │
│ │ Tolerance Height   │ 0.18 │     │ │
│ │ Text Placement                  │ │
│ │ Horizontal │Default       │ ▼ │ │ │
│ │ Vertical   │Centered      │ ▼ │ │ │
│ │ Relative Position  │ 0.00 │     │ │
│ │ Alignment                       │ │
│ │ │Orient Text Horizontally│ ▼ │   │ │
│ └─────────────────────────────────┘ │
│   ┌────┐  ┌──────┐  ┌──────┐        │
│   │ OK │  │Cancel│  │Help..│        │
│   └────┘  └──────┘  └──────┘        │
└─────────────────────────────────────┘
```

Figure 10.15:

The Text Location dialog box.

The Text Format Dialog Box

The Text Format dialog box, shown in figure 10.16, controls the dimension variables that determine the content of dimension text. The Length **S**caling box enables you to enter a factor that AutoCAD applies to the actual measured length to calculate the value shown by the dimension text. If you are drawing a 2X detail, you can enter a Length Scaling factor of .5, and the dimension text reflects the correct dimension.

The **R**ound Off box enables you to enter an increment for AutoCAD to round off dimensions independent of the UNITS settings. You can work with a coordinate display set to five decimal places, but have all dimensions appear to only three decimal places.

The Text Prefix and Text Suffix boxes enable you to enter text strings to add to the dimension text. For example, you might want to suffix basic dimensions with the word BASIC rather than draw a box around the text, and suffix reference dimensions with REF. rather than surround the text with parentheses.

The Zero Suppression block contains boxes that enable you to suppress the printing of zeros in dimension text when UNITS is set to Architectural.

The Tolerances box contains three radio buttons that control how dimension text reflects tolerance settings. None prints the basic dimension only; Variance adds a tolerance value to the end of the dimension text, and Limits replaces the dimension text with two values: the basic dimension plus the Upper Value and the basic dimension minus the Lower Value. Both the Upper Value and the Lower Value boxes contain constant tolerance values used in the tolerance text, or to calculate dimension limits.

The Alternate Units box enables you to control the display of an alternate, or reference, dimension text string that follows the primary dimension text. The number of decimal places and suffix are independent of the primary dimension text. Calculate the value shown in alternate units from the primary dimension by applying the scaling factor. The default value of 25.4 enables you to add alternate metric dimensions to the drawings you create in inches.

Figure 10.16:

The Text Format dialog box.

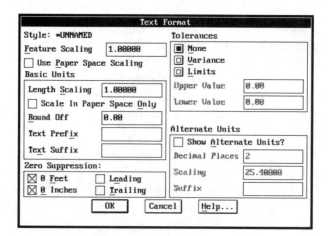

The Features Dialog Box

The Features dialog box displays the settings of all the dialog boxes described earlier, except for Text Format, in a single dialog box. If you have a large number of variables to change, you can do it with fewer keystrokes in the Features dialog box (see fig. 10.17).

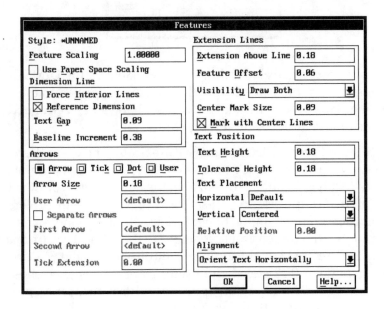

The Colors Dialog Box

You can use the Colors dialog box shown in figure 10.18 to set the colors of dimension lines, extension lines, and dimension text, as well as the overall scale of dimensions.

Scaling Dimensions

The default settings produce dimensions that are suitable for a drawing that is plotted at full scale (such as the mount plate), but you need to set different dimension scales for drawings that are plotted at larger or smaller scales. Setting a scale factor for sizing dimensions is similar to setting a scale for symbols that are defined at their desired plot size, such as a 3/8" bubble. You insert such symbols at the inverse of the plot scale.

Figure 10.18:

The Colors dialog box.

```
┌─────────────────────────────────────┐
│              Colors                  │
│ Style: *UNNAMED                      │
│ Feature Scaling         │1.00000   │ │
│ ☐ Use Paper Space Scaling            │
│ Dimension Line Color │BYBLOCK│ │    │
│ Extension Line Color │BYBLOCK│ │    │
│ Dimension Text Color │BYBLOCK│ │    │
│   ┌──────┐  ┌────────┐  ┌──────┐    │
│   │  OK  │  │ Cancel │  │Help...│   │
│   └──────┘  └────────┘  └──────┘    │
└─────────────────────────────────────┘
```

Multiply every size-related dimension variable by the DIMSCALE dimension variable value before the effects are applied to the drawing. This procedure enables you to change all size-related dimensioning variables by setting DIMSCALE.

DIMSCALE is controlled by the Feature Scaling boxes in the dimension variables dialog boxes. You set size-related parameters, such as text height and arrow size, to the actual sizes you want in your plotted output. Then you set Feature Scaling to the inverse of the plot scale. For example, to get 0.125-inch dimension text in a 1:12 plot, set the dimension text height to 0.125 and Feature Scaling to 12. The Text Height settings is multiplied by the Feature Scaling value. A 0.125 text height setting appears as 1.5 inches in the drawing (.125 x 12), but it appear as 0.125 inches when plotted at 1:12. The default setting for Feature Scaling is 1.

Dimensioning Circles, Arcs, and Angles

AutoCAD makes the dimensioning of objects and geometric relationships, easy and automatic. Even though you can dimension circles and arcs by using linear dimensions, AutoCAD includes three dimensioning commands to use specifically with circles and arcs: DIameter, RAdius, and CEnter. The ANgular command dimensions the angle between points or lines, or the angle of an arc or part of a circle.

The first command, DIameter, dimensions the diameter of a circle.

DIM Diameter. The Diameter command dimensions arcs and circles. The DIMCEN, DIMTIX, and DIMTOFL dimension variables control the location of the dimension text and whether or not dimension lines, center lines, and center marks are drawn, to create various styles of diameter dimensions.

The RAdius dimensioning command is almost identical to DIameter.

DIM RAdius. The RAdius dimensioning command dimensions arcs and circles. The DIMCEN, DIMTIX, and DIMTOFL dimension variables control the text location and whether or not dimension lines, center lines, and center marks are drawn, to create various styles of radius dimensions.

To use DIameter or RAdius, you must select a circle, arc, or arc polyline segment by picking a point. The diameter or radius dimension line passes through the center of the arc or circle and aligns with the pick point.

You can set DIMTIX OFF (the default) to force the text outside the circle or arc. Set DIMTIX ON to enable the text inside the circle or arc, if it fits. Set DIMTOFL ON to cause a radius or arc dimension line to be drawn, whether or not the text is outside the circle or arc. A DIMTOFL setting of OFF (the default) only draws the dimension line if the text is inside.

Set DIMCEN to 0 to suppress drawing a center mark. Set DIMCEN to a positive number to draw a center mark of that size. Set DIMCEN to a negative number to draw center lines, with a center mark the size of the number's absolute value.

Use the Diameter command to dimension the larger hole inside the six-bolt mounting hole pattern. Use RAdius to dimension one of the large fillets on the mount plate. The results are shown in figure 10.19.

Figure 10.19:

Diameter and radius dimensions.

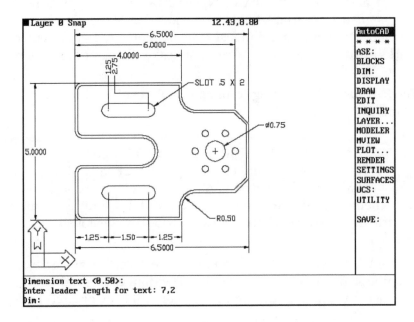

Dimensioning with DIameter and RAdius

Continue from the previous exercise, or edit an existing drawing named MTPLATE.

Command: **DIM** ⏎

Dim: **DIA** ⏎

Select arc or circle: *Pick large circle at about 45 degrees*

Dimension text <0.75>: *Press Enter*   Accepts the default text

Enter leader length for text: *Move cursor to see dimension drag, then enter 1.5 for leader length*

Dim: **RA** ⏎

Select arc or circle: *Pick the large*
(0.5") fillet at the bottom right on the outer
perimeter

Dimension text: *Press Enter*

Enter leader length for text: *Move cursor*
inside and outside the plate to see dimension drag,
and then pick point 7,2

DIameter only draws a leader if the dimension is outside the circle
or arc, but RAdius can draw the leader inside or outside the circle
or arc. You saw how you could drag the leader to either side of
the arc. You also can create an inside radius leader by entering a
negative leader length.

You saw how the DIameter dimension placed a center mark in the
circle. If the center mark, without a dimension, is all you want, use
the CEnter dimensioning command. CEnter draws only a center
mark or center lines and a center mark in the selected circle or arc.

DIM CEnter. The CEnter dimensioning command draws a
center mark (a cross) or center mark and center lines in
circles and arcs. The DIMCEN dimension variable controls
the center mark size and whether center lines also are drawn.

If DIMCEN is set to a positive value, CEnter draws a cross at the
circle's center. The larger the value of DIMCEN, the larger the
cross. If DIMCEN is set to a negative value, CEnter also draws
center lines that extend outside the circle. If DIMCEN is 0, trying
to use CEnter produces the message, DIMCEN = 0,0, not drawing
center cross. *Invalid*

Use a negative DIMCEN setting to place a center line and mark in
the circle you dimensioned in the previous exercise (see fig. 10.20).

Figure 10.20:

Center lines and mark drawn with negative DIMCEN.

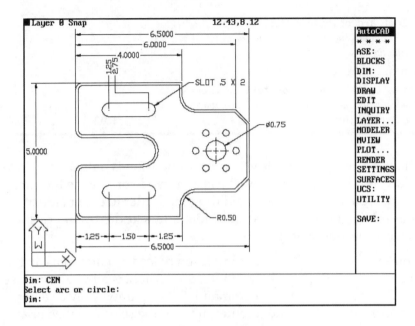

Placing Center Crosses with CEnter

Continue from the preceding exercise, or edit an existing drawing named MTPLATE and set UCS back to World.

```
Command: DIM ↵
Dim: DIMCEN ↵
Current value <0.09> New value: -.09 ↵   Assigns new DIMCEN value
Dim: CEN ↵
Select arc or circle: Pick any
point on the large circle
Dim: Press Ctrl-C *Cancel*                Exits from dimensioning mode
Command: QSAVE ↵                          Saves the drawing to the same
                                          name
```

Using ANgular Dimensioning

You can use the ANgular dimensioning command to dimension the angle between two lines, the angle subtended by an arc, or add an angular measurement to indicate part of a circle.

DIM ANgular. The ANgular dimensioning command dimensions an angle defined by picking two nonparallel lines or polyline segments, picking an arc or polyline arc segment, picking a circle and another point, or picking three points. All entity selection methods require selection by picking points.

ANgular Dimensioning Options

- **arc.** Pick an arc or polyline arc segment, then specify the dimension arc location and the dimension text location to dimension the angle. The extension lines pass from the center point to or through the end points.

- **circle.** Pick a circle, then specify a second angle endpoint, the dimension arc location, and the dimension text location to dimension the angle. The extension lines pass from the center point to or through the circle pick point and second angle endpoint.

- **line** and **Second line:.** Pick two nonparallel lines or polyline segments, then specify the dimension arc location and the dimension text location to dimension the angle between the lines from their intersection. This method is the only method for ANgular in Release 10, which initially prompts with `Select first line:.`

- **RETURN.** Press Enter and you are prompted for three points to determine the angle: `Angle vertex:`, `First angle endpoint:`, and `Second angle endpoint:`. Then you specify the dimension arc location and the dimension text location. The extension lines pass from the center point to or through the first and second angle endpoints.

- **Enter dimension line arc location (Text/Angle):.** Except for the two-line option, AutoCAD uses the point you specify for the dimension line arc location to determine whether to dimension the angle inside or outside the extension lines. For the two-line option, AutoCAD considers the lines to extend through their intersection, creating four possible angles to dimension. It uses the point you specify for the dimension line arc location to determine which angles to dimension, drawing any needed extension lines.

- **Dimension text <*default*>:.** This prompt is the standard default text prompt. Press Enter or enter an alternate value.

- **Enter text location:.** Specify the text location or press Enter to center the text in the dimension arc.

Try the ANgular dimensioning command to dimension the mount plate's lower-right chamfer and upper-right fillet, as shown in figure 10.21.

Dimensioning Angles with ANgular

Continue from the previous exercise, or edit an existing drawing named MTPLATE and set UCS back to World.

Command: **DIM** ↵

Dim: **ANG** ↵

Select arc, circle, line, or RETURN:
Pick chamfer line at ① (see fig. 10.21)

Figure 10.21:

Angular dimension.

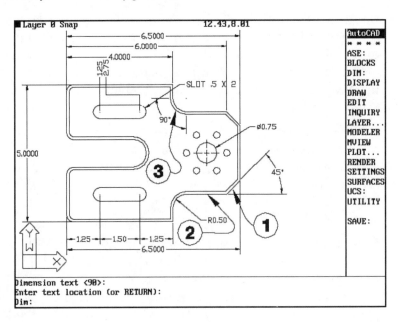

```
Second line: Pick horizontal line at ②
Enter dimension line arc location
(Text/Angle): Pick point 10,3.5
```
Dimension text <45>: *Press Enter*   Accepts the default text

Enter text location: *Press Enter*   Accepts the default location

Dim: **ANG** ⏎
```
Select arc, circle, line, or RETURN:
Pick the fillet arc of the inside
polyline at ③
Enter dimension line arc location
(Text/Angle): Pick point 5.5,6
```
Dimension text <90>: *Press Enter*

Enter text location: *Press Enter*

Dim: *Press Ctrl-C* *Cancel*

Command: **QSAVE** ⏎   Saves the drawing to the same name

Whether you realize it or not, you have been creating associative dimensions.

Introducing Associative Dimensions

An *associative dimension* is a single dimension entity. In AutoCAD, a single dimension entity consists of arrowheads, dimension lines, dimension text, and extension lines. There are many advantages to using associative dimensions. If you stretch one or more entities, any associative dimension related to the feature also changes automatically—you do not have to redimension it.

Setting the DIMASO dimension variable to ON (the default) makes dimensions associative. DIMASO affects linear, angular, ordinate, diameter, and radius dimensioning. Leaders and center marks are not associative. If DIMASO is ON when a dimension is created, the dimension is created as a single associative dimension entity. If DIMASO is OFF when a dimension is created, the dimension is created as individual arrowheads (blocks), dimension lines, dimension text, and extension lines, each component being a separate AutoCAD entity. Exploding an associative dimension with the AutoCAD EXPLODE command creates the same entities as creating a nonassociative dimension.

Using associative dimensions creates definition points on a layer named DEFPOINTS. Definition points link the dimension to the entity being dimensioned. You can snap to definition points with the NODe object snap mode. Definition points exist at each extension line origin and at the intersection of the dimension line with the second extension line origin.

You can use the AutoCAD STRETCH command to stretch associative dimensions or to move associative dimensioning text. If you catch a definition point in the STRETCH command's crossing window, the dimension is stretched. Although the dimension text does not have an actual definition point at the center, it behaves as if there were. You can use STRETCH to move dimension text by selecting it with a small crossing window centered on the text.

Several dimensioning commands are available for editing associative dimensions. Three are presented here, and others are covered later in the chapter.

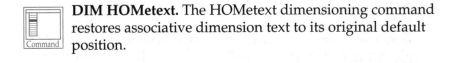

DIM HOMetext. The HOMetext dimensioning command restores associative dimension text to its original default position.

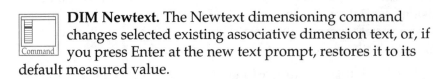

DIM Newtext. The Newtext dimensioning command changes selected existing associative dimension text, or, if you press Enter at the new text prompt, restores it to its default measured value.

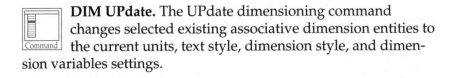

DIM UPdate. The UPdate dimensioning command changes selected existing associative dimension entities to the current units, text style, dimension style, and dimension variables settings.

Try stretching and editing some existing associative dimensions in the mount plate drawing. Use the UPDATE command to change the 6.5000 dimension at the bottom of the plate to the current two decimal places of precision, to increase its extension line offset by setting DIMEXO, and to add inch marks (") by setting DIMPOST. Stretching also updates dimensions to the current settings. Select and stretch the plate's left side and watch the dimensions across the top and bottom of the plate adjust and update to two decimal places. Use STRETCH to move the 4.5000 (or 4.50) dimension text above the plate. Use NEWTEXT to change the R0.50 radius dimension to R .5", and then change it back again. Use HOMETEXT to restore the 4.50" dimension text to its original position. The new text and the updated and stretched dimensions are shown in figure 10.22.

Changing and Stretching Associative Dimensions

Continue from the previous series of exercises.

Use UNDO and set a Mark to later undo
Back to later

Command: **DIM** ↵

Dim: **DIMEXO** ↵

Set to 0.18

Dim: **DIMPOST** ↵

Set to " (a quotation mark)

Dim: **UPDATE** ↵

Select objects: *Select the 6.5000 dimension at ① (see fig. 10.22)*

Select objects: *Press Enter*   Changes to 6.50" and the gaps between the extension lines and the plate increase

Dim: **EXIT** ↵   Exits from dimensioning mode

Command: **STRETCH** ↵

Select objects to stretch by window or polygon

Select objects: C *Select a Crossing window from ② to ③*

Select objects: *Press Enter*

Base point: *Pick any point*

Figure 10.22:

*Updated, stretched,
and new text
dimensions.*

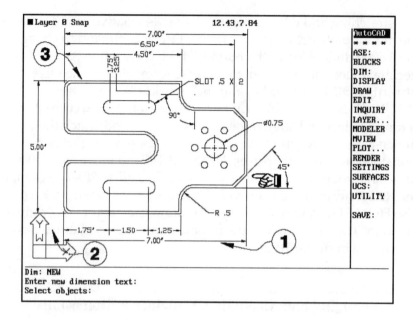

```
New point: @-.5,0 ⏎
```

Notice the affected dimensions' values and extension line offsets change

```
Command: STRETCH ⏎
```

*Use a tiny Crossing window to select the
4.50 dimension text above the plate, and then
move the text .75 to the right*

```
Command: DIM ⏎

Dim: NEW ⏎

Enter new dimension text: R .5" ⏎

Select objects: Select the R0.50 radius
dimension
```

```
Select objects: Press Enter              Changes the dimension to R .5"

Dim: NEW ⏎

Enter new dimension text: Press Enter    Changes the text back to its
                                         original value, updated to the
                                         current  dimension variable
                                         settings

Select objects: P ⏎                      Reselects the previously selected
                                         text
```

`Select objects:` *Press Enter*	Changes the text back to its original value, updated to the current dimension variable settings
`Dim: HOM` ⏎	
`Select objects:` *Pick the 4.50 dimension above the plate*	
`Select objects:` *Press Enter*	Returns the dimension to its default position
`Dim: EXIT` ⏎	
Use UNDO and undo Back	

Stretching an associative dimension or editing it with Newtext, HOMetext, or UPdate updates it to the current dimension variable settings. Because of this updating, you must take care to ensure that all dimension variables are set appropriately for the dimension(s) being edited before you update them.

Editing Associative Dimensions

In addition to standard commands that can change associative dimensions (such as STRETCH) and the HOMetext, Newtext, and UPdate dimensioning commands, AutoCAD includes several other dimensioning commands for editing the appearance of associative dimensions. TEdit changes the location of dimension text, TRotate (Text Rotate) rotates existing dimension text, and OBlique changes the angle of extension lines.

DIM TEdit. The DIM TEdit (DIMension Text Edit) relocates existing dimension text. You can drag the dimension text into place with your pointing device; specify left, right, or home (original) justification; or specify a text angle.

DIM TEdit Options

- **Left.** The Left option relocates linear, radius, and diameter dimension text. The exact text location varies depending on the vertical placement of the dimension.

431

- **Right.** The Right option relocates linear, radius, and diameter dimension text. The exact text location varies depending on the vertical placement of the dimension.

- **Home.** The Home option restores dimension text to its original location, similar to the HOMetext dimensioning command.

- **Angle.** The Angle option rotates dimension text to the angle you specify, similar to the TRotate dimensioning command.

- **Enter point.** This option relocates dimension text to the point you specify, similar to using the STRETCH command.

Another dimension command that enables you to edit dimension text is TRotate. As its name implies, TRotate rotates dimension text to the angle you specify.

 DIM TRotate. The DIM TRotate (Text Rotate) command rotates existing dimension text to any angle.

TEdit Angle produces the same result as TRotate, although TRotate can change more than one dimension at once.

The last command, OBlique, is useful for dimensioning isometric drawings or angling the dimension lines when they do not fit in a tight spot.

DIM OBlique. The OBlique dimensioning command changes existing associative dimension extension line angles without changing the dimension text value. Press Enter at the angle prompt to restore the default angle.

Try out a few dimension editing commands on some of your dimensions. Relocate the 4.00 dimension to the right with TEdit, and then rotate the 90-degree angle dimension to –45 degrees. None of the mount plate drawing's features are really suitable for an obliqued dimension, but try OBlique anyway, on the 5.00 dimension at the far left, as shown in figure 10.23.

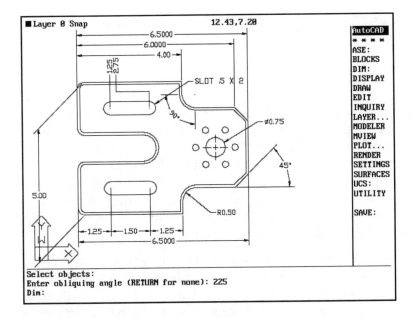

Figure 10.23:

Right-justified and rotated text and an obliqued dimension.

Editing Dimensions with TEdit, TRotate, and HOMetext

Command: **DIM** ↵

Dim: **TED** ↵

Select dimension: *Select the 4.00 dimension above the plate*

Enter text location (Left/Right/Home /Angle): *Move the cursor, noting how it drags the text, then enter* **R** ↵

Dim: **TR** ↵

Enter text angle: **-45** ↵

Select objects: *Select the 90-degree radius dimension*

Select objects: *Press Enter*   Aligns the text with the dimension line arc

Dim: **OBL** ↵

Select object: *Pick the 5.00 vertical dimension*

Select object: *Press Enter*

Enter obliquing angle   Moves the dimension
(RETURN for none): **225** ↵

Dim: **EXIT** ↵   Ends dimensioning mode

That exercise finishes this chapter's tour of dimensioning.

Summary

Although the resulting dimensioned drawing does not meet any "proper" standard, this chapter's tour of dimensioning covered all the major aspects of AutoCAD's dimensioning. You can make many more dimension variable settings, however, and you can use options to make AutoCAD's dimensioning conform to your standards. For a more complete discussion of these settings and options, see *Inside AutoCAD Release 12* (from New Riders Publishing), or the *AutoCAD Reference Manual*.

Associative dimensions are a real time-saver when you must edit dimensions. You can easily edit the value, style, or other characteristics of one or more dimensions with AutoCAD's wide range of dimensioning commands. Remember that when a dimension is exploded with the EXPLODE command, it becomes individual entities, such as lines, arrowhead blocks, and text. You cannot restore a dimension's associativity after it has been exploded.

Dimension styles help you establish, control, and enforce dimensioning standards. You can create and use standard styles for all of your common dimension types. Dimension styles have the added benefit of protecting associative dimensions from accidental changes and edits.

After you draw, annotate, and dimension a drawing, you are ready to plot it. Composing and plotting a final drawing is the topic of the final chapter.

Composing, Annotating, and Plotting

After you draw the geometry of your model, part, or floor plan, you compose the complete drawing image as you will plot it. A single model may be the subject of several plotted drawings. To compose a drawing, you define views, arrange views, and add text and drawing reference symbology. When the drawing has been composed, you can plot the drawing.

Composing a single drawing of a simple model that can be plotted full-scale is a straightforward task. If the model is much smaller, or much larger than the sheet on which you will plot the drawing, the task is more complex. Figure 11.1 shows the BRIDGE drawing from Chapter 5, composed for a plot, with three scaled paper space viewports.

Figure 11.1:

A multiview plot of the BRIDGE drawing.

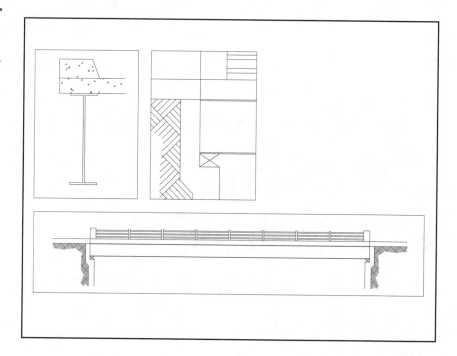

In this chapter, you use the concepts and commands you learned to compose and plot a finished drawing. You learn to perform the following procedures:

- Lay out, scale and label views, sections, and details to compose finished plots

- Compose and scale views and sections in paper space

- Add crosshatching and patterned fills

- Add dimensions in mview viewports, automatically adjusting dimension scales

- Add notes, schedules, and a title sheet in paper space

- Plot drawings

- Plot multiple drawings on a single sheet

Plotting a Basic Drawing

If your model is two-dimensional and can be plotted at full size, you can enter the dimensions, title block, text, and reference symbology without regard to scale factor. You can then plot the finished drawing. You initiate the plotting process by selecting Plot... from the File pull-down menu or by entering the PLOT command. The PLOT command displays the Plot Configuration dialog box, which is the control center for configuring plot devices and plots.

The Plot Configuration Dialog Box

The Plot Configuration dialog box contains six blocks of buttons and boxes. The Device and Default Information box lists the current plot device and includes a command button that displays the Device and Default Selection dialog box. This dialog box enables you to select an alternate plot device. The Pen Parameters block contains buttons that display additional dialog boxes: one to assign plotter pens to drawing colors, and another to specify how AutoCAD should sort drawing entities for plotting. The Additional Parameters block includes radio buttons for selecting the part of the drawing to be plotted, as well as other parameters.

The Paper Size and Orientation block contains buttons that enable you to describe the sheet of paper that you will use for the plot and the units used for the plot. The Scale, Rotation, and Origin block contains text entry boxes for calculating paper to model space scale, a check box to specify how the plot is to be fit on the paper, and a command button that displays the Plot Rotation and Origin dialog box. The Plot Rotation and Origin dialog box controls where the drawing will be located and oriented on the sheet.

The Plot Preview block contains buttons to verify that the plot will fit on the specified sheet of paper, and to preview its location and orientation. In other words, you can verify that the settings are correct without actually plotting the drawing. The Plot Configuration dialog box is shown in figure 11.2.

You cannot select a printer or plotter from the Plot Configuration dialog box if the device driver for that printer or plotter has not been loaded. Use the CONFIG command to configure AutoCAD to include any printers or plotters you may need.

Previewing a Plot

To preview a plot configuration, press one of the radio buttons (Partial or Full), and click the Preview command button. A partial preview shows you how the plot will fit on the paper, using the Preview Effective Plotting Area dialog box shown in figure 11.3. This dialog box displays quickly, but only verifies the dimensions of the paper and the effective plotting area.

Figure 11.2:

Plot Configuration dialog box.

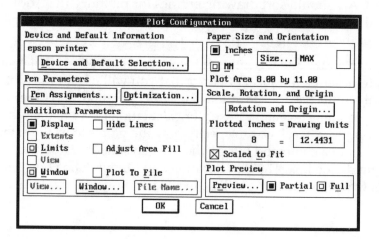

A **Fu**ll preview displays the plot on the screen, as it will be plotted on the paper. AutoCAD draws an outline of the usable part of the paper (allowing for the border that all plotters cannot use), and plots the drawing in that outline, according to the parameters you set in the Plot Configuration dialog box.

Figure 11.3:

Preview Effective Plotting Area dialog box.

```
┌─────────────────────────────────────────┐
│        Preview Effective Plotting Area   │
│                                           │
│              ┌──────────┐                 │
│              │          │                 │
│              │          │                 │
│              ├──────────┤                 │
│              │          │                 │
│              │          │                 │
│              └──────────┘                 │
│                                           │
│   ── Paper size: 8.00 wide by 11.00 high  │
│   ── Effective area: 8.00 wide by 5.79 high│
│                                           │
│   Warnings: 0                             │
│   ┌─────────────────────────────────┐    │
│   │                                 │    │
│   └─────────────────────────────────┘    │
│              ┌──────┐                     │
│              │  OK  │                     │
│              └──────┘                     │
└─────────────────────────────────────────┘
```

You can pan and zoom to examine details by using the **P**an and Zoom button on the Plot Preview dialog box that AutoCAD superimposes on the plot. The Plot Preview **P**an and Zoom mode works like the Dynamic option of the ZOOM command. When you are through with the preview, click on the **E**nd Preview button to redisplay the Plot Configuration dialog box. A full plot preview is shown in figure 11.4.

Before you can use Plot Preview correctly, you must have the proper printer and plotter selected and the paper size and orientation set.

Figure 11.4:

A full plot preview.

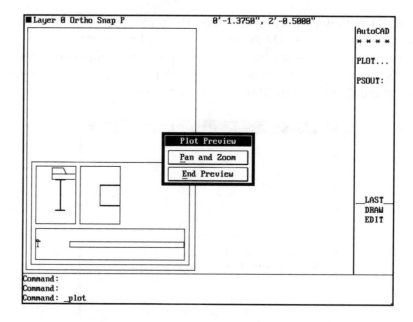

Composing Your Drawing in Paper Space

When you compose a drawing for plotting, you should take advantage of paper space. You used paper space in Chapter 5 to lay out three different views of the bridge in different mview viewports. You scaled those viewports so that the appropriate number of drawing units in each view equaled one paper space unit. You did this so that the drawing could be plotted at one to one from paper space.

Calculating Plot-Scale Factors and Sizes

When you model a design in AutoCAD, you draw it at full size. If the design is a house or other large object, the model may be 100' or more in size. To show such a large object on a small sheet of paper, you use ZOOM XP to scale the object's mview viewport.

The process of determining the paper size and viewport scale factor was discussed in Chapter 5 and will be reviewed here. Use the 92' bridge from Chapter 5 for an example.

First, paper size. To plot the 92' length of the bridge at a scale of 1"=4'-0" (or a plot-scale factor of 1/48: one plotted inch equals 48 drawing units) requires an area 23" long (1104"×1/48). A C size (17"×22") page will be too small, but a D size (34"×22") page is large enough for the span plus any notes or dimensions.

Second, viewport scale factor. To get an mview viewport with the bridge in it to plot at the proper one paper space unit to 48 drawing units scale, ZOOM XP the viewport at 0.020833333 (1/48). You followed these exact steps in Chapter 5 to scale each of the three viewports. The end section was scaled at 1"=1'-0" (1:12 or 0.08333333), the cross section was scaled 1-1/2"=1'-0" (1:8 or 0.125), and the elevation 1/4"=1'-0" (1:48 or 0.020833333).

The results of scaling the viewports in paper space is shown in figure 11.5. Your BRIDGE drawing is currently at this level of development.

Sizing Text, Symbols, and Dimensions

When adding text, symbols and dimensions to your drawing, remember to take advantage of paper space. Whether you are composing a single-view or multiview drawing, you use the calculated plot scale to set the height for text and symbols and the DIMSCALE setting for dimensions. If you have different plot scales for different views, you use different text height, DIMSCALE, and symbol-insertion scales for each view. DIMSCALE is explained later in the chapter.

Figure 11.5:

Three viewports scaled on a D-size sheet.

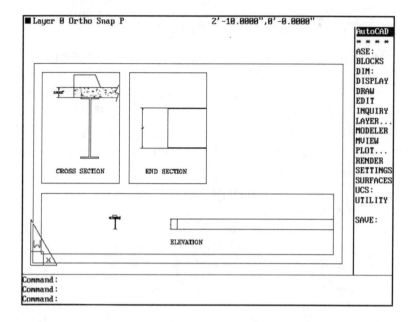

Before adding text or symbols to your drawing, answer this question: is it necessary to add the text or symbol in model space? If not, add the text in paper space, at the actual size you want the text when you plot at one to one. If you want or need to enter the text in model space, you need to consider the paper space viewport scale factor. If you add text at the desired plot height in model space, and then scale the viewport with ZOOM XP, the text will no longer be the correct size for plotting. The text in the viewport has been zoomed with all the other entities.

For text and unit-sized symbols drawn in model space, divide the desired plotted height by the ZOOM XP scale factor to determine the height in drawing units. For example, to get 1/8" plotted text with a 1/48 plot scale, set text size to 6 (1/8 divided by 1/48 plot-scale factor = 48/8 = 6). For symbols that are defined at their desired plot size, such as a 3/8" bubble, insert them at the inverse of the ZOOM XP scale. For paper space, just add the text of symbols at the desired plot height.

When you are dimensioning a drawing, you will need to enter the dimensions in model space. This enables you to take advantage of the associative nature of dimensions. When you add dimensions in model space, you have the same problems as you do with text and symbols added in model space. When you scale the viewport, the dimensions will not be the correct size for plotting. To get the correct text size, set dimension height to the inverse of the ZOOM XP scale factor. You can use the DIMSCALE command to set the dimension scale.

DIMSCALE has one other very useful feature. You can set DIMSCALE to 0 to get AutoCAD to scale dimensions for you. If you set DIMSCALE to 0 then scale your paper space viewport and add dimensions, the text, tick marks, and arrows will be scaled automatically.

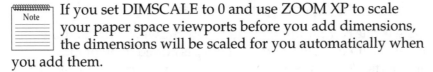 If you set DIMSCALE to 0 and use ZOOM XP to scale your paper space viewports before you add dimensions, the dimensions will be scaled for you automatically when you add them.

Composing a Single-View Plot

Composing a single-view plot is a simple matter. You can use paper space to compose the plot sheet and eliminate the need to scale notes, dimension, symbols, schedules, and titles.

In paper space, you insert a title block and border at 1:1 scale. You can add notes, schedules, and titles in paper space at their desired plotted height. You create an mview viewport to contain the drawing image, and use ZOOM *scale*XP to scale it by the plot-scale factor (for example, 0.0208333333XP for a 1/48 plot). You add dimensions in model space with DIMSCALE set to 0, so that AutoCAD sizes them to plot at the correct size. In effect, you compose the plot on the paper space sheet, so that when you plot it, what you see is what you get. You can then plot the drawing from paper space at 1:1 scale.

Composing Multiview Paper Space Plot Sheets

You can also use paper space to compose multiview plots. The process is the same as single-view plots from paper space, except that you create a separate mview viewport to contain each view. You use ZOOM *scale*XP to scale each viewport by the plot-scale factor calculated for that view. You annotate, and add symbols to each viewport by using its calculated scales and heights. Set DIMSCALE to 0 and dimension in model space after you have scaled the viewport.

Again, you compose the viewports on the paper space sheet, so that when you plot it, what you see is what you get. Then you plot the drawing from paper space at 1:1 scale.

There is one complication to multiview drawings. If you draw something in one viewport, the entity is added in all of the viewports. This is a problem if you are dimensioning a view. The dimensions will be added to the drawing in the viewport you are drawing in, at the appropriate scale factor. The dimension will also appear in the other viewports, but unless the viewports are at the same scale factor, the dimensions will be the wrong size for plotting. The solution is to add dimensions for each view to a different layer and then freeze the layer in the viewports in which you do not want the dimensions. This is done using a new layer feature, VP FREEZE, which is covered later in the chapter.

In the exercises for this chapter, you will use the paper space view of the BRIDGE drawing from Chapter 5. You will add dimensions and symbology to the bridge and control which viewports the dimensions and symbology appear in. The first task is to add a break line and hatching (symbology) to the cross section, as shown in figure 11.6.

Drawing a Break Line

Open the existing Bridge drawing.

Command: **PSPACE** ↵

Command: **ZOOM** ↵
Zoom Window from 1,7 to 11,1'9

Command: **MSPACE** ↵
*Make the cross section on the
left current*

Command: **LINE** ↵
*Draw a break from 2'7,0'10 to
2'4,0'4 to 2'7,0'3 to
2'5,-0'3*

Command: **QSAVE** ↵　　　　Saves the drawing to the same name

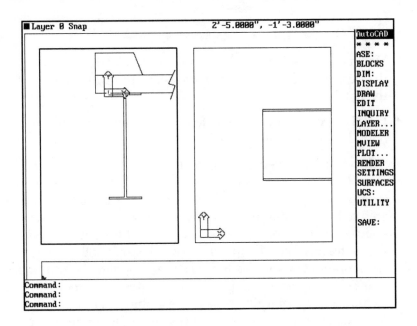

Figure 11.6:
A break line.

Using Crosshatches and Pattern Fills

Crosshatching and *pattern fills* make cross sections and other areas more readable by denoting materials, finishes, and other features or characteristics. You use the BHATCH command to hatch the area within a boundary.

BHATCH. The BHATCH command displays the Boundary Hatch dialog box, which is used to draw crosshatches or pattern fills in a boundary enclosure defined by selected existing entities. The selected entities should be contiguous to define a closed boundary without gaps or overlapping ends. AutoCAD's predefined hatch patterns are stored in the ACAD.PAT file. You can also define a user-specified array or grid of parallel lines as a hatch pattern.

BHATCH Dialog Box Options

- **Hatch Options.** This option displays the Hatch Options dialog box. Use this dialog box to select the pattern to use for the hatch.

- **Pick Points.** Use Pick Points to construct automatically a boundary for the hatch marks.

- **Select objects.** Select the objects to define the hatch boundaries. Each boundary should consist of a contiguous series of entities. If you select a block, all entities within it are considered to be hatch boundaries. Mview viewport borders can be selected as hatch boundaries. If you select text, attributes, shape, trace, or solid entities, the hatch stops at their perimeters, unless you use the Ignore style, described later in this chapter. The perimeters for text, attributes, and shapes include a small margin space for readability. For hatching complex areas or areas without clearly defined boundaries, trace perimeter with a polyline on a reference layer and select the polyline as the boundary.

- **View Selections.** This option highlights all selected objects and boundaries.

- **Preview Hatch.** Use Preview Hatch to see the hatching as it would result from your current selections.

- **Advanced Options.** Define the behavior of the Pick Points option.

Like blocks, patterns have a base point that defaults to 0,0. The alignment of the pattern is set by the UCS (and by the snap grid base point and angle). To control hatch-pattern placement precisely, set the UCS origin to the point where you want to place the pattern base point.

Using the Boundary Hatch Dialog Box

If you select Hatch from the Draw pull-down menu or type BHATCH at the keyboard, AutoCAD displays the Boundary Hatch dialog box. This menu enables you to set hatch-command defaults and to execute the BHATCH command. To define the area to be hatched, choose either the **P**ick Points < button or the **S**elect Objects < button in the Define Hatch Area block. You can use the View Selections < button to clear temporarily the dialog box from the screen, so that you can review the boundary selection. The Boundary Hatch dialog box is shown in figure 11.7.

```
┌─────────────────────────────────────────────┐
│              Boundary Hatch                   │
│ Pattern:      No hatch pattern selected        │
│   ┌──────────────────────┐                    │
│   │   Hatch Options...    │                    │
│   └──────────────────────┘                    │
│ Define Hatch Area                              │
│   ┌──────────────────────┐                    │
│   │    Pick Points <      │                    │
│   └──────────────────────┘                    │
│   ┌──────────────────────┐ ┌───────────────┐ │
│   │   Select Objects <    │ │ View selections < │
│   └──────────────────────┘ └───────────────┘ │
│   ┌──────────────────────┐ ┌───────────────┐ │
│   │   Preview Hatch <     │ │ Advanced Options... │
│   └──────────────────────┘ └───────────────┘ │
│   ┌──────┐ ┌────────┐ ┌─────────┐ ┌───────┐ │
│   │ Apply│ │ Cancel │ │ Another │ │ Help..│ │
│   └──────┘ └────────┘ └─────────┘ └───────┘ │
└─────────────────────────────────────────────┘
```

Figure 11.7:

Boundary Hatch dialog box.

Selecting Hatch Patterns

AutoCAD includes 53 predefined hatch patterns. You can view these in an icon menu by clicking on the Hatch **O**ptions button in the Boundary Hatch dialog box, which displays the Hatch Options dialog box, and then by clicking on the Pattern button in that dialog box. The first page of the icon menu is shown in figure 11.8.

Figure 11.8:

Hatch pattern icon menus.

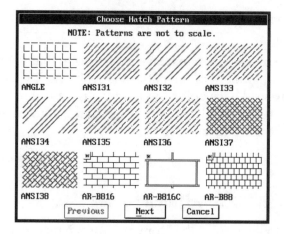

You can page through the icon menu by clicking on the **N**ext button. Select a pattern to clear the Choose Hatch Pattern icon menu and paste its name into the text box beside the Pattern button. If you know the name of the pattern you want, you can enter the pattern name by typing it in the text box in the Hatch Options dialog box. When you click on OK in the Hatch Options dialog box, the pattern name is pasted into the Boundary Hatch dialog box.

Selecting Hatch Styles

To hatch an area, you define one or more boundaries using entities in the drawing. These entities should form one or more closed boundaries. The hatch style you specify determines how Auto-CAD treats boundaries when you hatch. To specify a style, enter the pattern name followed by a comma and an N, O, or I (without intervening spaces).

You can also select the hatch style by clicking on one of the radio buttons in the Hatching Style block of the Hatch Options dialog box, shown in figure 11.9.

Figure 11.9:

Hatch Options dialog box.

The default style shown by the Hatching Style icon in the upper right corner illustrates **N**ormal style. If two or more boundaries lie inside each other or overlap, AutoCAD hatches every other boundary. If one boundary is inside another, for example, the inside boundary is hatched while everything else inside the outer boundary is hatched. If another boundary is inside the second, it is hatched, and so on.

If you click on the **I**gnore radio button, the Hatching Style icon illustrates the **I**gnore style. Everything within the outermost boundary is hatched. All inner boundaries are ignored.

If you click on the **O**uter radio button, the Hatching Style icon illustrates the **O**uter style. AutoCAD hatches from the outside boundary to the first inside boundary, and then stops.

Defining Hatch Boundaries

If the shape you want to hatch is relatively simple, you can use the entities that make up the shape to define the hatch boundary. If you use existing entities, they should not overlap or have gaps between them. Overlaps cause hatched areas outside the boundary and voids in the pattern; gaps cause the pattern to "leak" out of the boundary. Correct, overlapping, and gapping hatches are shown in figure 11.10.

Figure 11.10:

Correct, overlapping, and gapping hatches.

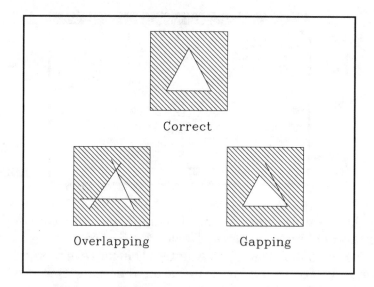

To ensure correct hatching, you may have to trim or break boundaries where they meet other entities to create contiguous closed boundaries. Often, however, it is easier to trace a polyline over the shape and then use the polyline as the boundary for the hatch. After the area is hatched, you can erase the boundary polyline, place it on a layer that is off or frozen, or keep it as part of the drawing.

Adding Patterns with HATCH

Continue from the previous exercise.

```
Command: LAYER ↵
```
Create a layer HATCH and set it current

Choose Draw, *then* Hatch

Choose Hatch **O**ptions, *then* **P**attern   Displays the Choose Hatch
                                                          Pattern dialog box

Click on **N**ext   Displays next page of patterns

Click on AR-CONC   Selects AR-CONC pattern

Click on OK

Click on **S**elect Objects

Select the bridge surface and break lines that are selected in figure 11.11.

```
Select Objects: ↵
Click on Apply                          Hatches the bridge surface
Command: QSAVE ↵
```

The hatched section is shown in figure 11.11.

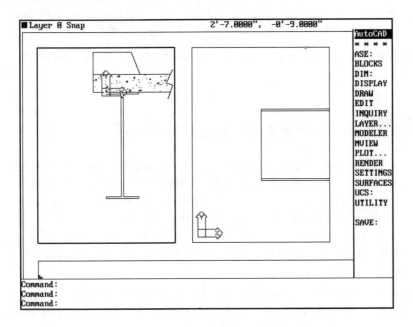

Figure 11.11:

Cross-hatched section.

Even with the minor inconvenience of having to adjust or define boundaries, the BHATCH command makes cross-hatching easy and takes much less time than manually performing the procedure.

Hatches are Blocks

Unless you specify their names with leading asterisks or select **E**xploded Hatch from the dialog box, hatches are inserted on the current layer as unique blocks. The hatch assumes the properties of the current layer. If you insert a hatch with a leading asterisk, it is drawn as lines with color and linetype BYLAYER on the current layer. If you explode a hatch block, however, the lines change to layer 0, with color BYBLOCK and linetype BYLAYER.

You can edit a hatch block in the same way as you edit other blocks, including the use of Autoedit. You can change color and layer directly, and you can change the linetype of internal hatch-line entities by changing the layer because they have BYLAYER linetypes. Commands such as ERASE, MOVE, and COPY edit the pattern as a whole, not as individual lines. If a hatch is exploded or created with *name, you can edit its individual lines.

Before you plot your drawing, you need to add notes and dimensions to it.

Adding Notes and Dimensions

Dimensions should be attached to the model, in model space, so that you can take advantage of their associations. You can use layers to control the visibility of dimensions, so that the dimensions that are pertinent to a particular view are only visible in that view's viewport. You can set feature scaling to 0 to ensure that all the dimensions plot at the same height, regardless of viewport scale.

There is no reason to attach notes and reference symbols—such as section cuts or keynote bubbles—to the model. Instead, they can be entered in paper space at full size.

Adding Dimensions to a Paper Space Plot Sheet

Continue from the previous exercise.

```
Command: LAYER ⏎
```
Create a DIMENSION layer and set it current

```
Command: DIM ⏎
```

```
Dim: DIMSCALE ⏎
```

Current value <1.0000> New value: 0   Sets DIMSCALE to scale
                                             dimensions automatically

```
Dim: VER ⏎
```

```
First extension line origin or RETURN
to select: ↵
```

```
Select line, arc, or circle
```
*Select the end of the bridge surface
at ① (see fig. 11.12)*

```
Dimension line location (Text/Angle):
```
Pick at -1'6,0'4

*Click in the right viewport to make it
active*

```
Dim: VER ↵
```

```
First extension line origin or RETURN
to select: ↵
```

```
Select line, arc, or circle
```
*Select the end of the girder at ②
(see fig. 11.12)*

```
Dimension line location (Text/Angle):
```
Pick at 23'5,-2'1

```
Dimension text <4'>: ↵
```

```
Dim: EXIT ↵
```

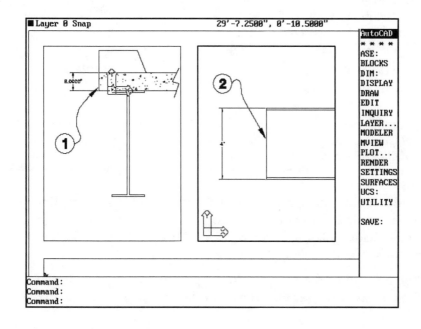

Figure 11.12:

*Paper space plot
sheet with scaled
dimensions.*

In spite of the difference in scales between the viewports, using DIMSCALE 0 made the sizes of dimension text and arrow heads correct in the viewport to which you added the dimension. You can continue to dimension the rest of the views or add text notes and symbols. Do not worry about the dimensions and hatches showing up in viewports where you do not want them—you can fix that before plotting as long as you put the hatch and dimensions on their own layers.

First, try adding some title text in paper space. You set text height to the desired plotted height, and enter the text, as shown in figure 11.13.

Entering Text in Paper Space

Continue from the previous exercise.

Command: **PSPACE** ↵

Command: **ZOOM** ↵
Use ZOOM then Previous

Command: **DTEXT** ↵

Justify/Style/<Start point>: **J** ↵

Align/Fit/Center/Middle/Right
/TL/TC/TR/ML/MC/MR/BL/BC/BR: **C** ↵

Center point: *Pick at 0'6,0'10*

Height <0'-0.8197">: **.4** ↵

Rotation angle <0.00> ↵

Text: **CROSS SECTION** ↵

Text: ↵

Command: **DTEXT** ↵
Add End SECTION at 1'2.875,0'10
Add ELEVATION at 1'5,0'3

Notice that paper space acts like a transparent sheet, enabling you to enter title text over the viewports. If you want, you can continue to add notes to the drawing and text to the title block in paper space.

You are almost ready to produce a plot of your bridge drawing. First, however, your viewports and layers need to be organized.

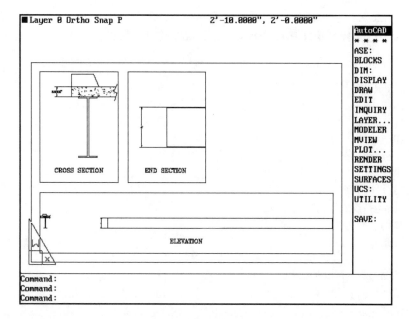

Figure 11.13:

Titles added in paper space.

Preparing MVIEW Viewports and Layers for Plotting

The bridge drawing has three visibility problems that must be fixed before plotting: lines that should be hidden show up in all viewports, the viewport borders show up, and the hatches and dimensions show up in all viewports. These problems can be fixed by using the MVIEW, CHPROP, and DDLMODES (or LAYER and VPLAYER) commands.

You can use the MVIEW Hideplot option to tell AutoCAD to perform a hidden-line removal in specific viewports when plotting. You can use CHPROP to move objects to different layers to control their visibility. These layers can be named uniquely, so that you can use VPLAYER or DDLMODES to freeze them in specific viewports. For example, the DIMENSION and HATCH layers enable you to have dimensions and annotations on those layers visible only in the cross section. You can also create a new layer named VP, for viewport borders, and freeze it.

455

Setting Hideplot and Viewport Layer Visibility for Plotting

Continue from the previous exercise, with paper space current.

Command: `MVIEW` ⏎

ON/OFF/Hideplot/Fit/2/3/4/Restore/   Selects the Hideplot
<First Point>: `H` ⏎   option

ON/OFF: `ON` ⏎

Select objects: *Select the bottom
viewport*

Select objects: ⏎   Ends object selection

Command: `LAYER` *or* `DDLMODES` ⏎
Create new layer VP, freeze VP

Command: `CHPROP` ⏎

Select objects: *Select all three
viewport boundary boxes*

Select objects: ⏎   Ends object selection

Change what property (Color/LAyer/   Selects the LAyer
LType/Thickness) ? `LA` ⏎   option

New layer <0>: `VP` ⏎

Change what property (Color/LAyer/   Removes the viewport
LType/Thickness) ? ⏎   borders

Command: `MSPACE` ⏎

Click in the right side viewport to set it current.

Command: `DDLMODES` ⏎

Click on layer 0, *then* Current   Makes 0 current
Click on layer DIMENSION *and* HATCH
Click on Cur VP: Frz
Click on OK

The section hatches, and dimensions disappear from the bottom
viewport.

Command: `PSPACE` ⏎

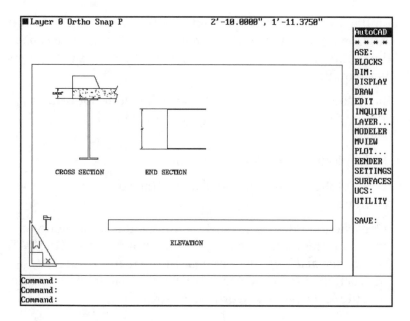

Now the drawing is ready to plot. Saving a plot view standardizes plotting and ensures that you do not plot the wrong area.

Plotting a Drawing

The goal for most design projects is a set of drawings to be used to build or manufacture the design. Thus, the printed or plotted drawing is often more important than the data stored in the drawing file. When you create a plot AutoCAD takes care of converting the drawing data into commands that drive the printer or plotter. Before you can plot a drawing, you need to perform some setup procedures.

Setting Up

The first step in plotting is plotter setup, which was probably done when AutoCAD was installed on your system. The first time you run AutoCAD, it leads you through a configuration menu and prompts you to set up plot devices. If you have a printer or a plotter, but you have not already configured it, you should do so now. Consult the AutoCAD *Installation and Performance Guide* and the plotter documentation for instructions, necessary options, or other requirements.

Use the following checklist to make sure the plotter or printer is ready to work the first time you use it (or if you later have problems):

- Is the plotter or printer plugged in?

- Is the plotter or printer connected to the correct port on the computer?

- Does the interface cable between the plotter or printer and the computer match the connections shown in the AutoCAD *Installation and Performance Guide* or the manufacturer's instructions for AutoCAD? Instructions that are not specific to AutoCAD may not work for AutoCAD.

- Has the plotter or printer been configured in AutoCAD?

- Does the plotter or printer self-test run properly, and is the output satisfactory?

Some of these items may seem obvious, but each of them has been the cause of calls to AutoCAD dealers for technical support. After you check these items, you need not check them again unless you have problems or make changes in the printer or plotter's setup.

The following list should be checked each time you create plots:

- Is the plotter or printer on, and are all switches and settings correctly set?

- Is the paper or other media loaded and properly aligned? Does it move freely without striking a wall, cables, or other obstructions?

- Is the plotter adjusted for that size of paper?

- Are the pens in the holder? Are they primed and flowing freely? If the plotter uses removable carousels, is the correct carousel in the plotter? Does the carousel type match the pen type? Are the correct pens for the media being used, and is the speed set so they work without skipping?

- If the plotter shares a single COM port with another device, such as a digitizer, has the selection switch been switched to the plotter, or has the cable been connected to the plotter?

- Does the plotter need to be in Remote mode to sense incoming commands?

After checking these items, you are ready to use the PLOT command.

Using the PLOT Command

Like AutoCAD's other commands, the PLOT commands can be accessed from the pull-down menus, screen menus, and the command line. In addition, you can use a script (a standard set of settings) to automate the plot process to batch-plot a series of drawings. For more information on scripts, consult the *AutoCAD Reference Manual* or the New Riders Publishing books: *Inside AutoCAD* and *Maximizing AutoCAD, Volume I.*

Regardless of how you access the PLOT command, its options are the same.

PLOT. The PLOT command plots to a plotter (such as a pen, electrostatic plotter, or a PostScript printer), or to a printer (such as a dot matrix or laser printer), or to a plot file. Layers must be on and thawed to be plotted or printer-plotted.

If you plot from model space, AutoCAD plots the image contained in the specified area to plot from the current viewpoint of the current viewport. If you plot from paper space, AutoCAD plots all active mview viewports and their contents in the specified paper space area to plot. Layer visibility and hidden-line removal in individual mview viewports are controlled with the VPLAYER command and the Hideplot option of the MVIEW command.

The output from AutoCAD's PLOT commands can be directed to a plot file instead of to a plotter or printer. Plot files can be used to import drawing images into other graphics, desktop-publishing programs, and word processing programs. Files can also be sent to a printer or plotter at a later time. This is sometimes done on networks that manage the flow of plot jobs, or by plot-spooling programs that minimize the time AutoCAD spends waiting for plots to finish.

Many parameters need to be set. Fortunately, the settings you make are stored as defaults for the next time you plot. If your drawings are standardized and plot setup is always the same, you can skip the setup options and begin plotting right away.

Try a plot of the BRIDGE drawing on a D-size (34×22) sheet of paper. If your plotter does not support a D-size sheet, use an A-size (8.5×11) sheet and cut the scale to a fourth. The current settings shown in the following exercise vary, depending on your plotter model.

Plotting a Drawing to Scale

Continue from the previous exercise

Command: **VIEW**
Save the current view to the name PLOT

Choose File, *then* Plot	Displays the Plot Configuration dialog box
Click on View...	Displays the View Name dialog box
Click on PLOT	Selects PLOT
Click on OK	Accepts the dialog box
Click on Size	Displays Paper Size and Orientation dialog box
Click on D size (34×22)	Selects D size paper
Click on OK	Accepts the dialog box
Click on Scaled to Fit	Turns it off

The scale is now 1 to 1. If Scale to Fit is off, leave it off to plot at 1 to 1.

Click on Plot Preview Full	Selects Full preview
Click on Preview	Displays the Drawing as it will plot (see fig. 11.15)

You should see your entire drawing because you are plotting a D size drawing 1 to 1. If you are using A size paper, change your Drawing Units in the Plot Configuration dialog box to .25.

Click on End Preview	Returns to Plot Configuration dialog box
Click on OK	Accepts the dialog box
Press RETURN to continue or S to Stop for hardware setup: ↵	
Vector sort done	
Command: QSAVE ↵	Saves the drawing to the same name

Understanding Plot Origin

A plotter's starting pen position is the *plotter origin*. The plot places the lower-left corner of the area to plot (display, extents, limits, view, or window) at the plotter origin. The rectangular boundary that defines the maximum plotting area for a sheet size is called its *hard clip limits*. You can determine your plotter's origin and hard clip limits by drawing and plotting a vertical line, erasing it, and then drawing and plotting a horizontal line (length is unimportant). Plot them on the same sheet, using Extents as area to plot and Fit as plot scale. They both start at the plotter origin and extend to the X or Y limits. Measure the distance from the lines to the sheet corner to determine the plotter origin. Measure the lines' lengths to determine your plotter's maximum area for that sheet size.

461

Figure 11.15:

The bridge drawing plotted.

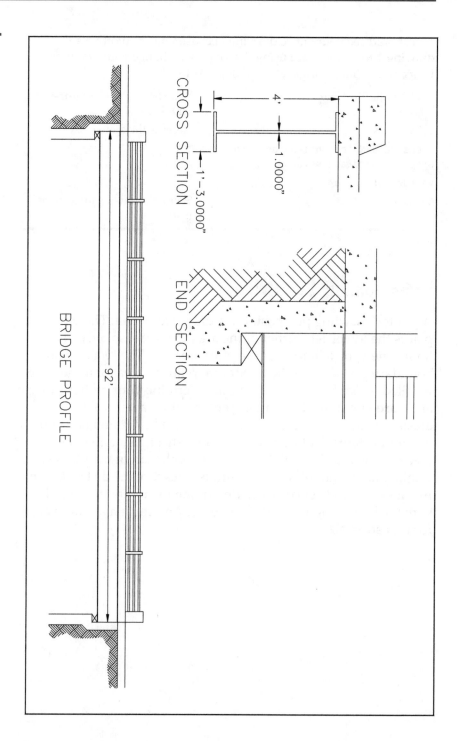

Standardizing Plots

Normally, AutoCAD places the lower-left corner of the part of the drawing you specify to plot at the plotter origin. If you standardize your plotting, you can always plot full-sheet plots at the default 0,0 plotter origin. Set limits to the sheet size, and define a view named PLOT with the lower-left corner at an offset from the lower-left corner of the limits. This offset should be equal to the X,Y distances from the lower-left corner of the sheet to the plotter origin for your plotter. Unless you plot at full scale or at 1:1 in paper space, convert this offset to drawing units (offset divided by scale factor). Set the upper-right corner to encompass the area you want to plot; anything outside the view (or outside your plotter's limits) is clipped. Make sure any title block you use fits in the window or view and is within your plotter's hard clip limits.

To plot a drawing at a particular point on the sheet, specify an X,Y displacement in plotter units at the plot-origin prompt. By specifying a different displacement for each view or detail, you can plot multiple images on a sheet, one at a time.

Controlling Pens, Line Weights, and Linetypes

In the previous plotting exercise, you entered **N** in response to the prompt to change settings for color and linetype. (Everything is plotted with the same pen at the same line weight.) Many drawings, however, need various line weights or colors and require different pens.

You can control three factors with the colors assigned to entities in a drawing when you plot. First, you can assign a different pen to each drawing color. Each pen can have a different tip width, color of ink, or speed. Assign the Pen color and linetype with the Pen Assignments dialog box from the Plot Configuration dialog box.

You can assign a different plotter pen number, plotter linetype, and pen speed to each color, depending on the features your plotter supports. The options are the following:

Pen Assignments Dialog Box Options

- **Pen.** Selects the pen number to use with a given color.

- **Ltype.** Selects the linetype to assign to a given color.

- **Speed.** Selects the pen speed settings.

- **Width.** Sets the width of the plotted line.

- **Pen Width.** Sets the width of the pen so that AutoCAD can adjust for the pen width.

- **Feature Legend.** Displays the Feature Legend dialog box. The dialog box shows all the linetypes available for the current plotter.

Entity color in the preceding settings applies to layer color settings as well. AutoCAD associates drawing colors with a pen, so that you can plot a specific entity or layer with a specific pen. To plot entities with a specific color, place the appropriate pen in the slot associated with the entity color. If you want to plot all red entities with red ink, for example, place a red pen in slot #1. Then, use the PLOT command to associate slot #1 with the color red. Note that the pen color and the entity color do not have to match. You are associating a pen with an entity color—the pen can have any color. With a single-pen plotter, AutoCAD pauses and prompts you to switch pens.

You can also control linetype when plotting. Just as you can assign a pen number to a specific color in the drawing, you can also assign a linetype to an entity color. Linetype 0 is continuous, which is the default. Plotter linetypes are independent of AutoCAD's software linetypes. You should generally define linetypes within the drawing editor by using the LINETYPE or LAYER commands. Plotter linetypes are useful for polylines whose segments are too short for AutoCAD's software linetypes to work or for plotting entities that do not support AutoCAD's software linetypes.

The third factor you can control when plotting is pen speed. Different pens require different speeds, depending on the type of pen, ink, and media, as well as the width of the pen. Because reduced plot time probably saves you money, experiment to find the fastest possible speed that gives you good plot results.

The fourth factor you can control is line width. By assigning different widths to lines you can get different weights of lines when you plot.

The final factor you can control is pen width. AutoCAD needs to know the pen tip width to control fills and wide polylines.

General Plotting Tips

The types of media you use depend on the projects you do, the quality needed for the output, and whether the plot is a check plot or final plot. For check plots, you can use inexpensive paper, even rolls of butcher paper. (Butcher paper is not smooth, so use roller-ball pens instead of ink pens or fiber-tip pens.)

The media you use for final plots or presentation is as much a matter of personal preference as pen type. The ink in plotter pens is different from that used in technical pens. For this reason, not all types of Mylar and vellum work well with plotter pens. Most media suppliers offer special Mylar and vellum for plotters.

Pen selection is also important. The three common types of plotter pens are roller-ball, fiber-tip, and liquid-ink pens. Roller-ball and fiber-tip pens are disposable—when the ink runs out or they dry up (because you forgot the cap), you can throw them away. Liquid-ink pens come in both reusable and disposable types. Disposable pens offer performance equal to reusable pens, but do not try to refill them—the points wear out.

In addition to the pens you choose, plot quality depends on three factors: pen/media combination, pen speed, and pen force. Pen speed is usually expressed in inches-per-second (ips) or centimeters-per-second (cps or cm/sec). Pen force is usually stated in grams.

Roller-ball pens have the fastest speed and can use the highest force. Plot quality is generally not as good as with other pen types; you may want to restrict roller-ball use to check plots. Fiber-tip pens offer better plot quality at a slightly reduced speed. Liquid-ink pens offer the best quality, but at the cost of even slower speeds. In general, roller-ball pens work well at 60 cps, fiber-tip pens at 40 to 50 cps, and liquid-ink pens at 10 to 30 cps.

Remember that Mylar wears out ink pen tips faster than vellum, and that all pens wear out, regardless of the material from which the tip is made. Jeweled points last the longest. Tungsten points also wear well. Cross-grooved pens can plot at higher speeds than plain-tipped pens can. Single-grooved pens do not work well.

Plotter Maintenance

You can do a few things periodically to ensure smooth operation of your plotter. First, clean the roller and pinch wheel every few months (or as needed) to remove paper fibers. Also, check to see if your plotter uses photo-diode sensors to measure paper size—there should be two of them if it does. Use a cotton swab dipped in alcohol to clean paper fibers off the glass covers that protect the sensors.

Keeping your pens working is simple—keep them capped when they are not in use. Even when the pens sit in the caps in a pen carousel, they are not sealed properly. Liquid-ink pens, in particular, dry up and clog if you do not keep them tightly capped. When you will not be using the plotter for a day or so, remove all pens from the carousel and place a cap on each one. These few simple tasks ensure that your plots come off without a hitch every time.

Summary

In this chapter, you finally created a plotted drawing. First, you had to call upon many of the commands you learned in earlier chapters. You coordinated PSPACE, MVIEW, VIEW, and the ZOOM XP scale option to lay out and scale views and a section on a multiview paper space plot sheet. You scaled dimensions in mview viewports to coordinate with the viewport-to-paper space scaling by setting DIMSCALE to 0. You learned to add cross-hatching by using the BHATCH command's XP scaling option to coordinate the hatch scale with the viewport-to-paper space scaling. You used DTEXT to add view labels and a title sheet.

You coordinated layers, colors, and linetypes, along with the MVIEW Hideplot option, and the VPLAYER and DDLMODES layer-visibility settings to control what was visible in each plotted viewport. Finally, you plotted the results.

By now you are an intermediate AutoCAD user, with enough skills to do almost any project. You gained basic computer skills and a good understanding of the way AutoCAD works. You are versatile—able to use any type of menu, dialog box, or the command line. The basic drawing and editing commands are familiar drafting tools. You can draw more accurately and efficiently in AutoCAD than you ever could manually. You know how to set up any type of drawing and how to use prototypes to reuse your setups.

You also learned to use more advanced commands and concepts, such as PLINE, PEDIT, paper space, UCSs, blocks, and xrefs. You know how advanced edit commands can enhance and fine-tune a drawing, as well as quickly duplicate or create simple or complex objects. You learned to pull this all together into a plotted multiview drawing, complete with dimensions and annotations.

Along the way, you accumulated many tips on small (but important) features and techniques. Because each chapter's exercises concentrated on specific aspects of AutoCAD, many of these tips, features, and techniques were not integrated into subsequent exercises. To integrate them would have complicated the exercises. In your own work, however, you should integrate all of what you learned to use AutoCAD most effectively and efficiently.

In this book's appendixes, you will find a reference list of AutoCAD commands; a table of system variables; and installation, configuration, and troubleshooting information.

You can also expand your knowledge and abilities with other books available from New Riders Publishing. *Inside AutoCAD* is a complete book on using AutoCAD. *Inside AutoCAD* is similar to this book, but it contains more in-depth tutorial/reference coverage that includes every AutoCAD concept, command, and feature. The *AutoCAD Reference Guide* (also available on disk) is an illustrated quick reference that covers every AutoCAD command. *AutoCAD: The Professional Reference* is a comprehensive reference guide that discusses in detail every AutoCAD concept, command, and feature. If you want to customize your AutoCAD system—to create your own menus, fonts, hatch patterns, linetypes, commands, and programs to automate AutoCAD—refer to *Maximizing AutoCAD Volume I: Customizing AutoCAD with Macros and Menus*, and *Maximizing AutoCAD Volume II: Inside AutoLISP*. With AutoCAD and the appropriate knowledge, the possibilities of what you can do are almost limitless.

Growing into 3D

Like the drawings you have done in previous chapters, most (if not all) of your design work is in two dimensions (2D), and you may never need to go beyond the flat world to three-dimensional modeling.

The chances are good, however, that 3D will benefit your work because it is often easier to design an object in 3D than it is to design and draw it in 2D. Once the 3D model is created, you can extract 2D views from it, creating finished drawings with little additional work. In this chapter, you learn how to apply some basic 3D concepts with many of AutoCAD's 3D commands to create the table drawing shown in figure 12.1.

AutoCAD has the following four kinds of three-dimensional drawing:

- 3D entities: points, lines, 3D polylines, and 3Dfaces.

- 2D entities: lines, arcs, polylines, and circles, which can be *extruded* into 3D by adding thickness to their profiles.

- 3D surfaces: 3D meshes and polygon faces.

- 3D solids: spheres, cones, and boxes created with the AME (Advanced Modelling Extensions) to AutoCAD.

In this chapter, you are introduced to AutoCAD's 3D concepts. You learn to:

- Create 3D objects by adding thickness to 2D entities, such as lines, arcs, polylines and circles

Figure 12.1:

A table drawn in 3D.

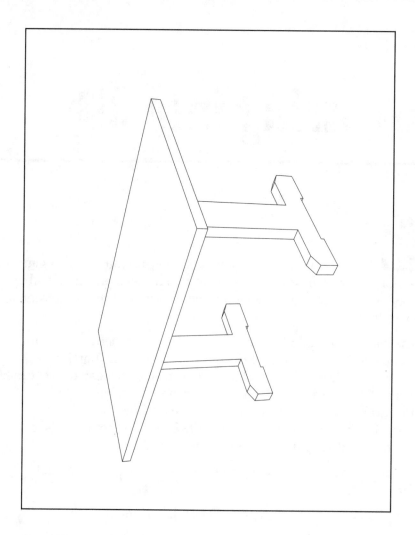

- Rotate and offset the UCS to any point and angle in 3D space
- Draw in 3D by using UCSs and by using Z coordinates in point entry and point filters
- Edit 3D objects with AutoCAD's normal editing commands
- Draw, edit, and view the 3D model from any point in space
- Put a skin on 3D models with surfacing commands
- Add realism by viewing 3D designs with their hidden lines removed and by viewing them in perspective

Adding a Third Dimension

In previous chapters, you dealt with 2D coordinates in the form X,Y. Adding a third dimension is as easy as adding another coordinate value for Z. Instead of entering a point as 2,5, for example, you can enter 2,5,3, indicating that the point lies three inches above the X,Y plane, along the Z axis. But just where is the Z axis?

Finding the Z Axis

You are already familiar with the X and Y axes. The Z axis runs through the 0,0,0 origin, perpendicular to the X and Y axes (see fig. 12.2). If you are looking down at the plane of X,Y axes in plan view, the positive Z axis comes up toward you and the negative Z axis goes away from you. This view is the default start-up display view in the WCS (World Coordinate System), with the Z axis perpendicular to the screen, positive Z values coming out of the screen toward you, and negative values going back into the screen.

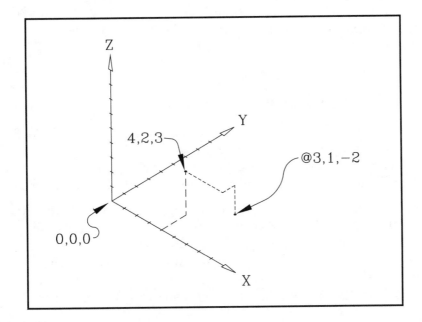

Figure 12.2:

3D axes and points.

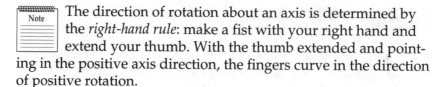

The direction of rotation about an axis is determined by the *right-hand rule*: make a fist with your right hand and extend your thumb. With the thumb extended and pointing in the positive axis direction, the fingers curve in the direction of positive rotation.

Entering 3D Coordinates

You have been drawing in 3D all along, even though the drawings were flat. Every time you enter or pick a point, you are specifying a 3D coordinate; if you do not otherwise specify the Z value, AutoCAD places the point in the X,Y plane of the current User Coordinate System (UCS). You can control the location of the Z coordinate by creating UCSs that are above or below the X,Y plane of the World Coordinate System (WCS). You can also control the Z of picked points by snapping to existing geometry with object snap or by using X,Y,Z point filters.

To type a 3D coordinate, enter its X,Y,Z value (such as **4.5,2,7.1**). To enter a relative 3D coordinate, add the @ sign in front of any 3D coordinates, as in **@2,5,3**.

Working in 3D would be tedious if you had to enter all your 3D coordinates in the WCS. The key to easy, flexible 3D work is AutoCAD's UCS.

Controlling 3D UCSs

The 0,0,0 origin of the default coordinate system, the WCS (World Coordinate System), is called the *global*, or *world*, origin. In previous chapters, working in 2D, you used the UCS to relocate the X,Y coordinates of the origin and to rotate (reorient) the X and Y axes.

In 3D, however, a UCS plays a much bigger role. Most AutoCAD entities—even 3D entities—are created in the orientation of the current UCS. By controlling the UCS orientation and origin, you can place any entity at any point and angle in 3D space. Think of the UCS as a sheet of glass on which you draw. Normally, the glass rests flat on your "table" when you draw. When you need to draw in a different plane, you simply pick the sheet of glass up, move it, rotate it, or tilt it to get the new orientation in which you need to draw. This plane, normally the X,Y plane of the current UCS, is called the current *construction plane*. The UCS command manipulates the location and orientation of the UCS and the construction plane.

UCS. The UCS (User Coordinate System) controls the location of 0,0,0 and the orientation of the X, Y, and Z axes. The World Coordinate System (WCS) is the default UCS. The DDUCS dialogue box also controls UCSs.

UCS Options

- **Origin.** Specify a new UCS origin point without changing orientation.

- **ZAxis.** Specify a new UCS origin point and reorient the Z axis by specifying a point on its positive portion.

- **3point.** Specify a new UCS origin point, and specify one point on the new positive X axis and one point anywhere in the positive portion of the new X,Y plane to set its orientation.

- **Entity.** Select an entity to define a new UCS with the same orientation as the entity. The origin varies with the type of entity. This option cannot be used with polygon meshes, 3D polylines, or viewport borders.

- **View.** Reorients a new UCS to the current viewpoint, parallel to the screen, without changing the origin.

- **X.** Specify a new UCS by rotating the Y and Z axes about the X axis.

- **Y.** Specify a new UCS by rotating the X and Z axes about the Y axis.

- **Z.** Specify a new UCS by rotating the X and Y axes about the Z axis.

- **Previous.** Restores the previous UCS. Repeat to step back—up to ten previous coordinate systems in paper space or ten in model space.

- **Restore.** Restores a previously saved named UCS. Enter a question mark for a listing of named UCSs.

- **Save.** Saves the current UCS. You specify a name (up to 31 characters). Enter a question mark for a list of named UCSs.

- **Delete.** Deletes a saved UCS by name. Enter a question mark for a list of named UCSs.

- **?.** Lists named UCSs. You can use wild cards to create a specific list. A current unnamed UCS is listed as *NO NAME*, unless it is the WCS (which is listed as *WORLD*).

- **World.** Restores the WCS.

 If you get "lost in space" when traveling through UCSs, restore the WCS with a plan view, and then take off again.

AutoCAD also includes an ELEV command and ELEVATION system variable, which can set the current construction plane to a Z elevation above or below the X,Y plane of the current UCS. The combination of UCS and ELEV can be confusing (elevation control may be dropped in a future release). To avoid confusion, use the UCS to control Z, and do not change the elevation.

Drawing in a 3D UCS

To see how easy the UCS command makes 3D drafting, drawing, and design, start a new drawing, make a block to provide visual orientation, and insert the block in several UCSs (see fig. 12.3).

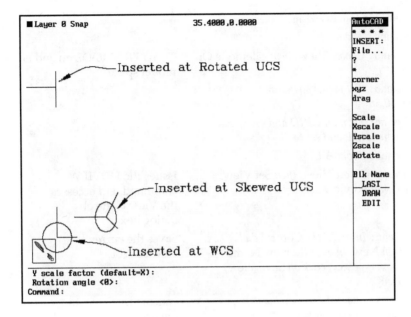

Figure 12.3:
*3DBLK blocks
inserted in UCSs.*

Making and Using UCSs

Start ACAD using the AB batch file.

Command: *Choose* File, *then* New, *and then enter* TABLE *in the* New Drawing Name: *edit box*	
Command: *Choose* View, *then* Tilemode, *then* Off	Turns TILEMODE off and changes to paper space
Set paper space LIMITS to 0,0 and 11,8.5	
Command: *Choose* View, *then* Mview, *then* 4 Viewports	Issues the MVIEW command
Command: _mview ON/OFF/Hideplot/Fit/2/3/4/Restore/ <First Point>: 4	
Fit/<First Point>: .25,.25 ↵	Specifies the lower left corner of viewport
Second Point: 10.5,8 ↵	Specifies the upper right corner of the viewport

Regenerating drawing.

Command: *Zoom all*

Command: *Choose* View, *then* Tilemode On   Turns TILEMODE on and enters model space

Command: *Set model space limits to -6,-6 and 60,36*

Command: *Turn on GRID and set 3, and turn on SNAP and set to .5*

Command: *Zoom All*

Command: *Choose* View, *then* Set View, *then* Named view   Issues the DDVIEW command and accesses the View Control dialog box

Command: *In the* View Control *dialog box, click on* New, *then in the* New Name *edit box, type* ALL, *click on* Save View, *then* OK   Saves the current view as ALL

Command: *Choose* Settings, *then* UCS, *then* Icon, *then* Origin   Sets the UCS icon to the origin

Command: *Draw a circle at 9,9 with radius 3*

Command: *Set entity color to red*

Command: *Draw a line from 9,9 to @4,0*

Command: *Set entity color to green*

Command: *Draw a line from 9,9 to @0,6*

Command: *Set entity color to blue*

Command: *Draw a line from 9,9 to @0,0,9*

Command: *Set entity color back to Bylayer*

Command: *Create a block named 3DBLK with insertion base point 9,9 and select all lines & circle*

Command: *Insert 3DBLK at 0,0 with default scale and rotation*

Command: *Insert 3BLK at 0,0,27 with default scale and rotation.*   Inserts the block above the first

Command: `UCS` ↵   Issues the UCS command

Origin/Zaxis/3point/Entity/view/X/Y/Z Prev/Restore/Save/Dal/?/<World>: 3 ↵   Specifies the 3point option

Origin point <0,0,0>: 10,4 ↵   Sets a location for the origin

```Point on positive portion of the```
 ```X-axis<11.0000,4.0000,```
 ```0.0000>: @6,-6,6 ↵```
	Specifies direction of the UCS's X axis

```Point on positive-Y portion of```
 ```the UCS X-Y plane```
 ```<10.7071,4.7071,0.0000>: @6,6,6 ↵```
	Specifies direction of the UCS's Y axis and UCS icon appears skewed

```Command:``` *Insert 3DBLK at 0,0* *(the new UCS origin)*	
```Command:``` *Choose* Settings, *then* UCS, *then* Presets	Accesses the UCS Orientation dialog box
In the UCS Orientation *dialog box, click on the* WCS (top left) *box, and then click on* OK	Sets the UCS to the WCS
```Command:``` *Choose* Settings, *then* UCS, *then* Origin	Starts the UCS command with the Origin option
```Origin/ZAxis/3point/Entity/View/X/Y/Z``` ```/Prev/Restore/Save/Del/?/<World>: o```	
```Origin point <0,0,0>: 0,30 ↵```	Moves the UCS origin to 0,30
```Command:``` *Choose* Settings, *then* UCS, *then* Axis, *then* Z	Starts the UCS command with the Z option

```Command: ucs```
 ```Origin/ZAxis/3point/Entity/View/X/Y/Z```
 ```/Prev/Restore/Save/Del/?/<World>: z```	

```Rotation angle about Z axis <0>: -90 ↵```	Specifies a -90 degree rotation for the UCS's Z axis
```Command:``` *Choose* Settings, *then* UCS, *then* Axis, *then* X	Starts the UCS command with the X option

```Command: ucs```
 ```Origin/ZAxis/3point/Entity/View/X/Y/Z```
 ```/Prev/Restore/Save/Del/?/<World>: x´```	

```Rotation angle about X axis <0>: 90 ↵```	Specifies a 90 degree rotation for the UCS's X axis and displays the broken pencil icon

```Grid too dense to display```
 ```Command:``` *Insert 3DBLK at 0,0 with default scale and rotation*
 Save the drawing (see fig. 12.3)	

In the last insertion, the circle appears edge-on: it looks like a line. The blue Z line goes to the left, the red X line points to the WCS origin, and the green Y line is seen as a point because it comes straight at you.

You can override the current UCS and cause AutoCAD to interpret a point with a WCS point by prefacing the point as an asterisk, (for example, *3,1,6). The format for overriding relative coordinates is similar (@*2,4,3 or @*3<90). For example, the last four UCS settings accomplished the same results as using the 3-point option with origin *0,30, selecting point *0,0 on the positive portion of the X-axis, and point *0,30,27 on the positive-Y portion of the UCS X-Y plane. The UCS has quite a few options, most of which relocate the origin or rotate the UCS in some way. You can often achieve the same result by using several different methods. Use whichever options are easiest for you to visualize—the UCS icon helps you visualize the results.

Interpreting the UCS Icon

The UCS icon is a visual reminder of the orientation of the UCS. It now displays as a broken pencil rather than as the usual X,Y icon. The broken pencil icon appears whenever the X,Y plane of the current UCS appears edge-on (or nearly so) to your viewpoint. The broken pencil icon indicates that drawing by picking points may be unpredictable. It does not appear at the origin, even with UCSICON ORigin set.

You learned to control the UCS icon in an earlier chapter, setting it to appear at the origin and turning it on and off. The following is a list of UCS icon shapes and indicators.

- **W.** A w appears in the Y arrow when the current UCS is the same as the WCS.

- **+.** A + (plus sign) appears in the intersection of the X and Y arrows when the UCS icon is located at the current UCS origin.

- **Box.** A box is formed by the intersecting lines of the X and Y arrows when the UCS icon is below your viewpoint (if you are viewing the UCS from the positive Z direction). The box disappears when you are viewing it from below.

- **Box with a broken pencil.** The X and Y arrows are replaced by a box with a broken pencil when the X,Y plane of the current UCS appears edge-on (or nearly so) to your viewpoint.

- **Cube in perspective.** A cube in perspective replaces the X and Y arrows when you are viewing the drawing in perspective.

- **Triangle.** A triangle replaces the X and Y arrows when you are in paper space.

Another way to visualize your 3D results is to view the drawing in 3D, rather than in a plan view.

Controlling the View with the VPOINT Command

The VPOINT command enables you to change your viewpoint relative to the origin. It changes the appearance of the display but does not change the model. It changes only your viewpoint— therefore, it changes the view you see of the model.

VPOINT. The VPOINT (ViewPOINT) command specifies a 3D viewpoint or X, Y, and Z angles for viewing a drawing. The default is a plan view 0,0,1 of the current UCS. You can define a viewpoint by entering a point value, using the Rotate option to enter an angle in the X,Y plane and an angle from the X,Y plane, or pressing Enter and picking the viewpoint by using a globe icon.

In addition to using menus, you can specify the viewpoint in three ways.

VPOINT Options

- **<0.0000,0.0000,1.0000>.** Enter a point to view from. Actually, VPOINT specifies the angle of view, not a specific point. You set the view direction relative to 0,0,0 by entering X,Y,Z coordinates that specify an angle from the origin from that point through the origin. No matter how you specify the viewpoint, you always look through the entire drawing toward the origin.

- **Rotate.** Specify the angle of view with two angles: the angle from the X axis in the X,Y plane and the angle from the X,Y plane towards the Z axis.

- **View point.** Press Enter at the initial prompt to display a globe and an axes tripod that assist in selecting a viewpoint.

 Note VPOINT displays only parallel projections and cannot control the distance at which you are viewing an object. The DVIEW command, which dynamically selects and controls a 3D viewpoint and viewing distance, can generate either parallel or perspective projections. DVIEW is an improvement on VPOINT.

Tip VPOINT uses the WCS origin if the WORLDVIEW system variable is on (set to 1, the default). Set WORLDVIEW off (0) to use the current UCS origin.

The easiest way to specify a viewpoint is to use the preset choices in the Viewpoint Presets dialog box. The icons enable you to view your model from any angle in 45-degree increments in the WCS X-Y plane and 10, 30, 45, 60, or 90 degrees above or below the X-Y plane. Click on the segment of the icon that corresponds to the angle from which you want to view your model.

Use the Viewpoint Presets dialog box to view the drawing from above and to the right. Then set the WCS current and use the Rotate option to view it from the front right (see fig. 12.4).

Using the Viewpoint Presets Dialog Box and Rotate Option

Continue from the previous exercise.

Command: *Choose* View, *then* Set View, *then* Viewpoint, *then* Presets	Accesses the Viewpoint Presets dialog box
From the Viewpoint Presets *dialog box, click on the 0 wedge, from the left figure, then the 30 wedge from the right figure*	Sets the viewpoint

`Command: ddvpoint`
`*** Switching to the WCS ***`
`*** Returning to the UCS ***`
	AutoCAD changes to the preset viewpoint

Command: *Choose* Settings, *then* UCS, *then* Presets	Accesses the UCS Orientation dialog box
In the UCS Orientation *dialog box, click on the WCS icon (top left) box, then click on OK*	
`Command: VPOINT ↵`	Issues the VPOINT command
`Rotate/<View point>` `<0.8660,0.0000,0.5000>: R ↵`	Specifies the Rotate option
`Enter angle in XY plane` `from X axis <0>: -20 ↵`	
`Enter angle from XY` `plane <30>: 24 ↵`	
`Regenerating drawing.`	
Command: *Zoom Center with point 0,30 and height 51*	
`Command: VIEW ↵`	Issues the VIEW command
`?/Delete/Restore/Save/Window: S ↵`	Specifies the Save option
View name to save: FRIGHT	Saves view with the name FRIGHT
Command: *Save the drawing*	

Figure 12.4:

Viewing from a front right viewpoint.

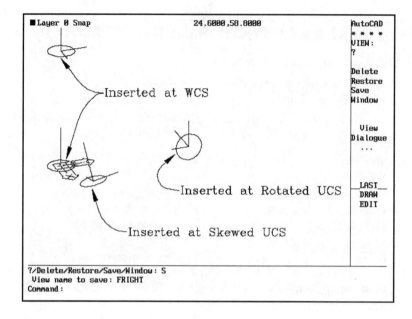

Your view should now show the insertions from an angle 20 degrees to the left and six degrees lower than the previous view.

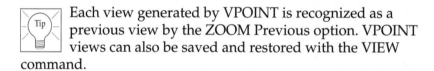 Each view generated by VPOINT is recognized as a previous view by the ZOOM Previous option. VPOINT views can also be saved and restored with the VIEW command.

Take a closer look at each of the Rotation options, listed in the following sections.

VPOINT Rotate Prompts Options

- **Enter angle in XY plane from X axis <0>:.** Specify a rotation angle to define the viewing direction relative to the X axis. If your drawing contains a box, a value of 0 gives you a view looking directly at the right side of the box. A value of 90 gives you a view of the back of the box, 180 is a view of the left side, and 270 gives you a view of the front of the box. You can enter any value in degrees—it does not have to be one of the four quadrant values listed previously.

- **Enter angle from XY plane <90>:.** Specify the angle for the viewpoint above or below the X-Y plane. A rotation angle of 0 gives you an elevation view of the box. An angle of 35 degrees gives you an isometric view, 90 degrees gives you a plan view, -90 degrees looks up from the bottom, and so on.

You can specify both angles at once with the globe icon, although it is not as precise as the Rotate option.

Using the VPOINT Globe

If you press Enter in response to the first VPOINT prompt, AutoCAD displays a globe icon and an axes tripod you can use to specify the viewpoint (see fig. 12.5). The globe consists of a cross surrounded by two circles. Consider the origin to be located at the center of a transparent globe. The center of the cross marks the north pole, the inner circle represents the equator, and the outer circle represents the south pole. The cross defines the four "straight" viewing directions: front, right side, back, and left side (looking north, west, south, and east, respectively). Picking the center of the cross gives a plan view.

Selecting a point inside the inner equator circle defines a viewpoint that is above the equator, looking down at an angle on your model. The closer the point is to the center of the cross, the greater is the angle above the X-Y plane. Picking a point exactly on the equator gives you a normal elevation view.

Picking a point between the circles gives a view that looks up at the origin from below. The closer the point is to the outer circle, the farther your viewpoint moves beneath the object. Picking on the outer circle gives a view looking straight up from below.

Try using the globe icon to specify a view looking up from below, in the negative X, Y, and Z directions. Watch the axes tripod as you move the cursor; it visually indicates the X,Y, and Z axes. The new viewpoint is shown in figure 12.6.

Using the VPOINT Screen Icon

Continue from the previous exercise.

Command: **VPOINT:** *Press Enter*

Rotate/<View point> <0.8585,-0.3125, 0.4067>: *Press Enter*

Move the pointing device until your display matches figure 12.5, and press the pick button.

Figure 12.5:

Picking a viewpoint with the globe icon.

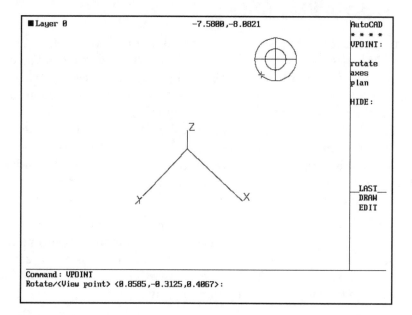

You now have a reversed view of the drawing. The lack of the box in the UCS icon tells you that you are looking up at it, not down.

Using the globe icon is the quickest way to define a viewpoint when you do not need an exact viewing direction or elevation angle.

Now that you can move your UCS and viewpoint around, drawing in 3D is much easier.

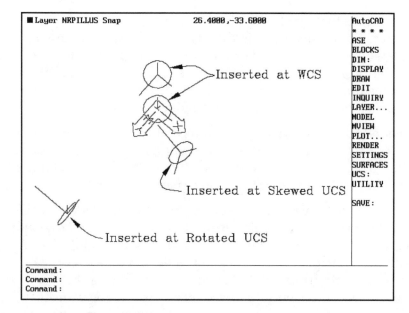

Figure 12.6:

Looking up at the drawing, from the southwest.

Drawing in 3D

You already know all the commands you need for drawing in 3D. Only one new command, PLAN, is introduced in this section. (PLAN sets the current viewpoint to a plan view.)

One new entity property, THICKNESS, is also introduced. (THICKNESS extrudes 2D objects to give them 3D thickness.) The rest of this section shows you how to manipulate views, UCSs, and viewpoints to create 3D drawings by using familiar drawing and editing commands, and by specifying 3D coordinates, object snaps, point filters, and 3D point entry.

3D Object Snaps and Point Filters

You have been using 3D object snaps all along—you just did not care about the Z coordinate (because it is always 0 in 2D). When working in 3D, you can take advantage of the fact that object snaps snap to the Z coordinate, as well as the X and Y coordinates.

This means that you have to be careful when snapping to one or more objects that align in the current view while occupying different points in space. For example, if snapping with object snap INT or ENDP mode to the corner of a box in plan view, will the upper or lower corner be found? Using object snaps in a diagonal viewpoint makes these ambiguous points easier to find.

Point filters enable you to pick points that match another point's X-, Y-, or Z-coordinate value. For example, you can use a point filter to draw a line that is horizontally or vertically aligned with another point, without it being on a snap increment.

You can enter any coordinate by any combination of X-, Y-, or Z-coordinate components. This is most useful when used to snap to one or two coordinate components of points in existing objects with object snap. To specify a point filter, enter it as .X or .XZ at any point-entry prompt. You are then prompted for the specified coordinate components, followed by any remaining coordinate components needed. You can use the following point filter options any time AutoCAD prompts for or expects a point.

Point Filter Options

- **.X.** Enter the X value of the next point.

- **.Y.** Enter the Y value of the next point.

- **.Z.** Enter the Z value of the next point.

- **.XY.** Enter the XY value of the next point.

- **.XZ.** Enter the XZ value of the next point.

- **.YZ.** Enter the YZ value of the next point.

Object snaps work extremely well in 3D when they are combined with point filters. In 3D, just as in 2D, point filters enable you to use the coordinate components of existing points in your drawing to build a new point. You can use any combination of existing X, Y, and Z values, and new values entered by the keyboard. You just enter .X, .Y, .Z, .XY, .XZ, or .YZ at any point-entry prompt to tell AutoCAD which coordinates to extract from the next point you enter, then AutoCAD prompts you for the remaining coordinate(s). For example, if you use the .X filter, AutoCAD reads the X-coordinate value of the point you pick, then prompts you for the Y- and Z-coordinate values. It combines these three values together to form a coordinate, which it applies to the command in progress.

Return to the front right viewpoint and begin drawing a table, using a combination of changed UCSs, relative point entry, 3D object snaps and XYZ point filters. Restore the FRIGHT view and draw a rectangle in the WCS using object snaps and point filters. This represents the top of a table (see fig. 12.7). The 3D blocks you inserted earlier give you something to snap to with object snaps, as well as provide visual points of reference until you draw more of the table.

Drawing with Object Snaps, Point Filters, and UCSs

Continue from the previous exercise.

Command: *Choose* View, *then* Set View, *then* Named view, *then select* FRIGHT, *then* Restore, *then click on* OK

Command: **LINE** ↵

From point: **.XY** ↵

of *Pick point 0,30 at the lower right block*

(need Z): **INS** ↵

of *Pick upper left block*   Snaps to block insertion point 27" above the .XY pick point.

To point: **INT** ↵

of *Pick the intersecting lines of the upper left block*

To point: **@54,0** ↵

To point: **.XZ** ↵   Uses the X and Z coordinate of picked point

of **@**   Taken from the last point

(need Y): **INS** ↵

of *Pick the lower right block*

To point: **C** ↵   Closes the lines

Figure 12.7:

A table top line.

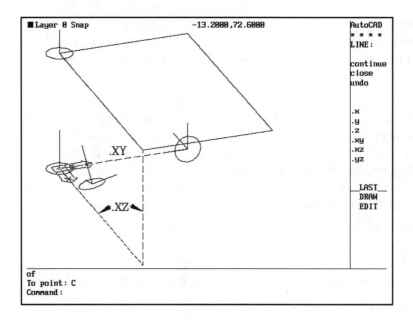

The resulting lines are parallel to the WCS, but they are 27 inches above it because they were object snapped to the 3D block at 0,0,27.

Now create a new UCS and draw the profile of a table leg using a polyline, as shown in figure 12.8.

Drawing a Table Leg in a New UCS

Command: **UCS** ↵

Origin/ZAxis/3point/Entity/View/X/Y/Z/   Specifies the
Prev/Restore/Save/Del/?/<World>: **3** ↵   3-point option.

Origin point <0,0,0>: **INS** ↵   Uses the INS object snap mode

of *Pick the skewed 3D block
at* ① *(see fig. 12.8)*

Point on positive portion of the X-axis Aligns X axis with
<11.0000,4.0000,0.0000>: **@0,1** ↵   the current Y axis

Point on positive-Y portion of the UCS
XY plane <9.0000,4.0000,0.0000>: **PERP** ↵

to *Pick table top line at* ②

Command: **UCS** ⏎

Origin/ZAxis/3point/Entity/View/X/Y/Z   Specifies the Save
/Prev/Restore/Save/Del/?/<World>: **S** ⏎   option

?/Desired UCS name: **LEG** ⏎   Specifies UCS name

Command: *Draw a PLINE from point 0,0 to points @6<0, @.5<90, @10<0, @.5<90, @6<0, @4<90, @8<-180, @17.5<90, @6<0, @3.5<90, @18<180, @3.5<270, @6<0, @17.5<270, @8<180 and Close*

Command: *Save the drawing*

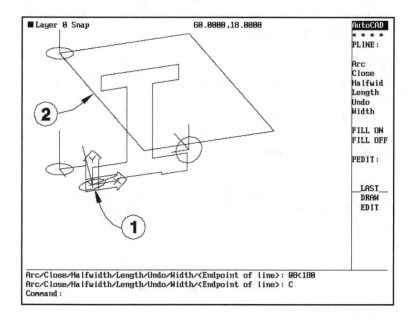

Figure 12.8:
A polyline table leg.

Now you have a rather flat table top and leg. They need some thickness to look realistically three-dimensional.

Adding Thickness to Entities

You can draw much of a 3D model by positioning 2D entities in various orientations within the model, and then *extruding* them to give the illusion of 3D substance. You can extrude lines, polylines, arcs, circles, and solids by applying a *thickness* to them. Thickness can be applied either before or after the entities are created. The thickness, if positive, extrudes the entity in its positive Z direction. A negative thickness extrudes the entity in its negative Z direction. If you draw a line in the X,Y plane with a thickness of 2", for example, the line appears as a rectangle two inches high, standing on edge to the X,Y plane. The length of the rectangle is the length of the line.

Thickness is an entity property like color, layer, and linetype. So far, all the entities you have drawn have a thickness of 0. You can draw an entity with a preset thickness by setting the THICKNESS system variable before you draw the entity. You can also use the DDEMODES Entity Modes dialog box to set thickness.

> **Note** Elevation is also an entity property. The ELEV command can be used to set both elevation and thickness. Because the ELEVATION system variable and ELEV command are likely to be dropped in future AutoCAD releases, however, you should avoid using them.

You can change an existing entity's thickness by using the CHPROP command. Try it in the next exercise to make the table top and leg two inches thick, as shown in figure 12.9.

Changing Thickness

Continue from the previous exercise.

*Select all entities using
a crossing window*

Command: *Choose* Modify, *then* Change, *then* Properties	Access the Change Properties dialog box
In the Thickness *text box,* enter 2.0, *and then click on* OK	Changes entity thickness to 2.0

Drawing in three dimensions is that simple! Now, the table top and leg each have a thickness of two inches. The 3D blocks are unaffected because blocks cannot be extruded. The top of the table top lines are now at 29" above the WCS origin; however, this table was supposed to have a top surface height of 27"—2" seems a bit thick. Try applying a negative thickness of 1.5" to the top.

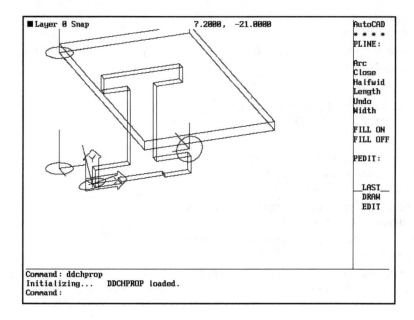

Figure 12.9:
A thicker table.

Extruding with a Negative Thickness

Command: *Select all four lines of top & set thickness to -1.5*

Command: *Erase all of the 3DBLKs except the one at WCS origin*

Command: *Save the drawing*

The table needs another leg. Use the THICKNESS system variable to set a thickness before you draw the table's right leg. You can easily draw it in your current view by object snapping to the left leg. You can copy the left leg, but try a different style of leg instead. Use an INT object snap mode to "trace" the top and bottom parts of the leg, skipping the middle support. After specifying the first point of each polyline, the rest of the points use the same Z elevation, regardless of the elevation of the coordinates entered or object snapped for them. The results are shown in figure 12.10.

Drawing with a Preset Thickness

Continue from the previous exercise.

```
Command: Set a running INTersection
object snap mode
Command: Set THICKNESS it to 2                     Sets default entity thickness
Command: PLINE ⏎
From point: .XY ⏎
of Pick corner of top of leg nearest upper left
of screen at ① (see fig. 12.10)
(need Z): 32 ⏎
Current line-width is 0.0000
Arc/Close/Halfwidth/Length/Undo/Width/
<Endpoint of line>: Pick ②
Arc/Close/Halfwidth/Length/Undo/Width/
<Endpoint of line>: Pick ③
Arc/Close/Halfwidth/Length/Undo/Width/
<Endpoint of line>: Pick ④
Arc/Close/Halfwidth/Length/Undo/Width/
<Endpoint of line>: C ⏎                             Closes the polyline
```

Next, repeat the process on the bottom part of the leg.

```
Command: PLINE ⏎
From point: 0,0,32 ⏎
Current line-width is 0.0000
Arc/Close/Halfwidth/Length/Undo/Width/
<End point of line>: Pick your way
around the base of the leg,
skipping the upright support, and
then close the polyline
Command: Save the drawing
```

You only had to specify one Z value for each polyline. Most 2D entities work the same way. For example, once you specify the first point of a circle or arc, the rest of the points must lie in the same plane, parallel to the current UCS. Therefore, even if you object snap to or specify a different Z value for the following points of the circle or arc, their Z values default to the first point's Z value.

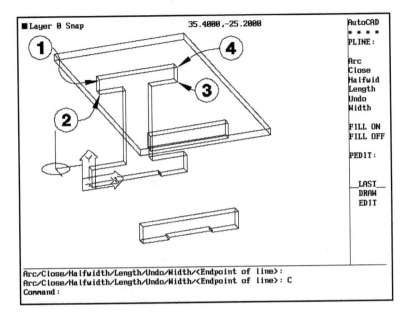

Figure 12.10:
Tracing the leg.

Try drawing an extruded circle to add a cylindrical upright to the second leg. It is easier to use object snap to snap it to the corner of the base and then move it, than it is to locate the final point for the circle (see fig. 12.11).

Drawing a 3D Circle

Continue from the previous exercise.

Command: *Set the UCS to World*

Command: **CIRCLE** ↵

3P/2P/TTR/<Center point>: *Pick the upper left corner of base at* ①
(see fig. 12.11)

Diameter/<Radius>: .875 ↵

Command: *Choose* Modify, *then* Change, *then* Properties, *and then select* Last *and change thickness to 17.5*

Command: *Set OSNAP to None*

Command: *Set THICKNESS back to 0*

Figure 12.11:

Cylinder drawn with circle and thickness.

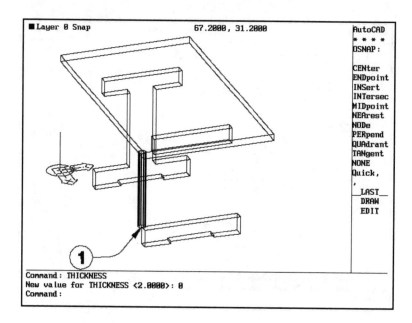

```
■Layer 0 Snap                        67.2000, 31.2000        AutoCAD
                                                             * * * *
                                                             OSNAP:

                                                             CENter
                                                             ENDpoint
                                                             INSert
                                                             INTersec
                                                             MIDpoint
                                                             NEArest
                                                             NODe
                                                             PERpend
                                                             QUAdrant
                                                             TANgent
                                                             NONE
                                                             Quick,
                                                             ,
                                                             _LAST__
                                                               DRAW
                                                               EDIT

Command: THICKNESS
New value for THICKNESS <2.0000>: 0
Command:
```

Now you need to move and array the cylinder to create four more leg supports, as shown in figure 12.12.

Editing in 3D

Most editing commands work like their 2D counterparts. In the next exercise, you use MOVE and ARRAY.

Moving and Arraying in 3D

Continue from the previous exercise.

Command: *Move the last entity a displacement of 1,3*

Command: *Array the last entity with a rectangular array of five rows, one column, and a distance of 4 between rows*

494

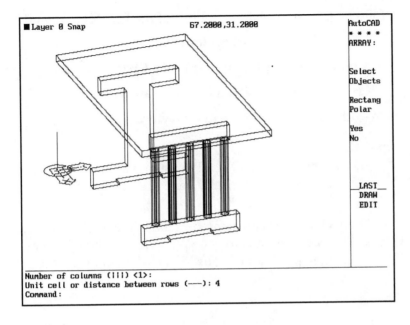

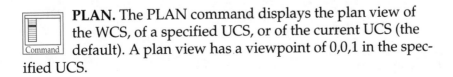

The only trick to editing in 3D is to make sure you have the right UCS. If your viewpoint does not align to the UCS, you will sometimes be surprised (and not necessarily pleased) by the results. AutoCAD does exactly what you tell it to do, not necessarily what you think you tell it to do.

Using multiple viewports, with a plan view in one viewport, is a good way to avoid surprises. The PLAN command makes it easy to get a plan view.

Using PLAN and Multiple Viewports in 3D

PLAN gives you a plan view of the current UCS, any named UCS, or the WCS.

PLAN. The PLAN command displays the plan view of the WCS, of a specified UCS, or of the current UCS (the default). A plan view has a viewpoint of 0,0,1 in the specified UCS.

The following sections list the options of the PLAN command.

PLAN Options

- **Current UCS.** Displays the current UCS in plan view.
- **UCS.** Displays any named UCS in plan view.
- **World.** Displays the WCS in plan view.

 If you set the UCSFOLLOW system variable to 1, every UCS change automatically generates a plan view.

Use the four viewports you created in the first exercise. Use the UCS and PLAN commands to get a plan view of the table (the WCS) in one viewport and of your LEG UCS in another (see fig. 12.13).

Using the PLAN Command

Continue from the previous exercise.

Command: *Set TILEMODE to 0*

Command: *Change to model space*

Click on the lower right viewport to make it current

Command: *Choose* View, *then* Set View, *then* Plan View, *then* Named UCS

`<Current UCS>/Ucs/World: U`

`?/Name of UCS: LEG ↵`   Specifies the saved LEG UCS

Command: *Zoom .8X (If the view did not fill the viewport, Zoom extents, then .8x)*

Command: *Save this view as RIGHT*

Click in upper left viewport to make it current.

Command: *Choose* View, *then* Set View, *then* Plan View, *then* World

`<Current UCS>/Ucs/World: W`

Command: *Zoom .8X*

*Click in lower left viewport
to make it current*

Command: *Set viewpoint to 0,-1,0
for a front view*

Command: *Save view as FRONT*

*Click in upper right viewport to make
it current*

Command: *Restore the* FRIGHT *view*

Command: *Save the drawing*

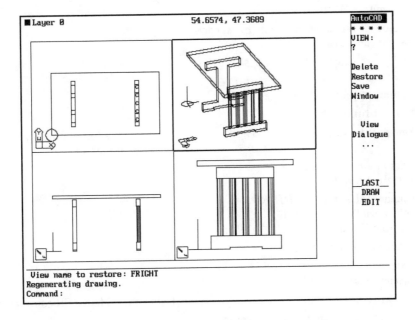

Figure 12.13:

*Plan views to the
WCS and LEG UCS
and a front view-
point.*

If you use the PLAN command, AutoCAD zooms All in the
current viewport, but if the extents have changed, the image may
not fill the viewport.

In this view, you can see a 0.5" gap between the leg and the table
top, which was caused by changing the top thickness from 2" to
-1.5" without adjusting the top of the leg. You can fix it with a 3D
STRETCH command. While you are at it, try another editing
command in 3D: CHAMFER. Chamfer the corners of the first leg
you drew (see fig. 12.14).

497

Stretching and Chamfering in 3D

Continue from the previous exercise.

*Click in lower right viewport
to make it current*

Command: *Choose* Settings, *then* UCS,
then Named UCS

In the UCS Control *dialog box,
select* LEG, *then click on* Current,
then OK

Command: **STRETCH** ↵

Select objects to stretch by window
Select objects: **C** ↵

*Make a crossing window from 0,24 to
21,27*

Select objects: *Press Enter*

Base point: *Pick any point*

New point: **@0,.5** ↵   Stretches the top of both legs to
                                          meet the table top

*Click in upper right viewport
to make it current*

Command: *Use the VPOINT Rotate
option to adjust the angle to
-35 from X-axis and 35 from X-Y plane*

Command: *Save the view as 3D*

Command: *Zoom Window to fill the
viewport with the left leg*

Command: **CHAMFER** ↵   Issues the CHAMFER command

View is not plan to UCS. Command
results may not be obvious.

Polyline/Distances/   Specifies the
<Select first line>: **D** ↵   distance option

Enter first chamfer distance   Sets the first
<0.0000>: **2.5** ↵   chamfer distance

Enter second chamfer distance   Accepts the first
<2.5000>: *Press Enter*   distance as the
                                          second distance

Command: *Press Enter*

498

```
View is not plan to UCS. Command
results may not be obvious.
Polyline/Distances/<Select first line>:
```
Pick one line near vertex ①
(see fig. 12.14)

`Select second line:` *Pick other line near vertex* ①

`Command:` *Repeat CHAMFER at vertex* ②

`Command:` *Set chamfer distances to 2 and 1*

`Command;` *Chamfer the lower left corner of the leg at* ③, *picking the horizontal line first*

`Command:` *Set chamfer distances to 1 and 2*

`Command:` *Chamfer the lower right corner at* ④, *picking the vertical line first*

`Command:` *Zoom Previous or All*

`Command:` *Save the drawing*

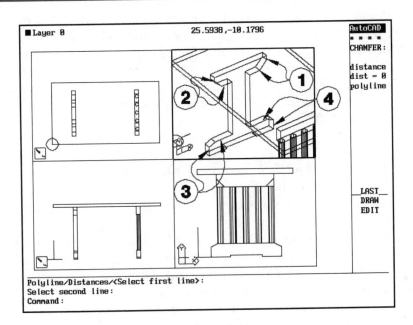

Figure 12.14:

Legs after using the 3D STRETCH and CHAMFER commands.

A *wireframe* model, such as the table you have just drawn, becomes more difficult to visualize as more and more entities are added to it. *Wireframe displays* show all lines and the edges of all surfaces, whether they should be hidden by another surface or not. Extremely complex 3D models are often impossible to comprehend in wireframe format. It helps if you add the illusion of solid surfaces to the 3D object.

Creating the Illusion of Solid 3D Surfaces

Surfaces appear transparent in wireframe displays. AutoCAD provides two ways to display images more realistically: hidden line removal and surface shading.

Removing Hidden Lines with HIDE

Hidden lines are lines that would be obscured by other surfaces if you were looking at a real object. When AutoCAD performs a hidden-line removal, it evaluates the entities in the drawing to determine which ones have surfaces and which surfaces should hide others. Then, it generates a view with the lines that should be removed from the display. The primary command for hidden-line removal is HIDE.

HIDE. The HIDE command calculates which edges should be obscured by other surfaces in a 3D drawing and removes those edges from the display. AutoCAD normally displays all edges of all entities. Only circles, wide polylines, solids, traces, 3D faces, 3D meshes, and extruded entities are treated as having opaque surfaces that hide other edges. Extruded 2D entities define surfaces by projecting their base lines in their extrusion direction by their thickness. Extruded circles, wide polylines, solids, and traces are treated as having top and bottom surfaces, as well as extruded edges.

Tip Entities on layers that are turned off are still considered by HIDE, and those entities may hide entities on visible layers. To avoid confusion, turn all layers on and freeze the layers you want excluded from hidden-line removal. Objects that intersect may not hide correctly unless you break or trim them to leave a tiny gap at the intersections. Hidden-line removal lasts only until the next regeneration.

Turn REGENAUTO off when using the HIDE command to suppress unnecessary regenerations. The MVIEW Hideplot option can turn hidden-line removal during plotting on and off in specific paper space viewports.

Try out the HIDE command on your table model. First, restore a single viewport for a larger view, then hide it (see fig. 12.15).

Using the HIDE Command

Continue from the previous exercise, with the upper right viewport current.

`Command:` *Set TILEMODE to 1*

`Command:` *Choose* Render, *then* Hide   Issues the HIDE command

`Regenerating drawing.`

Hiding lines: done 100%   AutoCAD counts off the lines as it calculates them

`Command:` *Save the drawing*

Most of the table does not yet have surfaces, so there are not many changes. If you look closely, you see that the extruded line representing the edge of the top hides a slice of the legs, the extruded polylines of the legs hide adjacent segments at their corners, and the extruded circles hide everything that they should.

To get a more realistic image, you need to add surfaces. A number of commands in AutoCAD draw surfaces in one way or another. Try the 3DFACE command to add a surface to the table top and underside.

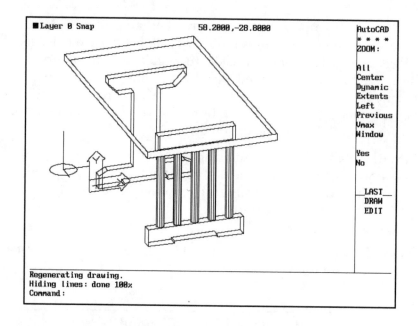

Surfacing with 3DFACE

The 3DFACE command draws triangular or quadrilateral surfaces. 3Dfaces always have four corner points, but the third and fourth points can coincide to create a triangular surface. The points can be located anywhere in 3D space. If they are coplanar (all in the same plane), however, the HIDE command treats the surface as opaque. If the points are not coplanar, the surface will be transparent and will not hide anything.

3DFACE. The 3DFACE command creates three- or four-sided 3D surfaces. Enter the points in a circular order. You can specify any Z coordinates for any corner point, creating nonplanar faces. If all points are coplanar, HIDE considers the face opaque.

To specify an invisible edge, enter an **I** at the first-point prompt of the edge. To create a triangular face, press Enter at the fourth-point prompt. The 3DFACE command repeats. It uses the previous third and fourth points as new first and second points; then it prompts for additional third and fourth points to draw another adjacent 3Dface. To exit, press Enter at the third-point prompt.

Use 3DFACE with object snaps to draw the top of the table. Pick your points carefully because object snap can snap to the top or bottom of the extruded lines of the table top (see fig. 12.16). Then, try another HIDE.

Using 3DFACE

Continue from the previous exercise.

Command: *Set an ENDpoint running object snap mode*

Command: *Choose* Draw, *then* 3D Surfaces, *then* 3D Face   Issues the 3DFACE command

First point: *Pick ① (see fig. 12.16)*

Second point: *Pick ②*

Third point: *Pick ③*

Fourth point: *Pick ④*

Third point: *Press Enter*   Ends the 3DFACE command.

Command: **HIDE** ↵   Issues the HIDE command

Regenerating drawing

Removing hidden lines: 175

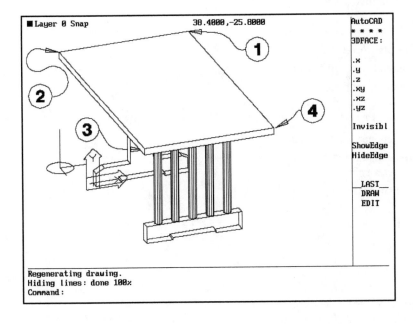

Figure 12.16:

3Dface table top with HIDE.

Surfacing the legs requires more work. The top was a simple rectangle, but the legs need several adjacent faces to cover them. The pick points for the bottom part are shown in figure 12.17. You can use the I option of the 3DFACE command to make the lines between faces invisible.

Before picking the first point of each edge you want to be invisible, enter an I. For example, if you want edge 2 to be hidden, enter an I before you select point 2, which is the first point of the second edge. Start the following exercise by erasing the right leg and restoring the RIGHT view. Also, because it is hard to see faces with invisible edges, temporarily set the entity color to red.

Creating 3Dfaces with Invisible Edges

Continue from the previous exercise, with OSNAP set to ENDP and the LEG UCS current.

Command: REGEN ↵

Makes the top of the leg visible to help erase it

Command: *Erase the entities of the right leg*

Command: *Choose* View, *then* Set View, *then* Named View

In the View Control *Dialog box, select RIGHT, and then click on* Restore, *then OK*

Command: *Set entity color to red*

Command: **3DFACE** ↵

First point: *Pick point* ①
(see fig. 12.17)

Second point: *Pick point* ②

Third point: **I** ↵
then pick point ③

Fourth point: *Pick point* ④

Third point: **I** ↵
then pick point ⑤

```
Fourth point: Pick point ⑥
Third point: Press Enter                    Ends the 3DFACE command
Command: 3DFACE ↵
First point: Pick point ⑤
Second point: I ↵
then pick point ⑦
Third point: I ↵
then pick point ⑧
Fourth point: I ↵
then pick point ⑥
Third point: Press Enter                    Ends the 3DFACE command
```

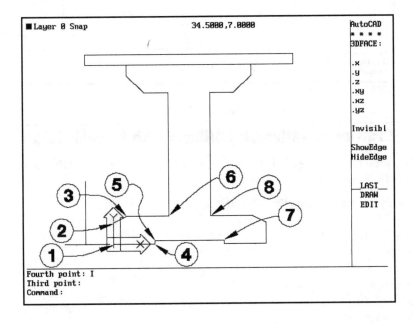

Figure 12.17:

Pick points for 3Dfaces.

Continue entering 3Dfaces, using the pick points shown in figure 12.18. You do not have to draw all of the faces; you can use MIRROR to copy some. After surfacing the leg, restore the 3D view.

Figure 12.18:

Pick points for more 3Dfaces.

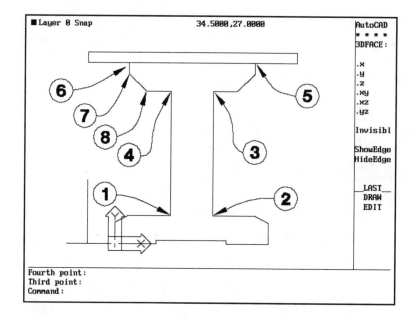

Drawing and Mirroring 3Dfaces with Invisible Edges

Continue from the previous exercise, with OSNAP set to ENDP and the LEG UCS current.

Command: *Choose* Draw, *then* 3D Surfaces,
then 3D Face

First point: I ↵
then pick point ①
(see fig. 12.18)

Second point: *Pick point* ②

Third point: I ↵
then pick point ③

Fourth point: I ↵
then pick point ④

Third point: *Press Enter*   Ends the 3DFACE command

Command: **3DFACE** ↵

First point: I ↵
then pick point ⑤

Second point: I ↵
then pick point ③

```
Third point: I ↵
```
then pick point ④
```
Fourth point: Pick point ⑥
```
Pick point ⑥
```
Third point: Pick point ⑦
```
Pick point ⑦
```
Fourth point: Pick point ⑧
```
Pick point ⑧
```
Third point: Press Enter
```
Press Enter   Ends the 3DFACE command
```
Command: MIRROR ↵
```
```
Select objects:Use Window to select the
```
Use Window to select the the entire left half of the leg
```
3 found.
```
```
Select objects: Press Enter
```
Press Enter   Ends object selection
```
First point of mirror line: MID ↵
```
of Pick the bottom center of the leg
```
Second point: @0,6 ↵
```
```
Delete old objects? <N> ↵
```
                                            Completes the surfacing
```
Command: Restore the view named 3D
```
Restore the view named 3D
```
Command: Set OSNAP back to NONE
```
Set OSNAP back to NONE
```
Command: Set COLOR back to BYLAYER
```
Set COLOR back to BYLAYER
```
Command: Save the drawing
```
Save the drawing

Finish the table with three quick COPY commands. By copying the faces, you save the time and trouble of drawing faces on the other side of the leg. After copying the faces, copy the entire left leg to create the right leg. Then, copy the 3Dface of the table top to close the underside of the top. Finally, perform a HIDE to check your surfaces (see fig. 12.19).

Copying Surfaces To Finish the Table

Continue from the previous exercise.

```
Command: COPY ↵
```
```
Select objects: W ↵
```
Use a window to select the 3Dfaces, but carefully pick the right edge so that it does not enclose the entire extruded polyline of the leg
```
9 found
```

```
Select objects: Press Enter
<Base point or displacement>
/Multiple: 0,0,2 ↵
Second point of displacement:
Press Enter                              Copies the objects
Command: HIDE ↵                          Checks the result of the copy
Command: REGEN ↵                         Regenerates the drawing so that
                                         you can select the entire leg

Select the entire leg
Command: DDCHPROP ↵
Set Color to BYLAYER
Command: Copy the entire leg with a
displacement of 0,0,32
Command: Copy the 3Dface on the table
top with a displacement of 0,-1.5,0
Command: HIDE ↵                          Checks the result
Command: SAVE ↵                          Saves the drawing
```

Figure 12.19:

Copied 3Dfaces and leg, with hidden lines removed.

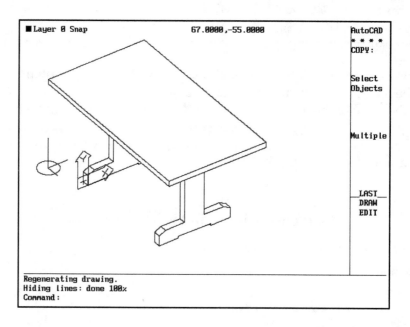

```
■Layer 0 Snap                  67.0000,-55.0000          AutoCAD
                                                         * * * *
                                                         COPY:

                                                         Select
                                                         Objects

                                                         Multiple

                                                         __LAST__
                                                         DRAW
                                                         EDIT

Regenerating drawing.
Hiding lines: done 100%
Command:
```

Now the table looks like a respectable first 3D project. You might want to add a cross support to keep it from wobbling, however.

The HIDE command is not the only command that can remove hidden lines, and the VPOINT command is not the only command that rotates your viewpoint. The DVIEW command does all this and more.

Viewing Dynamically in 3D

The DVIEW command enables you to display a model in parallel projection or in perspective. It provides a wealth of options for locating the *target point* (the point you are looking at), the *camera point* (the viewpoint where your "eye" is located), perspective distance, and many other factors. DVIEW takes all of the hard work out of drawing a perspective by calculating the image for you.

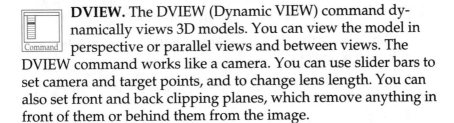

DVIEW. The DVIEW (Dynamic VIEW) command dynamically views 3D models. You can view the model in perspective or parallel views and between views. The DVIEW command works like a camera. You can use slider bars to set camera and target points, and to change lens length. You can also set front and back clipping planes, which remove anything in front of them or behind them from the image.

The following sections discuss the various DVIEW options.

DVIEW Options

- **Select objects.** Select the objects to drag in DVIEW, or press Enter to use the house-shaped DVIEWBLOCK to establish the viewpoint and options. Complex images do not drag well in DVIEW. If you select only a few representative entities, they drag smoothly in DVIEW. When you exit, the entire drawing regenerates from that viewpoint.

- **CAmera.** Rotate the camera around the target point by specifying the camera angle above or below the X,Y plane and from the X axis in the X,Y plane, similar to the VPOINT Rotate option.

- **TArget.** Rotate the target point around the camera by specifying the angle above or below the X,Y plane, and from the X axis in the X,Y plane.

- **Distance.** Specify the distance from the camera to the target, which turns perspective mode on.

- **POints.** Specify a camera point and target point to establish the angle of view. This option does not turn perspective mode on, but it does affect perspective if it is on.

- **PAn.** Specify two points to indicate a pan displacement. DVIEW pans the camera around the target in perspective mode. It pans both camera and target in parallel view.

- **Zoom.** Specify the lens length of the camera (changing the field of view, not the perspective) in perspective mode. The default lens length is 50mm. For a telephoto effect, use longer lens lengths; for a wide-angle effect, use a shorter lens length. In parallel view, the Zoom option zooms like ZOOM Center.

- **TWist.** Specify the view twist angle to rotate the camera around the line of sight.

- **CLip.** Sets front and back clipping planes, perpendicular to the line of sight.

- **Hide.** Removes hidden lines from the selection set.

- **Off.** Turns perspective mode off.

- **Undo.** Undoes the previous DVIEW option.

- **eXit.** Exits DVIEW and regenerates the drawing.

 Use the VIEW Save and Restore options to save and restore perspective views.

Most of the DVIEW options use slider bars for input. You move the cursor up and down or side to side to get the view you want, then pick. You can also enter a value on the prompt line. The coordinate display shows the current value as you slide. To set precise values, drag the slider to the approximate view you want, read the approximate value from the coordinate display, and enter the precise value at the prompt.

In general, DVIEW is a good substitute for VPOINT, and it is also the only way to get a perspective view in AutoCAD. Try setting a perspective view of the table (see fig. 12.20).

Creating a Perspective View

Continue from the previous exercise.

Command: *Choose* View, *then* Set View, *then* Dview	Issues the DVIEW command
Select objects: *Use a window to select the entire table*	
`*** Switching to the WCS ***`	
`CAmera/TArget/Distance/POints/PAn/Zoom /TWist/CLip/Hide/Off/Undo/<eXit>:` PO ↵	Specifies the POints option
`Enter target point <30.5387, 21.7554, 13.0745>:` .XZ ↵	
of MID ↵	
of *Pick the top right edge of table*	
(need Y): MID ↵	
of *Pick the top back edge of table*	
`Enter camera point <31.2097, 21.2855, 13.6481>:` @96,-84,21 ↵	Sets a new camera point
`CAmera/TArget/Distance/POints/PAn/Zoom /TWist/CLip/Hide/Off/Undo/<eXit>:` D ↵	Specifies the Distance option
`New camera/target distance <129.2788>:` *Drag the slider to about 120 on the coordinate display, then pick*	
`CAmera/TArget/Distance/POints/PAn/Zoom /TWist/CLip/Hide/Off/Undo/<eXit>:` PA ↵	Specifies the PAn option
`Displacement base point:` *Pick a point near the center of the view*	
`Second point:` *Drag the table up a little; the perspective changes as you drag it, then pick a point*	
`CAmera/TArget/Distance/POints/PAn/Zoom /TWist/CLip/Hide/Off/Undo/<eXit>:` Z ↵	Specifies the Zoom option
`Adjust lenslength <50.000mm>:` *Slide the lens length to about 60 on the coordinate display, then pick*	

CAmera/TArget/Distance/POints/PAn/Zoom /TWist/CLip/Hide/Off/Undo/<eXit>: *Press Enter*	Exits the DVIEW command
Regenerating drawing.	The hidden lines return
Command: *Erase the 3DBLK at the WCS origin*	
Command: *Set the UCS to World*	
Command: *Save the view as 3DPERSP*	
Command: **HIDE** ⏎	
Command: *Save the drawing*	

Figure 12.20:

The table in perspective.

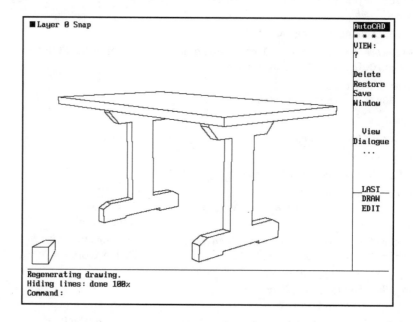

You now have a perspective view of the table. You cannot do much in perspective view because point picking is meaningless, but you can hide the drawing, shade it, view it, and plot it.

Tip — To draw while viewing a perspective, use multiple viewports with the perspective in one. The objects you draw appear in the perspective. In paper space, you can plot a perspective in one viewport and plot plan, front, and side views in other viewports.

Shading the View

Now that you have a perspective view, you can add shading to it.

If you have a 256-color display that uses AutoCAD's standard color scheme, you can create shaded images. *Shading* means that the surfaces are rendered as if a single light source behind your eyes is illuminating the model (as you look at it from directly in front of the screen).

Although the SHADE command does not provide the same quality as the AVE Render or AutoShade rendering program from Autodesk, it gives a good flat shading of the model. By setting system variables, you can adjust the ambient light ratio and the way in which SHADE displays surfaces and edges. The primary advantage of SHADE is that it is quick, readily available, and it does not cost extra. HIDE may be faster for simple drawings, but SHADE is faster for complex surfaces.

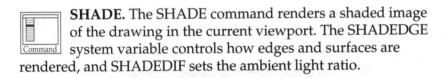

SHADE. The SHADE command renders a shaded image of the drawing in the current viewport. The SHADEDGE system variable controls how edges and surfaces are rendered, and SHADEDIF sets the ambient light ratio.

SHADE'S default lighting assumes 70 percent direct light, reflecting from a single light and 30 percent ambient background light. These percentages are controlled by the SHADEDIF system variable, from 0 to 100 direct. Higher values increase reflectivity and contrast. The intensity of the shading on a particular face is greatest if it is perpendicular to the light source, and it decreases as the angle of the face increases. Edges are highlighted in the background screen color if SHADEDGE is set to 1. Plain edges, SHADEDGE 0, usually look best.

Any display can produce two types of unshaded surface renderings. The default (SHADEDGE 3) draws faces filled with their original colors and highlights edges in the background screen color. This looks best on simple images. If SHADEDGE is 2, SHADE generates a simulated hidden-line removal, with faces in the background screen color and edges in the original colors of their faces. This looks as good as a slow HIDE. You cannot select entities after a SHADE (as you can with HIDE) until you regenerate the screen.

Try using the default settings of the SHADE command on the perspective image (see fig. 12.21).

Using the SHADE Command

Continue from the previous exercise.

Command: *Choose Render, then Shade*   Issues the SHADE command.

Regenerating drawing.

Shading complete.

Command: **END** ↵

Figure 12.21:

Perspective with SHADE.

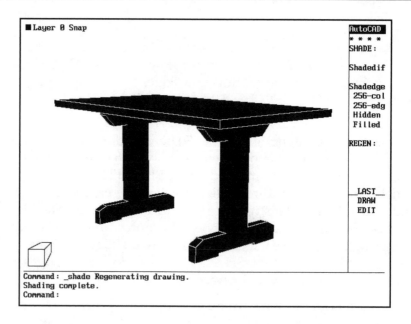

Now your table is complete!

Summary

Now that you have found the third dimension, you may find it easier to design an object in 3D than in 2D, or you may want to take advantage of the AVE Render, AutoShade, 3D Studio, or Autodesk Animator Pro programs from Autodesk to create stunning presentations to dazzle your clients or customers. Whatever your needs, you now know basic 3D concepts and you have learned how to use many of AutoCAD's 3D commands.

In this chapter, you learned to draw, edit, move, copy, and stretch 3D objects. You used the LINE command to draw in 3D by adding a Z coordinate. You learned to use 3D point entry and point filters. You learned to place the UCS at any point and angle in 3D space to create a construction plane where you can extrude many 2D entities into 3D. You used VPOINT, DVIEW, and PLAN to visualize, create, and present your 3D drawing from different viewpoints. You even used DVIEW to view a drawing in perspective. You surfaced your 3D model with the 3DFACE commands. Then, you viewed the surfaces realistically by removing hidden lines with the DVIEW and HIDE commands, and by shading their faces or surfaces with the SHADE command.

AutoCAD System Variables

Table A.1 presents the AutoCAD system variables. You can use this table to find AutoCAD's environment settings. These settings are available through the SETVAR command or AutoLISP's SETVAR and GETVAR functions. The system variable name and the default AutoCAD prototype drawing (ACAD.DWG) settings are shown. A brief description is provided for each variable, and the meaning is shown for each code flag.

Some variable names appear in italic; you use the SETVAR command to set their values. You can set all other variables directly by entering their name at the Command: prompt or indirectly through AutoLISP, ADS, or by using the command shown in the *Command Name* column. Variable names and features shown in bold are new to Release 12.

All values are saved with the drawing unless noted with (CFG) for ConFiGuration file, or (NS) for Not Saved. Variables marked (RO) are read only, which means that you cannot type their names or use SETVAR or the (setvar) function to change them.

Table A.1

AutoCAD System Variables

Variable Name	Default Setting	Command Name	Variable Description
ACADPREFIX	C:\ACAD;C:ACAD\SAMPLE;...		Directory search path set by DOS environment variable ACAD (NS),(RO)
ACADVER	12		The release number of your copy of AutoCAD
AFLAGS	0	**DDATTDEF**, ATTDEF	Current state of ATTDEF modes. The value is the sum of the following: 1 = Invisible 2 = Constant 4 = Verify 8 = Preset
ANGBASE	0	**DDUNITS**, UNITS	The direction of angle 0 in the current UCS
ANGDIR	0	**DDUNITS**, UNITS	The direction of angle measure: 1 = Clockwise 0 = Counterclockwise
APERTURE	10	**DDOSNAP**, APERTURE	Half the OSNAP target size in pixels (CFG)
AREA	0.0000	AREA, LIST	The last computed area in square drawing units
ATTDIA	0		Controls the attribute-entry method: 1 = DDATTE dialogue box 0 = Attribute prompts
ATTMODE	1	ATTDISP	Attribute display: 1 = Normal 2 = ON 3 = OFF

Variable Name	Default Setting	Command Name	Variable Description
ATTREQ	1		Attribute values used by Insert: 1 = Prompts for values 0 = Uses defaults
AUDITCTL	0		Controls the creation of an ADT log file containing AUDIT results: 0 = No file 1 = ADT file (CFG)
AUNITS	0	**DDUNITS**, UNITS	The angular unit display code: 0 = Decimal deg. 1 =Degrees/min/sec 2 = Grads 3 = Radians 4 = Surveyors
AUPREC	0	**DDUNITS**, UNITS	The number of angular units decimal places
BACKZ	0.0000	DVIEW	The DVIEW back clipping plane offset in drawing units. *See VIEWMODE* (RO)
BLIPMODE	1	BLIPMODE	Controls blip display: 1 = Blips 0 = No Blips
CDATE	19881202. 144648898	TIME	Current date and time in YYYYMMDD.HHMM SSmsec format (NS),(RO)
CECOLOR	BYLAYER	DDEMODES, COLOR	The current entity color (RO)
CELTYPE	BYLAYER	DDEMODES, LINETYPE	The current entity linetype (RO)

continues

Table A.1 Continued

AutoCAD System Variables

Variable Name	Default Setting	Command Name	Variable Description
CHAMFERA	0.0000	CHAMFER	The first chamfer distance
CHAMFERB	0.0000	CHAMFER	The second chamfer distance
CIRCLERAD	**0.0000**		**The default radius value for new circle entities: 0 = None (NS)**
CLAYER	0	DDLMODES, LAYER	The current layer (RO)
CMDACTIVE	**1**	**CMDACTIVE**	**Indicates that an AutoCAD command is active (used primarily by ADS): 1 = None 2 = Transparent 4 = Script 8 = Dialog box (NS),(RO)**
CMDECHO	1		Controls AutoCAD Command: prompt echoing by AutoLISP: 1 = Echo 0 = No Echo (NS)
CMDDIA	1		Controls whether the PLOT command issues dialog boxes or prompts; a nonzero setting issues dialog boxes; 0 issues prompts (CFG)
CMDNAMES	**""**		**Names of any active commands**

Variable Name	Default Setting	Command Name	Variable Description
COORDS	0	[^D] [F6]	Controls the updating of the coordinate display: 0 = Absolute upon picks 1 = Absolute continuously 2 = Relative only during prompts
CVPORT	1	VPORTS	The current viewport's number
DATE	2447498. 61620926	TIME	The current date and time in Julian format (NS),(RO)
DBMOD	**4**	**Most**	**Describes modifications to the current drawing database:** **0 = None** **1 = Entities** **2 = Symbol table** **4 = Database variable** **8 = Window** **15 = View** **(RO)**
DIASTAT	0	DD?????	The last dialog box exit code: 0 = Canceled 1 = OK button (RO)
DIMALT	0	**DDIM,** DIMALT	Controls the drawing of additional dimension text in an alternative-units system: 1 = On 0 = Off
DIMALTD	2	**DDIM,** DIMALTD	The decimal precision of dimension text when alternative units are used

continues

Table A.1 Continued

AutoCAD System Variables

Variable Name	Default Setting	Command Name	Variable Description
DIMALTF	25.4000	**DDIM,** DIMALTF	The scale factor for dimension text when alternative units are used
DIMAPOST	""	**DDIM,** DIMAPOST	The user-defined suffix for alternative dimension text (RO)
DIMASO	1	DIMASO	Controls the creation of associative dimensions: 1 = On 0 = Off
DIMASZ	0.1800	**DDIM,** DIMASZ	Controls the size of dimension arrows and affects the fit of dimension text inside dimension lines when DIMTSZ is set to 0
DIMBLK	"."	**DDIM,** DIMBLK	The name of the block to draw rather than an arrow or tick (RO)
DIMBLK1	""	**DDIM,** DIMBLK1	The name of the block for the first end of dimension lines. *See DIMSAH* (RO)
DIMBLK2	""	**DDIM,** DIMBLK2	The name of the block for the second end of dimension lines. *See DIMSAH* (RO)
DIMCEN	0.0900	**DDIM,** DIMCEN	Controls center marks or center lines drawn by radial DIM commands: Mark size = value Draw center lines = negative (mark size = absolute value)

Variable Name	Default Setting	Command Name	Variable Description
DIMCLRD	0	**DDIM,** DIMCLRD	The dimension line, arrow, and leader color number: 0 = BYBLOCK 256 = BYLAYER
DIMCLRE	0	**DDIM,** DIMCLRE	The dimension extension line's color
DIMCLRT	0	**DDIM,** DIMCLRT	The dimension text's color
DIMDLE	0.0000	**DDIM,** DIMDLE	The dimension line's extension distance beyond ticks when ticks are drawn (when DIMTSZ is nonzero)
DIMDLI	0.3800	**DDIM,** DIMDLI	The offset distance between successive continuing or baseline dimensions
DIMEXE	0.1800	**DDIM,** DIMEXE	The length of extension lines beyond dimension lines
DIMEXO	0.0625	**DDIM,** DIMEXO	The distance by which extension lines originate from dimensioned entity
DIMGAP	0.0900	**DDIM,** DIMGAP	The space between text and a dimension line; determines when text is placed outside a dimension **(Creates reference dimension outlines if negative)**
DIMLFAC	1.0000	**DDIM,** DIMLFAC	The overall linear dimensioning scale factor; if negative, acts as the absolute value applied to paper space viewports

continues

Table A.1 Continued

AutoCAD System Variables

Variable Name	Default Setting	Command Name	Variable Description
DIMLIM	0	**DDIM,** DIMLIM	Presents dimension limits as the default text: 1 = ON 0 = OFF *See DIMTP and DIMTM*
DIMPOST	""	**DDIM,** DIMPOST	The user-defined suffix for dimension text, such as "mm" (RO)
DIMRND	0.0000	**DDIM,** DIMRND	The rounding interval for linear dimension text
DIMSAH	0	**DDIM,** DIMSAH	Enables the use of DIMBLK1 and DIMBLK2 rather than DIMBLK or a default terminator: 1 = ON 0 = OFF
DIMSCALE	1.0000	**DDIM,** DIMSCALE	The overall scale factor applied to other dimension variables except tolerances, angles, measured lengths, or coordinates 0 = Paper space scale
DIMSE1	0	**DDIM,** DIMSE1	Suppresses the first extension line: 1 = On 0 = Off
DIMSE2	0	**DDIM,** DIMSE2	Suppresses the second extension line: 1 = On 0 = Off

Variable Name	Default Setting	Command Name	Variable Description
DIMSHO	0	DIMSHO	Determines whether associative dimension text is updated during dragging: 1 = On 0 = Off
DIMSOXD	0	**DDIM,** DIMSOXD	Suppresses the placement of dimension lines outside extension lines: 1 = On 0 = Off
DIMSTYLE	*UNNAMED	**DDIM,** Dim: SAVE	Holds the name of the current dimension style (RO)
DIMTAD	0	**DDIM,** DIMTAD	Places dimension text above the dimension line rather than within: 1 = On 0 = Off
DIMTIH	1	**DDIM,** DIMTIH	Forces dimension text inside the extension lines to be positioned horizontally rather than aligned: 1 = On 0 = Off
DIMTIX	0	**DDIM,** DIMTIX	Force dimension text inside the extension lines: 1 = O 0 = Off
DIMTM	0.0000	**DDIM,** DIMTM	The negative tolerance value used when DIMTOL or DIMLIM is on

continues

Table A.1 Continued

AutoCAD System Variables

Variable Name	Default Setting	Command Name	Variable Description
DIMTOFL	0	**DDIM,** DIMTOFL	Draws dimension lines between extension lines even if text is placed outside the extension lines: 1 = On 0 = Off
DIMTOH	1	**DDIM,** DIMTOH	Forces dimension text to be positioned horizontally rather than aligned when it falls outside the extension lines: 1 = On 0 = Off
DIMTOL	0	**DDIM,** DIMTOL	Appends tolerance values (DIMTP and DIMTM) to the default dimension text: 1 = On 0 = Off
DIMTP	0.0000	**DDIM,** DIMTP	The positive tolerance value used when DIMTOL or DIMLIM is on
DIMTSZ	0.0000	**DDIM,** DIMTSZ	When assigned a nonzero value, forces tick marks to be drawn (rather than arrowheads) at the size specified by the value; affects the placement of the dimension line and text between extension lines
DIMTVP	0.0000	**DDIM,** DIMTVP	Percentage of text height to offset dimension vertically
DIMTXT	0.1800	**DDIM,** DIMTXT	The dimension text height for non-fixed text styles

Variable Name	Default Setting	Command Name	Variable Description
DIMZIN	0	**DDIM**, DIMZIN	Suppresses the display of zero inches or zero feet in dimension text 0 = Feet and Inches 1 = Neither 2 = Inches Only 3 = Feet only
DISTANCE	0.0000	DIST	The last distance computed by the DISTANCE command (NS),(RO)
DONUTID	**0.5000**		**The default inner diameter for new DONUT entities; may be 0 (NS)**
DONUTOD	**1.0000**		**The default outer diameter for new DONUT entities; must be nonzero (NS)**
DRAGMODE	2	DRAGMODE	Controls object dragging on-screen: 0 = Off 1 = If requested 2 = Auto
DRAGP1	10		The regen-drag sampling rate (CFG)
DRAGP2	25		The fast-drag sampling rate (CFG)
DWGCODEPAGE			**The code page used for the drawing; the default setting in ASCII**
DWGNAME		UNNAMED	The current drawing name supplied by the user when the drawing was begun (RO)

continues

Table A.1 Continued

AutoCAD System Variables

Variable Name	Default Setting	Command Name	Variable Description
DWGTITLED	0	**NEW**	**Indicates whether the current drawing has been named or not** **1 = Yes** **0 = No** **(RO)**
DWGPREFIX	C:\ACAD\		The current drawing's drive and directory path (NS) (RO)
DWGWRITE	1	**OPEN**	**Indicates that the current drawing is opened as read-only:** **0 = No** **1 = Yes**
ELEVATION	0.0000	ELEV	The current elevation in the current UCS for the current space
ERRNO	0		An error number generated by AutoLISP and ADS applications (*See* the *AutoLISP Reference Manual* or the *ADS Programmer's Reference Manual*)
EXPERT	0		Suppresses successive levels of Are you sure? warnings: 0 = None 1 = REGEN/LAYER 2 = BLOCK/WBLOCK/ SAVE 3 = LINETYPE 4 = UCS/VPORT 5 = DIM

Variable Name	Default Setting	Command Name	Variable Description
EXTMAX	-1.0000E+20, -1.0000E+20		The X,Y coordinates of the drawing's upper right extents in the WCS (RO)
EXTMIN	1.0000E+20, 1.0000E+20		The X,Y coordinates of the drawing's lower left extents in the WCS (RO)
FILEDIA	1		Controls the display of the dialogue box for file name requests: 0 = Only when a tilde (~) is entered 1 = On (CFG)
FILLETRAD	0.0000	FILLET	The current fillet radius
FILLMODE	1	FILL	Turns on the display of fill traces, solids, and wide polylines: 1 = On 0 = Off
FRONTZ	0.0000	DVIEW	The DVIEW front clipping plane's offset, in drawing units; *see VIEWMODE* (RO)
GRIDMODE	0	DDRMODES, GRID	Controls grid display in the current viewport: 1 = On 0 = Off
GRIDUNIT	0.0000,0.0000	DDRMODES, GRID	The X,Y grid increment for the current viewport
GRIPBLOCK	**1**	**DDGRIPS**	**Controls the display of grips for entities in blocks: 1 = On 2 = Off (CFG)**

continues

Table A.1 Continued

AutoCAD System Variables

Variable Name	Default Setting	Command Name	Variable Description
GRIPCOLOR	5	**DDGRIPS**	The current color code of unselected grips; can be a value of 0 to 255 (CFG)
GRIPHOT	1	**DDGRIPS**	The current color code of selected grips; can be a value of 0 to 255 (CFG)
GRIPS	1	**DDSELECT**	Controls the display of entity grips and grip editing 1 = ON 0 = OFF (CFG)
GRIPSIZE	5	**DDGRIPS**	The size of the grip box in pixels; (CFG)
HANDLES	0	HANDLES	Controls the creation of entity handles for the current drawing: 1 = On 0 = Off (RO)
HELPFILE	""	**HELP**	The default help file's name; also set by the ACADHELP environment variable (NS)
HIGHLIGHT	1		Determines whether the current object selection set is highlighted: 1 = Off 2 = On (NS)

Variable Name	Default Setting	Command Name	Variable Description
HPANG	0	**BHATCH, HATCH**	**The default angle for new hatch patterns (NS)**
HPDOUBLE	0	**BHATCH, HATCH**	**Controls user-defined hatch-pattern doubling:** **1 = On** **0 = Off** **(NS)**
HPNAME	""	**BHATCH, HATCH**	**The default name for new hatch patterns (NS)**
HPSCALE	1.0000	**BHATCH, HATCH**	**The default scale factor for new hatch patterns; must be nonzero (NS)**
HPSPACE	1.0000	**BHATCH, HATCH**	**The default spacing for user-defined hatch patterns; must be nonzero (NS)**
INSBASE	0.0000, 0.0000	BASE	The insertion base point X,Y coordinate of the current drawing in the current space and the current UCS
INSNAME	""	**DDINSERT, INSERT**	**The default block name for new insertions (NS)**
LASTANGLE	0	ARC	The end angle of the last arc in the current space UCS (NS),(RO)
LASTPOINT	0.0000, 0.0000, 0.0000		The current space and UCS coordinate of the last point entered (recall with "@") (NS)
LENSLENGTH	50.0000	DVIEW	The current viewport perspective view lens length, in millimeters (RO)

continues

531

Table A.1 Continued

AutoCAD System Variables

Variable Name	Default Setting	Command Name	Variable Description
LIMCHECK	0	LIMITS	Controls limits checking for the current space: 1 = On 0 = Off
LIMMAX	12.0000, 9.0000	LIMITS	The upper right X,Y limit of current space, relative to the WCS
LIMMIN	0.0000, 0.0000	LIMITS	The lower left X,Y limit of current space, relative to the WCS
LOGINNAME	**""**	**CONFIG**	**The name entered by the user or configuration file during login to AutoCAD (CFG),(RO)**
LTSCALE	1.0000	LTSCALE	The global scale factor applied to linetypes
LUNITS	2	**DDUNITS,** UNITS	The linear units format: 1 = Scientific 2 = Decimal 3 = Engineering 4 = Architectural 5 = Fractional
LUPREC	4	**DDUNITS,** UNITS	Units precision decimal places or fraction denominator
MACROTRACE	**0**		**Controls the DIESEL macro-debugging display** **1 = On** **0 = Off**
MAXACTVP	16		The maximum number of viewports to regenerate (NS),(RO)

Variable Name	Default Setting	Command Name	Variable Description
MAXSORT	200		The maximum number of symbols and file names sorted in lists, up to 200 (CFG)
MENUCTL	**1**		**Command-line input-sensitive screen menu-page switching:** **1 = On** **0 = Off** **(CFG)**
MENUECHO	0		Suppresses the display of menu actions on the command line; the value is the sum of the following: 1 = Menu input 2 = Command prompts 4 = Disable ^P toggling (NS)
MENUNAME	ACAD	MENU	The current menu name, plus the drive/path if entered (RO)
MIRRTEXT	1		Controls reflection of text by the MIRROR command: 0 = Retain text direction 1 = Reflect text
MODEMACRO	**""**		**A DIESEL language expression to control status-line display**
OFFSETDIST	**-1.0000**	**OFFSET**	**The default distance for the OFFSET command; negative values enable the Through option (NS)**

continues

Table A.1 Continued

AutoCAD System Variables

Variable Name	Default Setting	Command Name	Variable Description
ORTHOMODE	0	[^O] [F8]	Sets the current Ortho mode state: 1 = On 0 = Off
OSMODE	0	**DDOSNAP,** OSNAP	The current object snap mode; the value is the sum of the following: 1 = Endp 2 = Mid 4 = Cen 8 = Node 16 = Quad 32 = Int 64 = Ins 128 = Perp 256 = Tan 512 = Near 1024 = Quick
PDMODE	0		Controls the graphic display of point entities
PDSIZE	0.0000		Controls the size of point graphic display
PERIMETER	0.0000	AREA, DBLIST, LIST	The last computed perimeter (NS)(RO)
PFACEVMAX	4		The maximum number of vertices per face in a PFACE mesh (NS),(RO)
PICKADD	**1**	**DDSELECT**	**Controls whether selected entities are added to, or replace (added with Shift+select) the current selection set:** **0 = Added** **1 = Replace** **(CFG)**

Variable Name	Default Setting	Command Name	Variable Description
PICKAUTO	0	**DDSELECT**	Controls the implied (AUTO) windowing for object selection: 1 = On 0 = Off (CFG)
PICKDRAG	0	**DDSELECT**	Determines whether the pick button must be depressed during window corner picking in set selection (MS Windows style): 1 = On 0 = OFF (CFG)
PICKFIRST	0	**DDSELECT**	Enables entity selection before command selection (noun/verb paradigm): 1 = On 0 = Off (CFG)
PICKBOX	3		Half the object-selection pick box size, in pixels (CFG)
PLATFORM	*Varies*		Indicates the version of AutoCAD in use: a string such as "386 DOS Extender," "Sun 4/SPARCstation," "Apple Macintosh," etc.
PLOTID	""	**PLOT**	The current plotter configuration description (CFG)
PLOTTER	0	**PLOT**	The current plotter configuration number (CFG)

continues

Table A.1 Continued

AutoCAD System Variables

Variable Name	Default Setting	Command Name	Variable Description
PLINEGEN	0		The control points for polyline generation of noncontinuous linetypes: 0 = Vertices 1 = End points
PLINEWID	0.0000	**PLINE**	The default width for new polyline entities
POLYSIDES	4	**POLYGON**	The default number of sides (3 to 1024) for new polygon entities (NS)
POPUPS	1		Determines whether the Advanced User Interface (dialog boxes, menu bar, pull-down menus, icon menus) is supported: 1 = Yes 0 = No (NS),(RO)
PSPROLOG	""		The name of the PostScript post-processing section of ACAD.PSF to be appended to the PSOUT command's output
PSQUALITY	75	**PSQUALITY**	The default quality setting for rendering of images by the PSIN command
PSLTSCALE	1		Paper-space scaling of model space linetypes: 1 = On 0 = Off (DWG)

Variable Name	Default Setting	Command Name	Variable Description
QTEXTMODE	0	QTEXT	Sets the current state of Quick text mode: 1 = On 0 = Off
REGENMODE	1	REGENAUTO	Indicates the current state of REGENAUTO: 1 = On 0 = Off
SAVEFILE	**AUTO.SV$**	**CONFIG**	**The default directory and file name for automatic file saves (CFG),(RO)**
SAVETIME	**120**	**CONFIG**	**The default interval between automatic file saves, in minutes (CFG)**
SAVENAME	**""**	**SAVEAS**	**The drawing name specified by the user to the last invocation of the SAVEAS command in the current session (NS), (RO)**
SCREENBOXES	**25**	**CONFIG**	**The number of available screen menu boxes in the current graphics screen area (RO)**
SCREENMODE	**0**	**[F1]**	**Indicates the active AutoCAD screen mode or window: 0 = Text 1 = Graphics 2 = Dual screen (RO)**
SCREENSIZE	572.0000, 414.0000		The size of current viewport, in pixels, X and Y (RO)

continues

Table A.1 Continued

AutoCAD System Variables

Variable Name	Default Setting	Command Name	Variable Description
SHADEDGE	3		Controls the display of edges and faces by the SHADE command: 0 = Faces shaded, edges unhighlighted 1 = Faces shaded, edges in background color 2 = Faces unfilled, edges in entity color 3 = Faces in entity color, edges in background
SHADEDIF	70		Specifies the ratio of diffuse-to-ambient light used by the SHADE command; expressed as a percentage of diffuse reflective light
SHPNAME	**""**	**SHAPE**	**The default shape name (NS)**
SKETCHINC	0.1000	SKETCH	The recording increment for SKETCH sements
SKPOLY	0		Controls the type of entities generated by SKETCH: 1 = Polylines 0 = Lines
SNAPANG	0	**DDRMODES,** SNAP	The angle of SNAP/GRID rotation in the current viewport, for the current UCS
SNAPBASE	0.0000, 0.0000	**DDRMODES,** SNAP	The X,Y base point of SNAP/GRID rotation in the current viewport, for the current UCS

Variable Name	Default Setting	Command Name	Variable Description
SNAPISOPAIR	0	**DDRMODES,** SNAP [^E]	The current isoplane for the current viewport: 0 = Left 1 = Top 2 = Right
SNAPMODE	0	**DDRMODES,** SNAP [^B] [F9]	Indicates the state of Snap for the current viewport: 1 = On 0 = Off
SNAPSTYL	0	**DDRMODES,** SNAP	The snap style for the current viewport: 1 = Isometric 0 = Standard
SNAPUNIT	1.0000, 1.0000	**DDRMODES,** SNAP	The snap X,Y increment for the current viewport
SOLAMEVER	**2.1**		**The Region Modeler software's version number**
SOLAREAU	**sq cm**		**The unit system for area calculations**
SOLAXCOL	**3**		**The color number of the SOLMOVE MCS icon**
SOLDELENT	**3**	**SOLIDIFY**	**Controls prompting for original entity deletion by SOLIDIFY command.** **1 = Don't delete** **2 = Ask** **3 = Delete**
SOLDISPLAY	**WIRE**	**SOLMESH, SOLWIRE**	**Controls the default display mode for new solids**
SOLHANGLE	**45.000000**	**SOLIDIFY**	**The default angle of new solid entity hatch patterns**

continues

Table A.1 Continued

AutoCAD System Variables

Variable Name	Default Setting	Command Name	Variable Description
SOLHPAT	U	SOLIDIFY	The default pattern name for new solid entity hatching
SOLHSIZE	1.000000	SOLIDIFY	The default scale for new solid entity hatch patterns
SOLLENGTH	cm	SOLLIST, SOLMASSP	The unit system for perimeter calculations
SOLMATCURR	MILD_ STEEL	SOLMAT	The default material assigned to new solid entities
SOLPAGELEN	25	SOLLIST, SOLMASSP, SOLMAT	The length of message pages, in lines
SOLRENDER	CSG	SHADE, SOLMESH, SOLWIRE	The display type for solids CSG = By primitive UNIFORM = As composite
SOLSERVMSG	3	MANY	The level of details displayed by Region Modeler messages 0 = None 1 = Errors 2 = Errors+progress 3 = All
SOLSOLIDIFY	3	MANY	Controls prompting for entity conversion to solid regions 1 = Don't convert 2 = Ask 3 = Convert

Variable Name	Default Setting	Command Name	Variable Description
SOLWDENS	4	**MANY**	Controls the number of edges used to represent curved solid surfaces displayed as wireframes (SOLWDENS*4)
SORTENTS	0	**DDSELECT**	The optimization codes for oct-tree spatial data-base organization; the value is the sum of the following: 0 = OFF 1 = Object selection 2 = OSNAP 4 = REDRAW 8 = MSLIDE 16 = REGEN 32 = PLOT 64 = PSOUT (CFG)
SPLFRAME	0		Controls the display of control polygons for spline-fit polylines, defining meshes of surface-fit polygon meshes, invisible 3D face edges: 1 = On 0 = Off
SPLINESEGS	8		The number of line segments in each spline curve
SPLINETYPE	6		Controls the spline type generated by the PEDIT command's Spline option: 5 = Quadratic B-Spline 6 = Cubic B-Spline

continues

541

Table A.1 Continued

AutoCAD System Variables

Variable Name	Default Setting	Command Name	Variable Description
SURFTAB1	6		The number of RULESURF and TABSURF tabulations, also the REVSURF and EDGESURF M-direction density
SURFTAB2	6		The REVSURF and EDGESURF N-direction density
SURFTYPE	6		Controls the type of surface generated by PEDIT smooth option: Quadratic B-Spline=5 Cubic B-Spline=6 Bézier=8
SURFU	6		The M-direction surface density of 3D polygon meshes
SURFV	6		The N-direction surface density 3D polygon meshes
SYSCODEPAGE	**ascii**		**The code page used by the system**
TABMODE	**0**	**TABLET, [F10]**	**Controls tablet mode: 1 = On 0 = Off**
TARGET	0.0000, 0.0000, 0.0000	DVIEW	The UCS coordinates of the current viewport's target point (RO)
TDCREATE	2447498. 61620031	TIME	The date and time of the current drawing's creation, in Julian format (RO)

Variable Name	Default Setting	Command Name	Variable Description
TDINDWG	0.00436285	TIME	The total amount of editing time elapsed in the current drawing, in Julian days (RO)
TDUPDATE	2447498. 61620031	TIME	The date and time when the file was last saved, in Julian format (RO)
TDUSRTIMER	0.00436667	TIME	User-controlled elapsed time in Julian days (RO)
TEMPPREFIX	""		The directory configured for placement of AutoCAD's temporary files; defaults to the drawing directory (NS),(RO)
TEXTEVAL	0		Controls the checking of text input (except by DTEXT) for AutoLISP expressions: 0 = Yes 1 = No (NS)
TEXTSIZE	0.2000	TEXT	The height applied to new text entities created with nonfixed-height text styles
TEXTSTYLE	STANDARD	TEXT, STYLE	The current text style's name (RO)
THICKNESS	0.0000		The current 3D extrusion thickness
TILEMODE	1	TILEMODE	Release 10 VPORT compatibility setting; enables/disables paper space and viewport entities: 1 = On 0 = Off

continues

Table A.1 Continued

AutoCAD System Variables

Variable Name	Default Setting	Command Name	Variable Description
TRACEWID	0.0500	TRACE	The current width of traces
TREEDEPTH	**3020**	**DDSELECT**	**The maximum number of node subdivisions for oct-tree spatial database organization in model space and paper space for the current drawing**
TREEMAX	**?**	**TREEMAX**	**The maximum number of entities nodes for oct-tree spatial database organization for the current AutoCAD configuration (CFG)**
UCSFOLLOW	0		Controls automatic display of the plan view in the current viewport when switching to a new UCS: 1 = On 0 = Off
UCSICON	1	UCSICON	Controls the UCS icon's display; the value is the sum of the following: 0 = Off 1 = On 2 = At origin
UCSNAME	""	**DDUCS**, UCS	The name of the current UCS for the current space: "" = Unnamed (RO)
UCSORG	0.0000, 0.0000, 0.0000	**DDUCS**, UCS	The WCS origin of the current UCS for the current space (RO)

Variable Name	Default Setting	Command Name	Variable Description
UCSXDIR	1.0000, 0.0000, 0.0000	**DDUCS**, UCS	The X direction of the current UCS (RO)
UCSYDIR	0.0000, 1.0000, 0.0000	**DDUCS**, UCS	The Y direction of the current UCS (RO)
UNDOCTL	**5**	**UNDO**	**The current state of UNDO; the value is the sum of the following:** **1 = Enabled** **2 = Single command** **4 = Auto mode** **8 = Group active** **(RO),(NS)**
UNDOMARKS	**0**	**UNDO**	**The current number of marks in the UNDO command's history (RO), (NS)**
UNITMODE	0		Controls the display of user input of fractions, feet and inches, and surveyor's angles: 0 = Per LUNITS 1 = As input
USERI1 - 5	0		User integer variables USERI1 to USERI5
USERR1 - 5	0.0000		User real-number variables USERR1 to USERR5
VIEWCTR	6.2518, 4.5000	ZOOM, PAN, VIEW	The X,Y center point coordinate of the current view in the current viewport (RO)
VIEWDIR	0.0000, 0.0000, 1.0000	DVIEW	The camera point offset from target in the WCS (RO)

continues

Table A.1 Continued

AutoCAD System Variables

Variable Name	Default Setting	Command Name	Variable Description
VIEWMODE	0	DVIEW, UCS	The current viewport's viewing mode; the value is the sum of the following: 1 = Perspective 2 = Front clipping on 4 = Back clipping on 8 = UCSFOLLOW On 16 = FRONTZ offset in use (RO)
VIEWSIZE	9.0000	ZOOM, VIEW	The current view's height, in drawing units (RO)
VIEWTWIST	0	DVIEW	The current viewport's view-twist angle (RO)
VISRETAIN			Controls retention of XREF file layer settings in the current drawing.
VSMAX	12.5036, 9.0000, 0.0000	ZOOM,PAN,VIEW	The upper right X,Y coordinate of the current viewport's virtual screen for the current UCS (NS),(RO)
VSMIN	0.0000, 0.0000, 0.0000	ZOOM,PAN,VIEW	The lower left X,Y coordinate of the current viewport's virtual screen for the current UCS (NS),(RO)
WORLDUCS	1	UCS	The current UCS, equivalent to WCS: 1 = True 0 = False (RO)

Variable Name	Default Setting	Command Name	Variable Description
WORLDVIEW	1	DVIEW,UCS	Controls the automatic changing of a UCS to the WCS during the DVIEW and VPOINT commands: 1 = On 0 = Off
XREFCTL	**0**		**Controls the creation of an XLG log file that contains XREF results:** **0 = No file** **1 = XLG file** **(CFG)**

Installation, Configuration, and Troubleshooting

This appendix provides answers to some of the most common problems encountered in installing and configuring AutoCAD and gives you a better understanding of the AutoCAD manuals. Because AutoCAD has become more and more complex with each release, this appendix cannot cover all the different operating environments, hardware configurations, and other variables. For complete information on the settings that you can make to fine-tune your particular system, see the *AutoCAD Interface, Installation and Performance Guide* or the *AutoCAD Reference Manual*. If you are running AutoCAD on a DOS-based system, you may find your answer in a DOS guide, such as *Microsoft MS-DOS User's Guide and Reference* or *Maximizing DOS 5* from New Riders Publishing.

For AutoCAD to run properly, you must set up your system environment properly. On UNIX-based systems, the system administrator is typically responsible for setting up and maintaining the operating environment, as well as setting up applications such as AutoCAD. On DOS systems, however, that responsibility often falls on the user. The first section of this appendix, therefore, examines the DOS bootup environment.

Setup for the DOS Environment

When a DOS system starts up, the computer system performs a self-test and checks the system's memory. It then looks for two system files. On MS-DOS systems, these files are called IO.SYS and MSDOS.SYS. These files are *hidden* and do not show up in a directory listing. IO.SYS controls interaction between the upper levels of the operating system and the hardware. MSDOS.SYS is the MS-DOS kernel—that is, it controls file input/output, memory allocation, and general operating system services. Then the command shell, COMMAND.COM, is loaded. The shell provides the internal portion of DOS—that is, those commands and functions that are loaded into (and remain in) the system's memory rather than existing as executable files on disk and is the interface to the kernel.

The operating system looks for two additional files—CONFIG.SYS and AUTOEXEC.BAT. CONFIG.SYS and AUTOEXEC.BAT enable you to customize your system's setup. These files generally are created by the person who sets up the system, and they often are created or modified by applications software during the application's installation. Because AutoCAD depends on the operating system environment, you should understand these two DOS files.

CONFIG.SYS primarily contains statements that define the system's hardware configuration. It often includes commands to load device drivers (programs that control a device such as a mouse), set the number of files that can be open concurrently, and allocate the number of disk buffers (temporary storage areas). Your system may or may not have a CONFIG.SYS file. Some systems require device drivers to configure their memory, hard disks, or other storage devices. Settings like buffers and files may not be necessary for DOS to boot successfully, but AutoCAD relies on them. DOS 5.0 creates a CONFIG.SYS file when it is installed.

Once the CONFIG.SYS file has been executed, DOS searches for a file called AUTOEXEC.BAT. While CONFIG.SYS primarily controls the hardware configuration of the system, AUTOEXEC.BAT controls the software environment. Statements commonly found in AUTOEXEC.BAT load device drivers with COM and EXE file extensions, set environment variables, and execute start-up commands. AUTOEXEC.BAT need not exist for the system to boot, but as with CONFIG.SYS, most systems will have an AUTOEXEC.BAT file.

Understanding CONFIG.SYS

CONFIG.SYS is a file that DOS executes automatically each time the operating system is booted. CONFIG.SYS must reside in the root directory of the boot drive, which in most DOS systems is drive C. The following is a typical minimum CONFIG.SYS file if you run an AutoCAD system:

```
FILES=40
SHELL=C:\DOS\COMMAND.COM /P /E:256
```

The FILES line defines the maximum number of files that may be open at one time. If the FILES setting is too low, AutoCAD may generate an error message when it attempts to open additional files. An increased value of FILES requires a relatively small amount of memory, so set FILES to a minimum of 40.

The SHELL line in the CONFIG.SYS file enables you to change the way COMMAND.COM functions. DOS requires a certain amount of RAM to store environment variable settings and other global information. AutoCAD also uses environment variables (a typical AutoCAD installation requires at least 256 bytes of environment space). The SHELL line in CONFIG.SYS changes the amount of memory allocated to the DOS environment. The previous example specifies an environment space of 256 bytes for DOS 3.3 or later. 256 is a good starting size. This number specifies the actual size setting. For 512 bytes, use 512. The maximum is 32768 bytes. Modify or add a SHELL line to your CONFIG.SYS file if you get an Out of environment space error. This error message may be difficult to see because often it scrolls off the screen quickly when the AUTOEXEC.BAT or the AutoCAD startup batch file (described later in this appendix) executes. Remember to substitute your boot drive for "C:" if your boot drive is not C. You must include the /P switch on the SHELL line to make COMMAND.COM reside in memory permanently, or the system will be unresponsive after booting.

Your CONFIG.SYS file will probably include other lines, particularly device drivers. For example, to configure memory and initialize a mouse, CONFIG.SYS might include the following lines:

```
DEVICE=C:\BOOT\EMM.SYS
DEVICE=C:\MOUSE\MOUSE.SYS
```

Understanding AUTOEXEC.BAT

AUTOEXEC.BAT is a standard batch file that resides in the root directory of the boot drive (typically drive C). DOS automatically looks for a file called AUTOEXEC.BAT when it boots. If DOS finds this file, it executes the statements contained in the file.

Usually, AUTOEXEC.BAT installs the TSR (terminate-and-stay-resident) device drivers, such as mouse and digitizer drivers, ADI drivers with COM and EXE extensions, and utility programs, such as DOSKEY. AUTOEXEC.BAT also sets the system prompt, sets global environment variables, and performs other standard start-up functions.

The following is a recommended minimum AUTOEXEC.BAT file:

```
PROMPT=$P$G
PATH C:\;C:\DOS
```

The preceding prompt statement causes DOS to always display the current directory in its prompt.

The PATH line should contain, at a minimum, your root directory and DOS directory. Your path probably includes other directories. You do not need to include the directory containing AutoCAD on your path if you execute AutoCAD explicitly from its directory.

In addition to a path and prompt statement, your AUTOEXEC.BAT file may include commands to load ADI drivers and other device drivers and to set environment variables.

Creating and Editing Environment Files

CONFIG.SYS and AUTOEXEC.BAT can be created or edited with any text editor that can read and write ASCII files. Before changing your CONFIG.SYS or AUTOEXEC.BAT files, make sure you have a backup of your current CONFIG.SYS file, as well as a bootable DOS floppy disk. If you make an error, you may need to reboot from a floppy disk and copy the backup files onto your hard disk.

ASCII Text Files

Many of the files used by the operating system and applications are stored in a simple text format called *ASCII* (American Standard Code for Information Interchange). ASCII files can be read by almost all word processors and text editors. Several DOS commands are designed specifically to work with ASCII files. Many applications (including AutoCAD) use ASCII files for data that can be modified by the user, but they have their own special formats for their other data files.

You can examine the contents of ASCII text files, such as your AUTOEXEC.BAT file, with the DOS TYPE command. TYPE displays other types of data files, but the contents may not be recognizable. Because other data files usually contain special characters that may cause your system to make strange noises, flash the screen, or even crash (forcing you to reboot), you should use TYPE only on files that you know are in ASCII format. The general format for using the TYPE command is as follows:

```
TYPE filename.ext
```

In the preceding syntax *filename.ext* is the name of the file (including the extension) that you want to display. The file name can include the path information. The command TYPE \AUTOEXEC.BAT displays the contents of the AUTOEXEC.BAT file located in the root directory of the current drive. If the file contains more information than fits on a single screen, you can use the command MORE < *filename.ext* to make the display pause after each full screen of information. The TYPE command does not accept wild cards.

If you do not have a text editor or word processor, you can create ASCII files with the DOS COPY command, using the following format:

```
COPY CON: filename.ext
```

The `filename.ext` parameter is the name of the file to be created. The CON: portion of the command stands for console and instructs the COPY command to take the information from the keyboard (the console) and copy it into the file specified. When you type this command and press Enter, the new file is created, and any further text you type is stored in it. Enter a Ctrl-Z character (hold down the Control key and press Z, then release); then press Enter to stop entering text and mark the end of the file. For example, the following would create the AUTOEXEC.BAT file shown earlier:

```
C:\>COPY CON: AUTOEXEC.BAT
PROMPT=$P$G
PATH C:\;C:\DOS
<^Z>
        1 File(s) copied
C:\>
```

This works for extremely simple files that do not need modification after their creation. Unfortunately, it has a number of limitations. Once you press Enter at the end of a line, you cannot change the line. You cannot edit an existing file. This makes it difficult to create long files. However, the advantages of this method are that it is always available to you in DOS, it is quick, and you can include special characters that may be difficult to enter in a word processor.

For editing files (rather than simply creating them), DOS includes the EDLIN (editor line) command. EDLIN has all the commands necessary for modifying an existing file, but it is primitive and tedious to use compared to most text editors and word processors. See your DOS manual or a book about DOS for information on its use.

DOS 5.0 includes a new full-screen, menu-based editor named EDIT for working with ASCII files.

Using the DOS 5.0 EDIT Command

EDIT has a complete help system, can be used with either a mouse or the keyboard, and offers a variety of keyboard shortcuts and useful features. The DOS command EDIT activates the program. You can include the name of the file to be edited at the DOS prompt, such as EDIT CONFIG.SYS, or you can use a menu to open any file. EDIT is more powerful and easier to use than EDLIN, and it offers many of the advantages of a word processor for editing text files.

If you are using an earlier version of DOS, use a commercial text editor or word processor to display, print, and edit ASCII files. Many people prefer using a word processor they are familiar with rather than using DOS commands to edit files.

Selecting Text Editors

To create or modify your CONFIG.SYS and AUTOEXEC.BAT files, you need a text editor capable of editing and saving ASCII files. You can create ASCII files with Norton's Editor, SideKick, PC Write, WordStar in non-document mode, the WordPerfect Library Program Editor, WordPerfect's DOS text file option, Microsoft Word in text-only format, and most other word processors.

The default format of most word processors is not ASCII, so be sure to create and save files in an ASCII format. Also be sure to specify the extension, such as SYS and BAT, because most word processors default to their own document file extension. If you have doubts about producing ASCII files, test your editor or word processor with the following steps.

Text Editor Test

Load your text editor or word processor. Get into its edit mode, and make a new file named TEXT.TXT. Write a paragraph of text, and copy it to get a few screens full. Save the file, and exit to DOS. Then test it by using the following exercises.

```
C:\>CD \directory ↵
```

Use the name of your text editor's directory or the name of the directory that contains TEXT.TXT for the lowercase directory in the previous line.

```
C:\IA-ACAD>TYPE TEXT.TXT ↵
```
Displays all the text you entered if your editor produced a standard ASCII file

```
C:\IA-ACAD>DEL TEXT.TXT ↵
```
Deletes the file

Your text editor is working fine if your text is identical to what you typed in your editor, and no extra characters or control codes, which might look like åÇäÆ^L, appear. If any "garbage" appears on-screen, particularly at the top or bottom of the file, then your text editor either is not suitable, or it is not configured correctly for use as an ASCII editor.

After you determine that your text editor can create and edit ASCII files, you are ready to customize your system's configuration files.

Recommended Hardware Configurations

The purpose for which you use AutoCAD will determine the type of hardware best suited to your application. Whether yours is an educational or production environment, an 80386-based system, or better, is required to run the DOS version of AutoCAD Release 12. If you are not using AutoCAD in a production environment, consider a 386SX system. If your drawings are not very large or complex, a 386SX will provide performance comparable to a full 30386DX system.

The following minimum configuration is recommended for the DOS version of AutoCAD:

- An 80386-based system (or better) for production use, or an 80386SX-based system for educational use.

- 640K conventional memory plus at least 8M or more

extended memory. AutoCAD 386 makes the best use of extended memory. AutoCAD also uses expanded memory in addition to the extended memory required, but extended memory is faster.

- A hard disk with at least 23M of free disk space before AutoCAD is installed. This includes space for AutoCAD's program files, along with your drawing files.

- One or more floppy disk drives with 1.2M or 1.44M capacity.

- PC or MS-DOS Version 3.3 or later (5.0 is recommended), with program files loaded in a hard disk directory called C:\DOS.

- AutoCAD program files loaded in a hard disk directory called C:\ACAD.

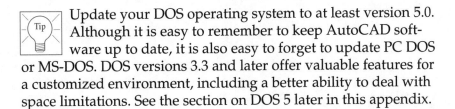 Update your DOS operating system to at least version 5.0. Although it is easy to remember to keep AutoCAD software up to date, it is also easy to forget to update PC DOS or MS-DOS. DOS versions 3.3 and later offer valuable features for a customized environment, including a better ability to deal with space limitations. See the section on DOS 5 later in this appendix.

AutoCAD Installation

AutoCAD Release 12 for DOS comes with a menu-driven installation program that automatically creates necessary directories, copies files, and personalizes AutoCAD for you. It also enables you to install only those groups of files that you want, which saves disk space if you do not want AME, ASE, ADS, IGES, AutoCAD Render, source, bonus, or sample files.

IMPORTANT! Before beginning any software installation, always make a backup copy of your software program disks (often called distribution disks). Install the software from the backup set of disks, not the originals. You also should keep a backup copy of your DOS distribution disks.

Backing Up Your Original Floppy Disks

Before making backup copies of your distribution disks, cover the notch (if any) in the upper right corner of 5 1/4-inch disks with a write-protect tab or piece of tape. For 3 1/2-inch disks, slide open the write-protect button on the back of the upper right corner. These measures will prevent accidental erasure or damage. You will need the same number and type of backup disks as your distribution set.

Using DISKCOPY To Back Up Your Disks

If you have only one floppy drive of the correct type, insert the first original (source) disk in it and type:

```
C:>CD \DOS ↵                        Changes to the \DOS directory
C:\DOS>DISKCOPY A: A: ↵
```

Use B in lieu of A, if you are using drive B. Then change disks when prompted.

If you have two disk drives that are the same size and density (both 5 1/4-inch or both 3 1/2-inch), place the first distribution disk in drive A and a backup (target) disk in drive B, and type:

```
C:>CD \DOS ↵
C:\DOS>DISKCOPY A: B: ↵             Copies everything on A: to B:
```

Repeat the process for each source disk.

The source disk is the disk you are copying (your original distribution disk), and the target disk is your duplicate (backup) disk. Your target disk does not have to be formatted. The DISKCOPY command formats it for you.

Preparing Your Hard Drive

A minimal configuration for AutoCAD Release 12 requires at least 11M of free space on your disk for executable and support files and 4M for working space. If you install the sample drawings, you will need an additional 2.6M. A complete installation, including ADS (which only developers need) and the Advanced Modeling Extension (AME) (an extra-cost option), AutoCAD SQL Extension (ASE), AutoCAD Render, and the AutoCAD tutorial requires a minimum of 23M. If you do not have enough space to install the files you have selected, the INSTALL program will warn you.

The installation program creates the necessary directories, so you do not need to create them beforehand. The INSTALL program prompts you to enter information about your installation that includes your name, company name, dealer name, and dealer's telephone number. You must enter each item, or INSTALL will not continue. This information will be written to your disk and become a permanent part of your AutoCAD executable file.

The INSTALL program is fully menu-driven, so you should have no difficulty installing AutoCAD. During the installation process, INSTALL will ask if you want it to create a start-up batch file called ACAD386.BAT. If this file is on your path (it is created in your root directory, so it should be), you will be able to enter ACAD386 at the DOS prompt to start AutoCAD from any current directory.

Installing AutoCAD Release 12

Insert Disk #1 in drive A.

`C:\>A:` ↵

`A:\>INSTALL` ↵

Follow the instructions and prompts.

If your source disk drive is other than drive A, substitute its drive letter for A. If your hard disk is not drive C, substitute its drive letter for C.

To finish the installation, run AutoCAD and configure your system. If any of your hardware requires an ADI driver, install it according to the manufacturer's instructions before configuring AutoCAD.

AutoCAD Configuration

If you have just installed AutoCAD, or if you need to reconfigure AutoCAD for a different hardware device, the AutoCAD configuration menu will prompt you to identify selected parameters for the appropriate video display, digitizer, plotter, and printer/plotter that make up your workstation configuration.

You must run AutoCAD to configure it. If you have not configured AutoCAD, it will skip to configuration automatically when you start the program. During a first-time configuration sequence, AutoCAD will automatically take you through the steps required to select your display, input device, plotter, and printer.

Using the Configuration Menu

If AutoCAD has already been configured once, you can examine your configuration setup by entering the CONFIG command from the AutoCAD command prompt. AutoCAD will display your current configuration and prompt you with the configuration menu.

Examining Your AutoCAD Configuration

Start AutoCAD. If you are using a start-up batch file, such as ACAD386.BAT or ACAD.BAT, type ACAD386 or ACAD and press Enter. If your AutoCAD directory is part of your path and AutoCAD's environment variables have been set, type ACAD and press Enter. Otherwise, change to your AutoCAD directory, type ACAD, and press Enter.

If AutoCAD has not been configured, it will prompt you through the choices, then display the current configuration.

To reconfigure AutoCAD, enter CONFIG at the command prompt.

```
Current AutoCAD configuration
   Video display:      Your current display
     Version: Your current display driver version
   Digitizer:          Your current input device
     Version: Your current input device driver version
```

```
   Plotter: Your current output device
      Port: Your current output device connection
      Version: Your current output device driver version
Press RETURN to continue: Press Return

Configuration menu
   0.  Exit to drawing editor
   1.  Show current configuration
   2.  Allow detailed configuration
   3.  Configure video display
   4.  Configure digitizer
   5.  Configure plotter
   6.  Configure system console
   7.  Configure operating parameters
Enter selection <0>:
```

During configuration, AutoCAD creates a configuration file called
ACAD.CFG in the current directory. This configuration file contains the settings of the CONFIG command and certain AutoCAD
system variables.

Reconfiguring Your System

Reconfiguring AutoCAD is simple and straightforward. AutoCAD
asks you several questions about your hardware setup, and
you respond with either answers or a number selection from
a list of choices that AutoCAD provides. Configuration is depen-
dent on your hardware.

To configure or change a device driver, simply select the item you
want to change from the configuration menu. AutoCAD then
prompts you for values to supply for each device.

Using ADI Drivers

ADI (Autodesk Device Interface) drivers are device driver programs for plotters, printers, digitizers, and video cards. The two
types of ADI drivers are real-mode ADI drivers and protected-
mode ADI drivers. Real-mode ADI drivers are memory-resident
(TSR, or terminate-and-stay-resident) programs that operate in

conventional memory. If you are using a real-mode ADI driver, you must install it in memory prior to starting AutoCAD. Install this type of driver by entering its name at the DOS prompt, just like any other program. You can install an ADI driver in your CONFIG.SYS file, AUTOEXEC.BAT file, or your AutoCAD start-up batch file. Examples of both files are shown in this appendix. You can configure AutoCAD for real-mode ADI drivers by choosing the proper ADI version from the configuration menu.

If you are using a protected-mode ADI driver, AutoCAD loads the driver automatically into extended memory. You do not need to load it prior to starting AutoCAD. AutoCAD automatically loads the names of protected-mode drivers into the configuration menu. To configure AutoCAD for a protected-mode driver, choose the correct driver from the configuration menu.

> **Note** For AutoCAD to load automatically the names of protected-mode ADI drivers into the configuration menu, the driver must be named with a magic prefix. The magic prefix identifies the type of protected-mode driver. AutoCAD searches for and then loads the driver names into an appropriate configuration menu based on the magic prefix.

See the *AutoCAD Interface, Installation and Performance Guide* for more information on protected-mode drivers and magic prefixes.

Start-Up Batch Files

You can preset several of AutoCAD's start-up settings that control its memory usage and support file search order. The installation program gave you the option of creating a start-up batch file called ACAD386.BAT. The following is a typical ACAD386.BAT file for Release 12:

```
SET  ACAD=C:\ACAD\SUPPORT;C:\ACAD\FONTS;C:\ACAD\ADS
SET  ACADCFG=C:\ACAD
SET  ACADDRV=C:\ACAD\DRV
C:\ACAD\ACAD  %1  %2
SET  ACAD=
SET  ACADCFG=
SET  ACADDRV=
```

The preceding start-up batch file sets AutoCAD file search paths, executes AutoCAD, then clears the environment variables when AutoCAD is exited.

A more sophisticated start-up batch file also can optimize AutoCAD's use of memory, specify other AutoCAD operating parameters, and control the current drawing directory.

Optimizing Memory and Controlling Directories

The following example shows a more sophisticated start-up batch file. You can create a file like this for each of your jobs or applications, each with a unique name. An explanation of the various types of memory follows this section.

The STARTUP.BAT file assumes that your AutoCAD program directory path is C:\ACAD. If it is not, substitute your own path.

Creating the STARTUP.BAT File

In the following example start-up batch file, the lines in italics represent the lines that should consist of settings or statements appropriate for your particular system. An explanation of each section follows the batch file listing. (Do not put any blank lines in your batch file, or it will not work.)

```
SET ACAD=C:\ACAD\SUPPORT;C:\ACAD\FONTS;C:\ACAD\ADS
SET ACADCFG=C:\ACAD
SET ACADDRV=C:\ACAD\DRV
```
Your version and hardware-dependent memory settings and other operating parameters go here.
```
C:
CD \PROJECT
\ACAD\ACAD %1 %2
CD\
SET ACAD=
SET ACADCFG=
SET ACADCFG=
```
Memory release statements go here.

SET ACAD=. Defines the directory that AutoCAD searches if it does not find a needed support file in the current directory. The support files include shape files, slide files, and other support files.

SET ACADCFG=. Defines the directory AutoCAD searches for configuration files. Create several configuration directories and corresponding start-up batch files if you must support more than one environment or more than one device, such as different graphics adapters.

SET ACADDRV=. Specifies the directory or directories AutoCAD searches for protected-mode ADI driver files. This variable must be set to a directory containing the protected-mode drivers if you want to use the dirvers. If your third-party drivers are installed in seperate directories, you can add the directory name to this variable. This makes updating AutoCAD or your drivers easier and helps to keep files organized.

Version and Hardware-Dependent Memory Settings:. The start-up file also can control the amount of memory AutoCAD uses (SET ACADMAXMEM=). Memory that is in use before you load AutoCAD is *not* available for AutoCAD's use.

> **Note** No memory settings are necessary for AutoCAD unless you want to limit the amount of memory AutoCAD uses so that other programs executed from within AutoCAD can use the free memory.

C:. ensures that you are on the right drive. Substitute another letter if AutoCAD is not on drive C.

CD \PROJECT:. This line instructs your system to change to the working directory (named PROJECT), but yours can change to any working directory. You can create multiple start-up batch files, each with its own CD command, for each project directory you use.

\ACAD\ACAD %1 %2. This line executes ACAD.EXE. If ACAD.EXE is on your path, you can use ACAD alone here; however, specifying the directory avoids having DOS search the path. The %1 and %2 are replaceable parameters for which you can enter a drawing name (%1) and script name (%2) when you run the STARTUP.BAT batch file. For example, to run a script with the name MYSCRIPT on a drawing MYDWG, enter **STARTUP MYDWG MYSCRIPT**, and the batch file executes this line as \ACAD\ACAD MYDWG MYSCRIPT. AutoCAD then executes MYSCRIPT at the main menu with MYDWG as the default drawing.

CD\. This line returns you to the root directory.

SET ACADDRV=, **SET ACADCFG=**, and **SET ACAD:.** Clear these settings, to avoid conflict with any other AutoCAD configurations that you might use and to free up environment space.

Memory Release Statements. Finally, if you made any other memory or environment settings, insert lines here to clear them as well.

Use **SET variable=** to clear any settings that you make in a start-up batch file, such as STARTUP.BAT. If you do not clear your settings, your other AutoCAD-related applications will find the settings and be directed to the wrong configuration and support files.

Consult the *AutoCAD Interface, Installation, and Performance Guide* for more information on memory settings for running AutoCAD. If you are unfamiliar with the various types of memory, the following descriptions should help.

Understanding Types of Memory

RAM memory is commonly expressed in bytes and bits. A bit is the smallest unit of storage, representing either a 0 or a 1. A byte is eight bits, and it represents a single alphanumeric character. You do not need to overly concern yourself with this or with data storage, but you need to know how much memory you have because AutoCAD needs a large amount. A given memory location is accessed by its *address*, commonly expressed in bytes (usually in K, or 1024-byte increments). For example, the lowest memory address is at 0K, and on a system with 1 megabyte of RAM, the maximum address is 1024K (which equals 1M).

The five types of memory are as follows (see fig. B.1):

- **Conventional memory.** This is the range of memory addresses from 0K to 1024K. Because the upper 384K of conventional memory is reserved (as explained in the next paragraph), the first 640K of memory addresses is often considered (incorrectly) to be where conventional memory ends. Conventional memory is most crucial for standard DOS applications, and one of the benefits of DOS version 5 is that it can make more memory between 0K and 640K available to applications.

- **Reserved I/O Address Space**, or **Upper Memory Area (UMA).** This area is the 384K of memory between 640K and 1024K. It is primarily reserved for video adapters and other peripheral device-address mapping (the device is assigned an address within that range). In addition, a range of memory is sometimes allocated from the UMA as an expanded-memory page frame, which is a range of memory that an expanded-memory manager uses to make expanded memory available to the system. Standard applications do not normally access this reserved memory area.

- **High Memory Area (HMA).** The HMA is either the 64K address range between 1024K and 1088K, or the 64K of memory addresses between the end of conventional memory at 1024K and the beginning of extended memory at 1088K. Only one program at a time may use the HMA. In DOS 5, a portion of the operating system may be loaded into this region.

- **Extended memory.** Sometimes referred to as XMS, this is the memory above the 1088K mark, which can be as much as 15 megabytes on 80286 systems and as much as 4 gigabytes on 80386 and 80486 systems. (A gigabyte is equal to 1024 megabytes.) This memory is addressed directly by applications that are specifically written to address it. A program called an *extended-memory manager* is used to manage extended memory access by applications.

- **Expanded memory.** Also referred to as EMS, expanded memory is memory configured for the Lotus/Intel/Microsoft

(LIM) expanded-memory specification (EMS). Physical expanded memory comes in the form of a card installed in the computer. All of the processor types can access expanded memory. A special driver must be used to permit applications to address this memory. On 80386 and 80486 systems, a device driver can be used to emulate expanded memory using extended memory.

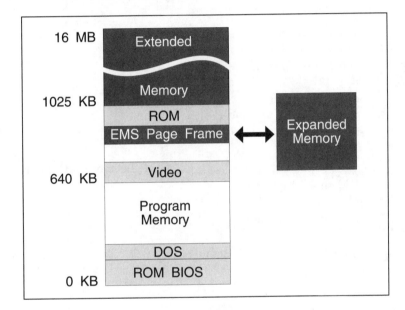

Figure B.1:
DOS memory map.

Using AutoCAD with Microsoft Windows

AutoCAD can run as a full-screen DOS application under Microsoft Windows 3.1. This arrangement enables you to switch between AutoCAD and Microsoft Windows applications. There are two steps to setting up Windows to work with AutoCAD. The first step is to add a line to the [386Enh] section of your Windows SYSTEM.INI file with a text editor. The second step is to create a PIF (Program Information File) for AutoCAD. The following exercise details these steps.

Setting Up Windows for AutoCAD

Start your word processor and open your Windows SYSTEM.INI file. The file is usually located in C:\WINDOWS. Then find the [386Enh] section and add the following line below the [386Enh] label:

```
device=c:\acad\pharlap.386
```

Start Windows and run the PIF Editor. The PIF Editor is usually located in the Main program group.

In the Program Filename:
text box, enter COMMAND.COM

In the Window Title: *text box,*
enter AutoCAD 12

In the Optional Parameters:
text box, enter /E:256 /C STARTUP.BAT

In the Start-up Directory: *text box,*
enter C:\PROJECT

Click on High Graphics   Highlights the radio button

In the EMS Memory: KB Limit
text box, enter 0

In the XMS Memory: KB Limit
text box, enter at least 2048

Leave all other settings at their default values.

Choose File, *then* Save

In the File Name: *text box,*
enter ACAD12.PIF

Choose File, *then* Exit

Select a program group to add the AutoCAD program item.

Choose File, *then* New
and click on OK

In the Command Line: *text box,*
enter ACAD12.PIF

Now Windows is set up to run AutoCAD. To start AutoCAD, double-click on the AutoCAD 12 icon.

Compatible Third-Party Memory Managers

Microsoft Windows uses a memory manager that is compatible with AutoCAD. HIMEM.SYS is the memory manager commonly used with Windows and DOS 5.

Quarterdeck Office Systems' QEMM memory manager, version 5.1 or greater, is compatible with AutoCAD and Windows. It also may give you more available conventional memory than HIMEM does.

In addition to QEMM, other third-party memory managers are compatible with both Windows and AutoCAD. Check the documentation for the memory manager, or consult the manufacturer to make sure the memory manager you are considering is compatible.

Problems and Solutions

This section offers some suggestions for dealing with common problems encountered in setting up and running AutoCAD.

Solving Problems with AutoCAD and DOS

- When errors occur, use the UNDO command to clean up the drawing and restore system variables. Then try again.

- Go back to the previous exercises to see if you made an error that did not show up immediately.

- Check defaults, such as snap, osnaps, aperture, current layer, and layer visibility.

- Check the *AutoCAD Reference Manual*.

- Call your AutoCAD dealer. If you have no current dealer, Autodesk can recommend one.

- Try the ACAD forum on CompuServe, the world's largest AutoCAD user group and most knowledgeable source of support.

- If you find a specific problem in this book, particularly a problem with an exercise, you can call New Riders Publishing at (503) 661-5745. Be ready to give us the page number where you are having the problem. We cannot give general AutoCAD support—your AutoCAD dealer can answer general AutoCAD questions.

Problems with CONFIG.SYS

If your CONFIG.SYS settings do not run smoothly, your only indication may be that some things do not work. If you get the error message:

```
Bad or missing FILENAME
```

DOS cannot find the file as it is specified. Check your spelling, syntax, and provide a full path.

```
Unrecognized command in CONFIG.SYS
```

The preceding message means that you made a syntax error, or that your version of DOS does not support the configuration command. Check your spelling.

Watch closely when you boot your system. These error messages flash by very quickly. If you suspect an error, temporarily rename your AUTOEXEC.BAT file so that the system stops after loading CONFIG.SYS. You can also try to send the screen messages to the printer by pressing Ctrl-Prtscr as soon as DOS starts reading the CONFIG.SYS file. Press Ctrl-Prtscr again to turn off the printer echo.

Problems with ADI Drivers

If you have a problem with a device that uses an ADI driver, suspect the driver first. Consult the driver's documentation, then contact your dealer or the manufacturer for help.

Problems with AUTOEXEC.BAT

Errors in AUTOEXEC.BAT are harder to troubleshoot, for many reasons. Often, the system just does not behave as you think it should. Here are some troubleshooting tips:

- Isolate errors by temporarily editing your AUTOEXEC.BAT file. You can disable a line with a leading colon, for example:

```
: NOW DOS WILL IGNORE THIS LINE!
```

- Many AUTOEXEC.BAT files use the command ECHO OFF or @ECHO OFF to turn off echo to the screen. Disable echo off to see what these files are doing. Put a leading colon on the line.

- Echo to the printer. Press Ctrl-Prtscr while booting to see what is happening.

- Make sure the prompt, path, and other environment settings precede any TSR (memory-resident) programs in the file.

- Check your path for completeness and syntax. Directories do not need to be in the path unless you want to execute files in them from other directories, or the program requires it.

- APPEND (DOS 3.3 or later) works like PATH to let programs find their support and overlay files in other directories. It uses about 5K of RAM. All files in an appended directory are recognized by programs as if they were in the current directory. If you use APPEND, use it cautiously. If you modify a file in an appended directory, the modified file will be written to the current directory, not to the appended directory. Loading an AutoCAD MNU file from an appended directory creates an MNX file in the current directory. AutoCAD searches an appended directory before completing its normal directory-search pattern, so appended support files get loaded instead of those in the current directory.

- SET environment errors are often obscure. Type SET and press Enter to see your current environment settings. If a setting is truncated or missing, you are probably out of environment space. Fix it in your CONFIG.SYS file. Do not use extraneous spaces in a SET statement.

- If you are fighting for memory, insert temporary commands in the AUTOEXEC.BAT file to check your available memory. Once you determine what uses how much, you can decide what to sacrifice. Use the following commands at appropriate points to display the remaining memory:

```
CHKDSK
PAUSE
```

Reboot to see the effect. Remove the commands when you are done.

Run **CHKDSK /F** at the DOS prompt on a regular basis. It will verify your hard disk file structure and free up any "lost clusters" found. Lost clusters are sometimes created when programs crash. Answer N when it asks if you want to convert the clusters to files. Do not run CHKDSK /F from the SHELL command while in AutoCAD.

If you have unusual occurrences or lockups, and you use TSRs, suspect the TSRs as your problem source. Cause and effect may be hard to pin down. Disable TSRs one at a time in your AUTOEXEC file. Reboot and test.

Problems with DOS Environment Space

If you run out of space to store DOS environment settings, you see the following error message:

```
Out of environment space
```

You may see this message when executing a batch file. An environment-space problem also may show up in unusual ways, such as a program failing to execute, AutoLISP not having room to load, or a block insertion not finding its file on disk. This occurs because the path; AutoCAD settings limiting extended or ex-panded memory; and AutoCAD configuration, memory, and support file settings are all environment settings.

To find out how much environment space you need:

- Type **SET>TEMP.$** at the DOS prompt.

- List the TEMP.$ file with the DIR command. The file size is the number of characters. Delete the file.

- Add the number of characters for new SET statements.

Include revisions to your AUTOEXEC.BAT and start-up files, such as IL.BAT.

- Add a safety margin of 10 percent.

DOS defaults the environment size to 160 bytes. The space expands if you type in settings, but it cannot expand during execution of a BAT file, including your AUTOEXEC.BAT file. Loading a memory-resident (TSR) program or utility (such as SIDEKICK, PROKEY, some RAM disks and print buffers, or the DOS PRINT and GRAPHICS commands) freezes the environment space to the current size. Fortunately, DOS 3.0 or later versions can easily expand the space. See the earlier section on CONFIG.SYS in this appendix for details.

Problem Memory Settings

So many variations of operating system environment settings and version-specific switches that deal with AutoCAD's memory usage exist that they cannot all be covered here. The wrong settings can cause random crashes and conflicts with other software. These settings and switches are explained in the *AutoCAD Interface, Installation, and Performance Guide*.

Losing Screen or Digitizer Configuration

Sometimes your digitizer configuration or screen gets disturbed when you are drawing. This can happen when you use memory-resident programs or AutoCAD's SHELL command to access other programs from AutoCAD. Rather than ending your drawing and starting again, use the REINIT command. The REINIT command displays a dialog box that enables you to re-initialize the digitizer and plotter port, digitizer, display, and ACAD.PGP file. If your display becomes garbled and you cannot see the dialog box clearly, type 3 and enter:

```
RE-INIT 8
```

This automatically re-initializes the display. It does not clear your UNDO stack, enabling you to reverse any errors that may have occurred while the screen was garbled.

Finding Support Files

When you ask AutoCAD to find a support file (such as a menu file), it searches in a particular order. A typical search order is as follows:

```
"STUFF.mnu":  Can't open file
   in C:\PROJECT\(current directory)
   or C:\DWGS\

   or C:\ACAD\SUPPORT\


   or C:\ACAD\
```

First the current directory.
Then the current drawing's directory.
Then the directory(ies) designated by SET ACAD=.
Last, the program directory, home of ACAD.EXE.

```
Enter another menu file name (or RETURN for none):
```

If you keep AutoCAD's search order in mind, it helps you avoid errors caused by AutoCAD's finding the wrong support files. Sometimes AutoCAD finds the wrong support files because the environment variable ACAD setting is in a start-up batch file. Make sure to clear your settings with SET ACAD= at the end of batch files. Remember that appended directories are always searched first.

Deciphering Current Directory Errors

If you use SHELL to change directories from within AutoCAD, you may get strange results. New drawings will not default to the changed current directory, yet the SAVE command defaults to save files in the changed current directory. Subsequent attempts to load support files (such as MNX files) can crash AutoCAD.

If you must change directories on SHELL excursions, automate the directory change with a batch file that also changes back to the original directory.

Solving AutoCAD SHELL Errors

Here are some common errors encountered in using AutoCAD's SHELL command:

```
SHELL error: insufficient memory for command
```

This message may be caused by an ill-behaved program executed during a previous SHELL or before entering AutoCAD. Some programs do not clean up after themselves—they leave a dirty environment behind that causes AutoCAD to believe (erroneously) that insufficient memory exists.

```
Unable to load XYZABC: insufficient memory
Program too big to fit in memory
```

If SHELL got this far, these are correct messages. You need to modify your system configuration to allow more conventional memory space. Try removing TSRs from memory as a first step. The second step is to use the SHROOM.COM utility that is in the AutoCAD SAMPLE subdirectory.

```
SHELL error in EXEC function (insufficient memory)
```

This error can be caused by not having enough free conventional memory to load DOS. The solutions are the same as those for the preceding error.

Dealing with Miscellaneous Problems

If you run under a multi-tasking environment, such as Software Carousel, DESQview, or Windows, you may get an error that claims a file should be in a directory in which it never was. For example, you may get:

```
Can't find overlay file D:\JOB231\ACAD.OVL
Retry, Abort?
```

Do not type an A unless you give up. Type R to retry. If that does not work, flip partitions and copy the file to the directory listed in the error message. You may need to try another R during the flip. Copy the file, flip back, and try R again.

```
Expanded memory disabled
```

When starting AutoCAD from DOS, the preceding error can be caused by a previously crashed AutoCAD program. Sometimes a crashed AutoCAD program (or another program) does not clear its claim on expanded memory. This causes the program to think that none is available. Reboot to clear it.

Handling File Errors

You may encounter file-error messages when AutoCAD cannot open a file. This may be caused by too few files requested in the FILES= statement of the CONFIG.SYS file, or by too many files left open by AutoLISP's OPEN function. This error can show up as the following:

```
Can't find overlay file C:\ACAD\ACAD.OVL      (Or any other file).
```

Tracing Errors

You are your best source for error diagnosis. When problems occur, record them so you can recognize patterns. Some trouble-shooting tips include the following:

- Use screen-capture programs to document the text screen.

- Echo the screen to the printer.

- Write down what you did in as much detail as possible, as far back as you can remember.

- Echo a copy of AutoCAD's STATUS screen to the printer.

- Check the DOS SET command settings and current directory by using SHELL.

Multiple DOS Configuration Files

Some programs do not run properly on a system setup for AutoCAD, and the opposite is also true. One solution is to use multiple DOS configuration files, switching between them when-ever necessary. Create one set of configuration files (CONFIG.SYS and AUTOEXEC.BAT) for AutoCAD and a second set for the alternate configuration. For example, create files called ACAD.SYS and ACADAUTO.BAT for use as your system configuration files when running AutoCAD. Then, create a set of files called ALT.SYS and ALTAUTO.BAT for use with the alternate configuration. Include in each file the appropriate commands and settings for each configuration.

Next, create a batch file that copies the correct configuration files to CONFIG.SYS and AUTOEXEC.BAT, then reboot the system. The following two batch files, called GOALT.BAT and GOACAD.BAT, offer examples of this process:

```
GOALT.BAT file:
COPY C:\ALT.SYS C:\CONFIG.SYS
COPY C:\ALTAUTO.BAT C:\AUTOEXEC.BAT
@ECHO REBOOT system to run the ALT configuration.
```

```
GOACAD.BAT file:
COPY C:\ACAD.SYS C:\CONFIG.SYS
COPY C:\ACADAUTO.BAT C:\AUTOEXEC.BAT
@ECHO REBOOT system to run AutoCAD.
```

To run AutoCAD, type GOACAD and press Enter. The correct configuration files are copied into place. Then, reboot the system by pressing Ctrl-Alt-Del. After the system has rebooted, start AutoCAD as you normally do. Use the same process to switch configuration files for the alternate configuration.

File Problems after a System Crash

When your system goes down unexpectedly in the middle of an AutoCAD session, you may end up with extraneous files on disk or with files locked and inaccessible.

First, run CHKDSK /F at the DOS prompt to restore any disk space occupied by abandoned files. Do not run CHKDSK /F from SHELL.

Removing Extraneous Swap Files

When AutoCAD 386 terminates abnormally, you may find files on your hard drive with names that are hexadecimal numbers, such as 092A314F.SWR or 103B272D (no extension). Typically, these files will have file sizes of 0K, 100K, or nearly 400K. Normally, AutoCAD erases these files whenever you exit the program. If the system locks up for some reason, the files will remain on your disk until you erase them.

Use the DOS DEL or ERASE commands to erase these files. You can erase all files with an extension of SWR by entering:

```
DEL *.SWR
```

If you have a number of these files without extensions, they will probably begin with the same one or two digits. For example, if they all begin with 0, you can delete them all by entering:

```
DEL 0*.
```

However, be aware that this will delete every file in the current directory that begins with 0 and has no extension. If you have data or other files in the current directory that do not have extensions and you wish to keep them, you have to erase the swap files one-by-one, or use a wild-card combination common to them all.

Unlocking Locked Files

If you have file locking enabled and your AutoCAD session terminates abnormally, the drawing file you were editing will still be locked. If you try to edit it again, you will be unable to do so.

To unlock a locked file, first verify that the file is not actually in use by someone else, such as on a network. If it is not, choose File, then Utilities to access the File Utilities dialog box. Click on Unlock file. A standard AutoCAD file dialog box will appear. Select all files you wish to unlock and click OK. AutoCAD will then unlock the files. The File Utilities dialog box will re-appear telling you how many files were unlocked.

Solving Login Errors

If, after a system crash, you get an AutoCAD Alert dialog box with the error message:

```
Login Failed:  The maximum number of users has been reached.
```

Try again later. You must restart AutoCAD with the same ACAD.CFG configuration file that was in use at the time of the crash. AutoCAD automatically repairs the situation.

Corrupted Drawings

If you receive an error message beginning with words like EREAD or SCANDR when trying to load a drawing, the file may be corrupted. If the drawing was made with Release 11 or 12, AutoCAD itself may be able to salvage some or all of it. Drawings created with prior releases will have to be recovered with a third-party utility or be redrawn.

The RECOVER command will try to recover as much of your drawing as possible. It will perform an automatic audit of the file and present you with the results in the drawing editor. Any warning messages AutoCAD displays are also written to a log file with the same name as the recovered drawing, but with an ADT extension, if the AUDITCTL system variable has been set to 1 (the default is 0).

Using AutoCAD's Standard Tablet Menu

AutoCAD comes with a standard tablet menu, shown in figure B.2, and includes a plastic template for an 11x11-inch digitizer tablet. To use the standard AutoCAD tablet menu, affix the AutoCAD standard plastic template to your digitizer and use the AutoCAD TABLET command to let the program know where the tablet "boxes" are located.

Figure B.2:

The standard AutoCAD tablet menu.

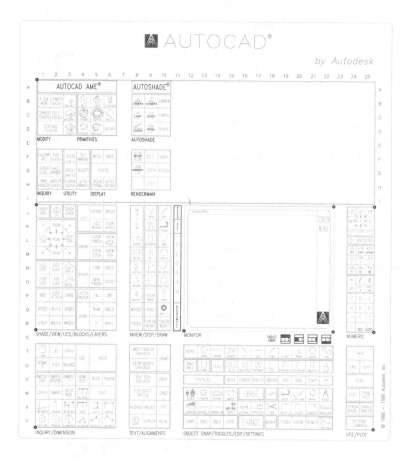

The TABLET.DWG Drawing

AutoCAD also comes with a drawing file, TABLET.DWG, which reproduces the plastic template menu. You can use this drawing to create a custom template drawing for your digitizer.

If you know how to edit drawings and customize the tablet menu, you can make your own tablet drawing, supporting the menu with your own tablet menu programs. If you customize your tablet menu, make a backup copy of TABLET.DWG, call it MYTABLET.DWG, and make your changes to the copy, not to the original.

Configuring Your Tablet Menu

This section assumes that you are using an 11x11-inch or larger digitizer that has been configured according to the *AutoCAD Interface, Installation, and Performance Guide*.

If you are using the AutoCAD template, place it on your digitizer. If you are using the plotted TABLET drawing, trim the drawing, leaving about a 1/2-inch border, and tape it to your digitizer. Because every tablet is different, and because every user trims and tapes differently, you must configure the tablet to let AutoCAD know exactly where the tablet commands are located on the surface of the tablet.

Use the TABLET command from inside the drawing editor to configure the tablet. You see a series of donuts—tablet pick points on the drawing (or template)—that you can use as a guide when picking each of the four menu areas prompted for by the TABLET command.

The standard menu is divided into four menu areas by columns and rows. In figure A.1, for example, the columns are numbered 1 to 25 across the top and the rows are lettered A to Y on the left. Menu area 1 is the top rectangular area. The first donut pick point is near A and 1 in the top left corner. Menu area 1 has 25 columns and 9 rows of menu "boxes."

To configure the tablet, pick three points for each menu area and enter the number of columns and rows. Use figure B.3 as a guide for picking points.

Figure B.3:

Configuring the AutoCAD standard tablet menu.

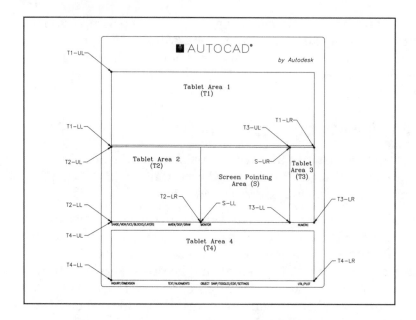

Configuring the AutoCAD Tablet Menu

Begin a NEW drawing named TEST.

The drawing screen appears with the screen menu.

```
Command: TABLET ⏎

Option (ON/OFF/CAL/CFG): CFG ⏎

Enter the number of tablet menus desired
(0-4) <0>: 4 ⏎

Digitize the upper left corner of menu area 1:
Pick point

Digitize the lower left corner of menu area 1:
Pick point

Digitize the lower right corner of menu area 1:
Pick point

Enter the number of columns for menu area 1:
25 ⏎

Enter the number of rows for menu area 1: 9 ⏎

Digitize the upper left corner of menu area 2:
Pick point
```

Digitize the lower left corner of menu area 2:	*Pick point*
Digitize the lower right corner of menu area 2:	*Pick point*
Enter the number of columns for menu area 2:11 ↵	
Enter the number of rows for menu area 2: 9 ↵	
Digitize the upper left corner of menu area 3:	*Pick point*
Digitize the lower left corner of menu area 3:	*Pick point*
Enter the number of columns for menu area 3:9 ↵	
Enter the number of rows for menu area 3: 13 ↵	
Digitize the upper left corner of menu area 4:	*Pick point*
Digitize the lower left corner of menu area 4:	*Pick point*
Digitize the lower right corner of menu area 4:	*Pick point*
Enter the number of columns for menu area 4:25 ↵	
Enter the number of rows for menu area 4: 7 ↵	
Do you want to respecify the screen pointing area (Y) *Press Enter*	
Digitize lower left corner of screen pointing area:	*Pick point*
Digitize upper right corner of screen pointing area:	*Pick point*

Try picking a few commands from the tablet and drawing in the screen pointing area to test the configuration.

Command: **QUIT** ↵	Quits the TEST drawing

The standard AutoCAD tablet menu is configured for your digitizer and the configuration parameters are stored on your disk in a file.

Swapping Tablet Menu Areas

The process of swapping a menu area changes its function from the default to a different, predefined menu. To swap a particular menu area, select one of the four corresponding tablet swap icons located on the digitizer overlay below the monitor area. The following list describes the default and alternate menus for each swap icon.

- **Menu Area 1**. Top menu area.

  Default. AME and AutoShade menus.

  Swap. Replaces AME and AutoShade menus with a blank menu area that can be used for personal applications and menu items.

- **Menu Area 2**. Left menu area.

  Default. Display commands are transparent, and VPOINT and DVIEW refer to the WCS.

  Swap. Display commands cancel a command in progress, and VPOINT and DVIEW refer to the current UCS.

- **Menu Area 3**. Right menu area.

  Default. American units.

  Swap. Metric units.

- **Menu Area 4**. Lower menu area.

  Default. Object snap picks are temporary.

  Swap. Changes object snap picks to running object snap picks.

When you swap a menu area, the corresponding asterisk in the screen menu below [AutoCAD] changes to a number to indicate which menu has been switched. The selecting of [AutoCAD] resets all menu areas to their defaults.

For more information on tablet swapping and customization, see *Maximizing AutoCAD, Volume I* from New Riders Publishing.

DOS Basics and Performance

To use AutoCAD, you should first know something about your computer and how it works. Most computer programs—applications such as AutoCAD or most word processors—require the user to understand basic computer functions. Some programs "insulate" the user from the computer system by performing these basic functions automatically, but such programs still are the exception rather than the norm.

Fortunately, getting started in AutoCAD requires only a modest knowledge of your system. If you are new to computers or to the DOS operating system, this appendix will help get you up to speed. If you already are familiar with DOS, skim this appendix to learn AutoCAD specifics.

You need to understand seven basic elements about your computer system. On the hardware side (the physical equipment that makes up the system), you need to know a bit about the following:

- The individually identifiable components, such as mouse or digitizer, video monitor, and printer or plotter

- The computer's internal processor

- The system's internal working memory

- The disk drives, where software programs and data (such as AutoCAD drawings) are stored

On the software side (the instructions that tell the system what to do), you need to know a bit about the following:

- The operating system's commands and utilities

- Data files (such as AutoCAD drawings) and how to manage them

- Applications software (such as the AutoCAD program) and how its commands and functions interact with the operating system

To begin, consider the difference between the two fundamental components of your computer system—hardware and software.

Hardware and Software

Hardware is your computer's physical equipment, including the keyboard, video monitor, disk drives, and any other tangible components it may have. *Software* is a set of instructions that controls these physical components. Software is stored electronically on disk or in the system's internal memory. The computer reads the software from the disk into memory where it exists only as electrical charges that tell the computer system how to function.

Hardware is divided into *system hardware* and *peripherals*. The system hardware includes the keyboard, monitor, central processing unit (CPU), internal working memory (RAM), and internal storage memory (usually disks). Peripherals include external storage memory (floppy disks or tape), digitizers, printers, plotters, modems, mice, and so on. The type of CPU, the amount and type of memory, and the storage capacity and speed of the disks are all related to the system's *performance*. Your monitor's resolution, image quality, and availability of color also affect your productivity when you do computer-aided design or drafting (CAD).

Other peripherals, which vary widely from system to system, also affect your productivity. For example, a digitizer generally offers quicker command entry and greater precision and flexibility than a mouse or keyboard. A printer often produces a drawing faster than a plotter, but the plotter produces a better-quality drawing.

Software can be categorized into two main groups: *operating system software* and *application software*. Operating system software provides various levels of interaction (called the *interface*) between the computer hardware and the user, as well as between the computer hardware and application software. *Application software* (often called programs, such as AutoCAD and AutoSHADE) is what you interact with the most. The operating system is general-purpose software, while a program is special-purpose software.

Picture a computer system as a stack of blocks. The top block represents your applications, below that is the operating system, and at the bottom is the system's hardware. Figure 1.1 illustrates this concept.

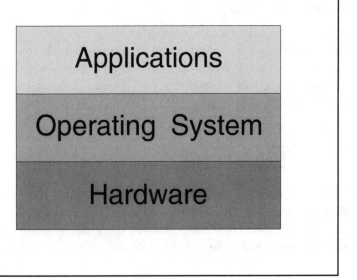

Figure 1.1:
The various levels of a typical computer system.

You deal most actively with the top block (your applications), while the operating system makes it all happen behind the scenes, or *transparently* for the user. On IBM-compatible systems, the operating system software is generally DOS (disk operating system). The standard DOS commands are the same whether you are using MS-DOS (Microsoft DOS), PC-DOS (IBM's version), or an OEM (original equipment manufacturer) version, which is slightly customized by the hardware supplier.

Many Levels of DOS

The operating system provides commands for managing your system and data. One of the most important functions of the operating system is to display a screen *prompt*, such as A:> or C:\>. A prompt is a cue that the system is ready to receive and execute a command. When you type a command after a prompt and press Enter, DOS interprets what you typed and acts accordingly. If what you typed is neither a valid DOS command nor a program name that DOS recognizes, the system displays an error message and repeats the prompt.

You generally have two *entry points* into your computer system. You can control it from within an application such as AutoCAD, or you can control it from the operating-system level. But before you learn to control the system, you should have an understanding of its hardware components.

The CPU and Memory

What many users perceive as the main body of the system, the CPU and memory, are physically two of the smallest components in the system. Nevertheless, they are the most important. The next section examines the first of these pieces—the brain of the system.

The Central Processing Unit

The central processing unit (CPU) is responsible for the work done in your computer. Most of the "computing" takes place in the CPU. The type of CPU in your computer system determines both its speed and its capabilities. Four classes of processors are used in IBM compatibles: the 8088 or 8086, the 80286, the 80386, and the 80486. The 80486 is the newest and most powerful CPU available.

The outdated 8088 and 8086 processors (used in the original IBM PC) and the 80286 (used in the IBM AT) are limited in their memory-management and processing capabilities compared to today's 80386 and 80486 CPUs. AutoCAD is a complex program that needs all the power you can afford. To run AutoCAD Release 12, you must have at least an 80386- or 80486-based system.

The 80386 requires a *math coprocessor* to run AutoCAD. A math coprocessor, also called an *FPU* (floating-point unit), processes floating-point math operations many times faster than the CPU. Math coprocessors manufactured by Intel have numbers the same as the CPU they were designed to work with except that the last digit is a 7. For example, the 80386 requires an 80387 FPU. The 80486 has a built-in math coprocessor and does not require an external one.

Note | References to the 80386 or 80486 mean the 80386DX and 80486DX parts. The 80386SX has half the data-transfer capacity of the 80386DX. For production AutoCAD use, the slight cost savings of an 80386SX are not worth the performance loss. Beware of the 80486SX; it is an 80486 with the FPU disabled! The money you save on it will be more than used up by the 80487 FPU you have to buy.

Computer systems are classified by the type of CPU because the CPU imposes absolute limits on performance and software compatibility. Memory is a more flexible resource, and you can easily improve a computer system's performance by adding more working memory.

589

Primary Storage Memory

Your computer system's primary storage area, or working *system memory*, is the CPU's workspace. When you copy a file from one disk to another, the file is momentarily stored in that system memory workspace before being copied to the destination disk. Programs use the same workspace for calculations or data manipulations. The applications software and operating system software must also be loaded into this workspace when they are executing. Because of the way in which the CPU retrieves data from it, this memory is called *random-access memory* (RAM).

Although RAM chips vary in type and storage capacity, what is important to system performance is the location of the memory and how the processor addresses it. (For more details about memory and for definitions of terms used in the following list, see Appendix B or your *AutoCAD Interface, Installation and Performance Guide*.)

The primary types of system memory are as follows:

- **Conventional memory.** The range for conventional memory is 0K to 1024K. (With personal computers, memory usually is measured in *kilobytes*, abbreviated as K. A kilobyte contains 1,024 bits of data.) All AutoCAD systems need at least 640K, but only part of that memory is actually available to AutoCAD because DOS uses part of it. DOS Version 5 can make more of this 640K available to applications than previous DOS versions.

- **Extended memory.** Sometimes referred to as *XMS*, extended memory is the memory over 1024K. A program called an *extended memory manager* (EMM) can manage your applications software's access to extended memory.

- **Expanded memory.** Also referred to as *EMS*, expanded memory may be on a physical expanded memory card installed in the computer or provided by an extended memory manager.

Extended and expanded memory are addressed directly only by applications, such as AutoCAD, that are specifically written for them. AutoCAD 386 needs extended memory. At least 8M

(8 *megabytes* equals 8192K) total system memory is recommended for AutoCAD 386, of which 7M will probably be configured as extended.

Secondary Storage

The system memory (RAM) provides a place for the CPU to manipulate data. But the system also must have a place to store that data, as well as application programs, operating system files, and so on. The system's secondary storage—its hard drives, floppy disks, tape drives, and CDs—serves that function. Because the floppy disk drive slot is visible on your computer but the hard disk is not, some users confuse hard disk storage with system RAM. Data is stored in the system's RAM storage as transient electrical charges, while data is stored as relatively permanent magnetic codes on a tangible, though hidden, disk. Hard disks work just like floppy disks, except they are much faster and have a much larger storage capacity, due to being manufactured more precisely and sealed airtight to eliminate dust. The more secondary storage available to the system, the more information you can store.

> **Note** Although secondary storage can consist of tape and various devices other than disks, the discussion will refer just to disks. Your main disk is probably a hard disk labeled C. If your hard disk is not drive C, substitute its drive letter wherever C is shown throughout the book.

Hard disks are useful for storing large amounts of data. Floppy disks are used to distribute software, transfer files between computers that are not connected by a network, and create backup copies of important files. Floppy disks (also called diskettes) come in two sizes. The older size is 5 1/4-inches, with a flexible jacket. At 3 1/2-inches, the newer size is smaller, with a hard plastic case. Each size comes in several *densities*. Density refers to the relative amount of information that can be stored on the disk. The standard DSDD (double-sided double-density) 5 1/4-inch floppy holds 360K; the standard DSDD (or just DD) 3 1/2-inch floppy holds 720K. High-density (HD) 5 1/4-inch floppies hold about 1.2M of information, and high-density 3 1/2-inch floppies hold approximately 1.44M. Drives that are designed for high-density disks usually can read and write to lower-density disks, but low-density drives cannot read high-density disks.

The combination of physical size and density determines the *format* of the disk. Any application you want to install and any data you want to copy on your system must be in the appropriate format. Most software manufacturers make their products available on both 5 1/4-inch and 3 1/2-inch floppies in standard densities.

The floppy disk is made of a flexible magnetic material similar to that used for audio tapes. Disk care is important. Avoid temperature extremes, do not touch the actual recording material, and store diskettes in sleeves or containers to avoid contamination by dirt. Handle 5 1/4-inch floppies carefully to avoid creasing the jacket, and do not write on the disk (or its label) with a ballpoint pen or pencil.

Hard disks are classified by their data-access speed (such as 15 milliseconds, or ms—lower is better), their data-transfer rate (such as 15M/sec—higher is better) and their total capacity (such as 40M—a suitable minimum for AutoCAD). Hard disks are protected from your touch, but be careful not to expose them to physical shock. Once you have purchased a hard disk, all that is really important to you is the amount of currently available storage space on the disk.

Referencing a Drive

A single computer system may have several storage devices connected to it at once. In fact, most systems have at least two disk drives. In DOS, disk drives are addressed by an identifying *drive letter*. If a system has only one floppy drive, that drive is referred to as drive A. If a second floppy drive is available, it is drive B. The first hard disk drive is referred to as drive C.

The drive letters are *logical* references, not physical. A single physical drive may be assigned more than one logical drive letter. A hard disk may be divided into several logical disks, each with its own drive letter.

An important concept with DOS is the *current drive*—the drive the system uses for its current operations unless you instruct it otherwise. Many programs and DOS commands work with information that is stored on the computer. If you do not specify a drive letter, DOS attempts to execute the command using information from the current drive.

> **Note** Most systems use the DOS command PROMPT PG to make the current directory appear as part of the DOS prompt—for example, C:\>. See "Checking the Current Directory" later in this chapter.

You reference a drive by its drive letter followed by a colon (:), such as **C:** for drive C. To change to a different current drive, simply enter the new drive letter followed by a colon and then press Enter. For example, to change from drive C to drive A, type **A:** and press Enter. If you are changing to a floppy disk drive, the floppy disk should be in the drive, ready for the system to use. See "Checking Disks with CHKDSK" for an example.

The DOS Operating System

Information management on your computer system occurs at two levels: in the processor and where files are organized and stored on disk. The control in the processor is automatic, though its efficiency is affected by which version of operating system you have and by the way the system is configured. File management, on the other hand, is an ongoing process that you are responsible for.

To obtain the best performance from your computer system, you should have an up-to-date operating system that is configured properly. To check your DOS version, type **VER** and press Enter at the DOS prompt. Your version is important because many programs benefit from or require features available only in DOS version 3.0 or later, and DOS 5 (the current version) has features that maximize the amount of memory available to applications.

Booting the System

Generally, a computer system must have a *system disk*. A system disk is one that contains all of the operating system files necessary to start the computer. Most systems are set up to start (boot) from a hard disk. Otherwise, you start the computer from a floppy disk containing these files. As the system starts, the operating system is copied from the disk to RAM, where the processor can use it.

Once the basic portion of the operating system has been installed, the system checks for any special configuration instructions in a file called CONFIG.SYS, which must be located on the system disk. The settings in CONFIG.SYS establish memory management and install device drivers. For more information about CONFIG.SYS and configuring your system for use with AutoCAD, see Appendix B.

After the system is configured, it searches for a file called AUTOEXEC.BAT (automatically executing batch file), which contains instructions about standard DOS commands that are to be automatically executed. Many of these commands control how the operating system manages file access; others set *system variables*. Programs use system variables to obtain information about your computer system's configuration. Appendix B tells you how to customize your AUTOEXEC.BAT file.

When the operating system is booted, it is ready for you to use its utility commands, organize your files and directories, or start your application programs. One of the first things you may want to do is check memory and disk space.

Checking Disks with CHKDSK

The DOS CHKDSK (check disk) command checks the total amount of storage space on a disk and the amount currently available. It also reports the total and available amounts of conventional RAM. To use the CHKDSK command, type **CHKDSK** at the DOS prompt and press Enter. To check a disk in a drive other than the current one, include the drive letter in the command, for example CHKDSK B:. CHKDSK works for any hard or floppy disk. The operating system will respond to your CHKDSK command with a report (in this case, for a hard disk) that looks something like the following:

```
Volume AUTOCAD1  created 04-18-1991 3:41p
Volume Serial Number is 169A-5C83

  65468416 bytes total disk space
   4270080 bytes in 3 hidden files
    118784 bytes in 53 directories
  32727040 bytes in 967 user files
    655360 bytes in bad sectors
  27697152 bytes available on disk

      2048 bytes in each allocation unit
     31967 total allocation units on disk
     13524 available allocation units on disk

    655360 total bytes memory
    181088 bytes free
```

Generally, the most useful information is the bytes available on disk line, which indicates how much room is available for new programs and data files. Although the figure is reported in bytes, it is much more convenient to think of available storage in terms of megabytes. To convert from bytes to megabytes, simply divide by 1,024,000 (or 1,000,000 for a rough estimate). In the sample listing, approximately 27.5M of free space is available on the hard disk.

CHKDSK provides other information about the hard disk. The first two lines identify the disk. The next section presents a summary of disk usage by reporting the total disk space and the number and total size of hidden files, directories, and user files.

The `bytes total disk space` line indicates the size of the hard disk (again, divide by 1,024,000 to convert to megabytes). Many disks have portions that are no longer usable, reported as `bytes in bad sectors`.

The final two lines indicate the amount of working RAM installed in the system and the amount currently available. The DOS 5 MEM command also reports this information.

> **Note** CHKDSK also reports any disk problems, for example lost clusters, which are usually harmless leftovers created when programs crash (terminate due to error or power failure). Enter **CHKDSK /F** at the DOS prompt and answer **Y** when DOS asks whether you want to convert the clusters to files in order to delete them. See your DOS manual for details.

Working with Directories and Files

Information on your computer is stored in *files*. They include documents, drawings, and other data files you create, as well as the support files for the operating system and various applications. *Support files*, such as AutoCAD's text font definition files, contain data used by the primary program.

You refer to files by their *file names*. To avoid sorting through several hundred files to find the one you need, you organize the files into groups, just as you organize your paper files in file folders and file cabinets. You do this by creating *directories* and *subdirectories*. Directories also have names by which you refer to them, and one directory can contain any number of other directories and files. The root directory, however, can only have 112 files and directories.

Most people use the terms *subdirectory* and *parent directory* when talking about the relationship between two directories. For example, if you have a directory named DRAWING within your ACAD directory, you can say that the DRAWING directory is a subdirectory of the ACAD directory or that the ACAD directory is the parent of the DRAWING directory.

Your hard disk probably is already organized into a collection of directories, with each program contained in its own subdirectory and with data files organized under their own directories and subdirectories. This organization is called the *directory structure* or the *directory tree*. Each subdirectory is a branch of the directory tree. The main directory that contains all the other directories, subdirectories, and files on your disk is called the *root directory*.

Displaying the Directory Tree

The DOS 3.3 or DOS 5 TREE command lists directories and subdirectories. Figure 1.2 shows a sample directory tree. In DOS 3.3, the listing starts with the root directory; in DOS 5, it starts with the current directory.

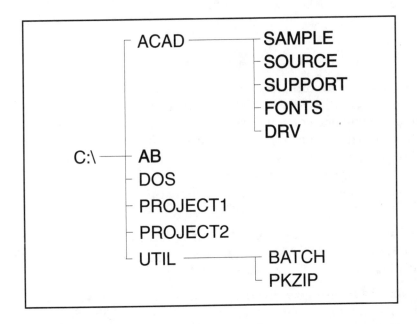

Figure 1.2:
A directory tree.

To specify a subdirectory or a file in a subdirectory, you need to specify the *path* of directory names that you follow from the root directory or current directory to the desired subdirectory. The full path name of a directory starts with the drive letter and the root directory. The root directory has no name but is indicated with a backslash (\). For example, the root directory of the first hard disk on your system is C:\. If the ACAD directory is a subdirectory of the root, it is specified as C:\ACAD. Subdirectories of ACAD are prefaced with additional backslashes. If the DRAWING directory is a subdirectory of C:\ACAD, you use the path name C:\ACAD\DRAWING. If drive C is the current drive, you can omit the drive designation, and the path name is simply \ACAD\DRAWING.

> **Note** You can abbreviate the current directory with a single period (.) and the parent directory with a double period (..). For example, if the current directory is \ACAD\DRAWING and if DRAWING2 is also a subdirectory of ACAD, you specify the path of DRAWING2 as ..\DRAWING2 instead of \ACAD\DRAWING2.

Checking the Current Directory

In working with directories, you always need to be aware of what your current directory is. Unless your AUTOEXEC.BAT file is set up to change the current directory, you will always start up in the root. You change the current directory with the CD (change directory) command or with an appropriate command from your application program. To change your directory, type **CD** *path* at the DOS prompt and press Enter, where *path* is the path of the desired directory.

Be careful not to lose track of the current directory. If you do lose track, you can enter CD without designating a path, and DOS will display the name of the current directory.

If your DOS prompt is the default (such as C>), and you want it to display the current directory (such as C:\>), try following the steps in the following exercise to reset it.

Setting the Prompt To Show the Current Directory

Type CD \ and press Enter at the DOS prompt to make sure the root directory is current.

```
C> PROMPT $P$G ↵
C:\>
```

Your prompt should now display a backslash, for the root directory.

You can put the PROMPT PG command in your AUTOEXEC.BAT file so that your prompt automatically displays the current path. See Appendix B for details.

Listing Directories and Files

The DOS DIR (directory) command lists the subdirectories and files in the current directory. It also lists the volume label of the current disk, the disk serial number (for DOS 4 and 5 hard disks only), and the name of the current directory. To display the listing, type DIR and press Enter. A listing might look like the following:

```
Volume in drive C has no label
Volume Serial Number is 2A35-17EB
Directory of  C:\AB1DOC

.             <DIR>      06-17-92    4:14p
..            <DIR>      06-17-92    4:14p
CMDREF        <DIR>      06-17-92   10:36p
PM            <DIR>      06-17-92    4:16p
AB1CHP02 DOC     16896  06-21-92    3:51p
AB1CHP03 DOC     24576  06-25-92   12:14p
AB1CHP04 DOC     26112  06-25-92    1:35p
AB1CHP05 DOC     27648  06-20-92   11:34a
AB1CHP06 DOC     25088  06-20-92   11:34a
AB1CHP01 DOC     66560  06-25-92    9:05p
       10 File(s)    67223552 bytes free
```

The directories, including the abbreviations for current directory (.) and parent directory (..), are indicated with <DIR>. The other items in the listing are files. File and directory names in DOS can contain up to eight characters, with an optional *extension* of up to three characters. In the preceding sample listing, the file names you see have DOC extensions. When you enter a file name at the DOS prompt, you must separate the name from its extension with a period, for example AB1CHP01.DOC. The directory listing on the screen does not show the periods.

The DIR /AD command in DOS 5 lists only subdirectories within the current directory. In other DOS versions, the command DIR *. lists all files or directories that do not have extensions. Because files often are named with extensions and directories are not, DIR *. usually lists only subdirectories.

Try listing your directories, and look for your AutoCAD directory.

Listing Directories

Type **CD ** and press Enter at the DOS prompt to make sure the root directory is current.

For DOS 5:

C:\>**DIR /AD** ↵   Displays a listing of directories

For DOS 5 or DOS 3:

C:\>**DIR *** ↵   Displays a listing of directories

Your listing will be similar to the following:

```
 Volume in drive C has no label
 Volume Serial Number is 2A35-17EB
 Directory of  C:\

ACAD          <DIR>      04-01-91    9:32p
BAT           <DIR>      11-30-90    9:04a
BOOT          <DIR>      11-30-90    8:14a
DOS           <DIR>      11-27-90    4:37p
DWG           <DIR>      12-18-90   10:45p
AB1DOC        <DIR>      06-17-91    4:14p
UTIL          <DIR>      12-15-90    9:16a
WORD          <DIR>      01-03-91    9:19a
         8 File(s)    66408448 bytes free
```

Try to identify your AutoCAD program directory. The one shown in the sample listing is ACAD.

Note If your AutoCAD program directory is not named ACAD, substitute its name wherever ACAD is shown throughout the book.

Many directory listings are too long to display on a single screen. The DIR /P command causes the listing to stop after each screen full of information. The DIR /W command lists names and extensions only, in a five-column-wide listing.

The /AD, /P and /W are *parameters* that modify the action of the directory command. Any number of parameters can be used with a single directory command. DOS 5 includes several additional parameters.

Using the DIR Command in DOS 5

The /O parameter organizes the DOS output into a sorted list. In addition to the parameter, you must specify how you want the files organized. The choices are:

```
N       Name
E       Extension
S       Size
D       Date and Time
```

For example, DIR /ON displays all of the files and directories sorted by name. DIR /OD displays the files sorted by date starting with the oldest file. You can use the minus sign to reverse the direction of any sort. DIR /O-D reverses the date order and displays the newest file first. DIR /OG groups the directories at the start of the listing.

DIR /S specifies that the contents of each subdirectory are displayed as an individual listing. The DIR /S command first displays the contents of the current directory (including all files and subdirectories); then the contents of the first directory in the list are displayed. If that subdirectory contains a subdirectory, its contents are then displayed, and so on.

Creating and Removing Directories

Many programs and applications automatically create directories during installation that store their program files. You also can create directories for your data files, using the MD or MKDIR command (make directory). To remove a directory, use the RD or RMDIR command (remove directory).

To use the MD (or MKDIR) command, enter the command followed by the name (or path) of the subdirectory to be created. For example, MD \ACAD\DRAWING will create the \ACAD\DRAWING directory. If you specify just the new directory name (with no path), a new subdirectory in the current directory is created. Unless a problem occurs, the MD command works quietly without giving you any feedback or messages.

The RD (or RMDIR) command works exactly like MD, except that it removes rather than creates the specified directory. You only can remove a directory that contains no files or subdirectories. Use the DEL command to remove any files before you remove the directory. If you enter DEL \ACAD\DRAWING*name.ext*, where *name* is a particular file name and *ext* is its extension, that particular file is deleted. If you enter DEL \ACAD\DRAWING*.*, all files in the DRAWING directory are removed.

Changing Directories

The CD or CHDIR (change directory) command changes the current directory. To move to a new directory, type CD (or CHDIR) followed by the path of the destination directory. For example, to move to the ACAD subdirectory, enter **CD \ACAD** (or **CHDIR \ACAD**). If you specify a drive letter, like **CD B:\PROJECTS**, it does not change to drive B, but changes the current directory of drive B. If you later change the current drive to drive B, you will find that PROJECTS is the current directory on drive B.

Several shortcuts for changing directories are available. Consider the parent directory \ACAD and its two subdirectories \ACAD\DRAWING and \ACAD\DRAWING2 as examples. If the destination directory is a subdirectory of the current directory, you can just enter **CD** followed by the subdirectory name.

When \ACAD is current, CD DRAWING changes to \ACAD\DRAWING. To move back up one level to the current directory's parent, enter **CD** and two periods. For example, enter **CD..** to change to \ACAD when \ACAD\DRAWING is current. If the current directory is \ACAD\DRAWING, you can move to DRAWING2 by entering CD ..\DRAWING2 instead of CD \ACAD\DRAWING2.

Most applications have their own methods and commands for moving between directories to locate a data file. Generally, you only need to use the CD command to locate and manage files in DOS or to change to an application's subdirectory before starting the application program.

File Management

All the information in your computer system is stored in the form of files. Program files with EXE, COM, and BAT extensions contain instructions that execute when you start up an application. The application program itself usually manages these files and any special support data files it needs. As you work, you create your own data files such as word processing documents, spreadsheets, or AutoCAD drawings.

Every file takes up storage space. In time, your disks begin to fill up. To maintain your system performance and avoid confusion, you should manage your files wisely. Proper file management includes naming your files properly, using subdirectories to organize your files, maintaining backup copies of your data files, and deleting unnecessary files.

Naming Files

File and directory names in DOS can be up to eight characters long with an optional extension of up to three characters. Permissible characters include all of the letters and numbers on your keyboard as well as the punctuation characters: ' ~ ! @ # $ ^ & ( ) _ - { }. A period separates the file name from the extension. Each combination of file name and extension must be unique within each directory.

Like most application programs, AutoCAD assigns certain specific extensions to its data files. The following are common file extensions you will see when working with AutoCAD:

- **DWG.** The DWG extension denotes an AutoCAD drawing file. AutoCAD assigns the DWG extension automatically—you do not need to assign it when you save a drawing. You just enter a file name, and AutoCAD adds the extension.

- **SCR.** An SCR file is an AutoCAD script file containing a list of AutoCAD commands. Script files are similar in concept to DOS batch files, except that they work within AutoCAD, not within DOS. You can automate many processes in AutoCAD with script files.

- **LSP.** LSP stands for an AutoCAD LISP file. AutoLISP is AutoCAD's programming language. By using LISP programs, you can automate complex tasks that cannot be performed with a script.

- **CFG.** The CFG extension denotes a configuration file containing information about your system hardware and software setup.

- **MNU.** MNU files are menu source files. You can customize your AutoCAD menu or create custom menus by creating and editing menu source files.

- **MNX.** Compiled menu files have the extension MNX. Before AutoCAD can use a menu, it compiles (translates) the menu source file (MNU file) into a more efficient form. AutoCAD then uses the MNX file as the menu file.

- **SHP.** Shape-definition source files have the extension SHP. Shapes include text fonts and simple symbols. You can create your own text styles by creating shape definition files.

- **SHX.** SHX stands for a compiled shape file. As with menus, AutoCAD compiles shape definitions into a more efficient form.

Using Wild Cards To Locate Files

DOS enables you to use wild cards when specifying file names. A wild card is a special character that represents one or a series of unknown characters. The asterisk matches any number of letters in either the file name or the extension. The question mark matches a single unknown character. For example, *.DWG matches any file with the DWG extension (AutoCAD drawings). R*.* matches any file that has a file name starting with the letter R, regardless of how many total letters are in the file name. R??.* matches any file with a three-letter file name that starts with R regardless of extension. Using *.* matches any file name. Wild cards are useful when listing files or when copying a group of files.

Note The asterisk makes DOS fill in the file name (or extension) from the asterisk's position to the end of the file name (up to the period) or extension. Any characters to the right of the asterisk are ignored.

You cannot place an asterisk between two letters to match characters at the beginning and end of a file name. For example, R*Z matches all files that start with the letter R, not just those that start with R and end with Z.

You can use wild cards with the DIR command to list certain types of files. The command DIR R* is the same as the DIR R*.* command and lists all file names starting with the letter R (regardless of their extension). The commands DIR, DIR *, DIR., DIR .*, and DIR *.* all produce a listing of all files in the directory. The command DIR *. lists only those files with a blank extension, which includes most directories.

Copying Files

An important aspect of file management is maintaining current *backups*. A backup is a duplicate set of files to use if you lose your current set. You should create a backup whenever the nuisance of re-creating your work would exceed the minor inconvenience of backing up your file(s)—in other words, almost always. The simplest way to create backups is to use the COPY command to duplicate the file(s) onto another disk (or, in AutoCAD, use the SAVE command to save a copy of a drawing to a different disk).

The COPY command can be used to replicate a file with a new name or to duplicate a file in a new location as a backup. To copy a series of files, use wild cards. The general form of the COPY command is as follows:

`COPY source target`

The *source* parameter is the file(s) to be copied and *target* is either the new name or the new location (or a combination of both). The command COPY TEMPLATE.DWG WORKING.DWG creates a duplicate of the file TEMPLATE.DWG with the name WORKING.DWG in the current directory. The command COPY TEMPLATE.DWG B: creates a backup of the TEMPLATE.DWG file, also named TEMPLATE.DWG, on the disk in the B drive.

Wild cards and paths are permitted within the COPY command. For example, the command COPY *.* B: copies all the files in the current directory to the disk in the B drive. The command COPY \ACAD\DRAWINGS*.* B: copies all the files in the \ACAD\DRAWINGS directory on the current drive to drive B. COPY *.DWG B: copies those files with a DWG extension (AutoCAD drawing files) from the current directory to the disk in the B drive.

> **Note** Restoring the directory organization, programs, and data of your entire system can be a huge task in the event of a major system failure or error. Backing up your entire system regularly with a tape drive or commercial backup program can make this task much easier if disaster strikes. Tape drives and backup programs are also good for backing up large sets of files.

Deleting Unwanted Files

File management includes getting rid of files that you no longer need on your system. Periodically, you should back up and delete the files that you are no longer using regularly. The DEL command (or its synonym ERASE) deletes files. DEL accepts both wild cards and path information. The command DEL OLD.DWG (or ERASE OLD.DWG) deletes the file OLD.DWG from the current directory. The command DEL \ACAD\DRAWINGS\OLD.DWG deletes the file OLD.DWG from the \ACAD\DRAWINGS directory. The command DEL \ACAD\DRAWINGS*.DWG removes all of the files with the extension DWG (AutoCAD drawing files) from the directory \ACAD\DRAWINGS. Obviously, you should be extremely careful when using wild cards with the DEL command. If you try to delete all of the files in a directory with the command DEL *.*, you see this prompt:

```
All files in directory will be deleted!
Are you sure (Y/N)?
```

You must enter a Y (upper- or lowercase does not matter in DOS) to confirm the deletion of all the files. You also can delete all files in a subdirectory by specifying the name of the directory rather than a file name. For example, the command DEL \ACAD\DRAWINGS is the same as DEL \ACAD\DRAWINGS*.*.

> **Note** You may unexpectedly get an `All files in directory will be deleted! Are you sure (Y/N)?` message when you did not intend to delete an entire directory. For example, accidentally entering DEL *A.* instead of DEL A*.* will delete the entire current directory instead of all files beginning with the letter A. If you make such a mistake and get the warning prompt, answer N to its message.

File Recovery

Sooner or later, when you are manipulating files, you will lose one. In DOS 5, you can sometimes restore a mistakenly deleted file with the UNDELETE command. However, any changes made to other files on the disk *after* the unintended deletion reduce your chances of successfully restoring the deleted file. The DOS 5 UNFORMAT command can retrieve information from a disk that has been formatted by mistake.

If you have an earlier version of DOS, you can use utility programs such as the Norton Utilities QU (Quick Unerase) or the PCTOOLS program to undelete files.

You may think you have lost or deleted a file when it was merely created in the wrong directory, or you may simply forget where you stored a file. In DOS 5, you can search multiple directories for files. Just add a /S to the DIR command, and it will search all subdirectories of the current directory (or path, if you specify a path). For example, the command DIR \ACAD*.DWG /S searches for and lists all drawing files in the \ACAD directory and all of its subdirectories.

With earlier versions of DOS, you can use utility programs, such as the Norton Utilities FF (Find File) or the PCTOOLS program, to search for files.

Executing Programs

Many common commands such as DIR and CD are built into the DOS COMMAND.COM file. Because COMMAND.COM is loaded when DOS is booted, these commands always are available at the DOS prompt. Other commands, application programs, and utility functions are contained in executable files (those with EXE extensions), command files (with COM extensions) and batch files (with BAT extensions). To execute EXE, COM, and BAT program files, enter their file names (with or without extensions) at the DOS prompt. Of course, DOS has to find the files to execute them.

> **Note** If you have EXE, COM, and/or BAT files with the same file names, DOS will first execute the EXE file. If no EXE file is found, DOS looks for a COM file, and if neither is found, it looks for a BAT file to execute.

You can enable DOS to find a program that is not located in the current directory in three ways. The first way is to use CD to change to another directory and then enter the program's file name. The second way is to enter the program's file name with the full path to its directory. For example, if ACAD.EXE is in C:\ACAD, you could enter \ACAD\ACAD to start AutoCAD from another current directory or enter C:\ACAD\ACAD to start AutoCAD from another drive. If the current directory is \ACAD\AB, you could start ACAD.EXE by entering ..ACAD instead of \ACAD\ACAD.

The third way to enable DOS to find a program that is not located in the current directory is to include the location of the program file in the PATH environment variable in your AUTOEXEC.BAT file. See Appendix B for more information.

Working with Files in AutoCAD

Most of AutoCAD's file functions are accessed by using the FILES command. The File Utilities dialog box provides an alternative to DOS (or your operating system) for managing your files. To display the File Utilities dialog box, enter the FILES command. You also can access the File Utilities by choosing File, then Utilities. Start AutoCAD and try using the File Utilities dialog box in the following exercise.

Accessing Files From AutoCAD

`C:\>CD \ACAD` ↵	Changes to the AutoCAD directory
`C:\ACAD>ACAD` ↵	Starts AutoCAD and displays the opening screen
Choose File, *then* Utilities	Accesses the File Utilities dialog box
Click on List files	Displays an AutoCAD file dialog box with all the DWG files in the current directory in the Files: scroll box
Click on Cancel, *then* Exit	Exits the file and File Utilities dialog box

The following is a list of the File Utilities dialog box options.

File Utilities

- **List files.** This option lists AutoCAD drawing files by default, but will list other files by changing the file display pattern.

- **Copy file.** This option enables you to copy a file from a drive and directory (source) into another drive and directory (destination). You also can specify a different name for the copied file. You can copy a file from one drive and directory to another and rename the file at the same time. This action will not delete the original file.

- **Rename files.** This option enables you to rename a file and (optionally) place the file in a different directory at the same time. Rename will copy a file from one directory to another (you can keep the same file name) and delete the original file.

- **Delete files.** The delete files option enables you to specify one or more files to delete. You are prompted to answer no or yes before each file is actually deleted.

- **Unlock file.** Option 6 enables you to unlock one or more files after a system crash, using wild-card options if you choose.

- **Exit.** This option closes the File Utilities dialog box

When you refer to a file name, do not forget to include the extension (such as DWG for drawing files).

> When you use the file utilities, do not delete the current drawing file (DWG), temporary files (AC, AC, or $A), or lock files (??K).

New computer users generally find AutoCAD's FILES menu helpful for manipulating files. Experienced users, however, may feel more comfortable with the operating system's file manipulation commands. When you are in an AutoCAD drawing, you can *shell out* to the operating system and execute operating system commands without exiting AutoCAD to execute those commands. You shell out with AutoCAD's SHELL or SH commands.

SHELL (or SH) functions as a gateway between AutoCAD, the operating system (such as DOS), and other external programs. If you press Enter once after typing SHELL or SH, AutoCAD presents an OS Command: prompt, at which you can issue a single operating system command and immediately return to AutoCAD. If you press Enter at the OS command prompt, you will stay in the operating system until you type EXIT and press Enter to return to AutoCAD. Once in the operating system, you can execute most operating system commands and software programs, depending on their memory requirements.

You can easily forget that you have shelled out of AutoCAD and into the operating system or another program. If you are shelled to the operating system, you will see a double "greater than" symbol (>>) at the command prompt instead of the normal single symbol.

AutoCAD 386 owners can use the SHROOM utility included with AutoCAD to increase the amount of memory SHELL provides for external programs. See the AutoCAD README.DOC and SHROOM.DOC files for more information.

The following lists the most common things to be aware of when working with the SHELL command:

- **Changing directories.** Make sure the current directory when you exit the SHELL command is the same directory as when you entered it.

- **CHKDSK.** Do not issue a CHKDSK /F when using SHELL.

- **Temporary files**. Do not delete temporary AutoCAD files with a $ symbol in the file name or extension or lock files with the extension ??K.

- **TSRs.** Do not load any RAM-resident or TSR programs from the shell. Load them before you start AutoCAD.

- **Resetting Ports.** Do not run programs (such as BASIC) that reset the I/O (input/output) ports.

Increasing AutoCAD Performance

Because AutoCAD accesses and manages your system resources efficiently, you do not need to tweak AutoCAD or your system to increase performance. Any general system performance enhancers will speed up AutoCAD. Four main bottlenecks commonly occur in computer systems: disk access, application workspace in RAM, graphics processing, and computing speed.

Speeding Up Disk Access

Because AutoCAD can be very disk-intensive (it accesses the disk frequently), your system's hard drive access speed affects AutoCAD's performance.

You can increase the disk access speed in several ways. The most inexpensive and dramatic way to increase disk performance is to use a disk cache. A *disk cache* is a TSR program that stores recent and frequently accessed disk information in RAM. Norton's N-CACHE, PCTOOLS' PC-CACHE, and Microsoft Windows 3.1's SMARTDRV.EXE are popular disk cache programs.

The amount of RAM allocated to the disk cache does not have to be large to significantly increase performance. A good starting size is 512K. Increasing the size of the cache will improve disk access; however, the amount of improvement diminishes quickly. AutoCAD can use the RAM more efficiently after a certain point.

When DOS stores files on your hard disk drive, it sometimes must break up the files and scatter them around the disk, rather than storing the file in contiguous (side-by-side) sectors (units of disk storage). The more files that are added to or deleted from the disk, the more likely your files are going to be fragmented. To maintain good disk performance, you should reorganize (*pack*, *defragment*, or *optimize*) the disk at least once a month. This reorders the files, moving the data for each file into contiguous sectors so DOS can access their contents more efficiently. You will find that periodically reorganizing your hard disk will improve performance in your other applications as well as in AutoCAD.

Several commercial disk management programs not only pack the disk but check and adjust other performance parameters of your hard drive, such as the disk's interleave factor (the ordering of the sectors on the disk). See any software dealer for recommendations. Before you pack your hard disk, make sure you have a complete backup of all files on the drive and that you know how to restore them in case of any problems.

Keep each of your software programs, like AutoCAD, in its own subdirectory. File access is faster, data files do not get mixed up, and future program upgrades are easier to install. Backing up your file system also is easier when programs are separated into individual directories. If you have more than one hard drive, consider installing software programs on one and using another for data. Because your software will be relatively static (the files will not change often), you need not defragment software directories as often as your data disk.

Another way to improve disk performance is to simply buy a faster disk drive.

Increasing Application Workspace

You also can enhance AutoCAD's performance cost-effectively by installing more RAM. When your drawings grow in size so that they no longer can fit in RAM while you work on them in AutoCAD, AutoCAD begins paging drawing and program data to disk. You begin to lose time as AutoCAD reads to and from your disk. The more RAM you can install in your computer, the longer you can put off paging. To determine how much RAM you might need, use this rule of thumb:

$3 \times$drawing size + 2M AutoCAD + 2M Windows

A 1M drawing would require 7M RAM to forestall paging. If you typically create 1M drawings, you should have 7M RAM (or more) to accommodate AutoCAD and maximize performance.

Free as much RAM as you possibly can before running AutoCAD, so that AutoCAD has as much RAM as possible. Load only those memory-resident TSR programs that you absolutely need.

Use a memory manager such MS-DOS 5's HIMEM.SYS or QEMM386.SYS from QuarterDesq Office Systems, along with DOS=HIGH and/or DOS's LOADHIGH or QEMM's LOADHI to maximize your available DOS memory. See an MS-DOS 5 or QEMM 386 manual, or *Maximizing DOS 5*, from New Riders Publishing for details.

Use Faster Video

A number of manufacturers offer video adapter boards that are optimized for AutoCAD, which will improve screen regeneration and redraw speed in AutoCAD. A number of these manufacturers as well as other third-party ADI driver developers offer software video drivers that optimize AutoCAD video performance. See your AutoCAD dealer for details.

Increasing Computing Speed

The only thing that can be done to increase computing speed is to use a faster CPU. Usually this means purchasing a new computer or at least a new motherboard. Some computers have upgradeable CPU modules or accept the INTEL DX2 line of CPUs.

Keep Up to Date

Although it is easy to remember to keep your AutoCAD software up to date, it also is easy to forget to update your DOS or ADI drivers. Keep in contact with your hardware manufacturer and AutoCAD dealer for updates. Install MS-DOS 5 if you are not using it already.

Other Tips

For other performance tips, see the *AutoCAD Interface, Installation and Performance Guide* and README.DOC file in your AutoCAD directory.

Index

T

New Riders Puts You on the Cutting Edge of Computer Information!

You'll Find All You Need To Know About Graphics with Books from New Riders!

New Riders Covers
All Your Operating System's Needs!

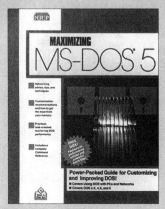

Maximizing MS-DOS 5
Through DOS 5
1-56205-013-3, 700 pp., 7³/₈ x 9¹/₄
$34.95 USA

Maximizing Windows 3.1
Windows 3.0 & 3.1
1-56205-044-3, 800 pp., 7³/₈ x 9¹/₄
$39.95 USA

More Titles from New Riders!

Inside OS/2, Release 2.0
Version 2.0
1-56205-045-1, 850 pp., 7³/₈ x 9¹/₄
$34.95 USA

Inside SCO UNIX
SCO Xenix 286, SCO Xenix 386, SCO UNIX/System V 386
1-56205-028-1, 600 pp., 7³/₈ x 9¹/₄
$29.95 USA

Inside Solaris SunOS
SunOS, Sun's version of UNIX for the SPARC workstation
1-56205-032-X, 750 pp., 7³/₈ x 9¹/₄
$29.95 USA

Inside Windows 3.1
Windows 3.0 & 3.1
1-56205-038-9, 750 pp., 7³/₈ x 9¹/₄
$29.95 USA

Maximizing Windows 3
Windows 3.0
1-56205-002-8, 704 pp., 7³/₈ x 9¹/₄
$39.95 USA

UNIX On Command
SCO UNIX, AT&T System V, & BSD 4.X
1-56205-027-3, 140 pp., 6³/₄ x 8¹/₂
$19.95 USA

Windows 3.1 Networking
Windows 3.0 & 3.1
1-56205-053-2, 350 pp., 7³/₈ x 9¹/₄
$22.95 USA

Windows 3.1 On Command
Windows 3.0 & 3.1
1-56205-047-8, 140 pp., 6³/₄ x 8¹/₂
$19.95 USA

Windows 3 On Command
Windows 3.0
1-56205-016-8, 140 pp., 6³/₄ x 8¹/₂
$19.95 USA

To Order, Call: (800) 428-5331
OR (317) 573-2500

NRP
NEW RIDERS
PUBLISHING

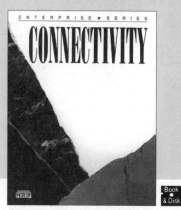
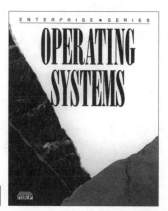